Cyber-Enabled Intelligence

Cyber-Enabled Intelligence

Edited by
Huansheng Ning
Liming Chen
Ata Ullah
Xiong Luo

CRC Press is an imprint of the
Taylor & Francis Group, an **informa** business

Color versions of the book's figures are available for download at CRC Press.com:
https://www.crcpress.com/Cyber-Enabled-Intelligence/Ning-Chen-Ullah-Luo/p/book/9780367184872

CRC Press
Taylor & Francis Group
6000 Broken Sound Parkway NW, Suite 300
Boca Raton, FL 33487-2742

First issued in paperback 2021

Printed on acid-free paper

ISBN-13: 978-0-367-18487-2 (hbk)
ISBN-13: 978-1-03-209033-7 (pbk)

Visit the Taylor & Francis Web site at
http://www.taylorandfrancis.com

and the CRC Press Web site at
http://www.crcpress.com

Contents

Editors

Huansheng Ning, PhD, earned his PhD from Beihang University in 2001. Currently, he is a professor and vice dean of the School of Computer and Communication Engineering, University of Science and Technology, Beijing, China. His current research focuses on Internet of Things, cyber philosophy, science and technology. Dr. Ning is the founder of Cyberspace and Cybermatics International Science and Technology Cooperation Base, and co-founder and vice chair of Beijing Engineering Research Center for Cyberspace Data Analysis and Applications. He serves as a steering committee member of *IEEE Internet of Things Journal* and associate editor of *IEEE System Journal*. He is co-chair of *IEEE Transactions on Cybermatics*. He hosted the 2013 World Cybermatics Congress and the 2015 Smart World Congress as the joint executive chair. Dr. Ning received the IEEE Computer Society Meritorious Service Award in 2013, and IEEE Computer Society Golden Core Award in 2014. He is an IET fellow and IEEE senior member.

Liming Chen, PhD, is professor of Computer Science in the School of Computer Science and Informatics at De Montfort University, Leicester, UK. He earned his BEng and MEng from Beijing Institute of Technology (BIT), China, and his PhD in Artificial Intelligence from De Montfort University, UK. His current research interests include data analytics, pervasive computing, artificial intelligence, and user-centered intelligent systems and their applications in smart healthcare. He is well published with more than 190 books, book chapters, journals/transactions, and conference and workshop articles in the above areas. Dr. Chen is an IET fellow, an IEEE senior member, a co-founder and co-director of the UK-China Gait and Health Innovation Institute at the DMU-USTB (University of Science and Technology Beijing, China) Joint Research Lab on Smart Healthcare and the IEEE CIS "User-centred Smart Systems" Task Force.

Ata Ullah, PhD, earned his BS and MS in Computer Science from COMSATS University, Islamabad, Pakistan, in 2005 and 2007, respectively, and PhD in Computer Science from IIUI, Pakistan, in 2016. From 2007 to 2008, he was a software engineer at Streaming Networks, Islamabad. Dr. Ullah contributed to the National University of Modern Languages (NUML), Islamabad, Pakistan as lecturer/head project committee from 2008 to 2015 and as assistant professor from 2015 to 2017 in the Department of Computer Science. From 2017 to 2018, he worked as a research fellow at the School of Computer and Communication Engineering, University of Science and Technology, Beijing, China. Dr. Ullah rejoined NUML in September 2018. He has supervised 112 projects. He has authored several papers in impact factor journals and contributed to books as well. He is also a reviewer and guest editor. His areas of interest are WSN, IoT, cyber physical social thinking (CPST) space, cyber-intelligence, and health services.

Xiong Luo, PhD, earned his PhD from Central South University, China, in 2004. From 2004 to 2005, he received postdoctoral fellowships from Tsinghua University, China. From 2012 to 2013, he was a visiting scholar at Arizona State University, USA. He currently works as a full professor in the School of Computer and Communication Engineering, University of Science and Technology, Beijing, China. His current research interests include machine learning, cloud computing, and cyber-physical systems. He has published extensively in his areas of interest in journals such as *IEEE Transactions on Industrial Informatics, IEEE Transactions on Human-Machine Systems, IEEE Transactions on Network Science and Engineering, IEEE Internet of Things Journal, and Future Generation Computer Systems*. Prof. Luo is a senior member of IEEE. He was a recipient of the 2002 IEEE CSS/Beijing Chapter Young Author Best Paper Award.

Contributors

Jorge Martinez Carracedo
School of Computing
Ulster University Jordanstown
Newtownabbey, United Kingdom

Fei Chang
The School of Computer and Communication Engineering
and
Beijing Engineering Research Center for Cyberspace Data Analysis and Applications
University of Science and Technology Beijing
Beijing, China

Xiaohui Chang
The School of Computer and Communication Engineering
and
Beijing Key Laboratory of Knowledge Engineering for Materials Science
University of Science and Technology Beijing (USTB)
Beijing, China

Feng Chen
Context, Intelligence and Interaction Research Group
De Montfort University
Leicester, United Kingdom

Liming Chen
Context, Intelligence and Interaction Research Group
De Montfort University
Leicester, United Kingdom

Maojian Chen
The School of Computer and Communication Engineering
and
Beijing Key Laboratory of Knowledge Engineering for Materials Science
University of Science and Technology Beijing (USTB)
Beijing, China

Pushpinder Kaur Chouhan
School of Computing
Ulster University Jordanstown
Newtownabbey, United Kingdom

Sahraoui Dhelim
The School of Computer and Communication Engineering
University of Science & Technology Beijing
Beijing, China

Dimitrios Giakoumis
Centre for Research & Technology Hellas
Information Technologies Institute
Thermi-Thessaloniki, Greece

Andreas Kargakos
Centre for Research & Technology Hellas
Information Technologies Institute
Thermi-Thessaloniki, Greece

Ioannis Kostavelis
Centre for Research & Technology Hellas
Information Technologies Institute
Thermi-Thessaloniki, Greece

Jürgen Kurths
Institute of Physics
Humboldt-University
Berlin, Germany

Ali Li
Beijing Engineering Research Center for Cyberspace Data Analysis and Applications
The University of Science and Technology Beijing
Beijing, China

and

School of Information and Electrical Engineering
Ludong University
Yantai, China

Ying Li
The School of Computer and Communication Engineering
and
Beijing Key Laboratory of Knowledge Engineering for Materials Science
University of Science and Technology Beijing (USTB)
Beijing, China

Ji Liu
Beijing Key Laboratory of Knowledge Engineering for Materials Science
University of Science and Technology Beijing (USTB)
Beijing, China

Liyuan Liu
The Second Hospital of Shandong University
Jinan, China

Xiong Luo
The School of Computer and Communication Engineering
and
Beijing Key Laboratory of Knowledge Engineering for Materials Science
University of Science and Technology Beijing (USTB)
Beijing, China

Muhammad Noman Malik
Department of Computer Science
National University of Modern Languages
Islamabad, Pakistan

Aamir Saeed Malik
Centre for Intelligent Signal and Imaging Research (CISIR)
Department of Electrical and Electronic Engineering
Universiti Teknologi Petronas
Seri Iskandar, Malaysia

Sally McClean
School of Computing
Ulster University Jordanstown
Newtownabbey, United Kingdom

Wooil M. Moon
Department of Geophysics
Faculty of Environment, Earth and Resources
University of Manitoba
Winnipeg, Manitoba, Canada

and

The School of Computer and Communication Engineering
University of Science and Technology Beijing
Beijing, China

Huansheng Ning
The School of Computer and Communication Engineering
and
Beijing Key Laboratory of Knowledge Engineering for Materials Science
University of Science & Technology Beijing
Beijing, China

Suli Ren
The School of Computer and Communication Engineering
University of Science and Technology Beijing
Beijing, China

Bryan Scotney
School of Computing
Ulster University Jordanstown
Newtownabbey, United Kingdom

Evangelos Skartados
Centre for Research & Technology Hellas
Information Technologies Institute
Thermi-Thessaloniki, Greece

Ahmad Rauf Subhani
Centre for Intelligent Signal and Imaging Research (CISIR)
Department of Electrical and Electronic Engineering
Universiti Teknologi Petronas
Seri Iskandar, Malaysia

Darpan Triboan
Context, Intelligence and Interaction Research Group
De Montfort University
Leicester, United Kingdom

Dimitrios Tzovaras
Centre for Research & Technology Hellas
Information Technologies Institute
Thermi-Thessaloniki, Greece

Ata Ullah
Department of Computer Science
National University of Modern Languages
Islamabad, Pakistan

Fei Wang
The Second Hospital of Shandong University
Jinan, China

Long Wang
The School of Computer and Communication Engineering
and
Beijing Key Laboratory of Knowledge Engineering for Materials Science
University of Science and Technology Beijing (USTB)
Beijing, China

Rui Wang
The School of Computer and Communication Engineering
and
Beijing Key Laboratory of Knowledge Engineering for Materials Science
and
Beijing Engineering Research Center for Cyberspace Data Analysis and Applications
The University of Science and Technology Beijing
Beijing, China

Weiping Wang
The School of Computer and Communication Engineering
and
Beijing Key Laboratory of Knowledge Engineering for Materials Science
University of Science and Technology Beijing (USTB)
Beijing, China

Zumin Wang
Department of Information Engineering
Dalian, China

Likun Xia
College of Information Engineering
Capita Normal University (CNU)
and
Beijing Advanced Innovation Center for Imaging Technology
Beijing, China

Yujuan Xiang
The Second Hospital of Shandong University
Jinan, China

Lei Xu
The University of Science and Technology Beijing
and
Beijing Engineering Research Center for Cyberspace Data Analysis and Applications
The University of Science and Technology Beijing
Beijing, China

Yang Xu
The School of Computer and Communication Engineering
and
Beijing Key Laboratory of Knowledge Engineering for Materials Science
University of Science and Technology Beijing (USTB)
Beijing, China

Jian Yang
The Department of Electronic Engineering
Tsinghua University
Beijing, China

Laurence T. Yang
Department of Computer Science
St. Francis Xavier University
Antigonish, Nova Scotia, Canada

Shunkun Yang
The School of Computer and Communication Engineering
University of Science & Technology Beijing
Beijing, China

Junjun Yin
Department of Electronic Engineering
Tsinghua University
and
The School of Computer and Communication Engineering
University of Science and Technology Beijing
Beijing, China

and

Department of Geophysics
Faculty of Environment, Earth and Resources
University of Manitoba
Winnipeg, Manitoba, Canada

Lixiang Yu
The Second Hospital of Shandong University
Jinan, China

Xin Yu
The School of Computer and Communication Engineering
and
Beijing Key Laboratory of Knowledge Engineering for Materials Science
University of Science and Technology Beijing
Beijing, China

Zhigang Yu
The Second Hospital of Shandong University
Jinan, China

and

Suzhou Institute of Shandong University
Suzhou, China

Raheel Zafar
Faculty of Engineering and Computer Science
National University of Modern Languages
Islamabad, Pakistan

Dandan Zhang
The School of Computer and Communication Engineering
and
Beijing Key Laboratory of Knowledge Engineering for Materials Science
University of Science and Technology Beijing (USTB)
Beijing, China

Wenbing Zhao
The Department of Electrical Engineering and Computer Science
Cleveland State University
Cleveland, Ohio

Fei Zhou
The Second Hospital of Shandong University
Jinan, China

Zhihao Zhou
The School of Computer and Communication Engineering
University of Science & Technology Beijing
Beijing, China

Tao Zhu
Department of Medical Informatics
School University of South China
Hengyang, China

Introduction

Generally we live in a complex and diverse physical space, in which we create and develop our interpersonal relationships, establishing social space via various interpersonal interactions. In addition, people use judgment and reasoning to reflect reality in the process of cognition, and explore the inner essential relationship and regularity of things to establish thinking space. With the rapid development of the Internet of Things, a new space, cyberspace, has quietly formed and become our fourth basic living space. The term *cyberspace* is a combination of *cybernetics* and *space*, referring to virtual reality in computers and computer networks. It was first created in the short story "Burning Chrome" and published in *Omni* magazine by William Gibson.[1] Later, it was popularized in the novel *Neuromancer*.[2]

As informatization and intellectualization have developed greatly in recent years, people realize that cyberspace interacts with the other three traditional spaces; therefore, cyber-physics-society-thinking (CPST)[3] space (Figure I.1) is gradually formed. Furthermore, objects in the CPST spaces establish dynamic and seamless interconnections, and accomplish physical interconnection, cyber interaction, social association, as well as thinking communication by the way of ubiquitous perception, computing communication convergence, which deeply promotes the integration of intelligence and the CPST space.

In recent years, with the increasing development of big data, social computing and brain informatics, artificial intelligence is gradually improved, penetrating into physical space, social space, cyberspace, and thinking space, thereby promoting the development and construction of these four spaces. And vice versa, the fusion and interaction of these four spaces drive the evolution of artificial intelligence. We call this cyber-enabled intelligence. It is different from intelligent networks and distributed intelligence, and it uses network data mining methods to analyze and model

---

[1] "Burning Chrome" is a short story written by William Gibson and first published in *Omni* in July 1982.

[2] *Neuromancer* is a 1984 science fiction novel by American Canadian writer William Gibson.

[3] H. Ning, H. Liu, J. Ma, L. T. Yang, and R. Huang, "Cybermatics: Cyber-physical-social-thinking hyperspace based science and technology," Future Generat. Comput. Syst., Aug. 2015. [Online]. Available: http://dx.doi.org/10.1016/j.future.2015.07.012

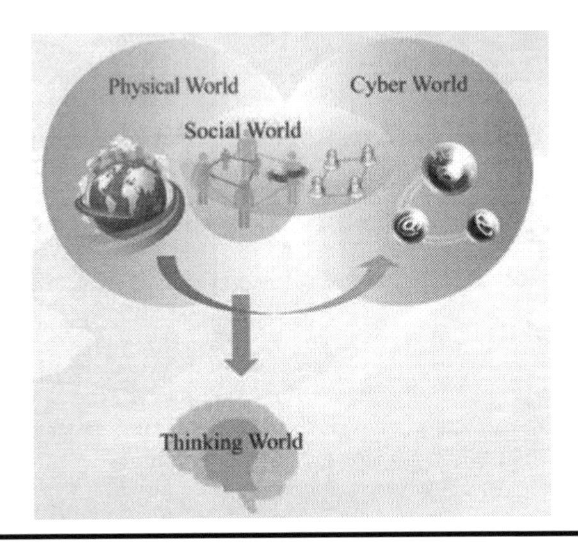

Figure I.1 The Cyber-Physical-Social-Thinking space.

evolutionary, self-similar and self-organizing dynamic networks like self-driving cars. If you want to go to the hospital, the cyberspace will automatically identify your request and manipulate a nearby car to stop at your location and take you to the hospital. Cyber-enabled intelligence consists of three components: cyber-enabled physical (CeP) intelligence, cyber-enabled social (CeS) intelligence, and cyber-enabled thinking (CeT) intelligence (Figure I.2).

CeP intelligence means cyber intelligence drives physical space to be more intelligent. It is achieved by means of lots of sensors hidden in physical entities. A variety of sensors transmit physical attributes in the form of data, and then the cyberspace will conduct intelligent analysis and processing of the data, generating the required information and accumulating knowledge, such as intelligent lighting. These messages produced by sensors interact in the CPST space, realizing intelligent identification and management, and achieve the cyber-enabled intelligence. The smart home we often talk about, with the residence as the platform that the multi-faceted interaction and integration of information in cyberspace, provides personalized services for the family.

In addition to physical properties, more social properties of physical objects are mapped to cyberspace. In cyberspace, the information that we got will be mined, generating a lot of knowledge, which would make social space smarter. This kind of intelligence is called CeS intelligence, and it supports cyberspace to help people in their daily lives. For example, social media is an interactive platform where individuals can create and share ideas and information, or find their own interests in a virtual community. Smart autobuses like Olli of IBM employ several social interaction foundations, including communication and advice. CeS intelligence can't get rid of the social space itself, and the development of

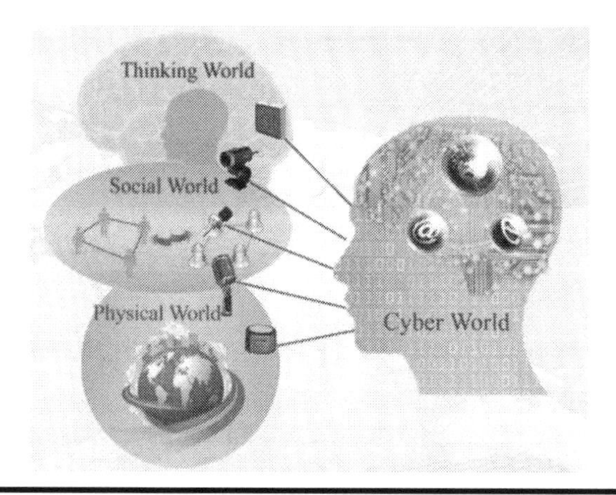

Figure I.2 Cyber-enabled intelligence.

cyberspace has profoundly affected social space. There is a new network presence in social space, such as the Social Network Service (SNS), which is representative of the existence of social networking. Compared with the traditional human social network, SNS breaks limitations of time and space and creates more possibilities for social space.

IoT realizes the deep convergence of physical space, cyberspace, social space, and thinking space, so cyber intelligence not only drives physical and social attributes, but also actuates thinking attributes such as analysis, synthesis, judgment, and reasoning, which utilize cyberspace to perform tasks autonomously and independently in the thinking space. Moreover, cyber intelligence promotes thinking space interacting with the other two spaces as well, achieving intelligence under mind control. We call it CeT intelligence. Further, under the impetus of cyber intelligence, a computer that has almost unlimited cloud computing power can nearly completely learn and think like a human, which jointly promotes a new era of artificial intelligence, such as the smart chat robot Zo.

This book consists of 15 chapters. Chapters 1 through 8 are about CeP intelligence. Chapter 9 is related to CeS intelligence, and Chapters 10 and 11 are related to aspects of CeT intelligence. The remaining chapters belong to hybrid intelligence. The chapters of this book are as follows:

- Chapter 1 performs on-road link quality estimation TPLE (Target-Prediction-based Link), and it dynamically calculates the track of a nearby vehicle target and estimates target impact on wireless link.
- Chapter 2 provides a distributed service-oriented architecture for a task, making each manufacturer provide service for their own products, and keeping data nodes collecting the information by themselves.
- Chapter 3 proposes a prediction-based data-sensing and -fusion scheme to reduce data transmission and maintain the required coverage level of sensors in WSN

(wireless sensor networks) while guaranteeing data confidentiality. How to utilize intelligence properly by developing effective schemes in WSN is explored.

- Chapter 4 proposes a scattering characterization by exploring the information contained in the three parameters (the average copolarization phase difference, amplitude ratio, and target coherence).
- Chapter 5 investigates the application of a level set method for the automated multiphase segmentation of multiband and polarimetric synthetic aperture radar (SAR) images.
- Chapter 6 discusses the development of a smart perception system, composed of a Ground Penetrating Radar and a surface rover-like mobile robot, which can autonomously perform sub-surface mapping.
- Chapter 7 points out researchers have embraced the aim of developing new interaction devices and technologies to facilitate the interactions of human with machines, and technology has raised computational power and intelligence through various interaction devices.
- Chapter 8 shows an approach that leverages ontology modeling techniques for generic and personalized activities of daily livings (ADLs) descriptions, incremental semantic reasoning and belief-based importance values for estimating confidence level.
- Chapter 9 puts forward a new model named BCRAM (a social-network-inspired breast cancer risk assessment model) that depends on epidemiological factors.
- Chapter 10 proposes a novel memristive multidirectional associative memory neural networks (MAMNNs) model with mixed time-varying delays.
- Chapter 11 tells us that decoding of the human brain is one of the most complex, difficult, and demanding research areas of the current era, and there have been many developments in brain research, especially in discriminating patterns of brain activities starting from simple to complex experiments.
- Chapter 12 investigates how to achieve fine-grained activity recognition in the context of application, and identification accuracy is improved by incorporating a nonlinear and local similarity measure. This model uses wearable sensors and a neural network (NN) learning algorithm.
- Chapter 13 proposes a comprehensive framework for the early detection of mental stress by analyzing variations in both electroencephalogram (EEG) and electrocardiogram (ECG) signals from 22 male subjects (mean age: 22.54 ± 1.53 years).
- Chapter 14 introduces various improved DV-HOP schemes with RSSI, and presents a new neural network (NN)-based node localization scheme named RHOP-ELM RCC.
- Chapter 15 presents the smart city architecture and association of the architecture layers to the security parameters, and discusses how situation assessment and cryptographic techniques can provide security in smart cities.

Chapter 1

TPLE: A Reliable Data Delivery Scheme for On-Road WSN Traffic Monitoring

Rui Wang, Fei Chang, and Suli Ren

Contents

1.1 Introduction

Traffic monitoring is an important part in modern city administration. Real-time road traffic data helps to improve transportation efficiency [1], such as road information broadcast and real-time weather publication.

Due to features of low cost, flexible deployment and easy maintenance, Wireless Sensor Networks are very suitable for establishment of extensive Intelligent Transportation Systems [2]. Some researches [2–5] have worked to collect on-road data by WSNs.

To realize a large-scale data collection by WSN upon on-road monitoring, there are still many challenges. One challenge is the reliability of data transmission from a sensor node to its destination in an on-road transportation environment. In a traffic on-road environment, the motor engines and other noises are much stronger as compare to other environments, especially the noise caused by motor engines. So reliable wireless data delivery in an on-road environment should take into account these obstacles.

We conducted an experiment to point out the aforementioned communication complexity. In that experiment, we used two sensor nodes equipped with CC1000 [6], one as sender and one as receiver. We set the distance between two sensor nodes to be 6m and set the radio power to be 0 dB/m. We conducted the same experiment in three different environments:

1. Two nodes placed in an indoor environment
2. Two sensor nodes placed in an outdoor non-traffic environment
3. Two sensor nodes placed alongside a road (where heavy traffic vehicles were running on the road)

Each experiment lasted ten minutes. As shown in Figure 1.1, the y axis shows package loss rate in the three different environments. We define 10 percentage points of its value as a span. You can see the package loss rate in environment is the minimum, and the maximum packet loss rate has achieved 64.15% where heavy traffic vehicles were running on the road. Figure 1.1 shows overall package loss rate. In the on-road context, the radio communication quality in the non-traffic outdoor environment is better than on the road with traffic. The only difference between the two scenarios is the busy vehicle targets running on the road.

Traditionally in wireless communication, link quality estimation is adopted to support the realization of reliable and low-delay data transmission. We argue that in an on-road traffic environment, the link quality cannot be described by existing link models. Apart from the normal factors that influence link quality, such as background noises, in an on-road traffic environment, the running vehicles are causing disruption to wireless links, especially the radio link used in wireless sensor networks. From Figure 1.1, by comparing scenarios b and c, almost 40% of sent packets are lost due to the noise of motor engines.

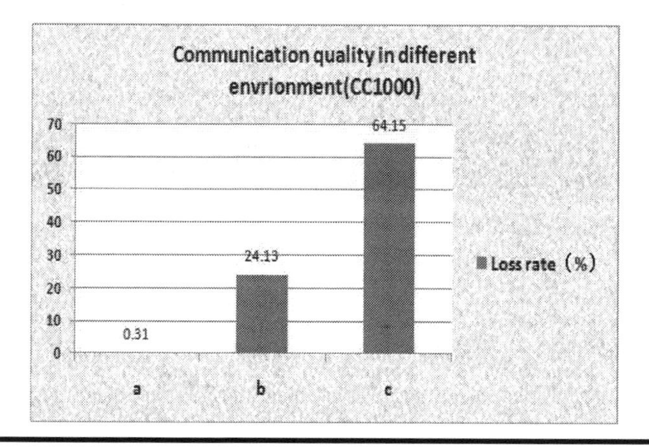

Figure 1.1 Radio loss rate in different settings.

From Figure 1.1:

1. The wireless communication quality in on-road environments is relatively poor with respect to other environments. The main reason for the worse radio communication quality is the noise of motor engines near the wireless environment.
2. The running and passing vehicles caused a huge distortion to the quality of the wireless links. The unstable and unpredictable nature of link quality gave rise to poor performance of data delivery, such as low delivery rate and high time delay.

In this paper we focus on the reliability of on-road data delivery. We have proposed and implemented a reliable data transmission scheme, called TPLE, which can conduct node data delivery according to real-time traffic position around the sensor node. Our proposed scheme can effectively estimate the link quality and bring good communication quality. Our contributions are as follows:

1. We proposed the TPLE scheme which can effectively deal with strong noises caused by on-road motor engines' targets.
2. With this scheme, we obtain relatively high radio communication quality with the acceptable cost of time delay with respect to data delivery.
3. We developed a real-time application to verify our proposed scheme; our system can be applied in pervasive on-road data collection.

1.2 Related Work

In this part, we briefly introduce the research of applying WSN in on-road monitoring and the research of reliable data delivery mechanisms. [2] proposed the idea of adopting WSN in on-road monitoring. The author proposed a single magnetic sensor–based solution for on-road vehicle identification. Also, a two sensor–based on-the-spot vehicle speed estimation scheme was proposed. In [3], the author proposed a data collection scheme to detect a vehicle on grass. Wireless radio delivers both raw measurements and in-network control information. Radio communication occurs mainly around those sensor nodes near the moving vehicle.

In the existing research related to WSN 802.11 networking, the challenges to achieving reliable data delivery are packet losses and errors. To handle these two challenges, solutions can be classified into two categories.

1.2.1 Frame-Based Solutions

In [4], the author proposed a solution for traffic light management. Communications occurred between the on-vehicle sensor and roadside relay, and the problem is that it needs continuous RSSI sampling, which is energy inefficient.

In [5], the author proposed a detection and classification solution for motor vehicles. The vehicle classification is accomplished by processing the data from multiple sensor nodes. A dynamic central node receives radio messages from correlated neighbors and performs the collaborative detection or classification tasks.

All of the aforementioned research by default assumed reliable wireless data delivery. However, as we mentioned earlier, the reliability of data delivery in terms of an on-road environment cannot be omitted to build a practical data collection system. The on-road environment presents new challenges to wireless link estimation research.

1.2.2 Physical-Based Solutions

COLLIE [7] detects collisions from weak signals for 802.11 networks by identifying error patterns within a physical-layer symbol. Moreover, COLLIE adopts a feedback of error packets from the receiver side. COLLIE is not applicable in the WSN field because the cost of this mechanism is too high related to overhead and energy consumption.

SoftRate [8] uses SoftPHY hints to estimate sudden changes in the BER so that collisions and packet losses can be detected. SoftRate needs to access the physical layer, which is difficult in WSN.

Present research on the chip error patterns on IEEE 802.15.4 standards shows that packet losses can be estimated [9]. Access to the physical layer is also essential here, making this solution impractical in WSN.

Based on research into packet loss estimation prediction in WSN with a joint RSSI-LQI-based classifier [10], the received packet can be classified into four categories: lost, successfully received, error by collision or error by weak signal. Then corresponding actions can be adopted to improve the reliability of the data delivery. The disadvantage of this scheme is solutions; [11–13] use RTS/CTS to ensure reliable data communication in 802.11 networks. The RTS/CTS overhead is relatively high and it is always disabled in WSN design.

In summary, the existing research in 802.11 networks on how to predict packet loss to realize reliable data delivery cannot be applied to WSN. Some researchers, such as [10], are trying to realize reliable data delivery. But as we have demonstrated in Figure 1.1, the noise and disturbance in an on-road context is much higher than typical WSN deployment sites, such as indoor [14], wildlife field [15] and outdoor [16,17] contexts. In this paper, we present our research on how to tackle the unprecedented scale of disruption in on-road WSN communication, and we also present our implementation of a Target Prediction–Based Link Quality estimation system which neither needed any overheads in the physical layer nor used RTS/CTS.

1.3 TPLE: Target Prediction–Based Link Quality Estimation Mechanism

In this section we propose a mechanism, namely TPLE for on-road data collection systems, to reliably deliver data. We first describe the ideas of TPLE, and then we describe the TPLE data collection procedures for data collection regarding on-road traffic. The framework of the TPLE is shown in Figure 1.2.

As shown in Figure 1.2, TPLE includes three parts: monitor model, state prediction and reliable delivery. The target can be sensed by sensor nodes when it comes, and the vector message about the incoming target which is produced by Anchor and its neighbors will be integrated to predict target state.

In detail, when the target is sensed by Anchor, it can produce a message of feature vector I, which includes the message of the time instant that the target is passing the Anchor and the signal strength of the monitoring target when the

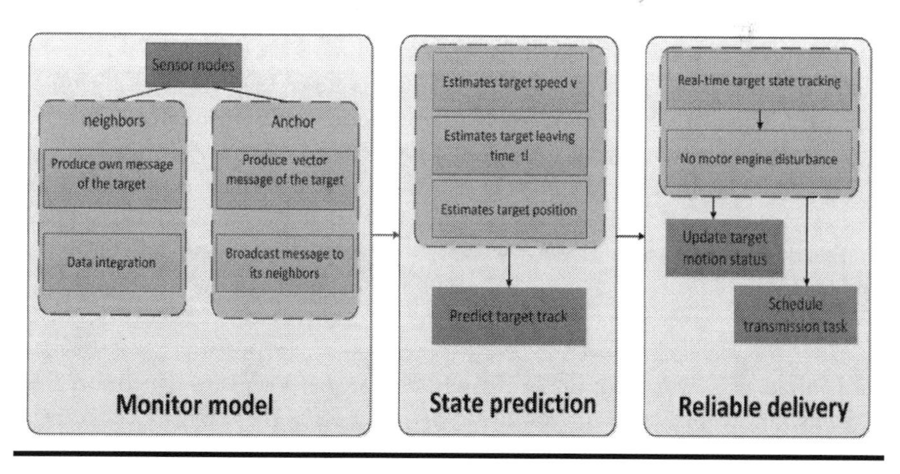

Figure 1.2 The framework of TPLE.

target reaches the Anchor. Then, the Anchor will broadcast feature vector I to its next neighbor node. When the next neighbor receives the I, in a short time, it can also produce a feature vector about the target, and will broadcast to its next neighbor node. We can estimate the target speed and calculate the leaving time when the target is out of the influential scope of each sensor by using such a form for message transmission of the feature vector. So, the sensor can reschedule the transmission tasks according to the state of the target. It's perfect to avoid the motor engine disturbance of the vehicle target when the sensors are involved in a task of delivering data and the radio communication quality can be greatly enhanced.

1.3.1 TPLE Algorithm for Link Quality Estimation

As we mentioned before, the extra complexity of an on-road traffic context lies in the unpredictable and sudden appearance of a vehicle target. Motor engines cause great disturbance to a wireless link when they are close to it.

According to our previous work in the on-road environment, the radio communication quality of a sensor node will decline when motor engines appear around a sensor. So an intelligent on-road data delivery scheme should be established for a radio communication task by reducing the disturbance of traffic motor targets.

Assume that a motor engine's magnetic field is like a disk having radius of R. The motion model of a nearby vehicle can be described as follows:

$$x_{k+1} = F_k x_k + G_k u_k + w_k \tag{1.1}$$

The measurement model of a sensor node is as follows:

$$z_k = H_k x_k + v_k \tag{1.2}$$

In these two equations, x_k is the state vector at time instant k, F_k is the target's matrix of state transition, G_k is the matrix of input noise, u_k is the dynamic noise, w_k is the process noise, Z_k is the measurement vector of the sensor node, H_k is the measurement matrix, and v_k is the measurement noise.

By adopting target tracking methods [18–20], such as Kalman filter [21], the target state such as speed and position can be estimated. According to the radius R of influential scope, the time instant when a target leaves the influential scope can be predicted. When a target's track is estimated by a sensor node, the sensor node can reschedule the transmission tasks and improve its quality.

Based on this idea, we propose a target prediction-based link quality estimation mechanism, namely TPLE. In TPLE mechanism, the downstream nodes can be informed of the appearance of an incoming vehicle target and dynamically calculate the link quality locally. By this mechanism, the radio communication quality can be greatly enhanced.

1.3.2 Reliable Data Delivery Scheme

In this part we describe the TPLE-based reliable data delivery scheme. First, we introduce a scenario that is very common in an on-road traffic monitoring environment. Figure 1.2 shows typical on-road monitoring settings. Several sensor nodes are deployed along a road, the sensor nodes are fixed in position, and the distance between two neighbor nodes is d (for simplicity, here we suppose the distance between neighbor nodes is equal in one system) [22]. Also, we suppose that the vehicle target is in a state of uniform rectilinear motion. We suppose the sensor nodes are synchronized with their local time in the system.

Here we introduce the concept of an Anchor. We define Anchor to be the first node in a monitoring system that notices the incoming target. According to [23], a sensor node can accurately report the time instant of a passing vehicle. When the vehicle target is monitored by a sensor node N_m, this sensor node can produce a message of feature vector I_m, where $I_m = \{t_{m,} s_m\}$. Here t_m is the time instant that the target passes a sensor node N_m, and s_m is the signal strength of the monitoring target when the target reaches a sensor node N_m. In Figure 1.3, N_1 is supposed to be the Anchor. When a vehicle target is identified by an Anchor, a message of feature vector I_1 will be broadcasted to its relevant neighbors N_2 in this figure.

As the data transmission process may fail, to accomplish the task successfully in a real system, a simple ACK-based retransmission mechanism for such acknowledgement providing Active Message in TinyOS [24] can be added in Anchor to ensure that this packet transmission process has been successfully performed.

As to the relevant neighbor, N_2 in Figure 1.3, it will be informed of the feature vector of an incoming target from upstream N_1. Meanwhile, in a short time, N_2 produces its own feature vector about that target I_2, $I_2 = \{t_2, s_2\}$. With the combination of I_1 and I_2, N_2 can obtain estimation of target speed locally:

$$\bar{v} = \frac{d}{|t_2 - t_1|} \tag{1.3}$$

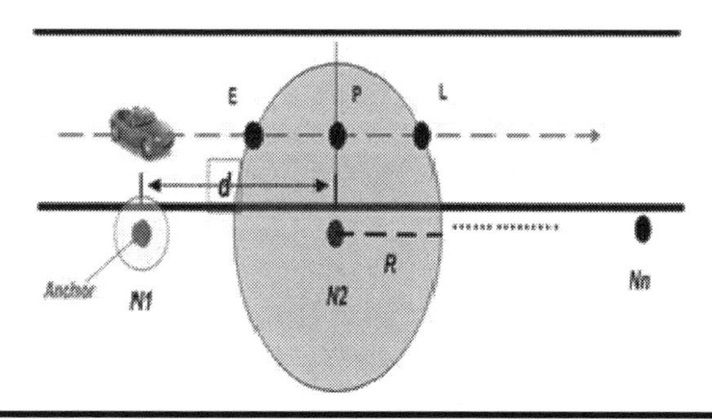

Figure 1.3 Monitoring settings.

where d is the distance between sensors N_1 and N_2; t_1 and t_2 are the time instants when the target reaches the sensors N_1 and N_2, respectively, and their value is derived from feature vector I_1 and I_2. With the estimated target speed $\bar{v}$, N_2 can predict the target track. The leaving time of the coming target can be estimated as

$$\overline{t_l} = t_2 + \frac{d_{PL}}{\bar{v}} \tag{1.4}$$

where d_{PL} is the distance between point P and point L. Because it is technically difficult to calculate the value of d_{PL}, we replace d_{PL} with R in (1.1), and get $\overline{t'_l}$. As $R > d_{PL}$, so $\overline{t'_l} \geq \overline{t_l}$. Besides simplicity, another advantage of this replacement is that the increased t_l assures package transmission, which to be scheduled upon the vehicle's leaving. The tradeoff of this replacement is a tiny increment in package delay. After this calculation of t_l, t_l can schedule its radio transmission tasks locally.

We define the Anchor to be the first node that discovers the incoming target. In some cases, the first physical node which is supposed to discover the vehicle target may miss the target and fail to report to relevant nodes. In such a case, the first discovery of that vehicle performs the role of Anchor and finishes the report task.

As all the sensor nodes in our system are homogenous, it is not difficult to implement the aforementioned mechanisms in a sensor node. Figure 1.4 indicates a chart of our proposed TPLE algorithm.

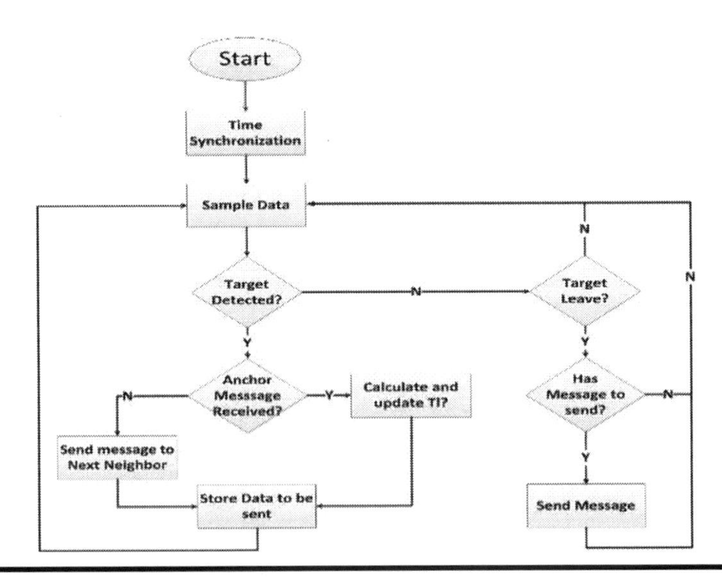

Figure 1.4 TPLE mechanism.

1.4 Verification and Experiment

Traditional wireless functionalities have been designed to employ a periodic sleep–wake sensor node mechanism in order to better save energy, in which every node in the sleep mode periodically wakes up to communicate with its neighbor nodes [25]. Once the communication is over, the node goes into sleep mode again until the next frame begins. But in traffic monitoring circumstance, the sensor nodes need to monitor targets frequently and communicate with neighbors during active time. Besides, a node cannot receive messages during sleep mode, so the messages targeted for such a node may be lost. In such a situation, the traditional duty cycle mechanism can neither save energy effectively nor improve transmission quality of the WSN—obviously. The TPLE algorithm we proposed can predict the target's status, then the active opportunity of sensor nodes can be estimated. Our algorithm does not need to monitor the target frequently, especially when data delivery occurs in an environment without motor engine disturbance. Therefore, our TPLE algorithm can effectively save WSN energy and improve data delivery quality. In this part we conducted both simulations and on-road experiments to verify our proposed scheme.

1.4.1 Simulations

We conduct computer simulations to verify our TPLE data delivery scheme. In our simulations, a sensor node is supposed to report its measurement when a vehicle target passes beside it.

1.4.1.1 Baseline Algorithms and Simulation Settings

We use two algorithms as comparison baselines, a simple acknowledgement-based single hop delivery provided by CC1000 radio stack (CRS) of Active Message in TinyOS [24] and the EWMA algorithm adopted in [26]. The maximal retransmission number in the MRS algorithm is set to be 3. The length of the temporal statistical window in EWMA is set to be 10 seconds. The EWMA algorithm sends a probing message every 0.5 second. In EWMA, a link is supposed to be good if the statistical package delivery rate is higher than 0.7.

The data delivery rate, average package delay, energy consumption and expected package retransmission lead to performance evaluations.

As vehicles are the largest disruptors of a link's quality, we adopt different traffic density (low, medium, high) simulations to evaluate performance. For small traffic density, we generate 5 vehicle appearances every minute; for medium density, 10 vehicles are generated every minute; and for high density, 20 vehicles are generated every minute. For each traffic density, we conducted 20 simulation groups.

The simulation settings are listed in Table 1.1. In Table 1.1, according to a large amount of on-road collected data, we set the radius of sensor nodes' radio influence

Table 1.1 Simulation Settings

Parameter	*Value*	*Description*
D_n2_n	6 m	Distance between neighbor nodes
V	5 m/s–15 m/s	Vehicle speed
$M_{in}D_{v2v}$	5 m	Minimal distance between two vehicles
R	4 m	Radius of a node's magnetic field
F1	0.8	Packet delivery rate without vehicle in influential scope
Pf	0.25	Packet delivery rate with vehicle in influential scope
Baud rate	19.2 kbps	Radio rate
Packet size	28 bytes	Radio packet size 0

to be 4 m, which means vehicles in this scope will reduce the sensor node's wireless communication quality. Also, we assigned 0.80, which is a relatively ideal radio communication quality in outdoor non-vehicle-appearance environments. The minimal distance between two vehicles is set to be 5 m, which is a normal setting if there is not a traffic jam. Moreover, our proposed TPLE mechanism is applicable in this assumption. The baud rate of a sensor node is assigned to be 19.2 kbps, which is a common rate in CC1000 radio communication module. The packet size has been fixed to 28 bytes, which is the standard packet size in TinyOS. We use baud rate and packet size to calculate packet delay between sender and receiver. We ignore other factors like transmission delay and software delay.

1.4.1.2 Data Delivery Rate

The data delivery rate is an important criterion for link quality. Figure 1.5 indicates the data delivery results in the simulation. The data delivery rate of our proposed TPLE scheme is higher than 94% in different traffic densities, which is ideal. The delivery rate of the CRS algorithm in all three traffic scenarios remains consistent to almost 70%. The reason is that the CRS algorithm does not consider link quality; the ACK mechanism is the only solution if one wants a high data delivery rate. As to the EWMA algorithm, although it takes link state into consideration, its link state estimation accurately reflects the real link status. In the high traffic density scenario, the performance of EWMA is mostly observed to be unstable because dense traffic introduces extra unpredictable factors for the link state estimation parts of EWMA.

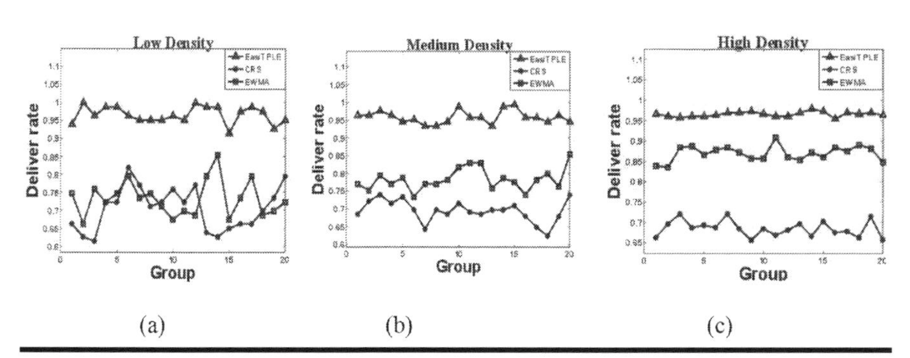

Figure 1.5 Data delivery rate simulation, where (a) represents the data delivery rate in low traffic density; (b) represents the data delivery rate in medium traffic density; (c) represents the data delivery in high traffic density. The representation of horizontal coordinates is the groups of simulation; the representation of vertical coordinates is the data delivery rate.

To summarize, our proposed TPLE scheme provides a stable and high data delivery rate for on-road sensors, and it deals well with the different traffic scenarios.

1.4.1.3 Average Packet Delivery Delay

Figure 1.6 indicates packet delay in simulation. The EWMA algorithm has the largest average packet delay because the link estimation in the EWMA algorithm enables wireless transmission when the statistical link quality is better than a threshold. The target-related information transmission experiences an unavoidable delay because of the statistical link quality estimation mechanism. The CRS

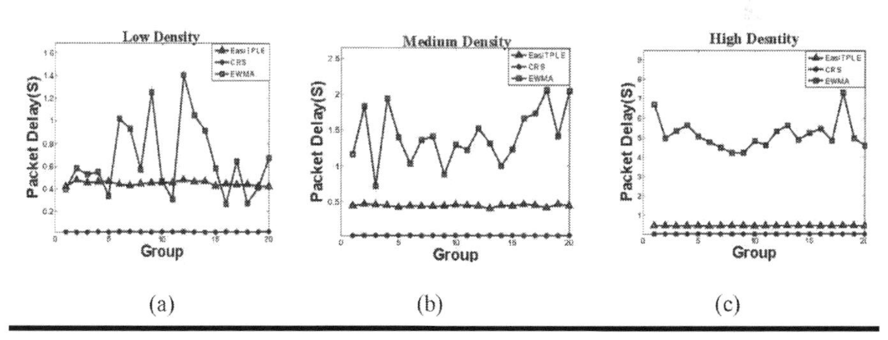

Figure 1.6 Packet delay simulation, where (a) represents the packet delay in low traffic density; (b) represents the packet delay in medium traffic density; (c) represents the packet delay in high traffic density. The representation of horizontal coordinates is the groups of simulation; the representation of vertical coordinates is the packet delay.

algorithm has the smallest delivery delay because it starts packet transmission once the target is detected. The cost of low packet delay is a relatively high retransmission number and low packet delivery rate. We will demonstrate it later. Our proposed TPLE has a relatively high delivery delay because it schedules the transmission task when the target leaves, which is unlike the immediate transmission seen in the CRS algorithm.

1.4.1.4 Average Packet Retransmission Number

Figure 1.7 indicates the average packet retransmission number in the simulation. From this figure, we can see along with the change in traffic density, the packet retransmission numbers of CRS and TPLE algorithms remains stable. TPLE has the lowest packet retransmission number, while the CRS algorithm has the highest retransmission number. The average retransmission number of the EWMA algorithm decreases as traffic density increases because more traffic results in more accurate link quality estimation, and transmission quality is improved. Compared with two baseline algorithms, TPLE has the least retransmission because it schedules radio communication tasks when there is a relatively good link quality.

1.4.1.4.1 Energy Consumption

Because radio communication requires the highest portion of a sensor node's energy, we use total packet number to evaluate energy consumption. In our algorithm, we use the CC1000 as a communication module. With its very low current

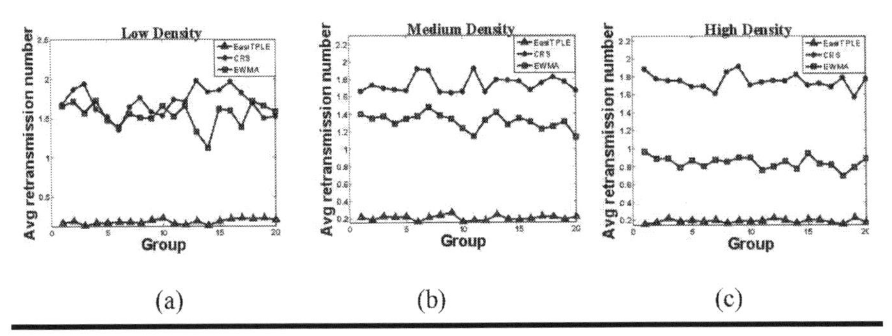

Figure 1.7 Average retransmission number, where (a) represents the packet retransmission number in low traffic density; (b) represents the packet retransmission number in medium traffic density; (c) represents the packet retransmission number in high traffic density. The representation of horizontal coordinates is the groups of simulation; the representation of vertical coordinates is the average packet retransmission number.

consumption, its unit energy consumption is the change of energy in unit time at a certain power. In the three algorithms (EWMA, CRS, and TPLE), we define the total packet number, the transmission power and the transmission time as the reference standard for energy consumption. The working power of the CC1000 can be set before the experiment. So, we can evaluate energy consumption according to the total packet number of the sensors. From Figure 1.8, we can see the EWMA algorithm definitely has the largest energy consumption because of the periodic link probing messages. As TPLE adopts the most effective link estimation mechanism, it consumes the least energy.

1.4.2 On-Road Verification Experiments

We also conducted real-world experiments to verify our proposed data delivery scheme. Based on the platform EasiTia [23], we implemented the TPLE algorithm in sensor nodes.

Then the sensor nodes were deployed along a road to detect and report vehicle messages. Figure 1.8 indicates our on-road experiment settings. We use four nodes along the road to perform data collection tasks, with two nodes on each side of the road. A sensor node is supposed to send its measurement about vehicle to a sink node.

We conducted three groups of experiments. Each experiment lasted 10 minutes. We used packet delay, packet delivery rate and retransmission number to evaluate our results. Table 1.2 indicates results of our on-road experiments. We compared the three algorithms (EWMA, CRS, and TPLE) in delivery rate, packet delay

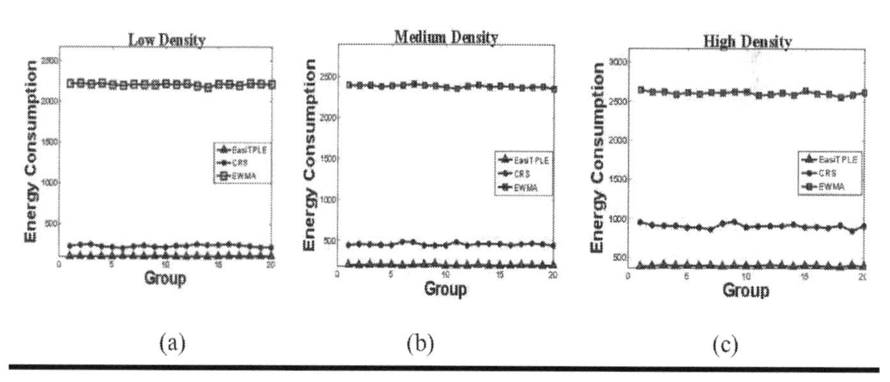

Figure 1.8 Energy cost simulation, where (a) represents the energy consumption in low traffic density; (b) represents the energy consumption in medium traffic density; (c) represents the energy consumption in high traffic density. The representation of horizontal coordinates is the groups of simulation; the representation of vertical coordinates is the energy.

Table 1.2 On-Road Experiment Results

	Delivery Rate %	*Packet Delay*	*Retransmission Number*
Group 1	82.54	1.08s	0.71
Group 2	85.87	0.84s	0.73
Group 3	94.11	0.81s	0.61

and retransmission number. In Table 1.2, Group 1, Group 2 and Group 3 represent the EWMA algorithm, the CRS algorithm and the TPLE algorithm, respectively. Each experiment of three algorithms is the same, and the result values of delivery rate, packet delay and retransmission number are the average values of all the experiments.

From this table we can see that the on-road data delivery rate of TPLE is not as good as the results in simulations, perhaps because of the inaccurate definition of the influential scope of the sensors' radio link. However, we can see that the packet delivery delay and average retransmission number is quite ideal, as indicated by our simulation.

Via both simulations and on-road experiments, we verified our proposed TPLE data delivery scheme. We demonstrated that our proposed scheme offered relatively better data delivery with less cost for small packet delivery. The delay is acceptable in an on-road monitoring environment (Figure 1.9).

Figure 1.9 On-road experiment scenario.

1.5 Conclusions

In this paper, we propose a TPLE mechanism to solve the motor engine–caused low link quality in an on-road traffic monitoring environment. TPLE estimates link quality by dynamically updated target motion status and schedules radio communication tasks when there is no motor engine disturbance. Simulation and on-road experiments demonstrate the good communication quality of TPLE in on-road environments.

Acknowledgments

This work was supported in part by the National Natural Science Foundation of China under Grant No. 61379134. Rui Wang and Fei Chang conceived and designed the experiments; Suli Ren performed the experiments; Rui Wang and Fei Chang contributed analysis tools; Suli Ren analyzed the data; Rui Wang, Fei Chang and Suli Ren wrote the paper. The authors declare no conflict of interest.

References

1. W.H. Lee, S.S. Tseng, and W.Y. Shieh, Collaborative real time traffic information generation and sharing framework for the intelligent transportation system, *Information Sciences*, 180(1), 62–70, 2010.
2. S. Coleri, S. Cheung, and P. Varaiya, Sensor networks for monitoring traffic, in *Allerton Conference on Communication, Control and Computing*, pp. 32–40, 2004.
3. T. He, S. Krishnamurthy, J. Stankovic, T. Abdelzahber, L. Luo, R. Stoleru, T. Yan, L. Gu, J. Hui, and B. Krogh, Energy efficient surveillance system using wireless sensor networks, in *Proceedings of the 2nd International Conference on Mobile Systems Applications and Services*, pp. 270–283, 2004.
4. C. Wenjie, C. Lifeng, C. Zhanglong, and T. Shiliang, A realtime dynamic traffic control system based on wireless sensor network, *34th International Conference on Parallel Processing Workshops*, 14–17 June 2005, Oslo, Norway, pp. 258–264, 2005.
5. L. Gu, D. Jia, P. Vicaire, T. Yan, L. Luo, A. Tirumala, Q. Cao et al. Light weight detection and classification for wireless sensor networks in realistic environments, in *Proceedings of the 3rd International Conference on Embedded Networked Sensor Systems*, p. 217, 2005.
6. T. Instruments, Cc1000: Single chip very low power transceiver, Revision A, 7th February, 2007.
7. S. Rayanchu, A. Mishra, D. Agrawal, S. Saha, and S. Banerjee, Diagnosing wireless packet losses in 802.11: Separating collision from weak signal, *IEEE INFOCOM 2008-The 27th Conference on Computer Communications*, pp. 735–743, 2008.
8. M. Vutukuru, H. Balakrishnan, and K. Jamieson, Cross layer wireless bit rate adaptation, in *ACM SIGCOMM Computer Communication Review*, 39(4), 3–14, 2009.
9. K. Wu, H. Tan, H.L. Ngan, Y. Liu, and L.M. Ni, Chip error pattern analysis in IEEE 802.15.4, *Mobile Computing IEEE Transactions on*, 11(4), 543–552, 2012.

10. Z.A. Eu, P. Lee, and H.P. Tan, Classification of packet transmissions outcomes in wireless sensor networks, in *IEEE International Conference on Communications*, pp. 1–5, 2011.
11. S.H. Wong, H. Yang, S. Lu, and V. Bharghavan, Robust rate adaptation for 802.11 wireless networks, in *Proceedings of the 12th Annual International Conference on Mobile Computing and Networking*, pp. 146–157, 2006.
12. S. Kim, L. Verma, S. Choi, and D. Qiao, Collision aware rate adaptation in multi rate WLAN: Design and implementation, *Computer Networks*, 54(17), 3011–3030, 2010.
13. M.A.Y. Khan, and D. Veitch, Isolating physical per for s-mart rate selection in 802.11, *Proceedings-IEEE INFOCOM*, pp. 1080–1088, 2009.
14. M. Sugano, T. Kawazoe, Y. Ohta, and M. Murata, Indoor localization system using RSSI measurement of wireless sensor network based on ZigBee standard, *Wireless & Optical Communications*, 1–6, 2006.
15. F. Viani, F. Robol, E. Giarola, G. Benedetti, S. De Vigili, and A. Massa, Advances in wildlife road-crossing early-alert system: New architecture and experimental validation, *The 8th European Conference on Antennas and Propagation (EuCAP 2014)*, pp. 3457–3461, 2014.
16. J. Suhonen, M. Kohvakka, M. Hannikainen, and T.D. Hannikainen, Design, implementation, and experiments on outdoor deployment of wireless sensor network for environmental monitoring, in *Embedded Computer Systems:Architectures, Modeling, and Simulation*, pp. 109–121, 2006.
17. M. Jin, X. Zhou, E. Luo, and X. Qing, Industrial-QoS-oriented remote wireless communication protocol for the internet of construction vehicles, *IEEE Transactions on Industrial Electronics*, 62(11), 2015.
18. T. Ghirmai, Distributed particle filter for target tracking: With reduced sensor communications, *Sensors*, 16, 1454, 2016.
19. Q. Zhang, and T.L. Song, Improved bearings-only multi-target tracking with GM-PHD filtering, *Sensors*, 16, 1469, 2016.
20. W. Zhu, W. Wang, and G. Yuan. An improved interacting multiple model filtering algorithm based on the cubature Kalman filter for maneuvering target tracking, *Sensors*, 16, 805, 2016.
21. R. Kalman, A new approach to linear filtering and prediction problems, *Journal of Basic Engineering*, 82(1), 167–175, 1960.
22. Q. Niu, X. Yang, S. Gao, P. Chen, and S. Chan, Achieving passive localization with traffic light schedules in urban road sensor networks, *Sensors*, 16, 1662, 2016.
23. R. Wang, L. Zhang, R. Sun, J. Gong, and L. Cui, Easitia: A pervasive traffic information acquisition system based on wireless sensor networks, *Intelligent Transportation Systems IEEE Transactions on*, 12(2), 615–621, 2011.
24. P. Levis, and D. Gay, *TinyOS programming*, Cambridge University Press, New York, 2009.
25. L. Wang, and K. Liu, An adaptive energy-efficient MAC protocol for wireless sensor networks[C], in *International Conference on Embedded Networked Sensor Systems* pp. 23–27, 2003.
26. M. Xue, H. Zhao, and J. Zhu, Research on EWMA based link quality evaluation algorithm for WSN, in *Cross Strait Quad-Regional Radio Science and Wireless Technology Conference*, pp. 757–759, 2011. IEEE.

Chapter 2

An Architecture for Aggregating Information from Distributed Data Nodes for Industrial Internet of Things

Tao Zhu, Sahraoui Dhelim, Zhihao Zhou, Shunkun Yang, and Huansheng Ning

Contents

2.1 Introduction

Internet of Things (IoT) covers a bundle of information and communication technologies, such as identification, sensing, communication and so forth. The ambitious vision of IoT is to interconnect any substantial entity in both the real and digital worlds by extending the Internet and using intelligent interfaces such that everything in IoT can communicate, be identified and interact [1,2]. Although this vision is still a long way from being completed, the development thus far has benefited many areas, including various industries such as healthcare services [3,4], supply chains [5,6], transportation [7] and so forth.

IoT enables an entirely new class of services, such as identification and tracking, with which the operation and role of many industrial systems are being transformed [8]. In [8], the authors surveyed some important IoT industrial applications. For example, using IoT, intelligent transportation systems can be created. From the office, transportation authorities can identify and track each vehicle with loads, monitor its movements, predict load conditions and even recommend driving directions to drivers [7]. In the food supply chain, products can be tracked all the way from farms to retailers, which is helpful in terms of food quality and safety management [9,10].

In these applications, a key fundamental functionality of IoT is to provide a product's information when the product's ID is read. The ID is generally written in radio-frequency identification (RFID) tags. To implement this functionality, there are two representative systems: the electronic product code (EPC) system and the ubiquitous ID (uID) system [11]. These two systems vary in many aspects, but they have a similar one-to-one (one ID, one record) architecture, as shown in Figure 2.1. Once a terminal reads a product's ID, it first forwards it to the ID resolution service, which is called Object Name Service in EPC system and uCode Resolution Server in uID system. The resolution service then returns to the terminal the address of a certain data node that issued the product's ID. This data node generally belongs to the product manufacturer, and we call it the source node of this product. Using this address, the terminal can find the information service provided by the node and obtain the target record from it. Since one ID can be associated to only one record from one data node, we call this a one-to-one architecture.

However, in many applications, a single product could have multiple records spreading over multiple distributed data nodes, and we need all the information to complete some operations [10,12]. For example, in a product supply chain, a product could leave a record at every data node where it arrives and is scanned [13].

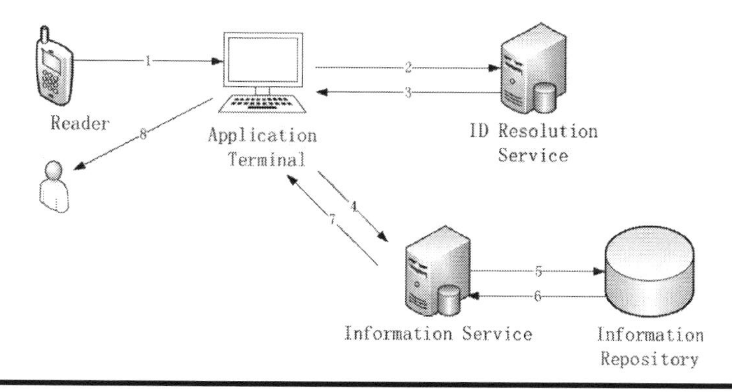

Figure 2.1 The classic one-to-one architecture.

The information from all these data nodes is needed to trace the product. The current one-to-one architecture does not directly support such functionality; therefore, supplementary components are indispensable for product tracing. In practice, aggregating information of an object from multiple distributed data nodes is a common task in many industrial applications [10]. Therefore, an architecture that can conveniently aggregate information from multiple distributed data nodes would facilitate many industrial IoT (IIoT) applications, and this is the motivation of our work.

Several requirements should be satisfied for the new architecture to be practical and feasible in multiple applications. First, scalability should be achieved since the development of IoT is very fast. Second, the heterogeneity of information across different applications and data nodes should be considered because we expect the architecture to have a relatively wide applicability. Third, the aggregating operation should clearly be efficient.

In this chapter, we propose a new architecture that attempts to satisfy these requirements. The proposed architecture is compatible with the existing IoT infrastructure, including both EPC and uID systems. In this architecture, each manufacturer provides service for their own products, and data nodes retain the information collected by themselves. Semantic technologies are adopted to handle problems of heterogeneity and serve as the foundation to support different applications. To validate the proposed architecture, we apply it to the problem of product tracing.

The remainder of this chapter is organized as follows. In Section 2.2, we briefly introduce the preliminaries needed in this paper. Then, in Section 2.3, we discuss some issues that should be addressed in the information aggregation architecture, which are also the criteria for evaluating an architecture. Section 2.4 details and discusses the proposed architecture. In Section 2.5, taking product tracing as an example, we explain how to use the proposed architecture in I IoT applications, in which the use of semantic web technologies is emphasized. Finally, Section 2.6 concludes the paper and presents directions for future work.

2.2 Preliminaries

2.2.1 Semantics for Internet of Things

Semantic technologies are focused on describing the meaning of information in a formal and machine-processable way, and the resulting descriptions are often called ontologies [14]. Some semantic technologies are used in our work. The Web Ontology Language (OWL) is designed to represent rich and complex knowledge about things, groups of things and relations between things. SWRL is the Semantic Web Rule Language that combines OWL and Rule ML, which is a sublanguage of the Rule Makeup Language designed for formalizing rules. Interested readers are encouraged to refer to related documents presented by W3C.

With rules, SWRL can express facts that hold only under specific conditions; these facts cannot be expressed using OWL alone. An SWRL rule is composed of two parts, antecedent (body) and consequent (head); if the antecedent holds, then the consequent must also hold. Here is an example of SWRL rules: any product whose expiration date is earlier than today is considered to be an expired product.

```
Product(?p1)^hasExpirationDate(?p1,?date)^SWRLB:greaterThan(today,?date) --> Expired(?p1)
```

Currently, there are some reasoners that support SWRL, for example, Pellet from Complexible Inc. Protégé is one of the best ontology editing tools, which can edit ontologies using a sophisticated GUI, and it supports Pellet and other reasoners.

In recent years, there has been an increasing trend of applying semantic technologies in I IoT [15–17]. A main reason for this trend is that the data generated in IoT have the same characters as the Web content. Barnaghi et al. reviewed some scenarios to demonstrate the importance of semantics to the search and development of IoT [15].

Interoperability: By casting knowledge into unambiguous and machine-processable ontologies, different stakeholders can access and interpret the data unambiguously.

Integration: By enabling interoperability, semantics technologies can support the seamless integration of data from different sources to create complex abstractions and environments.

Inference: Semantic web technologies allow logical reasoning, which is able to infer new information or knowledge from existing assertions and rules.

2.2.2 Product Tracing

Product tracing is one of the most important problems in modern supply chains [13]. Product manufacturers would like to know where their products go, and consumers might want to find where a problematic bottle of medicine came from. A supply chain is composed of a number of nodes, including factories, warehouses, and supermarkets. Data are generated when products move from one node to another.

The movement of a product is represented by a series of records distributed on different nodes. The basic schema for a record is (Product, Node, Start, End), which means that a *Product* arrives at and leaves a *Node* at *Start* and *End*, respectively. In [13], the problem of product tracing is defined in SQL language as follows.

Definition 1 (Product Tracing). Given product o and a time range tstart and tend, tracing o means the following:

```
SELECT r.Node, r.Start, r.End
FROM Record r
WHERE r. Product = o ORDER BY r.Start AND r.End ≥ tstart AND r.Start ≤ tend;
```

2.3 Information Aggregation from Federated Data Nodes in I IoT

From a system-level perspective, the Internet of Things is a radical distributed network system composed of numerous smart objects that produce and consume information [1]. Within this network, a large number of data nodes reside for collecting and storing information from the smart objects, and these data nodes are typically autonomous and could vary in many aspects. Due to this inherent feature of distribution, many applications in IoT often require information that is distributed on multiple data nodes, demanding these data nodes to cooperate and exchange the information to complete tasks.

In Industrial Internet of Things, aggregating information from distributed data nodes is common in many applications. In the healthcare industry, to comprehensively analyze a patient, we need to aggregate information from various IoT-based healthcare service providers that collect data of that patient using various sensors. In the food supply chain, to evaluate food safety, we need information about food production, processing, storage, distribution, and consumption. It is impossible for all this information to be stored in a single data node. Aggregating information from distributed data nodes is the basis of some key enabling technologies. The tractability of objects is key in many applications, such as supply chains, monitoring and surveillance. When the targeted object moves from one location to another, it leaves records collected by different data nodes.

Topology and Scalability: As in many other fields, such as federated database [18], in I IoT, the architectures for aggregating information from distributed data nodes can be classified into the centralized, the distributed and the P2P architectures [6,19]. The centralized architecture is by far the most impractical one because storing huge volumes of IoT data in a single node can lead to serious scalability issues; therefore, this type of architecture is beyond the scope of this paper. In the remainder of this paper, by centralized architectures, we refer to those architectures with a centralized management node and multiple distributed data nodes, as shown in Figure 2.2a. This centralized management node responds to all requests from all application terminals. However, as the request rate increases, this centralized node becomes the bottleneck of the system. By contrast, distributed architectures distribute the management service among a number of servers, as shown in Figure 2.2b. In this way, the bottleneck problem is relieved. In contrast to both types of architectures, every data node in P2P (also named self-organized) architectures is equipped with a management service to respond to requests for its own information, as shown in Figure 2.2c. There is no global state information that should be shared and coordinated among all nodes, and for a node, it only needs to maintain the connection with a limited number of neighboring nodes [20]. Generally, P2P architectures are considerably more scalable than centralized and distributed architectures [20].

Aggregation efficiency: Aggregation efficiency is another key issue. Although P2P is great at building large scalable systems, aggregation efficiency is its major drawback. Generally, the local data repository of a node is inadequate for supporting the aggregation requests; consequently, the requests must be forwarded to its neighboring nodes for further processing, the neighboring nodes forward the requests to their neighbors in turn, and the forwarding is recursively repeated until all related information is collected. The count of request forwarding would be large and unpredictable. By contrast, centralized architectures have no request forwarding problem because the sole management node possesses all the required information. For some distributed architectures, they also need a small number of forwarding among the management nodes for some requests, but property distribution schemes could avoid this problem and thus enhance the aggregation efficiency.

Heterogeneity: An inherent feature of IoT is heterogeneity. Distributed data nodes in an industrial application system in IoT could be heterogeneous in structure, scale, database management system and so forth. The service-oriented architecture (SOA) has proved to be a successful solution to handle the problem of structure heterogeneity [8,21]. Partners in an SOA comply with a set of agreed external interfaces and implement a stack of communication protocols.

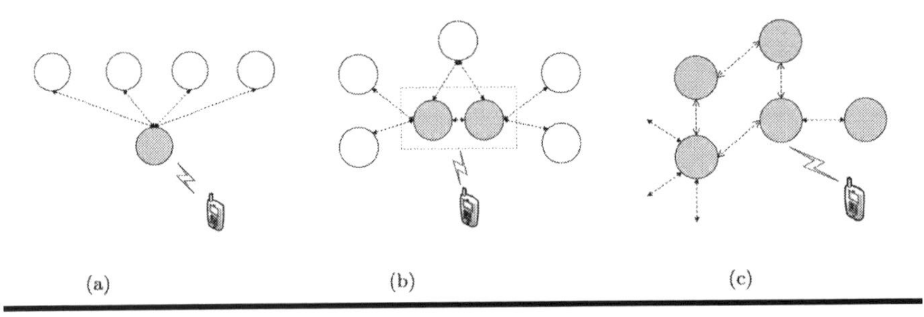

Figure 2.2 Architecture taxonomy. (a) Centralized, (b) Distributed, (c) P2P.

However, for information aggregation, semantic heterogeneity could be a more complex problem. Data nodes are autonomous, and they can choose their ways to store, interpret, and publish the data that they collected. When nodes differentiate in the meaning and use of data, representation of knowledge, semantic heterogeneity arises [15]. With semantic heterogeneity, a data node cannot understand the meaning of information provided by other nodes. We cannot extract the results from the aggregated data unless the semantic heterogeneity is addressed. Aggregating information from distributed data nodes is a common task among many I IoT applications. Building information aggregation architectures that support different applications is worthwhile but more challenging because we do not want to separate applications but rather wish that information from different applications could be shared with each other.

Availability: Availability is a common criterion for any system. A system should not break down simply because of the failure of a single node. In our case, data nodes are autonomous and heterogeneous. Their reliability should not be assumed. Therefore, the availability of the architecture should not rely on any single node.

2.4 The Proposed Information Aggregation Architecture

2.4.1 The Conceptual Design

Aiming to achieve information aggregation concerning a thing from multiple distributed data nodes, we propose a new architecture. Its conceptual design is illustrated in Figure 2.3.

Every data node assigns a globally unique URI to each information record that it collects during industrial applications. The form of the URI can be uCode, EPC code or any other type. Of course, resolution servers are able to locate the data node of a record by the record's URI, just as in the EPC/uID systems. This assignment is feasible. For example, uCode can be assigned for information and more abstract concepts that do not exist in the real world and for tangible objects and places in the real world.

The key component in Figure 2.3 is the query service that provides the UID list of all the information records related to a certain thing on request. For time efficiency, in this architecture, the query service is required to store the UID list in its local data repository. Therefore, it can instantly respond to the requests and does not need to call the other nodes.

With this conceptual design, the information aggregation procedure is divided into the following steps. In step 1, the terminal of a certain IoT application reads a thing's ID. In step 2, a request is forwarded to the query service with the thing's ID, and then the query service responds with a list of the URIs of

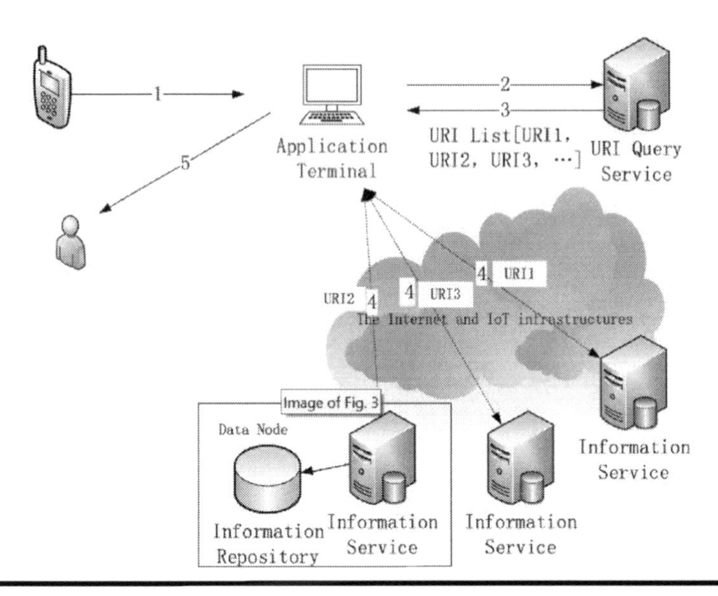

Figure 2.3 The conceptual design.

information records that need to be aggregated. Through the existing IoT infrastructures, it is easy to obtain an information record from a certain data node according to the record's URI. Therefore, in step 3, the terminal concurrently sends requests for all the records that spread on multiple distributed data nodes. In step 4, the aggregated records are integrated and processed, and then they are presented to users.

A major advantage of this conceptual design is the aggregation efficiency. The URI query service maintains the required URIs in its local information repository. To implement this basic design in the proposed architecture, other criteria, in addition to the aggregation efficiency discussed above, should also be addressed, particularly the scalability and heterogeneity.

To make the conceptual design scalable, we need a proper scheme to distribute the URI query service on different nodes. Because the volume of the data and the number of transactions in I IoT have been dramatically increasing, deploying the service on a centralized node would make that node the bottleneck of the system. However, distributing the URI query service on multiple nodes leads to the two following questions: (1) how does a terminal know which nodes to request for a certain thing? and (2) how does a query node know that it should maintain the URIs of which things?

Heterogeneity is the other important problem to be addressed. The difference of data nodes leads to heterogeneity. Data nodes can vary in structure, query language and capacity, among others. Another type of heterogeneity results in semantic difference, when nodes disagree in the meaning and usage of data, representation of knowledge. The problem of heterogeneity becomes more severe when the design is applied across multiple different applications, which means a larger number of data formats, services types and so forth.

In addition to the criteria discussed in Section 2.3, there is a special issue concerning the URI query service: how can returning unrelated URIs to the terminals be avoided? Terminals of a certain application would not want the information records generated in the other applications.

2.4.2 The Architectures of the Components

Considering the above criteria, we proposed the architecture illustrated in Figure 2.4. In this architecture, data nodes, query nodes and application terminals communicate with each other via the existing network infrastructures, including the Internet and various IoT systems.

With the existing network infrastructures, application terminals can quickly locate the source node of a product by its ID. Therefore, in this architecture, the URI query service is distributed on each source node, and each source node maintains the URIs for its own product. With this distribution scheme, for a certain product, application terminals can obtain the address of the query node by the ID resolution services provided by the existing IoT infrastructures.

In our architecture, we leverage the concept of service-oriented architecture and semantic web technologies to handle heterogeneity. SOA has been demonstrated to be successful in integrating heterogeneous systems. Semantic web technologies are useful in handling semantic heterogeneity. Moreover, we can use the reasoning ability of semantic web technologies to complete some tasks rather than developing additional software.

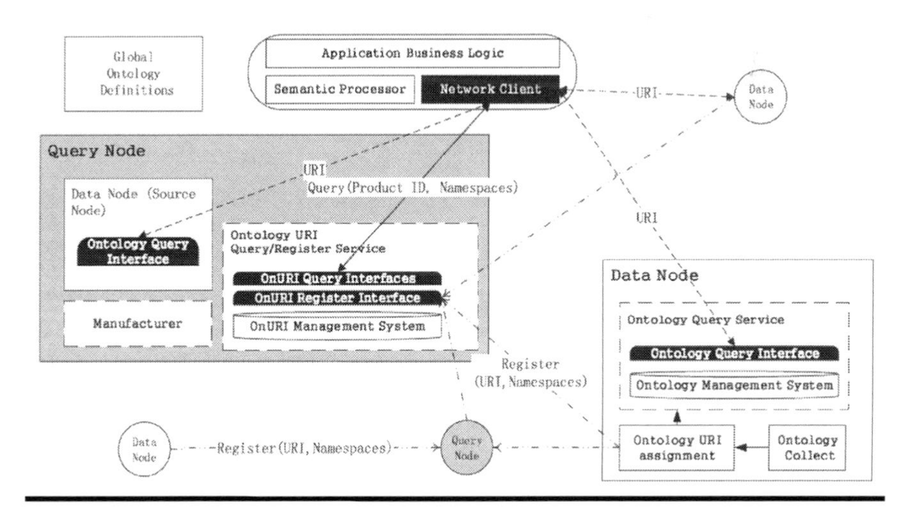

Figure 2.4 The architectures of the components.

2.4.2.1 Global Ontology Definitions

Note that semantics alone are not sufficient to solve the problem of semantic heterogeneity. All the partners involved in the architecture must follow the same ontological definitions. Ontologies from different applications are organized in different namespaces. Of course, some namespaces could be shared among multiple applications.

2.4.2.2 Data Node

A data node is composed of three essential functional components, i.e., ontology collect, ontology URI assignment and ontology query service. Data come from various sources, such as sensors, RFID readers, manually input and so forth. Ontology collect is the component that processes the data and represents data in the form of an ontology. Then, each ontological record is assigned a URI in the ontology URI assignment component. The ontology URI assignment component also analyzes what products are involved in each ontological record and then registers the URI at the source nodes of these products. Researchers have developed some systems to effectively store ontologies. For example, Lu et al. proposed a practical system to store ontologies in relational DBMS while simultaneously supporting reason and search [22].

For an ontological record, along with its URI, the namespaces that it used are also sent to the source nodes. The used namespaces are simple but very useful information that indicate what a record is about.

The ontology query service responds to requests from application terminals. This component is similar to the EPCIS in the EPC system and the application information services in the uID system. All the ontology query services of all data nodes provide the same ontology query interface for terminals to follow.

2.4.2.3 Node

In IoT, each manufacturer is required to provide a data node to maintain the product description of its own products for terminals to query. This data node is the source node of the products. In this architecture, each manufacturer is also required to provide an ontology URI query/register service for the its own products. Each query node is the combination of the data node and the ontology URI query/register service of a manufacturer. All the services of a query node should be accessed by the same IP address. In this way, application terminals can find the address of the service for a certain product through the resolution service of the IoT infrastructures. The ontology URI query/register service has two interfaces for external partners to follow. The OnURI register interface is for data nodes to register the URIs of ontologies about products. The OnURI query interface is for terminals to request the URI list of products. The URI data are maintained in the OnURI management system.

To avoid receiving unrelated URIs, application terminals tell the query node which namespaces they are interested in, and the query node excludes the corresponding URIs that are unrelated with those namespaces. Note that the terminals do not tell the query node about the application that they are interested in. Using namespaces as the selective condition is not only simple but also provides a flexible mechanism for sharing information among different applications.

2.4.2.4 Terminal

A network client that implements various network communication protocols is necessary for a terminal because there are various types of URIs. In addition, application terminals should be equipped with a semantic processor to support ontology processing and semantic reasoning. Based on the two components, it is the application business logic that implements the specific functionalities that the applications need.

2.4.3 Evaluations of the Proposed Architecture

Our proposed architecture is scalable and distributed. The URI register/query service is distributed on all the query nodes (manufacturers). Note that the number of query nodes is not fixed but rather increases with the scale of the system. There are two major merits of this distribution scheme. First, when new manufacturers join the system, although it means more products and more information to be addressed, it does not add additional workload to the existing query nodes. Second, the manufacturers know the scale of their own products; therefore, they could determine how much computational and storage capability the service should be equipped with. Another advantage is that the ontology data are not centrally maintained. Each data node only needs to take responsibility for the data collected by itself and has the ability to selectively share data with other trading partners. Since data are stored in each data node, the workload is naturally distributed.

Manufacturers are willing to provide such a register/query service because this architecture is helpful for them to collect information about their products. In some existing distributed architectures, manufacturers may have to initiate many queries to many nodes to know where the product information is. In contrast, under this architecture, manufacturers preserve all the information URIs of all their products. Furthermore, obtaining these URIs is very easy because they are offered spontaneously by the data nodes. Using data analysis techniques, this product information would provide manufacturers insights regarding many aspects.

The problems of heterogeneity are addressed in this architecture. First, it is a service-oriented architecture. Partners communicate using three agreed upon interfaces, and it does not matter what devices or software that a node adopts. Second, all the records are represented in the form of an ontology following common ontology definitions. Therefore, records can be shared and interpreted unambiguously among all the partners. Even information from different applications could be integrated seamlessly. Moreover, the reasoning ability of semantic technologies is capable of various tasks, and we do not need to develop additional software. For example, in the next section, we will show how to use SWRL to trace products.

The efficiency is another major advantage of this architecture. For any product, the URIs of all the related information have been published to the source node of the product by other data nodes and maintained in a local data repository. Therefore, it can instantly respond to requests from application terminals in real time. In contrast to the P2P architectures, a query may be propagated several times, and this significantly increases the processing time.

The availability of the architecture is supported by its feature of distribution. For centralized architectures, the breakdown of the centralized unit leads to the breakdown of the entire system. For the proposed architecture, the breakdown of any data node or any query node only affects the data or products of that node. However, data availability is the shortcoming. Data are strictly privately kept in each data node. The breakdown of a data node means that the data in this node are no longer available.

One major disadvantage of the architecture is that it could bring heavy network traffic when the ontological records to be transmitted are large. Another disadvantage is that it requires application terminals to possess good processing ability in case the data are too large and to support semantic analysis. Distributed reasoning could be a solution to relieve this problem [23].

2.5 Case Study: Product Tracing

In this section, taking product tracing as an example, we show how the proposed architecture works for aggregating product information from distributed data nodes in IIoT applications. Note that we have not yet implemented the architecture. The node architectures have been detailed above; thus, we focus on the ontology generation and register procedure and the aggregation procedure. Through this example, we would also like to demonstrate the capacity of semantic web technology in solving problems from industrial applications.

The problem of product tracing has been briefly introduced in the preliminaries section, and an artificial example is illustrated in Figure 2.5. In this example, after leaving the manufacturers, a phone and a camera are delivered via some warehouses and finally arrive at the retailer. A special situation occurs during the delivery process in that when the phone passes warehouse2, it is packed in a case with the camera. Now, the retailer employee wants to trace the phone (Listing 2.1).

All the participants in this application use the same ontology definitions. In this case, four main classes are defined in namespace “http://cybermatics.org/owl/product-tracing/,” denoted as *pt*, to represent product, data node, trace record and the package record; see Listing 2.1. In this paper, we use SWRL to express the ontology using a functional syntax.

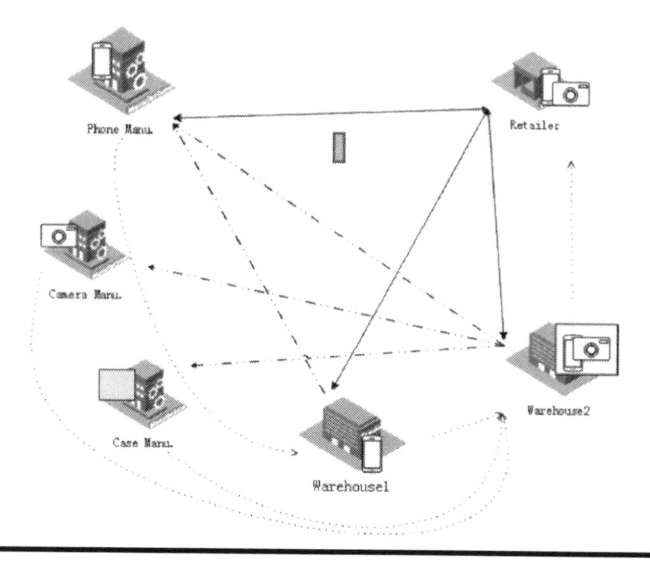

Figure 2.5 An example of product tracing.

```
Prefix(:=<http://cybermatics.org/owl/product-tracing/>)
...
Declaration( Class( :TraceRecord ))
Declaration( Class( :Node ))
Declaration( Class( :Product))
Declaration( Class( :PackRecord))
```

Listing 2.1 Classes declaration.

2.5.1 The Ontology Generation and Register Procedure

Within the proposed architecture, data nodes generate information about the phone in the form of an ontology and register them at the corresponding query node, i.e., the phone manufacturer. For this phone, the first and the authoritative piece of information is the product description generated by its manufacturer, which contains some basic information such as the product serial number, manufacturer and so forth. The manufacturer equips the phone with an RFID tag that contains a globally unique EPC, by which the product description can be addressed from elsewhere in IoT. In this sense, this ID is also the URI of the product description. The product description is written in ontology language as follows; see Listing 2.2.

When the phone leaves the phone manufacturer, it leaves a trace record 1, which records the phone ID, thee node name, and time information as follows; see Listing 2.3.

"pt:beginTime" and "pt:endTime" are data properties of the TraceRecord class indicating when the product is discovered and when it leaves the data node.

```
Prefix(pt:=<http://cybermatics.org/owl/product-tracing/>)
...
ClassAssertion(pt:Product :phone )
DataPropertyAssertion(pt:hasID :phone "urn:epc:1:2.24.400"^^xsd:anyURI)
DataPropertyAssertion( pt:producedBy :phone "phoneManu"^^xsd:string)
```

Listing 2.2 Product description.

```
Prefix(pt:=<http://cybermatics.org/owl/product-tracing/>)
...
ClassAssertion( pt:TraceRecord :phoneManu_record1 )
DataPropertyAssertion( pt:hasProductID :phoneManu_record1 "urn:epc:1:2.*.*"^^xsd:anyURI)
DataPropertyAssertion( pt:hasNodeName :phoneManu_record1 "phoneManu.")
DataPropertyAssertion( pt:beginTime :phoneManu_record1 "2016-3-20T21:32:52"^^xsd:dateTime)
DataPropertyAssertion( pt:endTime :record1 "2016-3-27T10:22:51"^^xsd:dateTime)
```

Listing 2.3 Tracing record.

The manufacturer publishes this piece of information using an HTTP URL and registers this URL along with the used namespaces, including *pt*, at its own ontology URI query/register server.

When the phone passes the next data node, i.e., warehousel, it leaves the trace record warehousel record1, as does the camera. Warehousel adopts the uID system, so it issues two different ucodes for the two records and registers the ucodes and *pt* at the phone manufacturer and the camera manufacturer, respectively; see Listing 2.4.

```
Prefix(pt:=<http://cybermatics.org/owl/product-tracing/>)
...
ClassAssertion( pt:TraceRecord :warehouse1_record1 )
ObjectPropertyAssertion(pt :hasProduct :record2 :phone)
DataPropertyAssertion( pt:beginTime :record1
    201"6-04-01T00:00:00"^^xsd:dateTime)
DataPropertyAssertion( pt:endTime :record1
    "2016-04-02T00:00:00""^^xsd:dateTime)
...
ClassAssertion( pt:TraceRecord :warehouse1_record2 )
ObjectPropertyAssertion(pt :hasProduct : warehouse1_record2:camera)
DataPropertyAssertion( pt:beginTime : warehouse1_record2
    "2016-04-01T12:00:00"^^xsd:dateTime)
DataPropertyAssertion( pt:endTime : warehouse1_record2
    "2016-04-02T00:00:00"^^xsd:dateTime)
```

Listing 2.4 Product tracing.

```
Prefix(pt:=<http://cybermatics.org/owl/product-tracing/>)
...
ClassAssertion( pt:TraceRecord :warehouse2_record1 )
ObjectPropertyAssertion(pt :hasProduct :warehouse2_record1 :case)
DataPropertyAssertion( pt:beginTime :warehouse2_record1
    "2016-04-11T00:00:00"^^xsd:dateTime)
DataPropertyAssertion( pt:endTime :warehouse2_record1
    "2016-04-12T00:00:00"^^xsd:dateTime)
ClassAssertion( pt:PackRecord :packRecord )
ObjectPropertyAssertion(pt :hasPackageNode :packRecord :warehouse2)
ObjectPropertyAssertion( pt:hasCase :packRecord :case)
ObjectPropertyAssertion( pt:hasPacked :packRecord :phone)
ObjectPropertyAssertion(pt :hasPacked :packRecord :camera)
```

Figure 2.6 The trace record of the case.

The warehouse2 data node observes a case passing by; then, it generates a trace record for the case. In addition, it also observes that the phone and the camera are packed in the case. Therefore, it appends the packing information to the trace record. The ontological expression of this piece of information is shown in Figure 2.6. The PackRecord class has a data property has Package Node, indicating the name of the data node where the packing information is collected. We assume that warehouse2 also adopts a uID system and issues a ucode for the record it collects. Since this ontology involves three products, warehouse2 registers the ucode of this record at the phone manufacturer, the camera manufacturer and the case manufacturer.

2.5.2 The Ontology Aggregation Procedure

Finally, the retailer receives the phone, and it wants to determine how the phone arrived. The application terminal first scans the RFID tag attached to the phone to obtain the ID. Then, by the resolution service of the EPC network, the terminal obtains the address of the query node of the phone manufacturer and sends an aggregation request to the ontology URI query service. The request content includes the product's ID and the namespace for product tracing, i.e., "http://cybermatics.org/owl/product-tracing/."

Once the query node receives the request, it generates the URI list, which is composed of all the URIs that have been registered with the phone's ID and the specific namespace. Then, the query node responds to the terminal with the OnURI list.

The terminal receives the response. Then, it checks the OnURI list. If the OnURI list is not empty, it concurrently initiates requests for the information addressed by the URIs; otherwise, it stops collecting further information. In this case, the list is not empty, and the URIs include http URL and ucodes. Therefore, the network client uses the corresponding network protocols to request information. The requests are initiated concurrently, and thus, the network transmission time does not increase with the number of URIs.

When each data node receives a request, it responds with the information addressed by the URI to the terminal.

Thus far, the terminal has collected all the information that involves the phone. The information contains the product description, two trace records of the phone, a trace record of the case, and a packing record. Note that what the retailer employee wants is to trace the phone. Therefore, before we present the collected information to the employee, the terminal needs to exclude the product description and understand that the trace record of the case is also a trace record of the phone.

We define a class name TraceRecord_phone for the phone. By the SWRL rule defined below, Pellet infers that any trace record has a product with a URI of "urn:epc:1:2.24.400" is an instance of TraceRecord_phone.

```
TraceRecord(?t)^Product(?p)^hasProduct(?r,?p)^
    hasID(?p,"urn:epc:1:2.24.400"^^xsd:anyURI)−>TraceRecord_phone(?t)
```

However, the trace record of the case in Figure 2.6 is also indispensable for tracing the phone. Then, another SWRL rule is defined as follows, which states that any trace record that has a case also has the products packed in the case if its node is the same as the package node. With this rule, Pellet can infer that the trace record that has the case in Figure 2.6 has the phone. Combined with the above rule, Pellet can select all the trace records for the phone.

```
hasNode(?r, ?n) ^ hasCase(?rt, ?c) ^ hasPacked(?rt, ?p) ^ Node(?n) ^
hasPackageNode(?rt, ?n) ^ hasProduct(?r, ?c) −> hasProduct(?r, ?p)
```

If someone wants to trace the camera, they can define a similar class and a rule for the camera. The inference result is shown in Figures 2.7 and 2.8, which indicates that all the trace records have been determined.

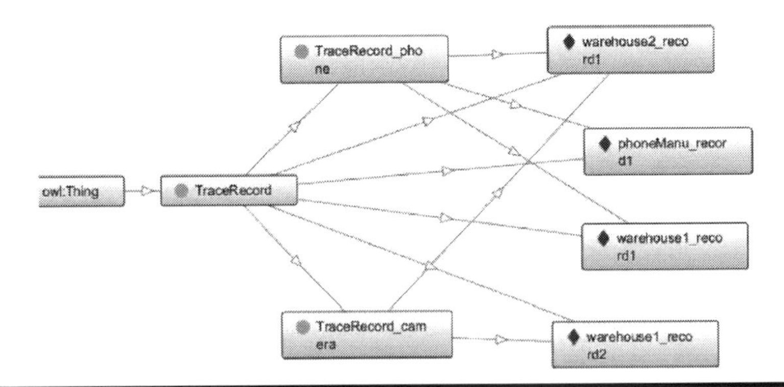

Figure 2.7 The inferred individuals of TraceRecord drawn by Protégé OntoGraf.

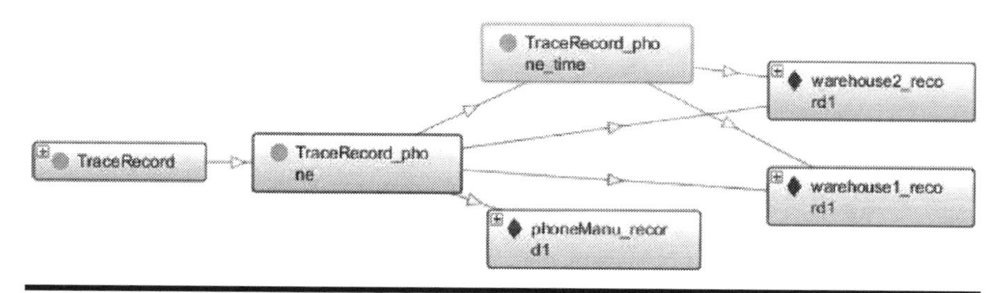

Figure 2.8 The result of product tracing drawn by Protégé OntoGraf.

However, according to the definition of production tracing, the records that do not satisfy the time constraint should be eliminated. Assuming that the retailer employee wants the record from April 1, 2016, to April 30, 2016, the constraint rule is as follows.

```
beginTime(?r, ?start) ^ endTime(?r, ?end) ^
    swrlb:greaterThanOrEqual(?end, "2016-04-01T00:00:00"^^xsd:dateTime) ^
    TraceRecord_phone(?r) ^ swrlb:lessThanOrEqual(?start, "2016-05-01T00:00:00"^^xsd:dateTime)
    -> TraceRecord_phone_time(?r)
```

Finally, from the result presented in Figure 2.8, it can be observed that Pellet has successfully excluded phoneManu_record1, and the task of tracing the phone has been completed.

2.6 Conclusion and Future Directions

In conclusion, the architecture proposed in this paper is a potential solution to the task of aggregating information from multiple data nodes, which is common in many IIoT applications. The architecture is scalable, because each query node (manufacturer) only takes responsibility for its own products, and each data node only for the data collected by itself. The architecture is also efficient. Query/Register requests are responded instantly, because the addresses of related nodes can be directly resolved with the product URIs. Information and node heterogeneity is addressed in the architecture with semantic and service-oriented technologies. We also propose to use ontology namespaces as the condition to select the interesting ontologies. This scheme can reduce the network traffic and would be a flexible mechanism to share data among different applications.

In the case study section, taking the problem of product tracing as an example, we show how to apply the proposed architecture to applications in IIoT. In this case, we detail the ontology generation and register procedure and the ontology aggregation procedure. The focus of this section is the use of semantic technologies, and it is shown that the reasoning ability of semantic technologies has the potential to support various important functionalities and thus to lay a solid foundation to support heterogeneous IIoT applications.

There are several important directions for future works. We have pointed out some disadvantages of the proposed architecture. The data availability is not solid, and in some cases, the network traffic could be heavy. Strategies are needed to relieve these problems. Moreover, before placing the architecture into practice, the security and privacy problems should be taken into consideration. In addition, evaluating the proposed architecture in other applications is also interesting.

Acknowledgments

This work is supported by the Fundamental Research Funds for the Central Universities (No. 06116073, No. 06105031) and the National Natural Science Foundation of China (No. 61471035).

References

1. Miorandi D, Sicari S, De Pellegrini F, Chlamtac I. Internet of Things: Vision, applications and research challenges. *Ad Hoc Netw.* 2012;10(7):1497–1516. doi:10.1016/j.adhoc.2012.02.016.
2. Atzori L, Iera A, Morabito G. The Internet of Things: A survey. *Comput. Netw.* 2010;54(15):2787–2805. doi:10.1016/j.comnet.2010.05.010.
3. Riazul Islam SM, Daehan Kwak, Humaun Kabir M, Hossain M, Kyung-Sup Kwak. The Internet of Things for health care: A comprehensive survey. *IEEE Access* 2015;3:678–708. doi:10.1109/ACCESS.2015.2437951.
4. Santos DFS, Almeida HO, Perkusich A. A personal connected health system for the Internet of Things based on the constrained application protocol. *Comput. Electr. Eng.* 2014;44:122–136. doi:10.1016/j.compeleceng.2015.02.020.
5. Fang S, Xu L, Zhu Y, Liu Y, Liu Z, Pei H et al. An integrated information system for snowmelt flood early-warning based on Internet of Things. *Inform. Syst. Front.* 2015;17(2):321–335. doi:10.1007/s10796-013-9466-1.
6. Agrawal R, Cheung A, Kailing K, Schönauer S. Towards traceability across sovereign, distributed RFID databases. *Proceedings of the International Database Engineering and Applications Symposium, IDEAS* 2006:174–184. doi:10.1109/IDEAS.2006.47.
7. Qin E, Long Y, Zhang C, Huang L. Cloud computing and the internet of things: Technology innovation in automobile service. *International Conference on Human Interface and the Management of Information* 2013:73–180.
8. Xu LD, He W, Li S. Internet of Things in industries: A survey. *IEEE Trans. Ind. Inf.* 2014;10(4):2233–2243. doi:10.1109/TII.2014.2300753.
9. Pang Z, Chen Q, Han W, Zheng L. Value-centric design of the Internet-of-Things solution for food supply chain: Value creation, sensor portfolio and information fusion. *Inf. Syst. Front.* 2012;17(2):289–319. doi:10.1007/s10796-012-9374-9.

10. Chen RY. Autonomous tracing system for backward design in food supply chain. *Food Control* 2015;51:70–84. doi:10.1016/j.foodcont.2014.11.004.
11. Koshizuka N, Sakamura K. Standards & emerging technologies ubiquitous ID. *Context* 2010;9(4):98–101. doi:10.1109/MPRV.2010.87.
12. Wu Y, Ranasinghe DC, Sheng QZ, Zeadally S, Yu J. RFID enabled traceability networks: A survey. *Distrib. Parallel Databases* 2011;29(5–6):397–443. doi:10.1007/s10619- 011-7084-9.
13. Wu Y, Sheng QZ, Shen H, Zeadally S. Modeling object flows from distributed and federated RFID data streams for efficient tracking and tracing. *IEEE Trans. Parallel Distrib. Syst.* 2013;24(10):2036–2045. doi:10.1109/TPDS.2013.99.
14. Hitzler P, Körtzsch M, Rudolph S. *Foundations of Semantic Web Technologies*. Boca Raton, FL: Chapman & Hall/CRC Press; 2009.
15. Barnaghi P, Wang W, Henson C, Taylor K. Semantics for the internet of things: Early progress and back to the future. *Int. J. Semantic Web Inf. Syst.* 2012;8:1–21. doi:10.4018/jswis.2012010101.
16. Chen L, Nugent C, Mulvenna M, Finlay D, Hong X. Semantic smart homes: Towards knowledge rich assisted living environments. *Stud. Comput. Intell.* 2009;189:279–296. doi:10.1007/978-3-642-00179-6_17.
17. Skillen KL, Chen L, Nugent CD, Donnelly MP, Burns W, Solheim I. Ontological user modelling and semantic rule-based reasoning for personalisation of help-On-Demand services in pervasive environments. *Future Gener. Comput. Syst.* 2014;34:97–109. doi:10.1016/j.future.2013.10.027.
18. Sheth AP, Larson JA. Federated database systems for managing distributed, heterogeneous, and autonomous databases. *ACM Comput. Surv.* 1990;22(3):183–236. doi:10.1145/96602.96604.
19. Cheung A, Railing K, Schönauer S. Theseos: A query engine for traceability across sovereign, distributed RFID databases. *Proceedings of the International Conference Data Engineering* 2007:1495–1496. doi:10.1109/ICDE.2007.369050.
20. Dressler F. A Study of self-organization mechanisms in ad hoc and sensor networks. *Comput. Commun.* 2008;31(13):3018–3029. doi:10.1016/j.comcom.2008.02.001.
21. Guinard D, Trifa V, Karnouskos S, Spiess P, Savio D. Interacting with the SOA-based internet of things: Discovery, query, selection, and on-demand provisioning of web services. *IEEE Trans. Serv. Comput.* 2010;3(3):223–235. doi:10.1109/TSC.2010.3.
22. Lu J, Ma L, Zhang L, Brunner J-S, Wang C, Pan Y et al. SOR: A practical system for ontology storage, reasoning and search. *Proceedings of the 33rd International Conference on Very Large Data Bases* 2007:1402–1405.
23. Oren E, Kotoulas S, Anadiotis G, Siebes R, ten Teije A, van Harmelen F. Marvin: Distributed reasoning over large-scale semantic web data. *J. Web Semant.* 2009;7(4):305–316. doi:10.1016/j.websem.2009.09.002.

Chapter 3

A Kernel Machine-Based Secure Data Sensing and Fusion Scheme in Wireless Sensor Networks for the Cyber-Physical Systems

Xiong Luo, Dandan Zhang, Laurence T. Yang, Ji Liu, Xiaohui Chang, and Huansheng Ning

Contents

3.1 Introduction

A cyber-physical system (CPS) as an integration of sensor networks with cyber resources responds intelligently to dynamic changes in the physical world, where the wireless sensor networks (WSNs) as one of the key components collect sensor data from the physical environment [1]. With the increasing presence and adoption of WSNs on the deployment of CPS, there has been a growing demand in data sensing and data fusion to properly utilize CPS intelligence. Then, by integrating WSNs from different domains, CPS has emerged as a promising direction to enrich the interactions between physical and virtual worlds [2,3]. A WSN is composed of spatially distributed autonomous sensors used to cooperatively monitor physical or environmental data, such as temperature, humidity, light, noise, pressure, speed and many others [4]. WSNs can be used for data sensing, disposing and transmitting [5]. While WSNs are employed for real-time monitoring, plenty of sensor nodes sense the data of fluctuant monitored objects within a valid range and send those data to the sink node and end-users [6,7]. More recently, WSNs have demonstrated many successful applications across a wide range of domains, such as military affairs, national security, national defense, environment monitoring, energy management and so on [8]. Thus, they are one of the key technologies to support sensing and actuation of CPS. WSNs are becoming a multidisciplinary research area attracting researchers from different fields, especially industrial areas.

In WSNs, the power module provides energy for nodes and once the nodes are deployed in many applications, it is almost impossible to recharge them. It is known that the process of wireless communication consumes most of the energy [9]. Since the data generated by sensor nodes during continuous sensing periods usually are of high temporal coherence, some data in the sustaining data sequence may be redundant, while causing unnecessary data transmission and wasting energy. The prediction-based data sensing and fusion schemes therefore have been proposed to process original data in the sensor nodes and reduce unnecessary transmissions [10]. To achieve the goal of extending the lifetime of the whole network, those schemes fully utilize the high temporal coherence of the sensed data to lessen the redundant transmissions and save the energy of sensor nodes [11,12]. In addition, since some problems like information leakage exist during data transmission, the security of data is also one of the key issues in WSNs.

Among the known data sensing and fusion methods, a delay-aware network structure for WSNs with in-network data fusion was proposed in [13]. The proposed structure organizes sensor nodes into clusters of different sizes so that each cluster can communicate with the fusion center in an interleaved manner. However, it cannot achieve the best effectiveness without knowing the minimum achievable compression ratio between the sizes of incoming and outgoing data. For different data sensing and fusion topologies (e.g., star, chain and tree), the optimal solutions were provided while computing the number of transmissions for each node in [14]. The distributed approximation algorithms were also presented for chain and tree topologies, but the model may be more complex as the size of the network increases. In [15], a distributed sensor fusion method was designed using a tree-based broadcasting strategy to improve the estimation efficiency and accuracy in WSN. Through the use of genetic machine learning algorithms, an implementation for data fusion techniques in WSNs was developed [16]. A quality-based multiple-sensor fusion approach was proposed in WSN [17]. However, there are also some improvements for these methods when the data set in WSN is more complex. In [18], the authors proposed a prediction-based temporal data fusion technique through the use of a first-order auto-regressive model. However, the prediction accuracy of this model is poor when the time series data set is few or nonlinear [19].

In order to avoid those limitations mentioned in the above data fusion approaches, some novel prediction-based data sensing and fusion schemes were presented with the help of grey model (GM) [20]. For instance, in [21], the authors presented a scheme GM-LSSVM. It implements the initial prediction using GM, and then utilizes the powerful nonlinear mapping capability of least squares support vector machine (LS-SVM) to improve prediction accuracy. LS-SVM is established using the structural risk minimization principle rather than the empirical error commonly implemented in neural networks. Then, LS-SVM can achieve higher generalization performance and higher precision accuracy than neural networks. But almost all nonlinear series system identification by LS-SVM is offline, and its model is trained periodically. It imposes a challenging obstacle while using LS-SVM to conduct the prediction for nonlinear time series online. Moreover, in GM-LSSVM, it just employs the prediction mechanism in all sensor nodes, then the sink node cannot get any data at some sampling periods. Therefore, this scheme cannot guarantee that the end-users are able to obtain the sensed data in every sampling point, and it is infeasible in most real-time monitoring applications. Motivated by [22], a novel scheme GM-OP-ELM through the combination of GM and optimally pruned extreme learning machine (OP-ELM) was proposed in [23]. Compared with GM-LSSVM, the computing speed of GM-OP-ELM improves greatly. With this scheme, prediction time can be saved immensely, but in some situations its accuracy may be lower than GM-LSSVM.

To improve prediction accuracy and guarantee transmission confidentiality, a novel prediction-based secure data sensing and fusion scheme using GM, kernel recursive least squares (KRLS) and the Blowfish algorithm (BA) is proposed in this paper to reduce the redundant transmission in WSNs. This scheme is called GM-KRLS. During the data sensing and fusion process, both the sink node and the sensor nodes must use the same small number of recent data items and prediction mechanism to predict the data of the next period, while guaranteeing that the data sequences in the sink node and the sensor nodes are synchronous. Then the end-users can get the accurate data of all sensor nodes from the sink node in every sampling period. When the prediction error is under the threshold defined by end-users, the sensor node does not need to send the sensed data to the sink node, then both the sink node and sensor node will consider the predicted data as the sensed data in this period; otherwise, the transmission between the sensor node and sink node will happen while encoding and decoding data based on BA [24,25]. In this way, unnecessary transmission is canceled to achieve the goal of secure data sensing and fusion. Moreover, in order to reduce the computational complexity and improve the accuracy of the prediction algorithm with a small number of data items, the proposed scheme employs GM to obtain the initial predicted value, then with the help of the KRLS learning algorithm [26], our scheme makes the predicted value approximate its actual value with high accuracy.

Through kernel function, KRLS puts original and nonlinear inputs into high-dimensional space to make them linear. It provides a generalization of the linear adaptive algorithm. As KRLS exhibits a growing memory structure embedded in the weight coefficients, it naturally creates a growing radial-basis function network, while learning the network topology and adapting the free parameters directly from data at the same time. Compared with the kernel least mean square (KLMS) algorithm as a typical kernel method, KRLS as an improved kernel machine learning algorithm has unique features where the learning rule is a beautiful combination of error-correction and memory-based learning [27,28]. Although KRLS and KLMS work in a similar way under the error-correction learning scheme, the former aims at minimizing the sum of squared estimation errors and the latter aims at minimizing the instantaneous value of the squared estimation. The convergence rate of KRLS is therefore relatively faster than that of KLMS. In consideration of the above reasons, we choose KRLS for data prediction in our scheme, and GM-KRLS may achieve high-accuracy data sensing and fusion with fast computing speed.

The rest of this paper is organized as follows. The related works are analyzed in Section 3.2. Section 3.3 describes the detailed secure data sensing and fusion scheme GM-KRLS. The simulation results and discussions are provided in Section 3.4. The conclusion is summarized in Section 3.5.

3.2 Related Work

3.2.1 Grey Model- (GM-) Based Prediction Method

The grey system represents a system in which the information about it is poor, incomplete, or uncertain. Under the system analysis scheme using GM, it can use only a few pieces of data to estimate an unknown system [29]. Meanwhile, the GM features a first-order differential equation used to characterize system behavior. Since the storage ability of a sensor node is limited, it is not easy to provide complete information for the whole WSN. It therefore can be treated as a grey system with uncertain or incomplete information in the process of data sensing and fusion.

As a single variable first-order model, GM(1,1) is the most commonly used grey model. In this paper, it is employed to conduct the initial prediction for those nodes in WSN. The prediction procedure of GM(1,1) can be summarized as follows [30,31]:

1. Define the original positive data sequence as follows:

$$\boldsymbol{x}^{(0)} = \left[x^{(0)}(1), x^{(0)}(2), \cdots, x^{(0)}(k), \cdots, x^{(0)}(n) \right] \tag{3.1}$$

   where $x^{(0)}(k)$ is the time series data at time k, and n represents the length of the data sequence.
2. Generate a new sequence $\boldsymbol{x}^{(1)}$ by the accumulated generating operation (AGO) for the initial sequence $\boldsymbol{x}^{(0)}$:

$$\boldsymbol{x}^{(1)} = \left[x^{(1)}(1), x^{(1)}(2), \cdots, x^{(1)}(k), \cdots, x^{(1)}(n) \right] \tag{3.2}$$

   where

$$x^{(1)}(k) = \sum_{i=1}^{k} x^{(0)}(i), k = 1, 2, \cdots, n$$

3. Form the first-order differential equation for $x^{(1)}(k)$ from $\boldsymbol{x}^{(1)}$:

$$\frac{\partial x^{(1)}(k)}{\partial k} + \omega x^{(1)}(k) = \vartheta \tag{3.3}$$

   where ω is the development coefficient, and ϑ denotes the grey input.
4. Use the ordinary least squares (OLS) method to estimate the gray parameters ω and ϑ in (3.3):

$$\begin{bmatrix} \hat{\omega} \\ \hat{\vartheta} \end{bmatrix} = \left(\mathbf{v}^T \mathbf{v} \right)^{-1} \mathbf{v}^T \tilde{\boldsymbol{n}} \tag{3.4}$$

   where $\hat{\omega}$ and $\hat{\vartheta}$ are the estimated gray parameters, respectively. Moreover,

$$\boldsymbol{v} = \begin{bmatrix} -\frac{1}{2}\left[x^{(1)}(2)+x^{(1)}(1)\right] & 1 \\ -\frac{1}{2}\left[x^{(1)}(3)+x^{(1)}(1)\right] & 1 \\ \vdots & \vdots \\ -\frac{1}{2}\left[x^{(1)}(n)+x^{(1)}(n-1)\right] & 1 \end{bmatrix}$$

and

$$\tilde{\boldsymbol{n}} = \left[x^{(0)}(2), x^{(0)}(3), \cdots, x^{(0)}(n)\right]^T$$

5. Obtain the predictive function by solving (3.3) and using the estimated parameters in (3.4):

$$\hat{x}^{(1)}(k) = \left(x^{(0)}(1) - \frac{\hat{\vartheta}}{\hat{\omega}}\right)e^{-\hat{\omega}(k-1)} + \frac{\hat{\vartheta}}{\hat{\omega}}, \ k = 1,2,\cdots \tag{3.5}$$

where $\hat{x}^{(1)}(k)$ is the predicted value of $x^{(1)}(k)$ at time k. Then, the predicted value $\hat{x}^{(1)}(k)$ at time k is:

$$\hat{x}^{(0)}(k) = \hat{x}^{(1)}(k) - \hat{x}^{(1)}(k-1) \tag{3.6}$$

where $\hat{x}^{(1)}(0)$ is set to 0.

Recently, some extension and optimization for GM(1,1) have been conducted and new grey prediction models were developed, such as the whitenization-based model GM(1,1, *Whi*) [32], an interval grey prediction model considering uncertain information [33].

3.2.2 Kernel Recursive Least Square (KRLS) Learning Algorithm

Adaptive algorithms can adjust their coefficients dynamically to adapt to the signal statistics in accordance with optimization algorithms. Consider an adaptive algorithm with M adjustable coefficients

$$y(i) = \boldsymbol{w}(i)^{\mathrm{T}}\boldsymbol{u}(i) \tag{3.7}$$

where $\boldsymbol{u}(i) = \left[u(i-D), u(i-D-1), \cdots, u(i-D-M+1)\right]^{\mathrm{T}}$ is the input vector; $\boldsymbol{w}(i) = \left[w_0(n), w_1(n), \cdots, w_{M-1}(n)\right]^{\mathrm{T}}$ is the coefficient vector; $y(i)$ denotes the output value and D is the prediction delay ($D \geq 1$).

Then the error sequence $e(i)$ can be formed as below:

$$e(i)=d(i)-y(i) \tag{3.8}$$

where $d(i)$ is a desired output and $e(i)$ can be used in optimization algorithms for updating the coefficients.

As the adaptive algorithms in kernel spaces have improved performance, kernel adaptive algorithms have been proposed in recent years. The kernel version of the recursive least square (RLS) is given as below.

Let $\kappa(\boldsymbol{u},\boldsymbol{v})$ be the kernel function. And the Gaussian kernel is defined as:

$$\kappa(\boldsymbol{u},\boldsymbol{v})=e^{-\zeta\|\boldsymbol{u}-\boldsymbol{v}\|^2} \tag{3.9}$$

where $\boldsymbol{u}$ and $\boldsymbol{v}$ are input vectors for kernel function, and ζ is a kernel parameter.

To derive RLS in reproducing kernel Hilbert space (RKHS), we utilize the Mercer theorem to transform the data $\boldsymbol{u}(i)$ into the feature space $\mathbb{F}$ as $\varphi(\boldsymbol{u}(i))$ (denoted as $\varphi(i)$) [27]. We formulate the RLS algorithm on the example sequence $\{d(1),d(2),\cdots\}$ and $\{\varphi(1),\varphi(2),\cdots\}$. At each iteration, the weight vector $\boldsymbol{w}(i)$ is the optimization solution of

$$\min_{\boldsymbol{w}}=\sum_{j=1}^{i}\beta^{i-j}|d(j)-\boldsymbol{w}^{\mathrm{T}}\varphi(j)|^2+\beta^i\lambda\|\boldsymbol{w}\|^2 \tag{3.10}$$

where λ is the regulation parameter, and β is the forgetting factor.

By introducing

$$\boldsymbol{d}(i)=[d(1),\cdots,d(i)]^{\mathrm{T}} \tag{3.11}$$

$$\phi(i)=[\varphi(1),\cdots,\varphi(i)] \tag{3.12}$$

We have

$$\boldsymbol{w}(i)=\left[\beta^i\lambda\mathrm{I}+\phi(i)\varsigma(i)(\phi(i))^{\mathrm{T}}\right]^{-1}\phi(i)\varsigma(i)\boldsymbol{d}(i) \tag{3.13}$$

where $\varsigma(i)=\mathrm{diag}\{\beta^{i-1},\beta^{i-2},\cdots,1\}$.

Furthermore, by using the matrix inversion lemma, (3.13) can be rewritten as

$$\boldsymbol{w}(i)=\phi(i)[\beta^i\lambda(\varsigma(i))^{-1}+(\phi(i))^{\mathrm{T}}\phi(i)]^{-1}\boldsymbol{d}(i) \tag{3.14}$$

The weight is explicitly expressed as a linear combination of the input data:

$$\boldsymbol{w}(i)=\phi(i)\boldsymbol{a}(i)$$

with

$$a(i)=\left[\beta^{i}\lambda\left(\varsigma(i)\right)^{-1}+\left(\phi(i)\right)^{\mathrm{T}}\phi\left(i\right)\right]^{-1}d(i) \tag{3.15}$$

Denote

$$\chi\left(i\right)=\left[\beta^{i}\lambda\left(\varsigma(i)\right)^{-1}+\left(\phi(i)\right)^{\mathrm{T}}\phi(i)\right]^{-1} \tag{3.16}$$

$\chi\left(i\right)$ can be expressed as follows:

$$\chi\left(i\right)=\left(r\left(i\right)\right)^{-1}\begin{bmatrix}\chi(i-1)r(i)+z(i)\left(z(i)\right)^{\mathrm{T}} & -z(i)\\ -\left(z(i)\right)^{\mathrm{T}} & 1\end{bmatrix} \tag{3.17}$$

where

$$z\left(i\right)=\chi\left(i-1\right)b\left(i\right) \tag{3.18}$$

$$r(i)=\beta^{i}\lambda+\kappa\left(u(i),u(i)\right)-\left(z(i)\right)^{\mathrm{T}}b(i) \tag{3.19}$$

and $a\left(i\right)$ can be calculated as follows:

$$a(i)=\begin{bmatrix}a(i-1)-z(i)\left(r(i)\right)^{-1}e(i)\\ \left(r(i)\right)^{-1}e(i)\end{bmatrix} \tag{3.20}$$

The KRLS algorithm can be summarized in Algorithm 1. As defined in this algorithm, a is a set of coefficients of the kernel expansion.

Algorithm 1: **KRLS**

Input: The original input data set u(i)
The desired output data set d(i)
Output: The predicted data set y(i)

1 $\chi\left(1\right)=(\lambda\beta+\kappa\left(u(1),u(1)\right)^{-1},a(1)=\chi\left(1\right)d(1),i=1$
2 **While** u(i) is available **do**
3 Calculate the output:

$$h(i)=\left[\kappa\left(u(i),u(1)\right),\cdots,\kappa\left(u(i),u(i-1)\right)^{\mathrm{T}}\right]$$

$y(i)=\left(h(i)\right)^{\mathrm{T}}a(i-1)$
4 Calculate the error: $e(i)=d(i)-h(i)^{\mathrm{T}}a(i-1)$

5 Update the coefficients: $z(i) = \chi(i-1)\boldsymbol{h}(i)$

$$r(i) = \beta^i \lambda + \kappa(\boldsymbol{u}(i), \boldsymbol{u}(i)) - (z(i))^T \boldsymbol{h}(i)$$

$$\chi(i) = r(i)^{-1} \begin{bmatrix} \chi(i-1)r(i) + z(i)(z(i))^T & -z(i) \\ -(z(i))^T & 1 \end{bmatrix}$$

$$\boldsymbol{a}(i) = \begin{bmatrix} a(i-1) - z(i)(r(i))^{-1} e(i) \\ (r(i))^{-1} e(i) \end{bmatrix}$$

6 $i = i + 1$

7 **End while**

Furthermore, some improvements on the basis of such basic KRLS have been achieved. For instance, by incorporating an online vector quantization method [28] or a forgetting technique in Bayesian inspired framework [34], the learning performance of KRLS can be improved. Then, those KRLS algorithms are particularly applicable to cases in which data arrives sequentially. From this point of view, this learning algorithm may have great potential to address our discussed issue in this paper.

3.2.3 Blowfish Algorithm (BA)

Every sensor node has a secret key which differs from other nodes. The sink node will generate a session key at the beginning and broadcast it to all sensor nodes. The sensor node will calculate a needham-schroeder symmetric key (NSSK) with its secret key and the session key for data encoding and decoding of this sensor node. Since the sink node knows all the secret keys of sensor nodes, it could calculate NSSKs to decode the data. Data transmissions between sink node and sensor nodes employ BA for encryption [35]. One run of data sensing, fusion, and transmission is listed below:

1. The sensor node senses data and employs the data sensing and fusion scheme to data prediction and fusion.
2. If the prediction error is below the threshold, both the sink node and sensor nodes consider the predicted data as actual data, and transmission is canceled. Otherwise, sensor node sends the actual data to sink node.
3. For the data need to be sent, the sensor node employs NSSK for encoding.
4. The sink node calculates NSSKs of sensor nodes and decodes data.

Bruce Schneier designed the BA, which is available in the public domain [24]. Since BA was first introduced in 1993, it has not been cracked yet, where Blowfish is a variable length key with 64-bit block cipher. From the application side, BA has demonstrated many successful applications across a wide range of domains.

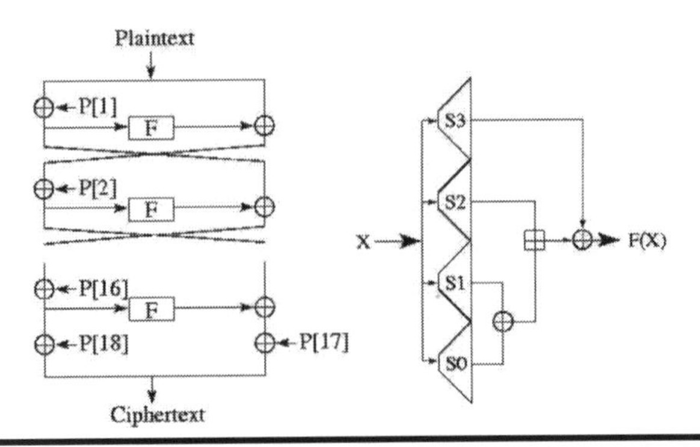

Figure 3.1 Schematic diagram of Blowfish algorithm.

As shown in Figure 3.1 [25], there are two parts of BA, i.e., the key expansion and the data encryption. The key expansion of BA begins with the P-array and S-box through the utilization of many sub-keys, while it converts a key of at most 448 bits into several sub-key arrays with 4168 bytes. Meanwhile data encryption is implemented through a 16-round network, where a key-dependent permutation as well as a key-dependent and data-dependent substitution are conducted in each round. All of the operations include XOR and additions on 32-bit words. Here, the F-function of BA is probably the most complex part of this algorithm because it is the only part of utilizing the S-box. More recently, to simplify the precessing complexity, a novel F-function was designed to generate dynamic S-box and XOR operator [36], and a new method was also developed to generate S-box and P-array [37].

Considering features of the above surveyed algorithms, the integration of those three methods in our proposed scheme may be an innovative case. Specifically, compared with other existing data fusion methods in WSNs, the proposed method has some unique advantages. Our contributions could be summarized as follows. Firstly, we employ GM to reduce random errors while using KRLS to improve prediction accuracy due to its powerful nonlinear mapping ability, and the combination of GM and KRLS is novel in kernel methods. Secondly, to guarantee data security, both the sink node and sensor node use the same prediction mechanism to reduce redundant data transmission; meanwhile, BA is introduced for data encoding and decoding. Thirdly, we use a small number of recent data items to predict the data of the next period in the data fusion scheme; thus, the increased data set may not influence the prediction effect. In this case, the proposed method may be effective in addressing some big-scale data sets.

3.3 Secure Data Sensing and Fusion Scheme GM-KRLS

3.3.1 The Scheme GM-KRLS

In consideration of the limited energy and storage as well as data security in sensor nodes, we present a prediction-based secure data sensing and fusion scheme, GM-KRLS, to reduce redundant data transmission, save energy with low computational cost and maintain data confidentiality. To guarantee that the data series in the sink node and the sensor nodes are synchronous in every period while conducing data sensing and fusion, both the sink node and the sensor nodes should employ the same data sequence and prediction mechanism [19]. Then the end-users can get the data of every sampling point in sensor nodes with low communication cost.

In the secure data sensing and fusion scheme, the data of the next period is predicted through our proposed method. The sensor node compares the sensed data with the predicted data. If the error between them is under the threshold ε, it is unnecessary for the sensor node to send the data to the sink node, and the energy is saved while achieving the goal of data fusion. Meanwhile, the sink node also employs the same prediction mechanism to predict the data of next period, and then considers the predicted data as the sensed data in the current period. Furthermore, the sensor node should transmit the sensed data to the sink node through the use of BA for encoding when the prediction error is beyond the threshold ε. It should be pointed that ε is defined by end-users and can be adjusted. Then the prediction accuracy will be influenced by different values of ε.

To improve prediction accuracy through the use of a few sample data items, in this paper, after obtaining the initial predicted data sequence via GM, the proposed method employs KRLS to make this predicted sequence approximate its actual value. Thus, the proposed secure data sensing and fusion scheme is presented in Figure 3.2 and a detailed description is listed as follows.

1. The sink node sends its acceptable prediction error threshold ε and the session key to all sensor nodes. In the first n periods, all sensor nodes transmit their sensed data to the sink node and calculate NSSKs with their keys and the session key. Then they construct the initial predicted data sequence.

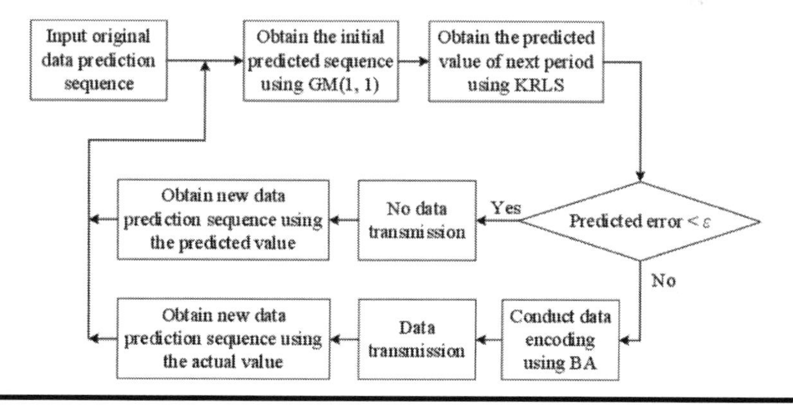

Figure 3.2 Schematic diagram of the proposed data sensing and fusion scheme.

2. Both the sink node and sensor node conduct prediction using the same data sequence and prediction mechanism. With the initial predicted data sequence of size n, a new data sequence of size $(n + 1)$ can be obtained via GM(1,1).
3. Train KRLS model with the initial predicted data sequence and the first n values of new data sequence being its input and output, respectively. And then the hidden relationships between those data sequences, i.e., the weight vector of KRLS, can be obtained.
4. With the hidden relationships obtained above, the KRLS algorithm takes the $(n + 1)$-th value of new data sequence generated by GM as input, and the predicted value of next period, i.e., the output of KRLS, could be obtained.
5. The sensor node senses the actual data of the next period.
6. Calculate the error between the actual data and the predicted data of the next period.
7. Compare the error with the threshold ε. If the error is less than ε, which means the error is acceptable, the sensor node does not send data to the sink node. Meanwhile, both the sink node and sensor node think of the predicted value as the actual value. Otherwise, the sensor node sends the actual value to the sink node using BA. Reconstruct the new data prediction sequence.
8. Specifically, if the sensor node does not send the data to the sink node within a fixed time T, the sensor node should send a beacon to the sink node. Loop (2)~(8) with the new data sequence.

On the whole, the proposed data sensing and fusion scheme can be summarized in Figure 3.3.

3.3.2 Complexity Analysis

We give an analysis of the time complexity of our proposed secure data sensing and fusion method. Let q be the number of samples in the proposed scheme. It is obvious that the main computation of our method is spent on GM(1,1) and KRLS learning. For every data sequence in GM, it will conduct calculations for n times to generate the new data sequence, where n denotes the length of the original data sequence. And q data sequences will be generated in the whole prediction process. Thus, the computational complexity of GM(1,1) is $O(qn)$. Similarly, for every training process of KRLS, the number of times we perform calculations equals the number of input vectors (i.e., n). Each input vector is used for calculating the coefficients of KRLS which could identify the relationship between input and output. Meanwhile, KRLS will be trained q times. The learning complexity of KRLS is also $O(qn)$ [27,38]. Thus, we can conclude that the complexity of our proposed scheme GM-KRLS is $O(qn)$.

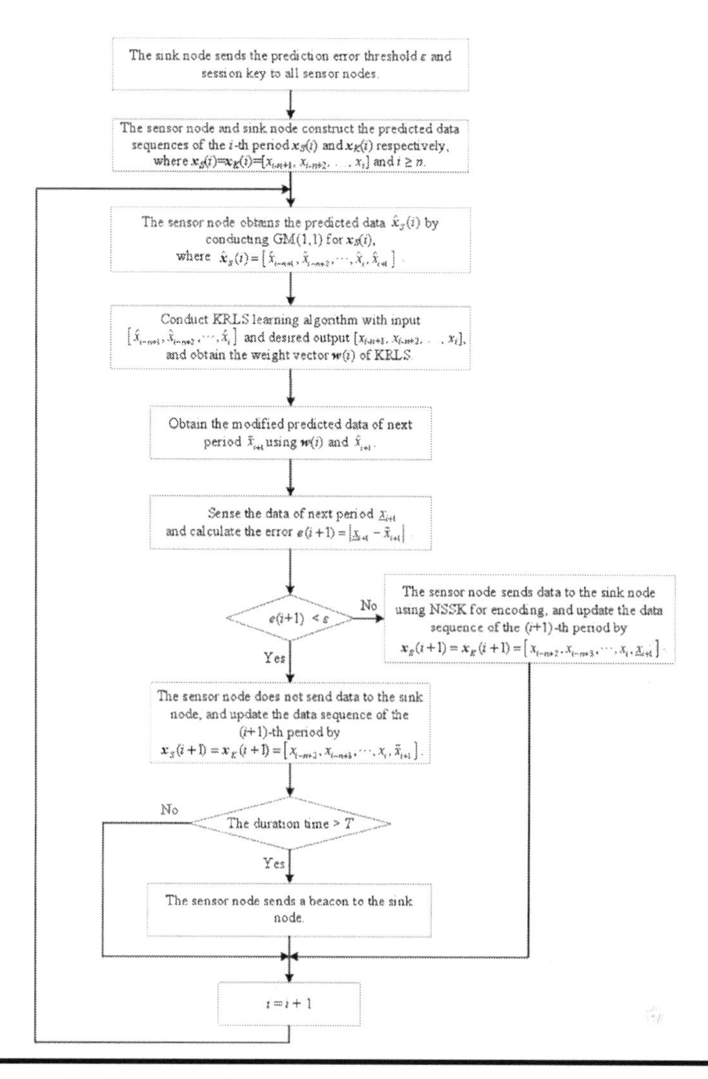

Figure 3.3 The flowchart of scheme GM-KRLS.

3.4 Simulation Results

In order to verify the effectiveness of the proposed data sensing and fusion scheme in WSN, three actual data sets are imported for simulation. We evaluate the performance of the scheme through prediction results and the successful prediction rate. GM is the basis of GM-LSSVM, GM-OP-ELM and GM-KRLS. GM-LSSVM and GM-OP-ELM seem to perform better than GM, however, they all have their own defects. GM-LSSVM spends much time in computation, and GM-OP-ELM may have a worse prediction accuracy in some situations, although its computational speed is quite fast. Therefore, in order to evaluate the computational efficiency and prediction accuracy of those schemes, we conduct simulations of our method compared with GM, GM-LSSVM and GM-OP-ELM. All the simulations are conducted in a MATLAB computing environment running in an Intel(R)Core(TM)i5-2410M, 2.30 GHz CPU. Here the algorithm LS-SVM designed in GM-LSSVM scheme is implemented by using a MATLAB Toolbox LS-SVM [39,40].

The actual data sets are collected from 54 sensors deployed in the Intel Berkeley research lab, and those sensors in the lab are distributed in accordance with Figure 3.4 [41]. This distribution of sensor nodes and the collected data sets are not only applied for theoretical research, they also have strong practicality in industrial areas. Each sensor node collects the humidity, temperature, light and voltage values once every 31 seconds. Humidity is measured by relative humidity, which is the product of the actual humidity value and 100. Light is in Lux where 1 Lux corresponds to moonlight, 400 Lux corresponds to a bright office and 100,000 Lux corresponds to full sunlight. We randomly choose a sensor node for the simulation and only its temperature, humidity and light data are employed. Since the voltage is always going on a downward tendency, it is not necessary to predict it. Each data set is extracted from the original temperature, humidity, and light data streams. It includes 2,000 continuous data items used in the following simulations. In our simulations, we choose the first 40 sampling points of each data set to construct the initial predicted data sequence. It means that n defined in Section 3.3 is set to 40, and we conduct predictions for the following 1,960 sampling points. In the proposed scheme, ε represents the requirements of end-users for data accuracy. Therefore, in our simulations, we test the successful prediction rate and the communication overhead of sensor nodes under different threshold ε.

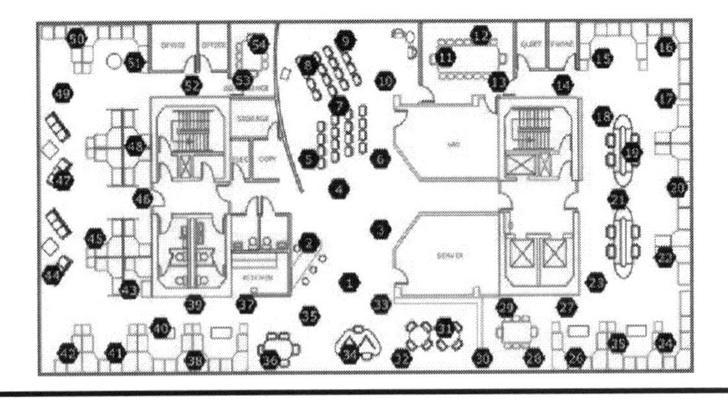

Figure 3.4 The distribution of the sensor nodes in Intel Berkeley Research lab.

3.4.1 Results of Temperature Data Set

The parameters of KRLS are set as follows: kernel parameter $\zeta = 0.01$, regularization parameter $\lambda = 0.0008$ and forgetting factor $\beta = 0.8$. The prediction results of the temperature data sequence are shown in Figure 3.5 when $\varepsilon = 0.17$. This figure shows the prediction values using GM-LSSVM, GM-OP-ELM and GM-KRLS schemes with the actual sensed data. It can be observed that the prediction values of these three methods are in good agreement with the actual values, which means they could achieve a good prediction effect. However, in some sampling points, the predicted values of GM-LSSVM and GM-OP-ELM vary hugely with a worse prediction effect. Thus, it is clear that the performance of GM-KRLS is better than that of others.

In addition, it is optional for choosing the threshold ε. In Figure 3.5 we choose the threshold as $\varepsilon = 0.17$, and it is nearly in the middle of the range we have set. Actually, we could change the value of ε; then the related simulation is also conducted when $\varepsilon = 0.33$ and similar results are obtained in Figure 3.6. It can be found that the prediction performance with $\varepsilon = 0.33$ is worse than that with $\varepsilon = 0.17$. Generally speaking, a smaller threshold means a high-quality prediction process with a smaller predicted error, and it also means a smaller successful prediction rate with more data transmission in WSN. After performing many runs for our method, we find in our simulation that 0.17 is a proper choice for the threshold, considering the practical requirement of tradeoff between the prediction effectiveness and the amount of transmitted data.

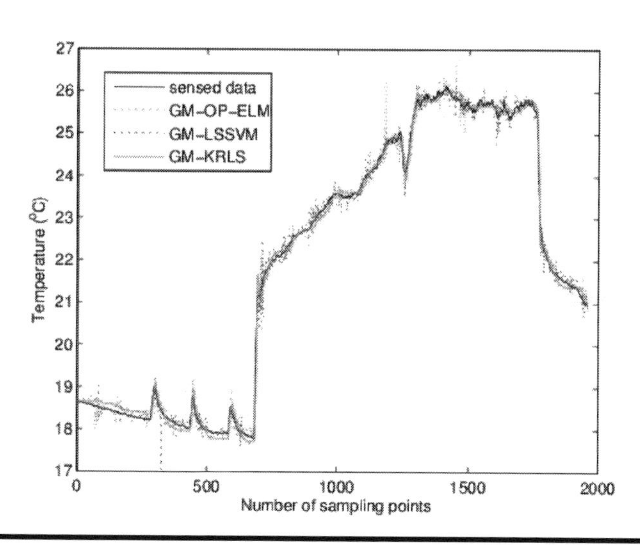

Figure 3.5 Prediction results of GM-OP-ELM, GM-LSSVM and GM-KRLS schemes for temperature items (ε = 0.17).

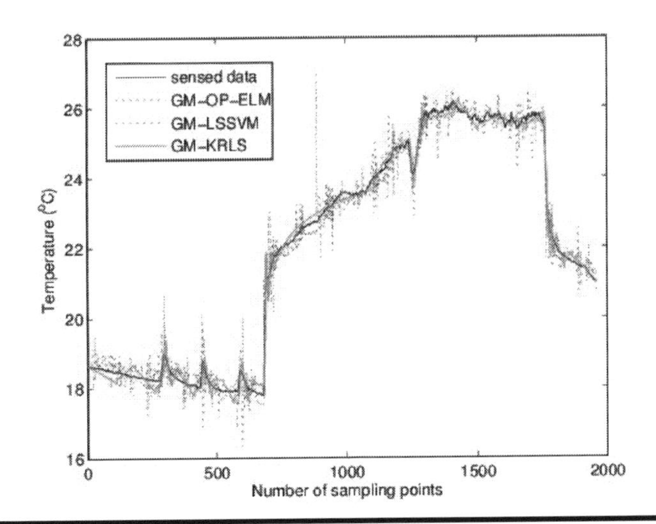

Figure 3.6 Prediction results of GM-OP-ELM, GM-LSSVM and GM-KRLS schemes for temperature items ($\varepsilon = 0.33$).

Figure 3.7 shows the successful prediction rate as the threshold ε changes. From this figure, it can be observed obviously that the bigger the value of the threshold is, the higher the successful prediction is. Furthermore, as the threshold changes, the successful prediction rate of GM-KRLS is always higher than that of other methods, which means that GM-KRLS has the best prediction effect. Meanwhile, it is known that the higher the successful prediction rate is, the less communication overhead will be produced. That is the goal of data sensing and fusion. Thus, it is obvious that the GM-OP-ELM and GM-LSSVM schemes outperform the GM-based scheme. It means that the GM-OP-ELM, GM-LSSVM and GM-KRLS schemes can save energy by improving prediction accuracy, and extend lifetime of the whole WSN simultaneously. Moreover, GM-KRLS seems to perform better when dealing with this issue.

Figure 3.8 shows the corresponding average error of these three schemes when the threshold ε changes. The average error can be used to evaluate the performance of the method, and a smaller average error indicates a better prediction effect. It can be found that the average errors of GM-KRLS are minimum and the errors of GM-OP-ELM are maximum. Thus, the overall prediction effect of GM-KRLS is best. Specifically, Figure 3.9 shows the predicted error of GM-KRLS at every sampling point when $\varepsilon = 0.17$. We can find that these errors are constrained within relatively tight bounds.

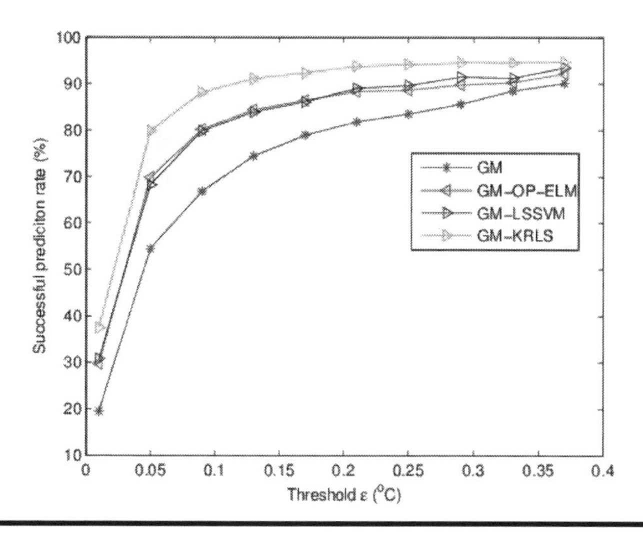

Figure 3.7 Successful prediction rate with different threshold of GM, GM-OP-ELM, GM-LSSVM and GM-KRLS schemes for temperature item.

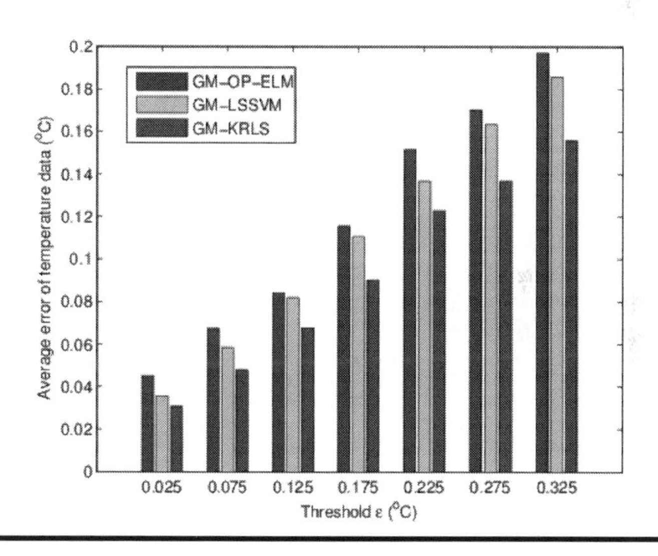

Figure 3.8 Average predicted error with different threshold of GM-OP-ELM, GM-LSSVM and GM-KRLS schemes for temperature item.

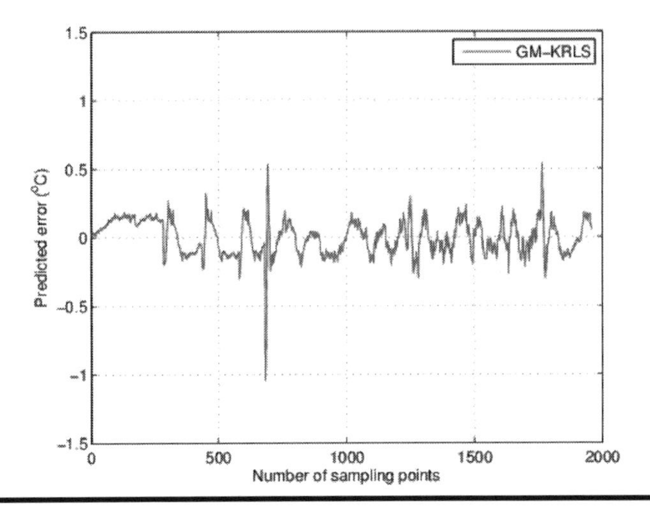

Figure 3.9 The predicted error of GM-KRLS scheme for temperature item ($\varepsilon = 0.17$).

3.4.2 Results of Humidity Data Set

The parameters of KRLS are set as follows: kernel parameter $\zeta = 0.03$, regularization parameter $\lambda = 0.0008$ and forgetting factor $\beta = 0.8$. Figure 3.10 depicts the actual humidity data of every sampling point and the prediction results using GM-OP-ELM, GM-LSSVM and GM-KRLS schemes when $\varepsilon = 0.17$. It is clear that the prediction values of three schemes almost follow the

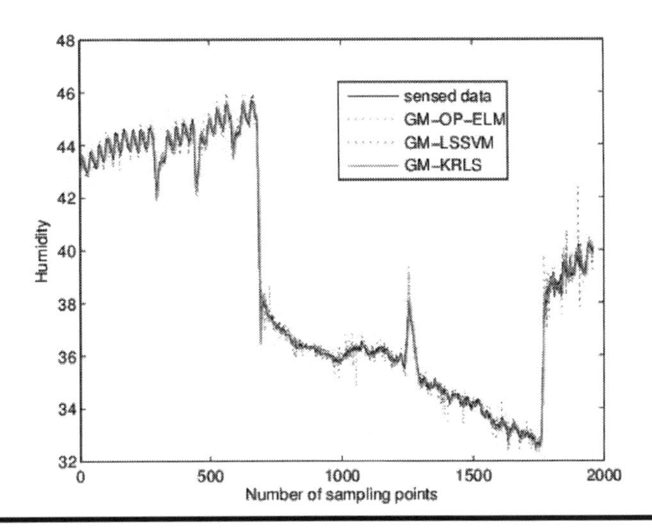

Figure 3.10 Prediction value of GM-OP-ELM, GM-LSSVM and GM-KRLS schemes for humidity items ($\varepsilon = 0.17$).

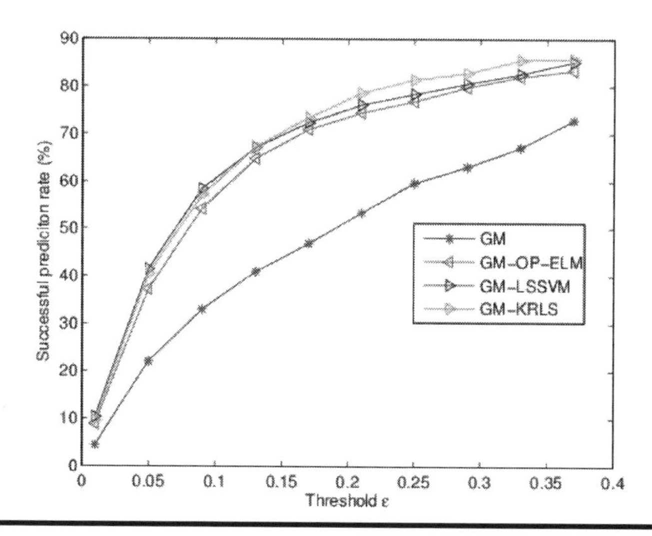

Figure 3.11 Successful prediction rate with different threshold of GM, GM-OP-ELM, GM-LSSVM and GM-KRLS schemes for humidity item.

actual sensed humidity data. Figure 3.11 shows the successful prediction rate under different threshold ε. The successful prediction rate of GM-OP-ELM is close to that of GM-LSSVM for the humidity data sequence, and GM-KRLS has a higher successful rate than other schemes.

Here Figure 3.12 shows the corresponding average error of these three schemes when the threshold ε changes. Figure 3.13 shows the predicted error of GM-KRLS at every sampling point when $\varepsilon = 0.17$.

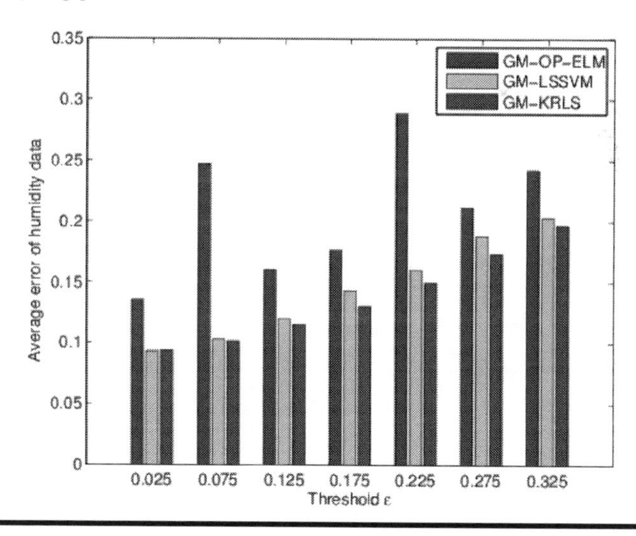

Figure 3.12 Average predicted error with different threshold of GM-OP-ELM, GM-LSSVM and GM-KRLS schemes for humidity item.

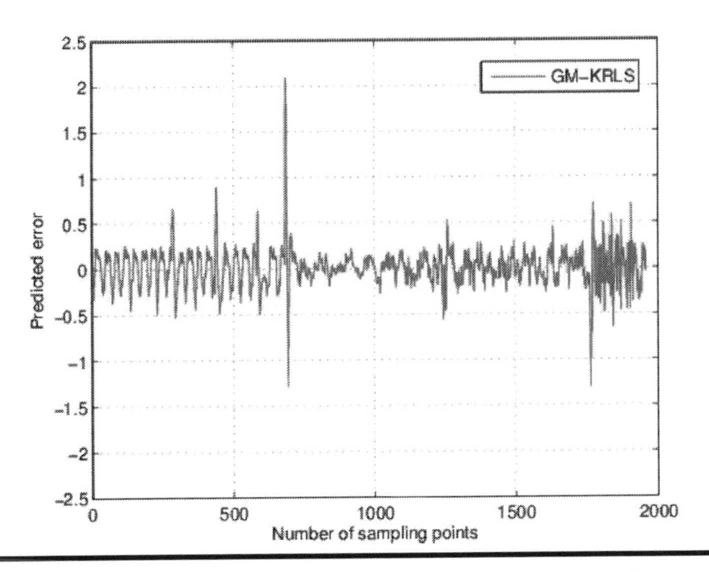

Figure 3.13 Average predicted error with different threshold of GM-OP-ELM, GM-LSSVM and GM-KRLS schemes for humidity item.

3.4.3 Results of Light Data Set

The parameters of KRLS are set as follows: kernel parameter $\zeta = 0.01$, regularization parameter $\lambda = 0.5$ and forgetting factor $\beta = 0.8$. Figure 3.14 displays the actual light sensed data and prediction value using GM-OP-ELM, GM-LSSVM and GM-KRLS schemes at every sampling point when $\varepsilon = 0.17$. It can be seen that this data sequence is nonlinear. Figure 3.15 shows the successful prediction rate under different threshold ε of GM, GM-OP-ELM, GM-LSSVM and GM-KRLS schemes for light data sequence. As we can see from this figure, the GM-KRLS also slightly outperforms GM-LSSVM and GM-OP-ELM for the high nonlinear light data items. Here, we can see that from Figure 3.14, the light data set is different from temperature and humidity data sets because its values vary within a relatively bigger range. Then, as a high-nonlinear and fluctuant time series data sequence, this light sensed data set has some complex characteristics. It results in a lower successful prediction rate with the threshold less than 0.4. However, our proposed method is still efficient since the successful prediction rate is higher than that of the other two GM-based methods. Furthermore, in order to verify the effectiveness of our scheme, we assign a series of bigger values to the threshold in Figure 3.15, where we can find that with the increase of threshold, GM-KRLS still performs better than the other three methods.

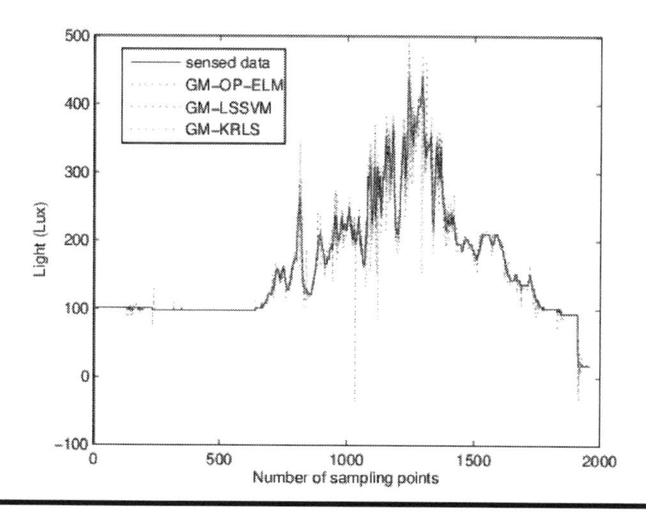

Figure 3.14 Prediction value of GM-OP-ELM, GM-LSSVM and GM-KRLS schemes for light item ($\varepsilon = 0.17$s).

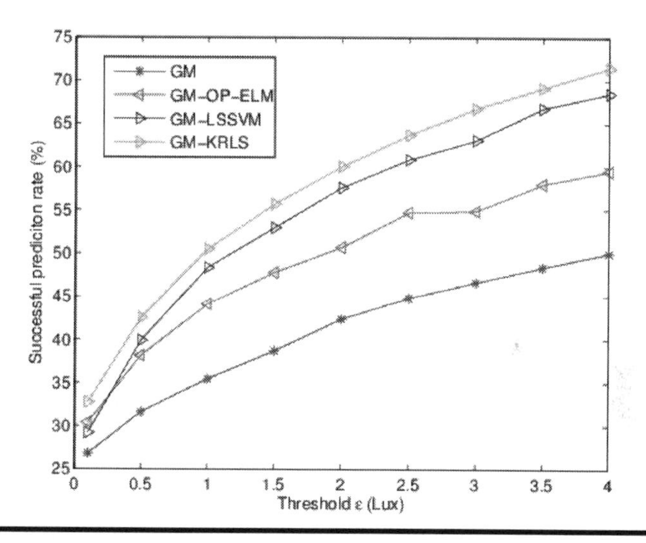

Figure 3.15 Successful prediction rate with different threshold of GM, GM-OP-ELM, GM-LSSVM and GM-KRLS schemes for light item.

In addition, Figure 3.16 shows the corresponding average error of these three schemes when the threshold ε changes. Figure 3.17 shows the predicted error of GM-KRLS at every sampling point when $\varepsilon = 0.17$.

In addition to the above evaluation for prediction accuracy of those schemes, we also provide a comparison for the computational time of GM-KRLS, GM-OP-ELM

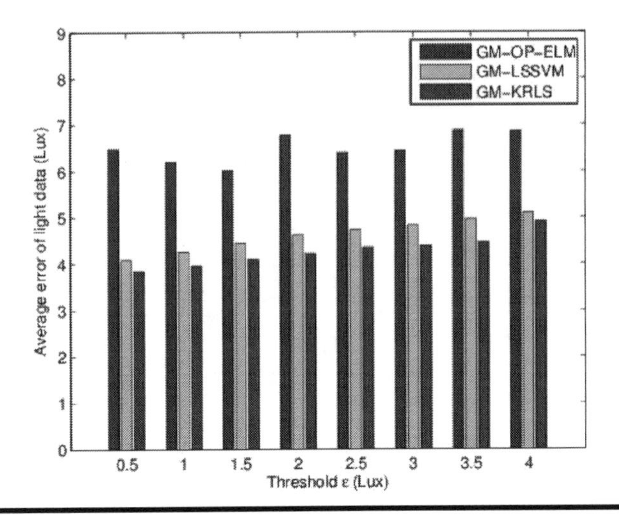

Figure 3.16 Average predicted error with different threshold of GM-OP-ELM, GM-LSSVM and GM-KRLS schemes for light item.

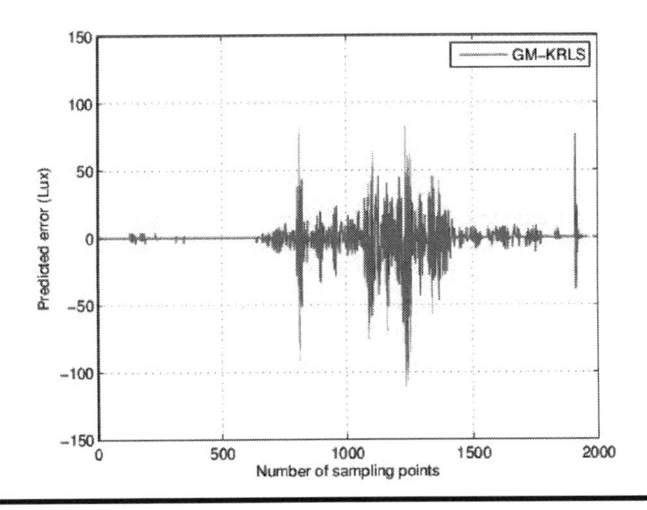

Figure 3.17 The predicted error of GM-KRLS scheme for light item ($\varepsilon = 0.17$).

and GM-LSSVM schemes in every prediction period for the three items. The results are listed in Figure 3.18. It can be observed that the computational time of GM-OP-ELM is the least, and the computational time of GM-KRLS is almost the same as that of GM-OP-ELM. But when compared with GM-LSSVM, GM-KRLS is more efficient since the computational time of GM-LSSVM is almost 10 times as much as that of GM-KRLS.

In consideration of the prediction accuracy and the computational time simultaneously, our proposed scheme GM-KRLS may be a competitive choice.

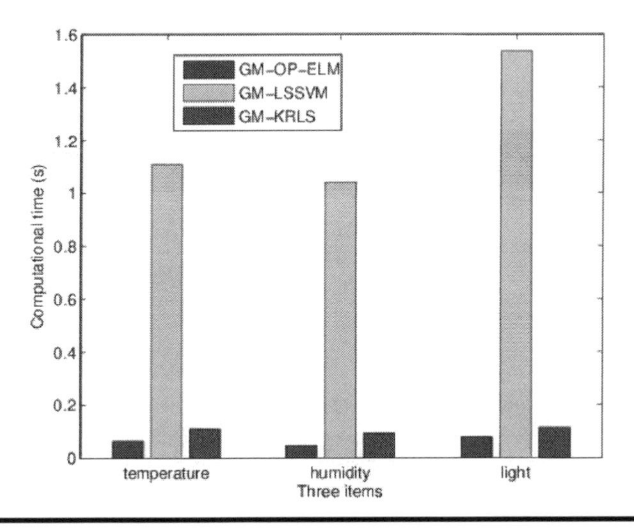

Figure 3.18 Computational time of GM-KRLS, GM-OP-ELM and GM-LSSVM schemes in every prediction period for three items.

Finally, it should be pointed out that although GM-OP-ELM performs better than GM-KRLS in terms of computational time, the former may suffer from design choices during implementation. Actually, ELM uses random projection spaces, while KRLS uses data-centered functional bases. It is difficult to set the design parameters optimally under the mathematical framework of ELM; practically, we need to conduct many trials and cross validation to select the number of hidden neurons and the nonlinear functions with the purpose of finding a good projection space. On the other hand, the KRLS learning algorithm can avoid such limitations by just mapping the data nonlinearly and deterministically to a Hilbert space, and adapting online the projection [38]. KRLS and its data-centered basis functions are therefore able to concentrate bases on the part of the functional space where the input data exists. In view of this, the scheme GM-KRLS has unique advantages under the current computational framework.

3.4.4 Results of Other Data Set

From the descriptions of the proposed data sensing and fusion scheme GM-KRLS, it can be observed that a data sequence with fixed length is used for data prediction of the next period. In this case, the prediction effect is closely related to the length of data sequence (i.e., n defined in Section 3.3) and the increase of the data set may not influence the algorithm effect. From this point of view, the proposed schema may be appropriate for other data sets with bigger size. Here we employ a larger temperature data set with 15,000 values to conduct simulation. When $\varepsilon = 0.17$, Figures 3.19 and 3.20 show the

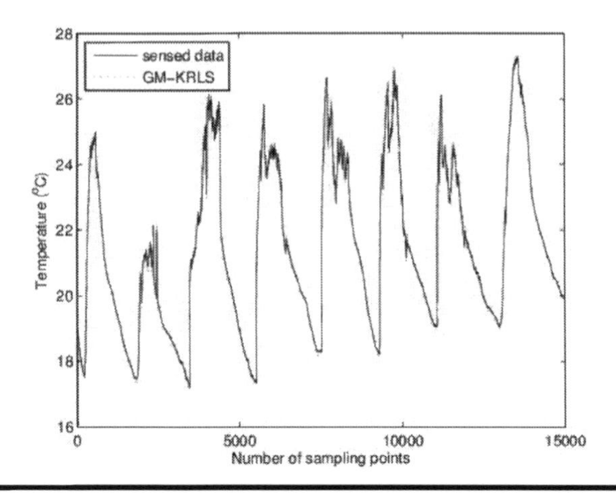

Figure 3.19 Prediction value of GM-KRLS scheme for a larger data set ($\varepsilon = 0.17$).

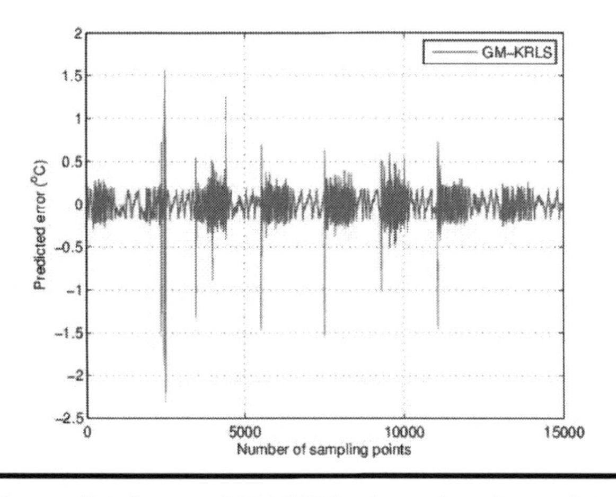

Figure 3.20 The predicted error of GM-KRLS scheme for a larger data set ($\varepsilon = 0.17$).

prediction effect and the predicted error at every sampling point, respectively. Here, the average error of GM-KRLS is 0.0873 within a relatively tight bound, which also verifies the effectiveness of the proposed method for a larger data set.

3.4.5 Results of Encoding and Decoding

In order to verify the effectiveness of BA, the simulation of encoding and decoding is also conducted. In this simulation, we choose four different data values with different NSSKs. The results are listed in Table 3.1. It can be found that BA plays an important role in guaranteeing the confidentiality under our proposed data sensing and fusion scheme.

Table 3.1 Simulation for Encoding and Decoding

NSSK	*Raw Data*	*After Encoding*	*After Decoding*
nikiisexcellent	25.341	160-102-23110-25-13-693551	25.341
nikiisexcellent	66.5	14015-15-71-117-46-26-23-111	66.5
nikiisexcellent	128	130-6689-5099-66504-75	128
nikiisexcellent	0.3861	16069-80-2711-104-11-106-82	0.3861
youyouisperfect	25.341	16063-82-22-88-98-666234	25.341
youyouisperfect	66.5	140-41116107-108470-112-88	66.5
youyouisperfect	128	130-44-127848-10940-5389	128
youyouisperfect	0.3861	160-123-63-121-127-19-50111	0.3861

3.4.6 Parameter Selections

In kernel methods, the parameter selections play an important role in the design of a learning algorithm. Here, taking the processing for light data set as an example, we explain how to choose proper parameters in simulations. As mentioned above, λ, ζ and β are three important parameters of KRLS in the GM-KRLS scheme. Firstly, we will choose an appropriate β after considering three different combinations of λ and ζ. Figure 3.21 shows the average predicted error in all three cases. It can be observed that the error is minimum when $\beta = 0.8$; thus, β is

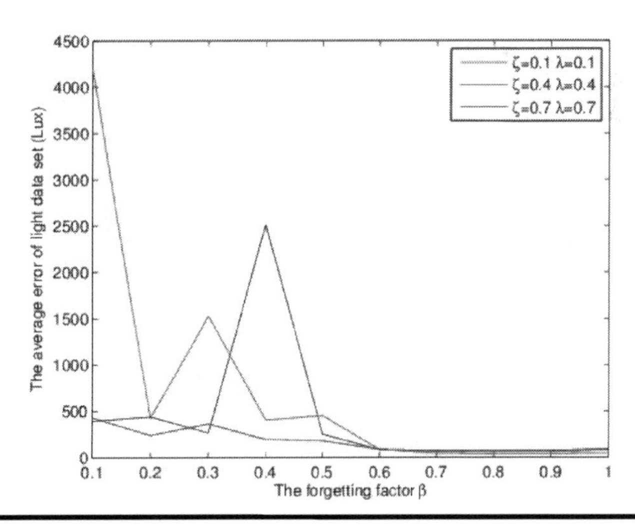

Figure 3.21 Predicted error with different β.

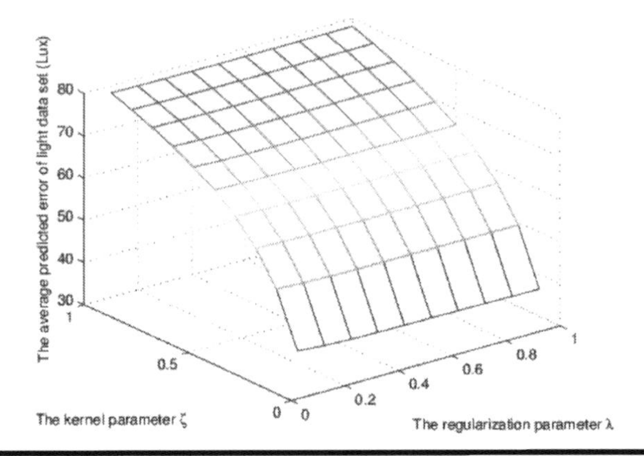

Figure 3.22 Predicted error with different ζ and λ ($\beta = 0.8$).

set to 0.8. Then, we vary the values of λ and ζ from 0.1 to 1.0 with a step value of 0.1. The average predicted error is shown in Figure 3.22. Here, the average error decreases when the ζ value is decreased from 1.0 to 0.1. Meanwhile, λ has rather little meaning for error. Therefore, we will select ζ first.

We vary the values of ζ from 0.005 to 0.1 with a step value of 0.005, where the λ value is randomly set to 0.1. Figure 3.23 shows the average predicted error with different ζ. Obviously, the ζ value of 0.01 achieves the best performance, and this is why we use $\zeta = 0.01$ as the default setting in this simulation. Now, we only have an unknown value of λ. Figure 3.24 shows the average predicted error while changing the values of λ. According to this figure, we set $\lambda = 0.5$; then the minimum predicted error can be obtained. So far, three parameters are selected. Similarly, those parameters of GM-KRLS in processing temperature and humidity data sets could be selected.

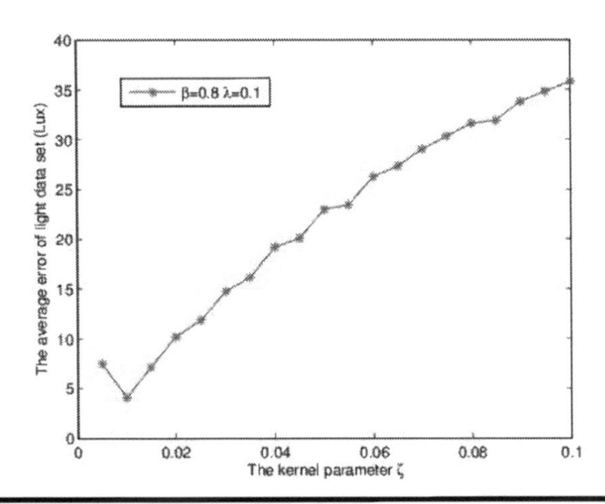

Figure 3.23 Predicted error with different ζ.

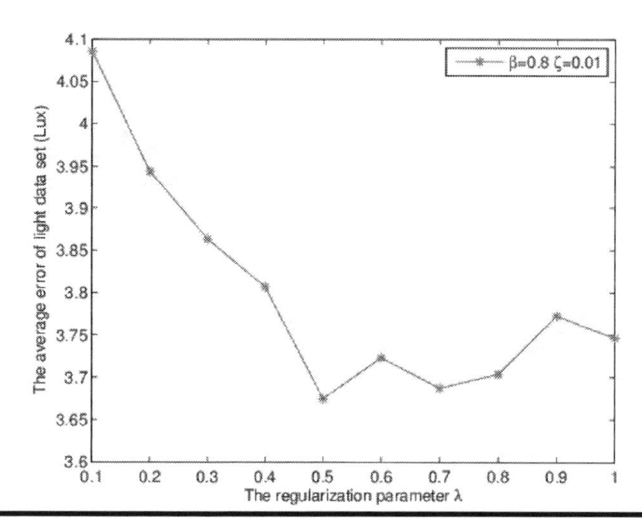

Figure 3.24 Predicted error with different λ.

3.5 Conclusion

In WSNs, prediction-based secure data sensing and fusion are effective in reducing redundant data communications, saving the energy of sensor nodes, keeping data confidentiality and enhancing the lifetime of network. Considering that the data sensed by the sensor nodes are of high temporal redundancy and the sensor nodes have limited energy, storage capacity and data processing ability, a novel prediction method based on secure data sensing and fusion scheme GM-KRLS using GM, KRLS and BA is proposed in this paper to deal with those issues mentioned above. In order to guarantee data synchronization between sensor nodes and sink node, the proposed scheme develops a prediction mechanism. During the data sensing and fusion process, the GM-KRLS firstly uses GM to implement the initial prediction with a small number of data items, then employs the KRLS learning algorithm to modify the predicted value with lower computational cost and higher successful prediction rate. Meanwhile, BA is used for data encoding and decoding during the transmission process. It can be found from simulation results that the proposed scheme can improve prediction accuracy and reduce the energy consumption caused by redundant transmission. GM-KRLS performs better than GM-LSSVM and GM-OP-ELM in terms of accuracy; moreover, its computational speed is close to GM-OP-ELM but much faster than GM-LSSVM. For high nonlinear and fluctuant time series data sequences (such as the data set of light in Section 3.4), GM-KRLS has significant advantages over other schemes. The confidentiality of data values is guaranteed by means of reducing transmission and encoding data. In view of those issues mentioned above, compared with other schemes, GM-KRLS may be a better choice in industry WSNs on the deployment of CPSs.

References

1. L. A. Tang, J. Han, G. Jiang, Mining sensor data in cyber-physical systems, *Tsinghua Sci. Tech.* 19(2014)225–234.
2. F. J. Wu, Y. F. Kao, Y. C. Tseng, From wireless sensor networks towards cyber physical systems, *Pervasive Mob. Comput.* 7(2011)397–413.
3. H. S. Ning, H. Liu, J. H. Ma, L. T. Yang, R. H. Huang, Cyber-physical-social-thinking hyperspace based science and technology, *Future Gener. Comput. Syst.* 2015. doi:10.1016/j.future.2015.07.012.
4. C. Zhu, L. Shu, T. Hara, L. Wang, S. Nishio, L. T. Yang, A survey on communication and data management issues in mobile sensor networks, *Wireless Commun. Mobile Comput.* 14(2014)19–36.
5. R. Tan, G. Xing, B. Liu, J. Wang, X. Jia, Exploiting data fusion to improve the coverage of wireless sensor networks, *IEEE ACM Trans. Networking*, 20(2012)450–462.
6. P. Ji, C. Wu, Y. Zhang, F. Chen, A low-energy adaptive clustering routing protocol of wireless sensor networks, in: *Proceedings of the 7th International Conference on Wireless Communications, Networking and Mobile Computing*, Wuhan, China, 2011, pp. 1–4.
7. M. Li, Z. Li, A. V. Vasilakos, A survey on topology control in wireless sensor networks: Taxonomy, comparative study, and open issues, *Proc. IEEE*, 101(2013)2538–2557.
8. Y. Nam, S. Rho, B. G. Lee, Intelligent context-aware energy management using the incremental simultaneous method in future wireless sensor networks and computing systems, *EURASIP J. Wirel. Commun. Netw.* 2013(2013)10.
9. G. Anastasi, M. Conti, M. Di Francesco, A. Passarella, Energy conservation in wireless sensor networks: A survey, *Ad Hoc Netw.* 7(2009)537–568.
10. E. F. Nakamura, A. A. F. Loureiro, A. C. Frery, Information fusion for wireless sensor networks: Methods, models, and classifications, *ACM Comput. Surv.* 39(2007).
11. H. Li, K. Li, W. Qu, S. Ivan, Secure and energy-efficient data aggregation with malicious aggregator identification in wireless sensor networks, *Future Gener. Comput. Syst.* 37(2014)108–116.
12. R. H. David, G. S. Antonio-Javier, G. S. Felipe, G. H. Joan, On the improvement of wireless mesh sensor network performance under hidden terminal problems, *Future Gener. Comput. Syst.* 45(2015)95–113.
13. C. T. Cheng, H. Leung, P. Maupin, A delay-aware network structure for wireless sensor networks with in-network data fusion, *IEEE Sensors J.* 13(2013)1622–1631.
14. H. Luo, H. X. Tao, H. D. Ma, S. K. Das, Data fusion with desired reliability in wireless sensor networks, *IEEE Trans. Parallel Distrib. Syst.* 22(2011)501–513.
15. C. L. Chen, J. Yan, N. Lu, Y. Wang, X. Yang, X. Guan, Ubiquitous monitoring for industrial cyber-physical systems over relay assisted wireless sensor networks, *IEEE Trans. Emerg. Top. Comput.* 3(2015)352–362.
16. A. R. Pinto, C. Montez, G. Arajo, F. Vasques, P. Portugal, An approach to implement data fusion techniques in wireless sensor networks using genetic machine learning algorithms, *Inf. Fusion* 15(2014)90–101.
17. O. Kreibich, J. Neuzil, R. Smid, Quality-based multiple-sensor fusion in an industrial wireless sensor network for MCM, *IEEE Trans. Industrial Electronics*, 61(2014)4903–4911.

18. A. Hui, L. Cui, Forecast-based temporal data aggregation in wireless sensor networks, *Comput. Eng. Appl.* 43(2007)121–125.
19. J. Kang, L. Tang, X. Zuo, X. Zhang, H. Li, GMSVM-based prediction for temporal data aggregation in sensor networks, in: *Proceedings of the 5th International Conference on Wireless Communications, Networking and Mobile Computing*, Beijing, China, 2009, pp. 1–4.
20. N. M. Xie, T. X. Yao, S. F. Liu, Multi-variable grey dynamic forecasting model based on complex network, in: *Proceedings of International Conference on Management Science and Engineering*, Moscow, Russia, 2009, pp. 213–219.
21. R Wang, J. Tang, D. Wu, Q. Sun, GM-LSSVM based data aggregation in WSN, *Comput. Eng. Des.* 33(2012)3371–3375.
22. Y. Miche, A. Sorjamaa, P. Bas, O. Simula, C. Jutten, A. Lendasse, OP-ELM: optimally pruned extreme learning machine, *IEEE Trans. Neural Networks* 21(2010)158–162.
23. X. Luo, X. H. Chang, A novel data fusion scheme using grey model and extreme learning machine in wireless sensor networks, *Int. J. Control Autom. Syst.* 13(2015)539–546.
24. B. Schneier. The Blowfish encryption algorithm. Available: http://www.schneier.com/blowfish.html Accessed June, 2015.
25. T. Y. Nie, T. Zhang, A study of DES and Blowfish encryption algorithm, in: *Proceedings of IEEE Region 10 Annual International Conference*, Singapore, 2009.
26. Y. Engel, S. Mannor, R. Meir, The kernel recursive least-squares algorithm, *IEEE Trans. Signal Process.* 52(2004)2275–2285.
27. W. F. Liu, J. C. Principe, S. Haykin, *Kernel Adaptive Filtering.* Wiley, Hoboken, NJ, 2011.
28. B. D. Chen, S. L. Zhao, P. P. Zhu, J. C. Principe, Quantized kernel recursive least squares algorithm, *IEEE Trans. Neural Networks Learn. Sys.* 24(2013)1484–1491.
29. F. M. Tseng, H. C. Yu, G. H. Tzeng, Applied hybrid grey model to forecast seasonal time series, *Technol. Forecast. Soc. Change* 67(2001)291–302.
30. Y. H. Wang, Y. G. Dang, X. J. Pu, Improved unequal interval grey model and its applications, *J. Syst. Eng. Electron.* 22(2011)445–451.
31. B. Zeng, C. Li, G. Chen, X. J. Long, Equivalency and unbiasedness of grey prediction models, *J. Syst. Eng. Electron.* 26(2015)110–118.
32. S. F. Liu, Y. Lin, *Grey Systems Theory and Applications.* Springer-Verlag, Berlin, Germany, 2010.
33. B. Zeng, G. Chen, S. F. Liu, A novel interval grey prediction model considering uncertain information, *J. Franklin Inst.* 350(2013)3400–3416.
34. S. Van Vaerenbergh, M. Lazaro-Gredilla, I. Santamaria, Kernel recursive least-squares tracker for time-varying regression, *IEEE Trans. Neural Networks Learn. Sys.* 23(2012)1313–1326.
35. G. Kumar, M. Rai, G. S. Lee, Implementation of cipher block chaining in wireless sensor networks for security enhancement, *Int. J. Secur. Appl.* 6(2012)57–72.
36. L. M. Jawad, G. Sulong, Chaotic map-embedded Blowfish algorithm for security enhancement of colour image encryption, *Nonlinear Dyn.* 81(2015)2079–2093.
37. A. Abd El-Sadek, T. A. El-Garf, M. M. Fouad, Speech encryption applying a modified Blowfish algorithm, in: *Proceedings of the 2nd International Conference on Engineering and Technology*, Cairo, Egypt, 2014, pp. 1–6.

38. J. C. Principe, B. Chen, Universal approximation with convex optimization: gimmick or reality? *IEEE Comput. Intell. Mag.* 10(2015)68–77.
39. J. A. K. Suykens, T. Van Gestel, J. De Brabanter, B. De Moor, J. Vandewalle, *Least Squares Support Vector Machines*. World Scientific, Singapore, 2002.
40. LS-SVMlab Toolbox. Available: http://www.esat.kuleuven.be/sista/lssvmlab/ Accessed June, 2015.
41. S. Madden. Intel Berkeley research lab data. Available: http://db.csail.mit.edu/labdata/labdata.html Accessed June 2015.

Chapter 4

Novel Model-Based Method for Identification of Scattering Mechanisms in Polarimetric SAR Data

Junjun Yin, Wooil M. Moon, and Jian Yang

Contents

4.1 Introduction

SYNTHETIC aperture radar (SAR) has all-weather imaging capability without sunlight and widely varying swath imaging modes in many SAR systems in operation [1]. Recently, an increasing number of space-borne SAR systems has been launched into Earth's orbit and various new missions are being planned. Typical SAR systems available for civilian use include C-band RADARSAT-2, L-band ALOS/PALSAR-2 (launched in May 2014), X-band TerraSAR-X/TanDem-X, and the X-band COSMO-SkyMed satellite constellation. Some future SAR missions include the RADARSAT Constellation (RCM) and L-band SAOCOM-1/2. As more and more SAR data become available to a large number of users, it is becoming critical to develop effective automatic techniques for SAR image interpretation.

SAR polarimetry is an advanced technique for extracting more detailed and quantitative physical information to characterize scattering mechanisms of various surface targets and features. In fully polarimetric SAR systems, SAR antennae transmit two orthogonally polarized signals and receive fully backscattered vector signals from surface scatterers, allowing development of different physical models for identification and separation of scatterers. Many scattering decomposition methods [2–7] in terms of both coherent and incoherent categories and parameter retrieval techniques have been developed for the interpretation of target physical scattering mechanisms (PSMs) that can be approximated from the backscattered polarimetric SAR signal received. Among the target decomposition methods, Cloude-Pottier's *H/alpha* decomposition provides a simple but effective method for target scattering mechanism identification and classification, and has been investigated widely in many applications. The *H/alpha* plane has been developed in several forms, such as the *H/alpha*-Wishart classifier [8] and the combination of the fuzzy *c*-means (FCM) algorithm with the *H/alpha* plane [9]. *H* and *alpha* are also commonly used parameters in machine learning-based classifiers, e.g., support vector machines [10,11] and neural networks [12].

Both *H* and *alpha* are rotation invariant parameters. However, in the *H/alpha* classification plane, only a few scatterers would fall in the zones with high *alpha* angles, which means that scatterers are more likely to concentrate in the regions with low and medium *alpha* angles, not be distributed separately over the whole *alpha* axis. The limited distribution range may result in small within-class distance, which is not favorable for target classification. In addition, *H* measures the scattering randomness. But it is difficult for *H* to discriminate between the multiple reflections arising from both forests and urban areas, because both areas can generate high entropy values.

In [13], a cylindrical coordinate system is used to represent target scattering properties, where three polarimetric parameters, i.e., the Bragg alpha angle [14–16], the average co-polarization phase difference (CPD), and the average amplitude ratio, are included. The Bragg alpha angle was first proposed in Cloude and Corr (2002) as a material indicator [15]. We extended the application of the Bragg alpha angle to the more general scattering case, in which the form of the Bragg alpha angle can be seen as the scattering ratio, denoted by α_B in this paper. Compared to *alpha*, α_B. has better discrimination capability for the rotated urban areas (i.e., building alignments not in the radar azimuth direction) and forests [13]. α_B shows similar physical interpretation for polarimetric SAR images as the polarization *alpha*. When the scattering mechanism deviates from surface scattering to double-bounce scattering, α_B increases from 0° and finally reaches 90° [17]. For the ocean surface description, we used RADARSAT-2 data for testing. It showed that α_B distributes in the interval $\left[0 \quad 35°\right]$ for the ocean surface when radar incidence angle ranges from 20° to 50° [17], and that α_B is very effective for ship detection. By investigating the expansion of the formula of α_B of symmetric scatterers, a new approach for scattering type classification is proposed in this study.

This study is organized as follows. Three polarimetric SAR data sets used for demonstration are described in Section 4.2. A new polarimetric parameter and the proposed scatter diagram with its definition of classification boundaries are introduced and discussed in Section 4.3. Experiment validations and comparisons are given in Section 4.4. Summary of results is presented in Section 4.5.

4.2 Data Sets and Pre-processing

Fully polarimetric RADARSAT-2 data acquired over the San Francisco Bay area, USA, and Fuzhou, China, are used to test the performance of the proposed method for target scattering characterization. These data sets were received in single look complex (SLC) product format, and were filtered using the refined Lee filter [18] with the window size of 7 in PolSARpro to reduce the speckle noise. Basic information of the test data is listed in Table 4.1, and Pauli-Basis images as well as corresponding Google Earth images of the test sites are shown in Figure 4.1. The San Francisco Bay test area is a well-known one and has been investigated for demonstration in many previous studies [10,19]. There are mainly three classes, i.e., forest, ocean, and urban areas.

Table 4.1 Technical Parameters of RADARSAT-2 Fully Polarimetric SAR Data

Location	*Incidence Angle (in degrees)*	*Pixel Number*	*Pixel Spacing (m)*	*Acquisition Date*
San Francisco Bay	28.02° – 29.82°	1453×1387	4.7×4.8	Apr. 9, 2008
Fuzhou, China (Data1)	34.43° – 36.03°	6120×3332	4.7×4.8	Oct. 20, 2013
Fuzhou, China (Data2)	34.43° – 36.03°	6120×3332	4.7×4.8	Nov. 13, 2013

Note: Data1 and Data2 denote the data acquired on different dates.

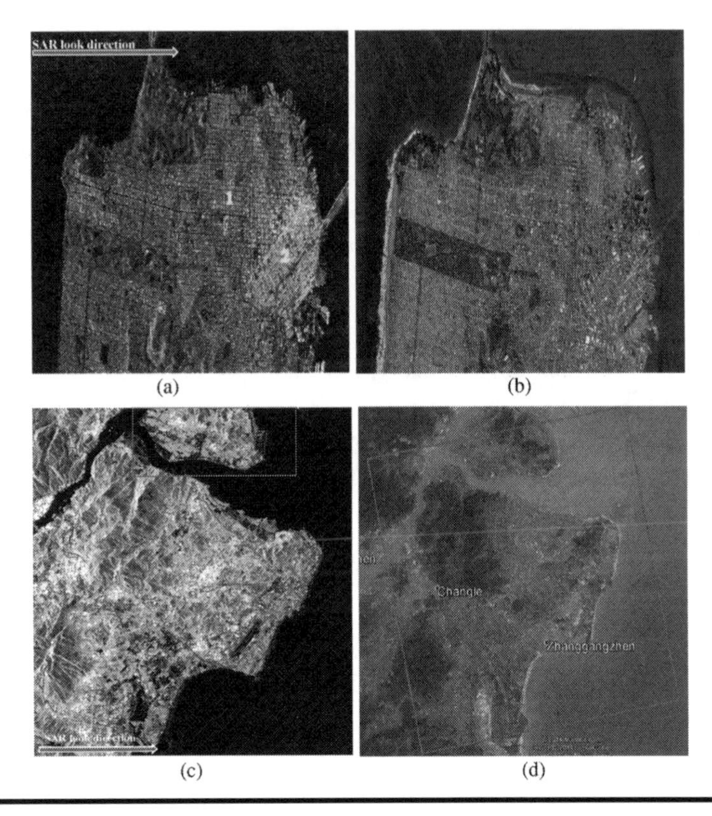

Figure 4.1 RADARSAT-2 Pauli-basis images of (a) the San Francisco Bay area (Apr. 9, 2008) and (c) Fuzhou, China (Oct. 20, 2013). Corresponding Google Earth images are shown in (b) and (d). The outlined area in (c) is a subarea of interest.

For urban areas, due to different man-made building structures and alignments (relative to the radar azimuth direction), two building block themes, as denoted by 1 and 2 in Figure 4.1a, can be clearly observed. The Fuzhou test area is more complicated. It consists of small town (or urban) areas scattered at the foot of mountains, mountainous forests, agriculture areas, water bodies, and coastal grass areas. The island shown in Figure 4.1c, with large farmland, is a region of interest. These test data sets are going to be used for demonstration in Section 4.3.

4.3 The Proposed Method

4.3.1 Trihedral, Dihedral, and X-Bragg Scattering Models

Canonical scattering matrices, e.g., the trihedral ($n = 1$) and dihedral ($n = 2$) scattering models in (4.1), are fundamental elements for understanding polarimetric SAR images. The trihedral and dihedral reflections have a π phase shift on the co-polarized ratios, as shown in (4.2), and can be shown on a unit circle in the polar

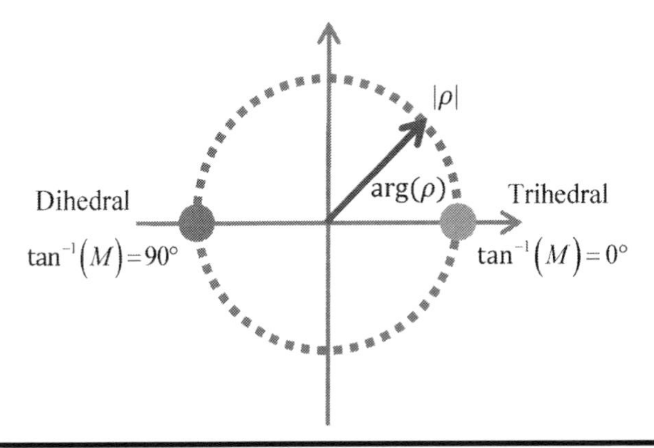

Figure 4.2 The co-polarized ratio ρ represented in the polar coordinate system. M is the parameter defined in (4.5).

coordinate system, as shown in Figure 4.2. The complex co-polarized ratio ρ is of great potential for scattering mechanism characterization.

$$\boldsymbol{S} = \begin{bmatrix} S_{\mathrm{HH}} & S_{\mathrm{HV}} \\ S_{\mathrm{VH}} & S_{\mathrm{VV}} \end{bmatrix} = \begin{bmatrix} 1 & 0 \\ 0 & (-1)^{n+1} \end{bmatrix} \tag{4.1}$$

$$\rho_{\mathrm{Trihedral}} = \frac{S_{\mathrm{VV}}}{S_{\mathrm{HH}}} = 1e^{j0}; \qquad \rho_{\mathrm{Dihedral}} = \frac{S_{\mathrm{VV}}}{S_{\mathrm{HH}}} = 1e^{j\pi}. \tag{4.2}$$

The scattering matrix $\boldsymbol{S}$ cannot describe the backscatter depolarization caused by the randomness of natural scattering media, and thus backscatter of polarimetric SAR signal is usually represented by the coherency (or equivalent covariance) matrix, defined as follows under the reflection reciprocity theorem.

$$\boldsymbol{T} = \vec{k}_{\mathrm{p}} \vec{k}_{\mathrm{p}}^{\mathrm{H}} = \begin{bmatrix} T_{11} & T_{12} & T_{13} \\ T_{12}^{*} & T_{22} & T_{23} \\ T_{13}^{*} & T_{23}^{*} & T_{33} \end{bmatrix}, \tag{4.3}$$

where $\vec{k}_{\mathrm{P}} = \left(1/\sqrt{2}\right)\left[S_{\mathrm{HH}} + S_{\mathrm{VV}} \quad S_{\mathrm{HH}} S_{\mathrm{VV}} \quad 2S_{\mathrm{HV}}\right]^{T}$ is the Pauli-basis vector and $<\cdots>$ and H denote the spatial average and matrix transpose conjugate, respectively. Under this form, another example whose scattering mechanism is mainly determined by ρ is shown in (4.4), which is the X-Bragg scattering model [14,15]. This model can be applied to a wide range of surface roughness conditions compared to the small perturbation model, and can also accommodate the surface roughness induced depolarization.

$$\boldsymbol{T}_{\text{X-Bragg}} = \begin{bmatrix} C_1 & C_2\text{sinc}(2\beta_1) & 0 \\ C_2^*\text{sinc}(2\beta_1) & C_3\left(1+\text{sinc}(4\beta_1)\right) & 0 \\ 0 & 0 & C_3\left(1-\text{sinc}(4\beta_1)\right) \end{bmatrix}, \quad (4.4)$$

where:

$$\begin{cases} C_1 = \left|S_{\text{HH}} + S_{\text{VV}}\right|^2 / 2 \\ C_2 = \left(S_{\text{HH}} + S_{\text{VV}}\right)\left(S_{\text{HH}} - S_{\text{VV}}\right)^* / 2; \\ C_3 = \left|S_{\text{HH}} - S_{\text{VV}}\right|^2 / 4 \end{cases}$$

and β_1 is the distribution width of the random surface slope. From this model, the material indicator M [15] was defined as follows:

$$M = \frac{T_{22} + T_{33}}{T_{11}} = \frac{\left|S_{\text{HH}} - S_{\text{VV}}\right|^2}{\left|S_{\text{HH}} + S_{\text{VV}}\right|^2} = \frac{\left|\rho - 1\right|^2}{\left|\rho + 1\right|^2}. \quad (4.5)$$

M is rotation invariant. Under the X-Bragg scattering model where backscatter from rough surface is modeled by Bragg coefficients, $\arctan(M)$ distributes in the interval $\left[0 \quad 45°\right]$. In [15] in the case of Bragg or X-Bragg scattering, $\arctan(M)$ is referred to as the Bragg alpha angle. If standing free of the Bragg scattering background, we can notice that for the trihedral and dihedral scattering models in (4.1), $\arctan(M)$ is equal to $0°$ and $90°$, respectively. Further, if the target backscatter, e.g., double-bounce scattering, is modeled by Fresnel coefficients, where the phase of the co-polarized ratio tends to be π, then according to (4.5), $\arctan(M)$ becomes larger than $45°$. Note that for deterministic scattering models with single scattering mechanisms (e.g., the scattering models presented in this section), the information contained in $\arctan(M)$ is identical to that in the co-polarization ratio ρ. However, backscatter from natural scatterers is a random process, and thus the exact relationship in (4.5) does not hold. In the next section, we continue to discuss the extension of arctan (M) to the general distributed target scattering case.

4.3.2 New Parameter to Represent the Randomness

An arbitrary symmetric scatterer can be represented by

$$\boldsymbol{T} = \boldsymbol{Q}(2\theta)^T \begin{bmatrix} t_{11} & t_{12} & 0 \\ t_{12}^* & t_{22} & 0 \\ 0 & 0 & t_{33} \end{bmatrix} \boldsymbol{Q}(2\theta), \quad (4.6)$$

where:

$$
\begin{aligned}
t_{11} &= \left|S_{\mathrm{HH}} + S_{\mathrm{VV}}\right|^2 \\
t_{22} + t_{33} &= \left|S_{\mathrm{HH}} - S_{\mathrm{VV}}\right|^2 \qquad ; \\
t_{12} &= \left(S_{\mathrm{HH}} + S_{\mathrm{VV}}\right)\left(S_{\mathrm{HH}} - S_{\mathrm{VV}}\right)^*
\end{aligned}
$$

$\theta \in \left[-\pi/4 \quad \pi/4\right]$ is the target orientation angle; t_{11}, t_{22}, t_{33}, and t_{12} are the coherency matrix elements in standard orientation (i.e., the target orientation angle θ is 0° 0); and $Q(2\theta)$ is the rotation matrix given by

$$
Q(2\theta) = \begin{bmatrix} 1 & 0 & 0 \\ 0 & cos2\theta & sin2\theta \\ 0 & -sin2\theta & cos2\theta \end{bmatrix}.
$$

The coherency matrix T permits depolarization, which is related to the energy dispersion from the co-polarized channels to the cross-polarized channel. Assuming that $\boldsymbol{T}$ is with 0° orientation angle, we let

$$
\alpha_{\mathrm{B}} = \arctan\left(\frac{T_{22} + T_{33}}{T_{11}}\right). \tag{4.7}
$$

Then the following relationship can be obtained (see the Appendix 4A).

$$
\alpha_{\mathrm{B}} = \arctan\left(\frac{\left|\rho_r - 1\right|^2 + 2\left|\rho_r\right| cos\phi_r \left(1 - \left|r_{\mathrm{c}}\right|\right)}{\left|\rho_r + 1\right|^2 - 2\left|\rho_r\right| cos\phi_r \left(1 - \left|r_{\mathrm{c}}\right|\right)}\right), \tag{4.8}
$$

where

$$
\rho_r = \left|\rho_r\right| e^{j\phi_r} = \sqrt{\frac{\left|S_{\mathrm{VV}}\right|^2}{\left|S_{\mathrm{HH}}\right|^2}} e^{j(\phi_{\mathrm{VV}} - \phi_{\mathrm{HH}})}, \tag{4.9}
$$

and

$$
r_{\mathrm{c}} = \frac{S_{\mathrm{HH}} S_{\mathrm{VV}}^*}{\sqrt{\left|S_{\mathrm{HH}}\right|^2 \left|S_{\mathrm{VV}}\right|^2}}.
$$

$\left|\rho_r\right|$ and ϕ_r are the average co-polarized amplitude ratio and the average CPD, respectively. α_{B} belongs to the interval $\left[0° \quad 90°\right]$. Equation (4.8) shows that α_{B} is greatly affected by the amplitude of the co-polarized coherence (correlation coefficient) $|r_c|$, which is the most important parameter affecting the noise variance of the co-polarized amplitude ratio and the phase difference [20]. When $|r_c|$ is small, both the amplitude ratio and the phase difference variances are large, indicating that the scattering is inhomogeneous with difference in backscattering behaviors. For high coherence areas where $|r_c|$ is large, all scattering is likely to come from a single mechanism, and in this case α_B is mainly determined by ρ_r. If we let $|r_c|=1$, an ideal value without considering the scattering randomness in α_B is given by

$$\alpha_0 = \arctan\left(\frac{|\rho_r - 1|^2}{|\rho_r + 1|^2}\right). \tag{4.10}$$

In practice, $|r_c|$ is always smaller than 1 for random backscatter. Therefore, we define a new parameter $\Delta\alpha_B$ to measure the effect of the scattering coherence on the estimation of α_B, as follows.

$$\Delta\alpha_B = \alpha_B - \alpha_0. \tag{4.11}$$

From (4.8), it can be noticed that when $|r_c|$ decreases, α_B deviates away from its ideal value α_0. When $|r_c|=0$, α_B distributes around 45°. By using simulated data which is Wishart statistically distributed with 4 number of looks, Figure 4.3 shows as an example the variation of $\Delta\alpha_B$ and α_B versus the co-polarized coherence $|r_c|$ for two classes of extreme scatterers, for which the corresponding covariance matrices are with ρ_r equal to 1 and –1, respectively. In the diagram shown in Figure 4.3, two ideal models are located at $(0° \quad 0°)$ and $(0° \quad 90°)$, respectively. As $|r_c|$ varies, two tilt lines can thus be generated. When $|r_c|$ reduces, the two points move away from the vertical line where $\Delta\alpha_B = 0°$. $|\Delta\alpha_B|$ increases with the decreasing $|r_c|$. In this study, we use $\Delta\alpha_B$ to measure the scattering randomness of scatterers. It is observed that the trihedral-like (the blue line) and dihedral-like (the red line) scatterers distribute on the right and left parts of the $\Delta\alpha_B / \alpha_B$ plane, respectively. Natural scatterers with the property of surface scattering can generally be regarded as originating from the trihedral point, while scatterers with double-bounce scattering originate from the dihedral point. In the case of surface and volume scattering, where the co-polarized phase difference $|\phi_r|$ is smaller than 90°, $\Delta\alpha_B$ is larger than 0°; while in the case of double-bounce scattering, where $|\phi_r|$ is larger than 90°, $\Delta\alpha_B$ is smaller than 0°.

Note that although α_B is rotation invariant (T_{11} and $T_{22}+T_{33}$ are independent of θ), the average co-polarized ratio ρ_r is significantly affected by θ [13]. Due to the effect of the orientation angle θ, pixels dominated by double-bounce scattering may have absolute CPD values smaller than 90°, which would have an impact on the determination of whether the scattering mechanism is dominated by surface or double-bounce scattering [7]. To eliminate the orientation effect on the identification of

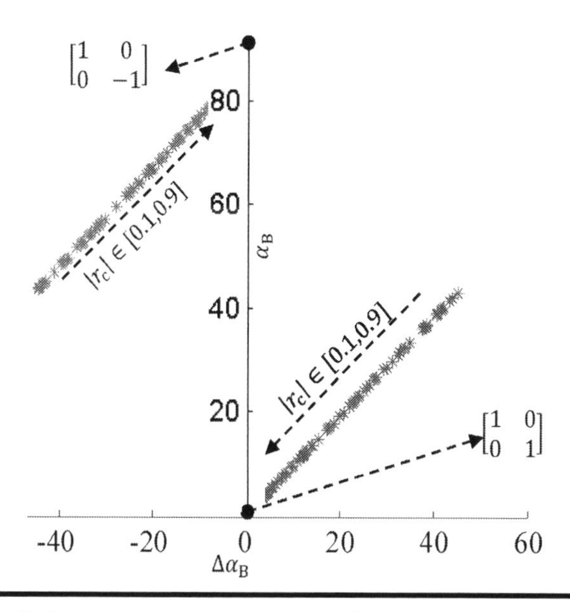

Figure 4.3 Variations of $\Delta\alpha_B$ and α_B versus r_c for the trihedral-like and dihedral-like scatterers by using simulated data, which are based the Wishart distribution (4 looks) and the covariance matrices $|S_{HH}|^2 \begin{bmatrix} 1 & \rho_r|r_c| \\ \rho_r^*|r_c| & |\rho_r|^2 \end{bmatrix}$ with $\rho_r = 1$ and $\rho_r = -1$, respectively.

scattering mechanisms, before extracting ρ_r, a de-orientation procedure is needed to rotate the coherency matrix $\boldsymbol{T}$ to be with 0° orientation angle [7,21].

RADARSAT-2 data acquired over the San Francisco Bay area are used to show the distribution plots of ρ_r and α_B as well as the relationship between $\Delta\alpha_B$, α_B, and α_0. Four typical theme areas are outlined in Figure 4.4a, denoting different scattering types, i.e., ocean surface Bragg scattering, forest vegetation scattering, urban double-bounce dominated scattering, and the scattering from urban areas rotated 45° relative to the azimuth direction. In Figure 4.4b–f, the cylindrical coordinate system is employed for representation, with the co-polarized ratio ρ_r displayed on the polar coordinate plane and α_B displayed on the height axis. Note that the de-orientation procedure [21] was applied. It is observed that pixels from the ocean surface and forests are distributed on the right part of the unit co-polarized ratio circle (the red circle), which means that the absolute CPD values of these scatterers are smaller than 90°. Pixels from urban areas are mostly distributed on the left part of the unit circle, suggesting that most pixels are with the property of $|\phi_r| > 90°$. The broad CPD distributions in Figure 4.4d–e suggest that multiple scatterers are present in urban areas, but the urban area is still experiencing substantial double-bounce scattering. It is also noted that scattering processes in the

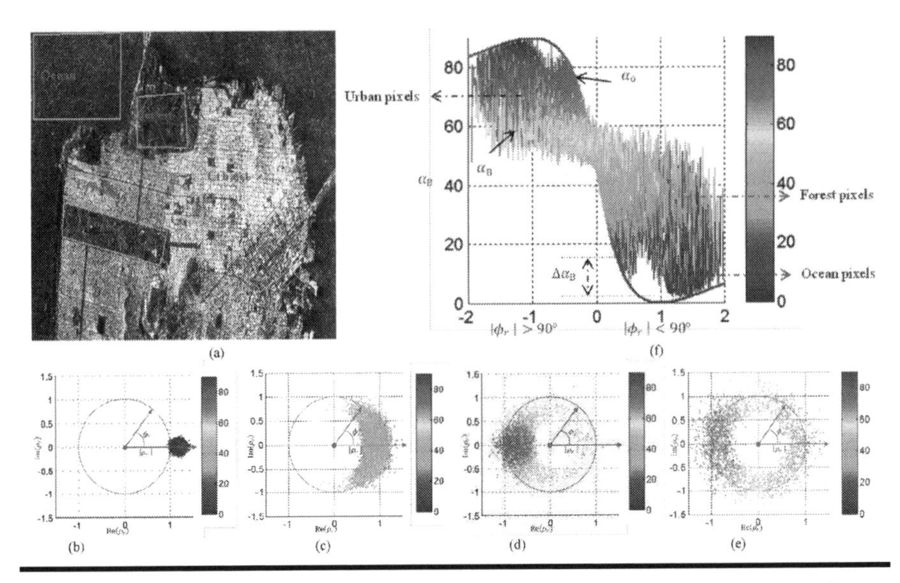

Figure 4.4 Distribution plots of ρ_r and α_B for the four typical scattering classes outlined in (a). Urban1 and Urban2 denote areas with man-made building structures aligned at 0° and 45°, respectively, relative to the radar azimuth direction. For better display, the 3-dimensional scatter plots are projected onto 2-dimensional planes. (b)–(e) are shown in the polar coordinate system with $|\rho_r|$ shown on the radial coordinate and ϕ_r shown the angular coordinate. The color bar indicates α_B values of the vertical axis of the cylindrical coordinate system. (f) Distribution plots of the four areas. The smooth curve in (f) represents the ideal α_0. (b) The ocean surface. (c) Forests. (d) The Urban1 area. (e) The Urban2 area.

Urban2 area (Figure 4.4e) are more complex than those in the Urban1 area because the rotated urban area has a larger CPD variation. The average α_B values for the four areas of Figure 4.4b–e are 3.4°, 41.1°, 50.2°, and 54.7°, respectively. Pixels of the ocean surface are distributed outside of the unit circle, indicating that $|\rho_r|$ is larger than 1, which is consistent with Bragg scattering coefficients. The majority of urban pixels are distributed inside of the unit circle, indicating that $|\rho_r|$ is smaller than 1, which is consistent with Fresnel scattering coefficients [13]. When $|\phi_r| < 90°$, the estimated α_B is larger than its ideal value α_0, and the corresponding $\Delta\alpha_B$ is larger than 0° (Figure 4.4f). For pixels dominated by double-bounce scattering ($|\phi_r| > 90°$), the estimated α_B is smaller than its ideal value α_0 (Figure 4.4f), and thus the corresponding $\Delta\alpha_B$ is smaller than 0°.

Figure 4.4b–f demonstrates that different theme classes are distributed in different regions of the 3-dimentional $\alpha_B / |\rho_r| / \phi_r$ system. However, it is difficult for this system to intuitively represent the scattering randomness. Thus in this study, we propose to use the simplified diagram, as shown in Figure 4.3, to classify the target scattering. Classification boundaries are introduced in the next section.

4.3.3 New Target Scattering Mechanism Classification Diagram

α_B and $\Delta\alpha_B$ have similar physical interpretations for target characterization as the polarization H and *alpha*. We also classify the scatterers into 8 basic scattering mechanisms. The proposed $\Delta\alpha_B/\alpha_B$ segmentation plane is shown in Figure 4.5a, and the *H/alpha* plane in Figure 4.5b. The $\Delta\alpha_B$ / α_B classification boundaries are determined based on both the *H/alpha* scattering plane and typical scattering models. There exist one-to-one correspondences between the classification zones of the $\Delta\alpha_B/\alpha_B$ and *H/alpha* planes.

1. Classification Boundaries of α_B: Classification boundaries of α_B for different scattering mechanisms are determined by statistical averages of real polarimetric SAR data according to the polarization *alpha*. The corresponding relationship between α_B and *alpha* is shown in Figure 4.6 for the San Francisco Bay area. Thresholds of α_B are calculated from the average of the pixels whose alpha values are at the *alpha* boundaries. For separation of zones 7, 8, and 9, boundaries of α_B are estimated as 40° and 50°; for separation of zones 4, 5, and 6, boundaries of α_B are estimated as 35°and 52.5°; and for separation of zones 1 and 2, boundaries of α_B are estimated as 60°. To test the validity of α_B boundaries, we use α_B with its thresholds to substitute *alpha* in the *H/alpha* plane. The result of the H/α_B classification is consistent with that of the *H/alpha* classification. Experiments show that the overall classification agreements between H/α_B and *H/alpha* results are 97.8%, 88.62%,

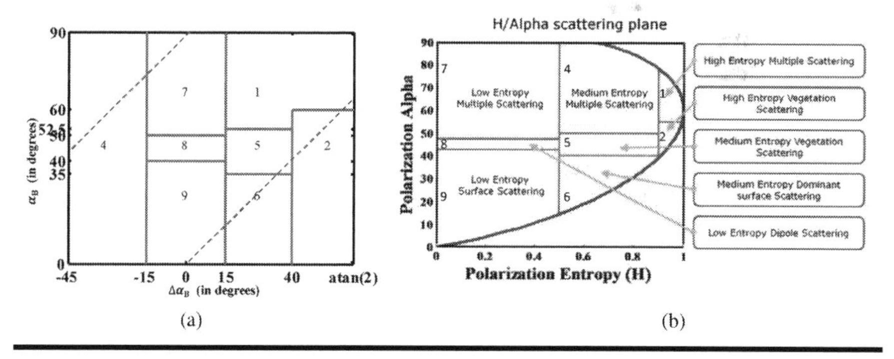

Figure 4.5 (a) The proposed $\Delta\alpha_B/\alpha_B$ classification plane. The values displayed on the axes indicate the zone boundaries. The dashed diagonal lines are tilted boundaries of the scatter diagram but they do not affect the classification. (b) The classic *H/alpha* plane. The zone numbers in the $\Delta\alpha_B/\alpha_B$ and the *H/alpha* planes have one-to-one correspondences.

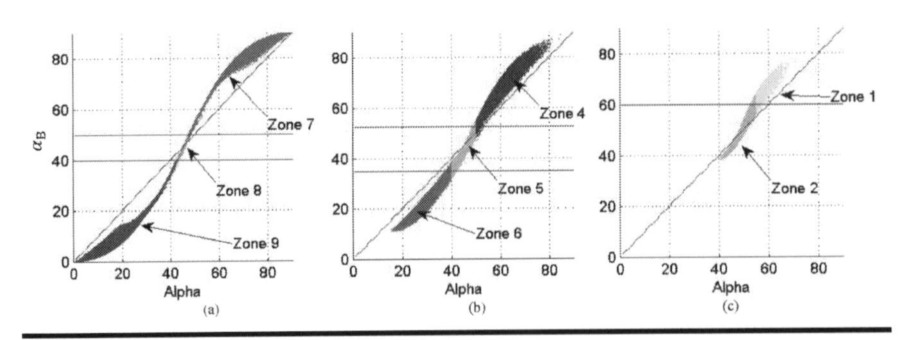

Figure 4.6 Scatter plots of α_B and *alpha* for (a) low entropy classes, (b) medium entropy classes, and (c) high entropy classes.

and 89.96%, respectively, for the RADARSAT-2 San Francisco data, Fuzhou Data1, and Data2. Further testing with several other RADARSAT-2 data shows that the lowest classification agreement between H/α_B and *H*/*alpha* results is 88.54%. This indicates that the selected boundaries for α_B are effective for identification of the basic scattering classes.

2. Classification Boundaries of $\Delta\alpha_B$: As discussed above, $\Delta\alpha_B$ is closely related to the co-polarized coherence. For homogeneous areas where target scattering diversity varies little, i.e., H is small and $|r_c|$ is large, $|\Delta\alpha_B|$ is small; and for heterogeneous areas where the backscattering process consists of a mixture of scattering mechanisms, i.e., H is large and $|r_c|$ is small, $|\Delta\alpha_B|$ is large. We use 3 physical models and the typical values of H ($H = 0.5$ and $H = 0.9$) to determine the thresholds of $\Delta\alpha_B$ to characterize the low, medium, and high heterogeneous scattering. The rightmost boundary of $\Delta\alpha_B$ is determined by a typical volume scattering model $\boldsymbol{T}_{\mathrm{vol1}}$ [15] as shown in (4.12). This model exhibits scattering azimuthal symmetry, in which the average co-polarized ratio ρ_r is 1, corresponding to an ideal α_0 value of 0°. When the volume shape parameter a varies from [5] to 1, α_B becomes smaller from its maximum $\mathrm{atan}(2) \approx 63.4°$ to its minimum 0°. Thus, the rightmost boundary of $\Delta\alpha_B$ is set to 63.4°. The leftmost boundary of $\Delta\alpha_B$ is estimated by the double-bounce scattering model $\boldsymbol{T}_{\mathrm{d}}$ [4] in (4.12). Canonical dihedral reflection has an ideal α_0 value of 90°. For the general double-bounce scattering, an extreme situation occurs at $\alpha = 1$. In this case, α_B reaches its smallest value 45°. Thus, the leftmost boundary of $\Delta\alpha_B$ is set to –45°.

$$\boldsymbol{T}_{\mathrm{vol1}} = \begin{bmatrix} 1+a & 0 & 0 \\ 0 & 1-a & 0 \\ 0 & 0 & 1-a \end{bmatrix}, \quad a \in [0 \quad 1];$$

$$\boldsymbol{T}_{\mathrm{d}} = \begin{bmatrix} |\alpha|^2 & \alpha & 0 \\ \alpha^* & 1 & 0 \\ 0 & 0 & 0 \end{bmatrix}, \quad \alpha \in [0 \quad 1]. \tag{4.12}$$

A generalized volume scattering model proposed in Cloude (2010) [15], as shown in (4.13), is used to calculate the other thresholds of $\Delta\alpha_{\mathrm{B}}$. This model exhibits scattering reflection symmetry. It is selected because it is applicable to a wide range of scattering situations from pure surface scattering to extreme volume scattering with the variations of model parameters.

$$\boldsymbol{T}_{\mathrm{vol2}} = \begin{bmatrix} e_{11} & e_{12} & 0 \\ e_{12}^* & e_{22} & 0 \\ 0 & 0 & e_{33} \end{bmatrix}, \tag{4.13}$$

where

$$\begin{cases} e_{11} = 2 + \dfrac{4}{3}X + \dfrac{4}{15}X^2 \\ e_{12} = \mathrm{sinc}(2\Delta)\left(\dfrac{2}{3}X + \dfrac{4}{15}X^2\right) \\ e_{22} = \dfrac{2}{15}X^2\left(1 + \mathrm{sinc}(4\Delta)\right) \\ e_{33} = \dfrac{2}{15}X^2\left(1 - \mathrm{sinc}(4\Delta)\right) \end{cases};$$

$X > 0$ is a depolarization factor, indicating the degree of particle anisotropy; $\Delta \in [0 \quad 90°]$ is the distribution width of particle orientations. By varying both X and Δ, the relationship between H and $|\Delta\alpha_{\mathrm{B}}|$ can be obtained. $|\Delta\alpha_{\mathrm{B}}|$ increases with increasing H. When $H = 0.5$, the median value of $|\Delta\alpha_{\mathrm{B}}|$ is 15°; and when $H = 0.9$, the median value of $|\Delta\alpha_{\mathrm{B}}|$ is 40°. Here, the median value of $|\Delta\alpha_{\mathrm{B}}|$ is not affected by X and Δ. Since $\Delta\alpha_{\mathrm{B}}$ can be either positive or negative, ±15° and ±40° are set as the thresholds of $\Delta\alpha_{\mathrm{B}}$. However, in practice, only a few pixels would fall in the interval $[-45° \quad -40°]$ in the $\Delta\alpha_{\mathrm{B}}$ image. Thus, the threshold of –40° is cancelled. Finally, the $\Delta\alpha_{\mathrm{B}}/\alpha_{\mathrm{B}}$ scatter diagram is divided into 8 regions as the *H*/*alpha* plane.

In Figure 4.3, we showed that two tilt lines are generated when $|r_{\mathrm{c}}|$ varies from 0.1 to 0.9. The tilt lines correspond to two scattering cases. It is easy to prove that the red and blue slant lines are the tilt boundaries of the $\Delta\alpha_{\mathrm{B}}/\alpha_{\mathrm{B}}$ scatter diagram, as follows. For a fixed α_{B} and an arbitrary ρ_r, according to equations (4.7) and (4.10), $\Delta\alpha_{\mathrm{B}}$ achieves its maximum (i.e., the blue line in Figure 4.3) only when $\rho_r = 1$;

and similarly, $\Delta\alpha_{\mathrm{B}}$ achieves its minimum (i.e., the red line in Figure 4.3) only when $\rho_r = -1$. Hence, these two lines are the tilt boundaries of the $\Delta\alpha_{\mathrm{B}} / \alpha_{\mathrm{B}}$ scatter diagram. The tilt boundaries are given by

$$\begin{aligned} \alpha_{\mathrm{B}} &= \Delta\alpha_{\mathrm{B}} & \Delta\alpha_{\mathrm{B}} &\in \left(0^\circ \quad 63.4^\circ\right] \\ \alpha_{\mathrm{B}} &= 90^\circ + \Delta\alpha_{\mathrm{B}} & \Delta\alpha_{\mathrm{B}} &\in \left[-45^\circ \quad 0^\circ\right) \end{aligned}. \tag{4.14}$$

In summary, we propose a new method for scattering mechanism classification. This method provides a simple classification scheme as the *H*/*alpha* plane. It does not, however, have the backscattered power information. Similar to the *H*/*alpha* method, the proposed method can also be used as an initial step for further advanced statistical classifiers such as the Wishart classifier. The stepwise procedure of the proposed method is summarized as follows. Note that the tilt boundaries do not affect the classification.

1. Rotate the coherency matrix $\boldsymbol{T}$ to be with 0° orientation angle [21];
2. Calculate α_{B}, $|\rho_r|$ and ϕ_r using (4.7) and (4.9), respectively;
3. Calculate $\Delta\alpha_{\mathrm{B}}$ using (4.11); and
4. Classify the given data into 8 scattering mechanisms based on the diagram shown in Figure 4.5a.

4.4 Experiments

Data sets introduced in Section 4.2 are used for validation. Experiments are carried out from the following aspects: (1) capability of the parameters for discriminating different areas; (2) comparison of classification results of the $\Delta\alpha_{\mathrm{B}}/\alpha_{\mathrm{B}}$ and *H*/*alpha* methods; (3) evaluation of $\Delta\alpha_{\mathrm{B}}/\alpha_{\mathrm{B}}$ and *H*/*alpha* initializations for the classic Wishart classifier; and (4) stability of $\Delta\alpha_{\mathrm{B}}/\alpha_{\mathrm{B}}$ and *H*/*alpha* methods for analyzing multi-temporal data. Computations involving *H* and *alpha* as well as the *H*/*alpha*-Wishart classification [8] are computed using PolSARpro. Iteration of the Wishart classifier is set to stop when the total number of pixels switching between classes is less than 1% of the total number of pixels.

Figure 4.7a–b shows images of *H* and $\Delta\alpha_{\mathrm{B}}$ of the San Francisco Bay data. The outlined areas with forest and rotated urban themes can be clearly distinguished in the $\Delta\alpha_{\mathrm{B}}$ image, while *H* could hardly discriminate these two classes. Figure 4.7c–f shows the probability distributions of different parameters. For the forested and rotated urban areas, the difference in average *alpha* values is 7.95°, while the difference in average α_{B} is 13.56°. If one uses the distributions shown in Figure 4.7c–f to classify the two classes, misclassification rates (i.e., the overlapping area under the two curves) of *H* and *alpha* are 61.3% and 32.2%, respectively, while $\Delta\alpha_{\mathrm{B}}$ and α_{B} have much smaller misclassification rates of 40.8% and 30.1%, respectively. It shows that compared to *H*, $\Delta\alpha_{\mathrm{B}}$ is more efficient in separating forests from the oriented urban area.

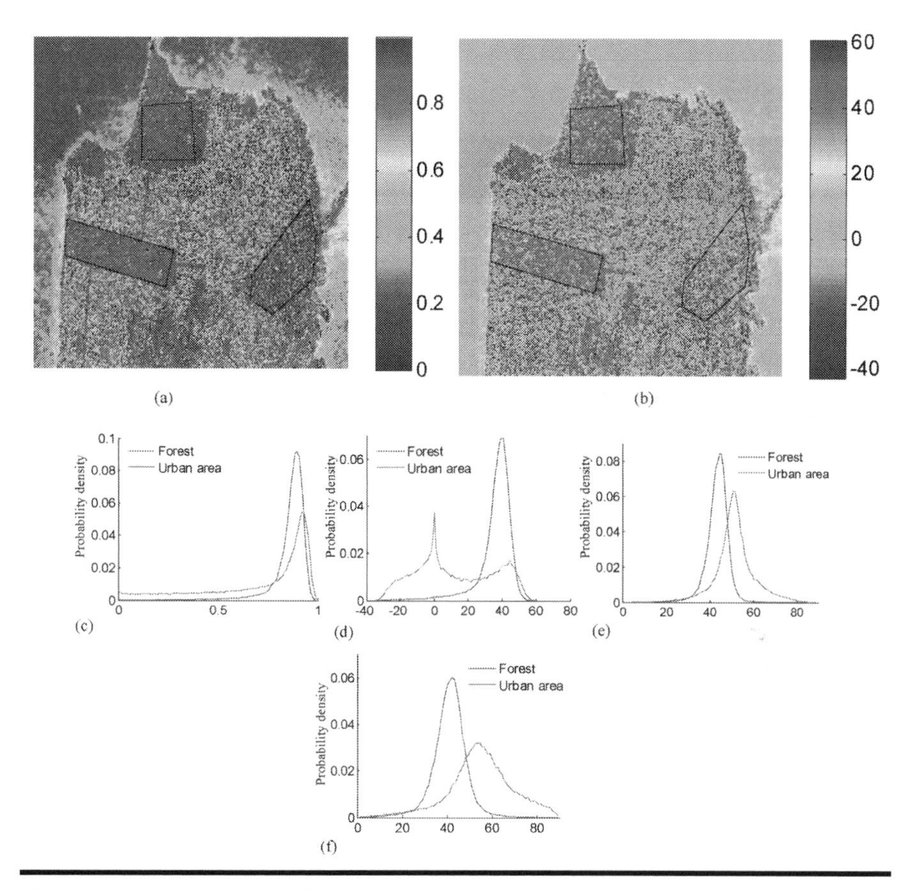

Figure 4.7 Comparison of *H* and *alpha* versus $\Delta\alpha_B$ and α_B. (a) The *H* image. (b) The $\Delta\alpha_B$ image. Histograms of (c) *H*, (d) $\Delta\alpha_B$, (e) *alpha*, and (f) α_B for the forest and rotated urban area themes.

Classification results of *H*/*alpha* and $\Delta\alpha_B/\alpha_B$ methods are shown in Figure 4.8. By visual inspection, it shows that the $\Delta\alpha_B/\alpha_B$ method classified more urban pixels into zones 4 and 7 (labeled in the red color), which represent double-bounce scattering events. The four typical themes outlined in Figure 4.4a are used to assess the performance of $\Delta\alpha_B/\alpha_B$ and *H*/*alpha* classifiers. The selected theme areas in this investigation are predominantly the ocean surface, forests, urban, and rotated urban areas. Table 4.2 shows the percentages of the classified scattering mechanisms of each area. The classification accuracy (CA) is calculated based on the physical interpretation of scattering mechanisms of the predominant scatterers of each area. For example, the ocean surface is generally regarded as being dominated by surface scattering, and thus pixels classified into zone 9 are used to calculate the corresponding CA. Similarly, the CA for forest theme areas is estimated from the pixels classified into zones 2 and 5, and the CA for urban theme areas is estimated from the pixels assigned to zones 7 and 4 [3,8].

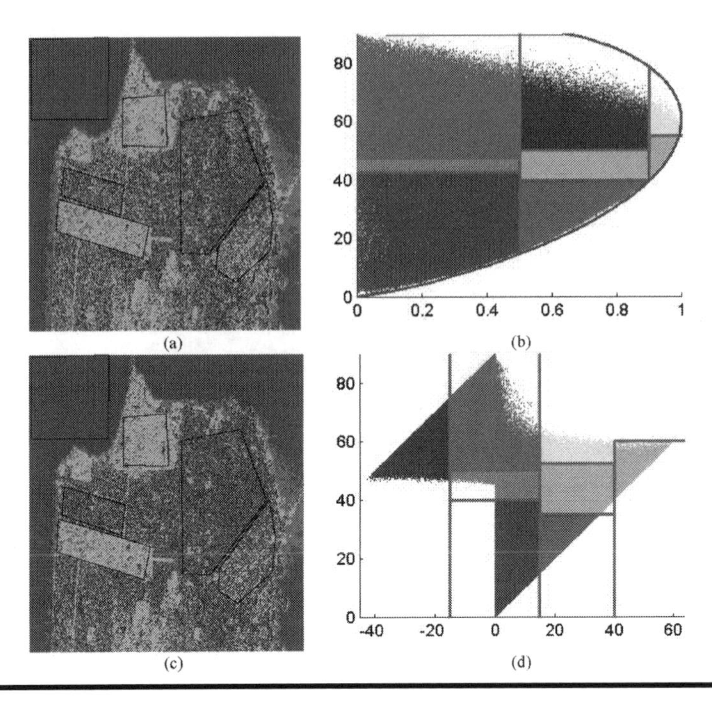

Figure 4.8 (a) Classification results of RADARSAT-2 data of the San Francisco Bay area using the *H/alpha* scattering plane. (b) The *H/alpha* scatter plot. (c) Classification results by the $\Delta\alpha_B/\alpha_B$ scattering plane. (d) The $\Delta\alpha_B/\alpha_B$ scatter plot. Colors in *H/alpha* and $\Delta\alpha_B/\alpha_B$ diagrams correspond to each other. The outlined areas (see Fig. 4(a)) will be used for the assessment in Table 4.2.

It is observed that the $\Delta\alpha_B/\alpha_B$ method provides higher accuracies for the identification of predominant scattering types, especially for urban areas. Significant differences between the $\Delta\alpha_B/\alpha_B$ and *H/alpha* classifications can be found in zones 4 and 7. Zone 4 and zone 7 in both *H/alpha* and $\Delta\alpha_B/\alpha_B$ planes correspond to the double-bounce reflections and the dihedral reflections, respectively. However, in urban areas, the *H/alpha* method could only detect 36.27% urban class pixels for the Urban2 area, while the $\Delta\alpha_B/\alpha_B$ method outperforms by 13.86%. In Urbanl, the *H/alpha* method classified a large number of pixels into zone 5, and in Urban2 a large number of pixels were assigned to zone 2. However, scattering objects in scattering zones 2 and 5 are generally recognized as vegetation scattering. In comparison, the $\Delta\alpha_B/\alpha_B$ method assigned the majority of urban pixels into zone 7. The difference between the results of $\Delta\alpha_B/\alpha_B$ and *H/alpha* methods is mainly due to the effect of CPD. In the $\Delta\alpha_B/\alpha_B$ diagram, the CPDs of different scattering types are actually integrated in the calculation of $\Delta\alpha_B$; while H is only related to the normalized intensity information of orthogonal scattering mechanisms. By incorporating the distinguished characteristic of CPD, the $\Delta\alpha_B/\alpha_B$ method has the

Table 4.2 Classification Accuracies (in Percentage) of the *H/alpha* Method and the $\Delta\alpha_B/\alpha_B$ Method for Four Typical Regions

The H/alpha Method										
%	*z*1	*z*2	*z*4	*z*5	*z*6	*z*7	*z*8	*z*9	CA	Overall accuracy
Ocean	0	0	0	0	0.11	0	0	**99.89**	**99.89**	**64.27**
Forest	0.11	**32.93**	1.93	**45.44**	17.32	0.58	0.14	1.56	**78.37**	
Urban1	0.06	0.34	**19.89**	29.16	7.71	**24.26**	4.47	14.10	**44.15**	
Urban2	4.77	28.22	**22.69**	19.13	3.58	**13.58**	2.16	5.87	**36.27**	
The $\Delta\alpha_B/\alpha_B$ Method										
%	*z*1	*z*2	*z*4	*z*5	*z*6	*z*7	*z*8	*z*9	CA	Overall accuracy
Ocean	0	0	0	0	0.01	0	0	**99.99**	**99.99**	**68.77**
Forest	0.62	**37.70**	0.67	**40.73**	13.46	2.93	0.72	3.18	**78.43**	
Urban1	0.11	2.68	**11.73**	11.69	5.45	**39.04**	12.01	17.28	**50.77**	
Urban2	5.23	17.52	**7.39**	13.16	2.48	**42.74**	3.95	7.52	**50.13**	

Note: The four areas were outlined in Figure 4.4a. $z1-z9$ are the segmentation zones in both *H*/*alpha* and $\Delta\alpha_B/\alpha_B$ planes, where $zi(i=1\cdots9)$ denotes Zone *i*.

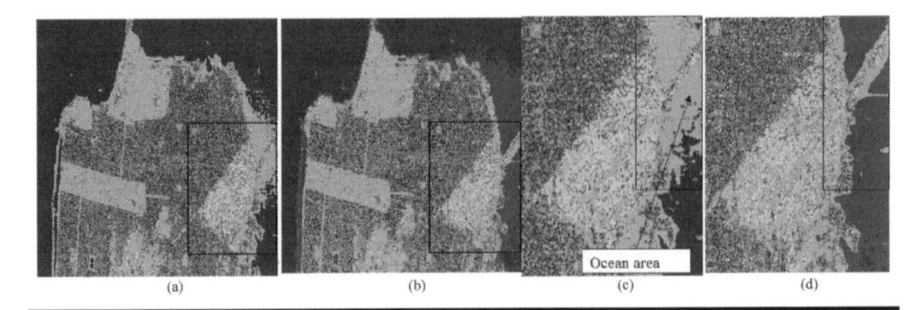

Figure 4.9 The Wishart classifier results of RADARSAT-2 data of the San Francisco Bay area, initialized by the *H/alpha* plane is shown in (a), and by the $\Delta\alpha_B/\alpha_B$ plane in (b). (c) and (d) are zoomed-in images corresponding to (a) and (b), respectively.

advantage of providing better separation for areas dominated by double-bounce scattering and areas dominated by vegetation scattering. This can also be observed in Figure 4.5, where zones 4 and 7 have a larger spatial distance away from zones 5 and 2 in the $\Delta\alpha_B/\alpha_B$ plane than in the *H/alpha* plane.

When classification results of *H/alpha* and $\Delta\alpha_B/\alpha_B$ methods are taken as initial partitions for the Wishart classifier, the iteration results are shown in Figure 4.9. A difference can be clearly observed between these two results, as detailed in Figure 4.9c and d. In the result obtained by the *H/alpha* initialization, a part of the ocean surface is classified as forests; while in the result initialized by the $\Delta\alpha_B/\alpha_B$ plane, there is no such misclassification. Results of *H/alpha*-Wishart and $\Delta\alpha_B/\alpha_B$-Wishart classifiers are compared in Table 4.3. Note that after the iteration of the Wishart classifier, pixels classified into class $i\left(i=1\ldots9\right)$ no longer correspond to the i-th zone of the scattering diagrams, so we define the final iteration result as class $ci\left(i=1\ldots9\right)$, with each class ci corresponding to the i-th initialization zone i. Since this is an unsupervised classification, we do not have prior knowledge about the land cover types. Therefore, for each test area, the class that has the maximum classified pixel number is selected as the correct classification for this area such that the classification performance can be assessed. For example, class $c2$ accounts for majority pixels for the forested area, and therefore CA of forests is calculated from pixels assigned into $c2$. In this way, the *H / alpha*-Wishart and the $\Delta\alpha_B/\alpha_B$-Wishart methods have classification rates of 81.93% and 87.71%, respectively, for the forest theme (see Table 4.3). However, in the Urban1 area, no single class takes up a significant majority of pixels. After applying the Wishart-distribution-based cluster merging criterion [8,22], which is usually used to measure the between-class distance, it is found that $c5$ has the minimum distance with $c4$. Therefore, pixels in $c5$ and $c4$ are merged to calculate the CA for the Urban1 area. From Table 4.3, it is observed that the $\Delta\alpha_B/\alpha_B$ initialization outperforms the *H / alpha* initialization for the Wishart classifier by producing 4.17% higher overall accuracy.

Table 4.3 Classification Results of the Iterative Wishart Classifier for the San Francisco Bay Area

Initialization by the *H/alpha* Method										
%	*c*1	*c*2	*c*4	*c*5	*c*6	*c*7	*c*8	*c*9	CA	Overall accuracy
Ocean	0	0.23	0	0	0.08	0	0	**99.69**	**99.69**	**73.83**
Forest	7.63	**81.93**	0.43	8.65	0.89	0.10	0.34	0.03	**81.93**	
Urban1	4.76	1.17	**20.79**	**37.18**	15.67	3.60	16.84	0	**57.97**	
Urban2	**61.43**	14.37	1.41	9.09	0.82	9.24	3.65	0	**61.43**	
Initialization by the $\Delta\alpha_B/\alpha_B$ Method										
%	*c*1	*c*2	*c*4	*c*5	*c*6	*c*7	*c*8	*c*9	CA	Overall accuracy
Ocean	0	0.05	0.03	0	1.09	0	0.01	**98.81**	**98.81**	**78.0**
Forest	4.39	**87.71**	0.93	6.22	0.26	0.11	0.38	0	**87.71**	
Urban1	6.20	1.49	**31.30**	**36.55**	0	4.23	20.24	0	**67.85**	
Urban2	**53.84**	27.18	1.05	6.41	0	8.85	2.68	0	**53.84**	

Note: The four typical class areas are outlined in Figure 4.4a. class $ci(i=1\cdots 9)$ corresponds to the result initialized by Zone $i(i=1\cdots 9)$.

Terrain cover types of the Fuzhou area are complicated. Since the studied methods are pixel-based approaches, there exist many isolated classified pixels, especially for areas with complicated topography. After obtaining the classified results, a simple morphological process is applied. The objective of this processing is to eliminate the isolated classified pixels so as to have a clearer observation of the results. The morphological processing does not change the classification results, described as follows. If a pixel located at (x, y) has class label $i(i = 1 \ldots 9)$, then a moving window centered at (x, y) is used to count the pixel number of each class in this moving window. If the label of the class whose pixel number is maximum in this window is also i, then the classified label for pixel (x, y) remains unchanged, otherwise this pixel is assigned a flag number 0 and will be excluded in assessment. In this approach, it is easier to observe and detect the predominant (or primary) classes in the area. A 51 × 51 window is used.

We have two multi-temporal data sets collected over the Fuzhou area. The overall classification agreement estimated using the iterative Wishart classifier for the two data sets is 56.87% when the *H*/*alpha* initialization is used, and is 78.25% when the $\Delta\alpha_B/\alpha_B$ initialization is used, indicating that the $\Delta\alpha_B/\alpha_B$ initialization is more stable.

The subarea outlined in Figure 4.1c contains four typical target areas: urban areas, forests, water, and agriculture areas. The Pauli-basis image and classification results are shown in Figure 4.10. Classification accuracies of *H*/*alpha*-Wishart and $\Delta\alpha_B/\alpha_B$-Wishart methods for these classes are compared in Table 4.4, where classification rates are calculated in the same way as those in Table 4.3. Each theme

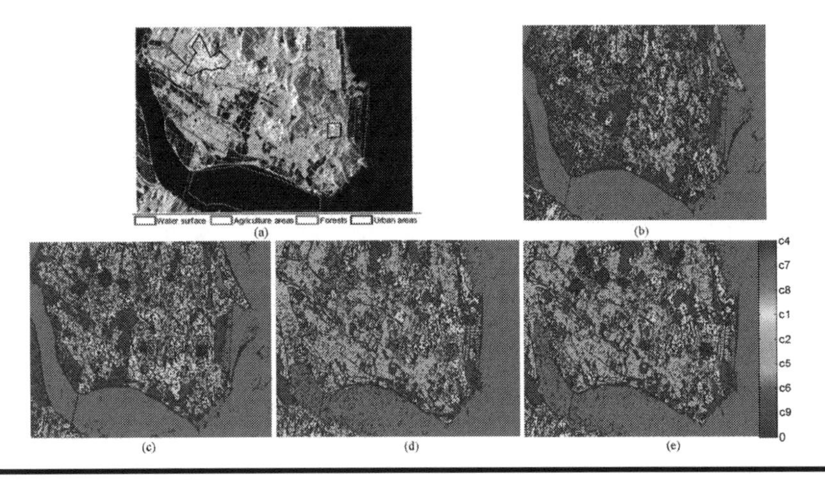

Figure 4.10 (a) The Pauli-basis image of a subset area of Fuzhou data, where the outlined areas are used as testing data for the evaluation in Table 4.4. Classification results of *H*/*alpha*-Wishart and $\Delta\alpha_B/\alpha_B$-Wishart methods of Data1 (acquired on Oct. 20, 2013) are shown in (b) and (c), respectively; results of *H*/*alpha*-Wishart and $\Delta\alpha_B/\alpha_B$-Wishart methods of Data2 (acquired on Nov. 13, 2013) are shown in (d) and (e), respectively.

Table 4.4 Comparison of Land Cover Classification Results (%) for the Island Subarea of Fuzhou

Data and Classifier	*Classes*	*c1*	*c2*	*c4*	*c5*	*c6*	*c7*	*c8*	*c9*	*CA*	*Overall Accuracy*
(Data1) *H/alpha*-Wishart	Water	0	0	0	0	**100**	0	0	0	**100**	**76.85**
	Field	3.02	0.02	0	**50.57**	0	0	46.14	0.24	**50.57**	
	Forest	**0.37**	**89.34**	0	1.37	0	0	8.91	0	**89.71**	
	Urban	44.47	1.30	**30.86**	0	0	0	23.37	0	**30.86**	
(Data1) $\Delta\alpha_B/\alpha_B$-Wishart	Water	0	0	0	0	**100**	0	0	0	**100**	**84.28**
	Field	42.32	0	0	**57.68**	0	0	0	0	**57.68**	
	Forest	**51.78**	**45.88**	0	2.34	0	0	0	0	**97.66**	
	Urban	5.19	0.14	**68.47**	20.50	0	0	5.69	0	**68.47**	
(Data2) *H/alpha*-Wishart	Water	0	0.74	0	0	**99.26**	0	0	0	**99.26**	**96.15**
	Field	0.03	0	0	**99.97**	0	0	0	0	**99.97**	
	Forest	**67.8**	0	0	1.04	0	0	0	**31.16**	**98.69**	
	Urban	2.38	0	0	11.07	0	**67.03**	19.51	0	**67.03**	
(Data2) $\Delta\alpha_B/\alpha_B$-Wishart	Water	0	0.03	0	0	**99.97**	0	0	0	99.97	**96.65**
	Field	0.25	0	0	**99.75**	0	0	0	0	99.75	
	Forest	**56.54**	0	0	0.42	0	0	0	**43.05**	99.59	
	Urban	3.03	0	**70.02**	11.77	0	0	15.19	0	70.02	

Note: Data shown in Figure 4.10a. Data1 were acquired on October 20, 2013, and Data2 were acquired on November 13, 2013.

area except the forests uses a single class to represent. Forests are mainly contributed by two classes. However, for data sets acquired at different dates, the two classes are different. For Data1 (acquired on October 20, 2013), *c*1 and *c*2 has the smallest between-class distance, measured by the Wishart distance; while for Data2 (acquired on November 13, 2013), *c*1 and *c*9 has the smallest between-class distance. The different appearance of the two data sets for forest classification results is probably due to the different weather conditions. Data1 was acquired on a clear day, while Data2 was acquired on a rainy day. Urban pixels are mainly classified into *c*4 or *c*7, which are obtained iteratively from zone 4 or zone 7, respectively. It is observed from Table 4.4 that the Wishart classifier appears to perform better when the $\Delta\alpha_B/\alpha_B$ method is used for initialization, especially for Data1, where an improvement of 7.4% overall accuracy is obtained in comparison with that of the *H*/*alpha* initialization.

The ground truth information over the whole Fuzhou study area is unavailable. We only consider the classified result of urban areas. Scattering properties of urban areas are comparatively more stable than those from areas of natural scatterers under different weather conditions [23]. Increasingly, urban area identification is becoming an important SAR application. In the Fuzhou SAR image, one can see that urban settlements are distributed sparsely over the whole study area, often with agriculture fields around. The ground reference map for urban areas is delineated manually using the Google Earth image. Figure 4.11a shows the bounding boxes (i.e., the minimum bounding rectangle of an area) of the urban reference data. According to Table 4.4, unsupervised classification results *c*4 and *c*7 are recognized as the urban class. Figure 4.11b–e shows the results of *H*/*alpha*-Wishart and $\Delta\alpha_B/\alpha_B$-Wishart methods, where the detected urban class is denoted by bounding boxes. In Figure 4.11b, it is seen that the *H*/*alpha*-Wishart method classified some mountain ridges into the urban class. This kind of misclassification is not found in the other three results. Table 4.5 gives the classified accuracies of the urban class. For both data sets, the $\Delta\alpha_B/\alpha_B$-Wishart classification demonstrates a significant improvement on the producer's accuracy. In comparison with the *H*/*alpha*-Wishart classification, it makes an improvement as high as 24.91% for Data1 and makes an improvement of 7.02% for Data2. The user's accuracies of both methods are higher than 90%. Difference between user's accuracies of the two methods is not significant.

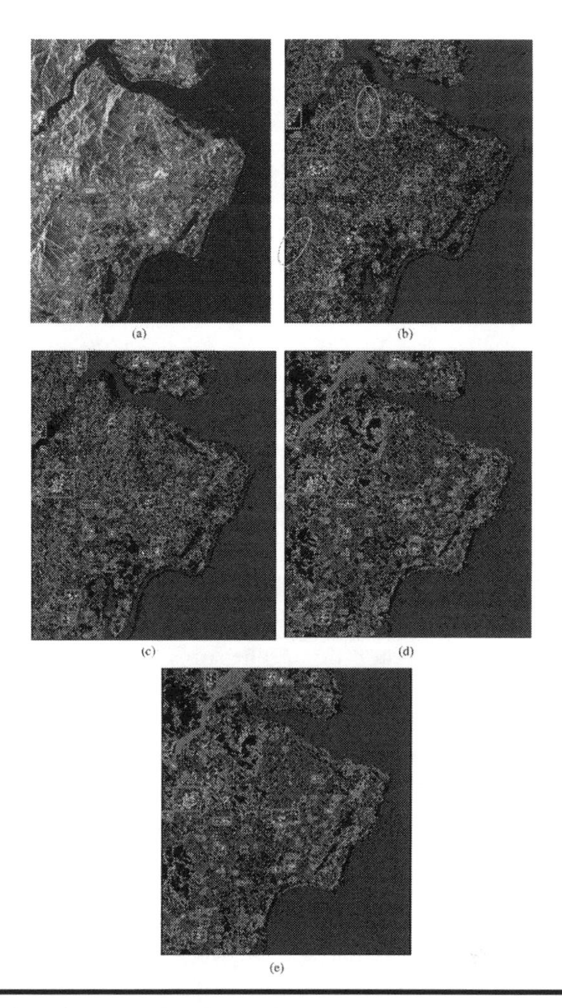

Figure 4.11 Classified results for urban areas. (a) Bounding boxes of the urban reference data. For Data1, results obtained by *H/alpha*-Wishart and $\Delta\alpha_B/\alpha_B$-Wishart methods are shown in (b) and (c), respectively; for Data2, results obtained by *H/alpha*-Wishart and $\Delta\alpha_B/\alpha_B$-Wishart methods are shown in (d) and (e), respectively. Rectangles are the bounding boxes of the identified urban pixels. In (b)-(e), the background is the final classification results. The outlined areas by ellipses in (b) indicate mountain ridges.

Table 4.5 Classification Accuracies for the Urban Class of the Fuzhou Data

Data1 (%)	*User's Accuracy*	*Producer's Accuracy*	*Data2 (%)*	*User's Accuracy*	*Producer's Accuracy*
H/*alpha*-Wishart	93.91	48.44		99.41	63.10
$\Delta\alpha_B/\alpha_B$-Wishart	97.98	73.35		99.33	70.12

Note: Data1 were acquired on October 20, 2013, and Data2 were acquired on November 13, 2013.

4.5 Summary

In this study, we proposed a simple but effective new approach for target scattering classification. This unsupervised classification method contains two polarimetric parameters: the scattering ratio α_B, and a new parameter $\Delta\alpha_B$, which is defined from the co-polarization ratio and coherence. In comparison with the polarization H, $\Delta\alpha_B$ shows better separation capability for forests and rotated urban areas. Compared with the *H*/*alpha* plane, the proposed $\Delta\alpha_B/\alpha_B$ plane performs better in identifying the predominant scattering mechanisms for the given region. The new plane can also be used as an initial processing step for further advanced statistical classifications. We demonstrated its effectiveness using three RADARSAT-2 fully polarimetric SAR data sets. It also shows that the new method is more stable when applied to multi-temporal polarimetric SAR data. In addition, the calculation of the proposed parameter is straightforward and the present method is easy to implement.

The $\Delta\alpha_B/\alpha_B$ method has similar physical interpretation for polarimetric SAR data as the *H*/*alpha* method. The main difference is that $\Delta\alpha_B$ uses negative values to characterize the scattering randomness for urban areas by taking CPD into account. In general, classification results of the *H*/*alpha* and $\Delta\alpha_B/\alpha_B$ methods are in relatively higher consistency. Test results of processing limited RADARSAT-2 data show that the minimum overall classification agreement is approximately 75% or better.

Appendix 4A

By assuming the reflection symmetric matrix $\boldsymbol{T}$ is at 0° orientation angle, then (4.7) can be written as

$$\alpha_B = \arctan\left(\frac{|S_{HH} - S_{VV}|^2}{|S_{HH} + S_{VV}|^2}\right). \tag{4A.1}$$

Expanding the right part of (4A.1) and dividing both the numerator and denominator by $|S_{\mathrm{HH}}|^2$ lead to

$$\alpha_{\mathrm{B}} = \arctan\left(\frac{1+\dfrac{|S_{\mathrm{VV}}|^2}{|S_{\mathrm{HH}}|^2}-2\dfrac{\mathrm{Re}\left(S_{\mathrm{HH}}S_{\mathrm{VV}}^*\right)}{|S_{\mathrm{HH}}|^2}}{1+\dfrac{|S_{\mathrm{VV}}|^2}{|S_{\mathrm{HH}}|^2}+2\dfrac{\mathrm{Re}\left(S_{\mathrm{HH}}S_{\mathrm{VV}}^*\right)}{|S_{\mathrm{HH}}|^2}}\right), \tag{4A.2}$$

where $\mathrm{Re}(\Delta)$ indicates the real part of a complex number. Substituting $S_{\mathrm{HH}}S_{\mathrm{VV}}^*$ by $r_c\sqrt{|S_{\mathrm{HH}}|^2|S_{\mathrm{VV}}|^2}$ and using the definition of ρ_r in (4.9), this yields

$$\begin{aligned}\alpha_{\mathrm{B}} &= \arctan\left(\frac{1+|\rho_r|^2-2\,\mathrm{Re}\left(r_c|\rho_r|\right)}{1+|\rho_r|^2+2\,\mathrm{Re}\left(r_c|\rho_r|\right)}\right) = \arctan\left(\frac{1+|\rho_r|^2-2|r_c||\rho_r|cos\phi_r}{1+|\rho_r|^2+2|r_c||\rho_r|cos\phi_r}\right)\\ &= \arctan\left(\frac{|\rho_r-1|^2+2|\rho_r|cos\phi_r\left(1-|r_c|\right)}{|\rho_r+1|^2+2|\rho_r|cos\phi_r\left(1-|r_c|\right)}\right)\end{aligned} \tag{4A.3}$$

Note that $|\rho_r|$ and ϕ_r are the average co-polarized amplitude ratio and the average CPD, respectively.

Acknowledgement

The authors are very grateful to the anonymous reviewers for their careful review which helped greatly improve this paper.

References

1. A. Moreira, P. Prats-Iraola, M. Younis, G. Krieger, I. Hajnsek, and K. Papathanassiou, "A tutorial on synthetic aperture radar," *IEEE Geosci. RemoteSens. Magazine*, pp. 6–43, 2013.
2. R. Touzi, "Target scattering decomposition in terms of roll-invariant target parameters," *IEEE Trans. Geosci. Remote Sens.*, vol. 45, no. 1, pp. 73–84, 2007.
3. S. R. Cloude and E. Pottier, "An entropy based classification scheme for land applications of polarimetric SAR," *IEEE Trans. Geosci. Remote Sens.*, vol. 35, no. 1, pp. 68–78, 1997.
4. A. Freeman and S. L. Durden, "A three-component scattering model for polarimetric SAR data," *IEEE Trans. Geosci. Remote Sens.*, vol. 36, no. 3, pp. 963–973, 1998.

5. A. Freeman, "Fitting a two-component scattering model to polarimetric SAR data from forests," *IEEE Trans. Geosci. Remote Sens.*, vol. 45, no. 8, pp. 2583–2592, 2007.
6. Y. Yamaguchi, T. Moriyama, M. Ishido, and H. Yamada, "Four-component scattering model for polarimetric SAR image decomposition," *IEEE Trans. Geosci. Remote Sens.*, vol. 43, no. 8, pp. 1699–1706, 2005.
7. Y. Yamaguchi, A. Sato, W.-M. Boerner, R. Sato, and H. Yamada, "Four-component scattering power decomposition with rotation of coherency matrix," *IEEE Trans. Geosci. Remote Sens.*, vol. 49, no. 6, pp. 2251–2258, 2011.
8. J.-S. Lee, M. R. Grunes, T. L. Anisworth, L.-J. Du, D. L. Schuler, and S. R. Cloude, "Unsupervised classification using polarimetric decomposition and the complex Wishart classifier," *IEEE Trans. Geosci. Remote Sens.*, vol. 37, no. 5, pp. 2249–2258, 1999.
9. S.-E. Park and W. M. Moon, "Unsupervised classification of scattering mechanisms in polarimetric SAR data using fuzzy logic in entropy and alpha plane," *IEEE Trans. Geosci. Remote Sens.*, vol. 45, no. 8, pp. 2652–2664, 2007.
10. M. Salehi, M. R. Sahebi, and Y. Maghsoudi, "Improving the accuracy of urban land cover classification using Radarsat-2 PolSAR data," *IEEE J. Sel. Top. Appl. Earth Obs. Remote Sens.*, vol. 7, no. 4, pp. 1394–1401, 2014.
11. A. Bhattacharya and R. Touzi, "Polarimetric SAR urban classification using the Touzi target scattering decomposition," *Can. J. Remote Sens.*, vol. 37, no. 4, pp. 323–332, 2011.
12. O. Antropov, Y. Rauste, H. Astola, T. Häme, and M. T. Hallikainen, "Land cover and soil type mapping from spaceborne PolSAR data at L-band with probabilistic neural network," *IEEE Trans. Geosci. Remote Sens.*, vol. 52, no. 9, pp. 5256–5270, 2014.
13. J. Yin and J. Yang, "New method for symmetric target scattering characterization in polarimetric SAR images," in *Proc. APSAR*, Tsukuba, Japan, pp. 597–600, 2013.
14. I. Hajnsek, E. Pottier, and S. R. Cloude, "Inversion of surface parameters from polarimetric SAR," *IEEE Trans. Geosci. Remote Sens.*, vol. 41, no. 4, pp. 727–744, 2003.
15. S. R. Cloude, *Polarisation: Applications in Remote Sensing.* 1st-edition, New York, Oxford University Press, Chapter 3 and Chapter 4, pp. 115–189, 2010.
16. S. R. Cloude and D. G. Corr, "A new parameter for soil moisture estimation," in *Proc. IGARSS*, Toronto, Canada, vol. 1, pp. 641–643, 2002.
17. J. Yin, J. Yang, Z.-S. Zhou, and J. Song, "The extended-Bragg scattering model-based method for ship and oil-spill observation using compact polarimetric SAR," *IEEE J. Sel. Top. Appl. Earth Obs. Remote Sens.*, vol. 8, no. 1, 2014.
18. J. S. Lee, M. R. Grunes, and G. de Grandi, "Polarimetric SAR speckle filtering and its impact on terrain classification," *IEEE Trans. Geosci. Remote Sens.*, vol. 37, no. 5, pp. 2363–2373, 1999.
19. K.-Y. Lee, Y. Oh, and Y. Kim, "Phase-difference of urban area in polarimetric SAR images," *Electron. Lett.*, vol. 48, no. 21, 2012.
20. J. S. Lee and E. Pottier, *Polarimetric Radar Imaging, From Basics to Applications.* Optical Science and Engineering Series, Boca Raton, FL, CRC Press, Chapter 4, p. 143, 2008.
21. J.-S. Lee, D. L. Schuler, and T. L. Ainsworth, "Polarimetric SAR data compensation for terrain azimuth slope variation," *IEEE Trans. Geosci. Remote Sens.*, vol. 38, no. 5, pp. 2153–2163, 2000.

22. J.-S. Lee, M. R. Grunes, E. Pottier, and L. Ferro-Famil, "Unsupervised terrain classification preserving polarimetric scattering characteristics," *IEEE Trans. Geosci. Remote Sens.*, vol. 42, no. 4, pp. 722–731, 2004.
23. O. Antropov, Y. Rauste, and T. Häme, "Volume scattering modeling in PolSAR decompositions: study of ALOS PALSAR data over Boreal Forest," *IEEE Trans. Geosci. Remote Sens.*, vol. 49, no. 10, pp. 3838–3848, 2011.

Chapter 5

A Modified Level Set Approach for Segmentation of Multi-Band Polarimetric SAR Images

Junjun Yin and Jian Yang

Contents

5.1 Introduction

Terrain classification [1–5] and image segmentation [6,7] are critical issues in the automated analysis of synthetic aperture radar (SAR) images. In polarimetric radar remote sensing, several approaches have been developed for forest/non-forest discrimination [8], oil-spill detection and segmentation [9], and agricultural crop classification [10]. Considering the effect of speckle, which is a natural phenomenon in SAR imagery [4], the applications of SAR data are challenged. To achieve better results, multiple sources of information such as multi-polarization, multi-frequency [5,11,12], optical imagery [8], and digital elevation models are generally combined in a processing framework to maximize application potential. Meanwhile, numerous SAR statistical models have been developed to fit SAR images with different resolutions for different observation scenarios. For example, the classic Gaussian/Wishart distribution is typically used to model homogeneous areas. For the high resolution images in which the central limit theorem is not always applicable, heterogeneous clutter models [13,14] are usually applied by incorporating a local random variable (usually representing the texture). This paper mainly focuses on segmenting homogenous areas. A widely accepted class of techniques for this type of polarimetric SAR image classification and segmentation is usually based on maximum-likelihood (ML) approximation and the complex Gaussian/Wishart distribution. These techniques include the supervised Wishart classifier [5], unsupervised classifiers with different initialization methods (e.g., polarization entropy H and the polarization angle α [1], H/α/anisotropy [2], and Freeman's decomposition [3]), and segmentation methods such as level set-based methods [15,16] and the spectral graph partitioning method [6]. Pixel-based classification methods do not use spatial information of the scene and pixel neighboring relations. Thus adding a segmentation step for pixel grouping may substantially improve partitioning of the image into homogeneous regions.

Studies on active contour models implemented via the level set method have been conducted recently to address SAR image segmentation [15,16] and sea target detection [17,18] problems. The active contour model was first proposed by Kass et al. (1987). This model is used to detect objects in a given image by evolving a curve. The curve depends on the gradient of the image to stop its evolution on the boundary of the desired object. Traditional active contour models are parameterized contour models, which are not suitable for characterizing automatic topological changes of curves. Consequently, the level set method introduced by Osher and Sethian [19] is widely used to deal with the curve evolution problem. This method implicitly represents the evolving curve as the zero-level curve of a function defined in a higher dimension. By this means, the evolution of the level set function is equal to a partial differential equation (PDE). This type of method, which minimizes a certain functional energy defined on a level set function, is known as the variational level set method. Early techniques were edge-driven methods [20,21], in which the image gradient is used to locate the boundaries of the desired object. Later, region-based methods [22–24], which are more robust to noise and initial contour conditions, were proposed. These methods are based on the additive noise model, which is invalid when describing SAR images with multiplicative speckle noise. In [16–18], level set methods were investigated for SAR intensity images regarding the issues of image segmentation, ship detection, and oil spill segmentation, respectively. For the multi-polarization case, only a few studies on level set methods can be found in the literature. In [15], a multi-phase level set method was proposed for polarimetric SAR image segmentation based on ML approximation and the complex Wishart/Gaussian distribution. The active contour model presented in [15] consists of a region-based term related to the speckle distribution and a classic curve boundary length term, which is not related to the image edge information. This method can guarantee segmentation from an arbitrary initial partition.

In addition to the speckle statistical model and polarimetric scattering mechanisms, the edge is an important fundamental textural feature [11,25,26] for SAR images. The edge provides immediate information on adjacent homogeneous regions. A popular edge detector for SAR intensity images is a Gamma distribution-based detector [25], which provides a constant false-alarm rate (CFAR). Then this detector is generalized in the polarimetric case with the complex Wishart distribution [11]. The edge information is the primary driver in the conventional boundary-based level set methods, such as the classic geodesic active contour (GAC) model [21], which uses an edge-stopping indicator to stop the evolving curve on desired boundaries. However, the GAC model cannot be applied to SAR images because the image gradient-based edge detector usually results in significant errors, e.g., a large number of false edges appear in high intensity regions, and a lot of real edges are lost in low intensity regions.

Two aspects are mostly considered in active contour-based methods: the energy functional defined on active contours and the multi-phase extension scheme [15,27]. In general, the energy functional consists of at least two terms, namely, the noise distribution model and the length term of the dynamic curves. These terms should be balanced to achieve efficient performance. The parameter for each term in traditional formulations is determined by experience to demonstrate its effect. The parameter is set manually for different images, thus resulting in the lack of flexibility and robustness of the methods. Few studies have addressed the problem on parameter setting. In multi-phase extensions, an efficient algorithm should converge accurately and rapidly. In [27], a multi-phase level set framework was proposed by using the Mumford-Shah model [22], wherein two approximations, namely, piecewise constant and piecewise smooth models, were presented. This multi-phase method uses a few level sets to represent multiple phases, and the problems of vacuum and overlapping can be avoided. In the present study, we employ the piecewise constant model, which is a simplified case of the piecewise smooth optimal approximation, for polarimetric SAR image segmentation. Compared with the multi-phase method introduced in [15], although the complexity of the PDEs of the piecewise constant model increases with the number of partitions, the additional computational cost at each iteration is mainly on addition and subtraction operations, which can be ignored if a limited number of initial curves is used.

Many polarimetric SAR sensors are in operation with multiple frequencies, e.g., C-band, L-band, and P-band. These frequencies provide different levels of information over the same scene due to their different sensitivities to the scattering medium and the target structure. Therefore, it is also of importance to investigate the improvement by using the combined multi-band data in the level set framework. In this study, we focus on the level set method for multi-phase segmentation of multi-band polarimetric SAR data. An active contour model is proposed by considering the edge information, which is provided by the polarimetric CFAR edge detector [11]. This edge detector is employed to take into account the reliability of the contour information and to speed up the curve evolution, thereby allowing for computational efficiency. The proposed model consists of two terms: a region-based statistical term and a weighted boundary length term. This model is then embedded into the piecewise constant level set framework for multi-phase segmentation.

This paper is organized as follows. In Section 5.2, we introduce the proposed active contour model and its implementation via the level set. The multi-phase method with an arbitrary number of initial curves is incorporated in the proposed model. Section 5.3 presents the validation experiments implemented on both synthetic and real multi-band polarimetric SAR data. Quantitative comparisons and evaluations are also provided. Conclusions are given in Section 5.4.

5.2 Methodology

Active contour models are based on the variational method and the technique of PDE. The basic idea is to deform a curve to the boundary of an object under the constraints of an energy functional minimization from a given image. The level set method is used extensively to deal with the curve evolution problem because it allows automatic changing of topologies, and is convenient for incorporating different forms of information extracted from an image into a certain energy functional.

5.2.1 Maximum a Posteriori (MAP)-Based Statistical Active Contour Model and Level Set Formulation

We start the analysis from a simple two-region problem. We assume that $\Omega \in R^2$ is the domain of a polarimetric SAR image. The polarimetric information is most commonly represented by the covariance matrix, which is a semi-definite positive Hermitian matrix denoted by $\boldsymbol{T}$ [1]. Let $P(\boldsymbol{T} \mid \boldsymbol{V})$ be the probability distribution of $\boldsymbol{T}$ in a homogeneous region and $\boldsymbol{V}$ be a parameter associated with the region statistic. For the image to be partitioned by a curve C, we aim to maximize

$P(\boldsymbol{V}_i\,|\,\boldsymbol{T})$ by using a Bayesian estimation, which leads to the classical MAP estimator, where $i \in [1,2]$, and $\boldsymbol{V}_1$ and $\boldsymbol{V}_2$ are the respective statistics inside and outside curve C. Maximizing $P(\boldsymbol{V}_i|\boldsymbol{T})$ amounts to maximizing $P(C\,|\,\boldsymbol{T})$. Thus we obtain $P(C\,|\,\boldsymbol{T}) = P(\boldsymbol{T}\,|\,C)P(C)/P(\boldsymbol{T})$ from the Bayes' rule. Assume that the partitioning curve C follows a Gibbs prior [28], i.e., $P(C) = Z^{-1}\exp(-u\phi(C))$, where Z and u are normalizing constants, and ϕ is a non-negative given function. Maximizing the likelihood term amounts to minimizing the minus-log-likelihood function. Hence, we obtain the following energy functional for the whole domain:

$$\begin{aligned} F(C) &= -\ln\big(P(\boldsymbol{T}\,|\,C)\big) + u\phi(C) + \ln\big(P(\boldsymbol{T})\big) + \ln(Z) \\ &= \int_{\Omega\backslash C} -\ln\left(\prod_{i=1}^{2} P(\boldsymbol{T}\,|\,\boldsymbol{V}_i)\right) d\Omega + u\phi(C) \\ &\quad + \int_{\Omega} \Big(\ln\big(P(\boldsymbol{T})\big) + \ln(Z)\Big) d\Omega. \end{aligned} \tag{5.1}$$

$\ln(P(\boldsymbol{T}))$ and $\ln(Z)$ are constants that are independent of curve C; thus, both are discarded. $\phi(C)$ is a function related to the segmentation boundary C. $\phi(C)$ is often considered as a classic regularizing term defined as the length of curve C, i.e., $\phi(C) = \text{length}(C) = \oint_C ds$. This definition is adopted in [15,16], and [23], which are all primarily region-driven methods (i.e., region statistics are dominant). In classical geometric and geodesic active contour models [20,21], which are boundary-driven methods, the edge information is the main factor for constructing image energy and locating the dynamic curve on desired boundaries. The GAC model [21] has a minimization problem as $\min_C \left\{E(C) = \oint_C g(C)\,ds + v\int_{inside(C)} g(x,y)\,dxdy\right\}$, where v is a constant acting as a balloon force term, and g is an edge indicator. The edge indicator is generally defined by a positive and monotonically decreasing function depending on curve C to account for strong image edges. From this we propose to incorporate edge information in an active contour model to obtain an accurate boundary location.

The edge indicator g should be positive on homogeneous regions and nearly zero on sharp edges. A typical g for additive noise is defined on the gradient of an image that is smoothed by a Gaussian kernel function [21]. This gradient-based edge indicator is not suitable for SAR images with multiplicative noise. Moreover, the Gaussian convolution used to smooth the image may blur the edges. Thus, we simply define the edge indicator g as a function of an existing edge image R without considering the Gaussian kernel as follows:

$$g = \frac{1+k}{1+k\left(R/T_f\right)^2}, \tag{5.2}$$

where k is a constant, R is an edge detector, and T_f is a threshold corresponding to a given probability of false alarms, which is used to measure the reliability of the detected edges. g can be regarded as a weighted edge function for speeding up or slowing down the curve evolution. When g reaches its minimum at the edges with the highest reliabilities, the evolving speed of the curve is low, thus ensuring a gradual change in curve changes to avoid errors. When g reaches its maximum in homogeneous regions, the curve evolves rapidly, thereby accelerating curve propagation. The edge detector R should be robust and efficient to detect edges in images accurately. A CFAR edge detector for polarimetric SAR data was proposed in [11]. This detector is based on the Wishart distribution and can be applied to a wide range of SAR data, including single intensity, dual, and full polarimetric SAR data at multiple bands, as well as their combinations. In the present study, we investigate the level set method for segmentation of multi-band polarimetric data; therefore, the CFAR edge detector (refer to [11] for more details) is adopted to calculate the edge indicator g, as shown in (5.2).

Let $\phi(C)=g(C)\cdot\text{length}(C)=\oint_C g(C)ds$. Consequently, the two-region partitioning problem shown in (5.1) from curve C can be rewritten as follows:

$$E_{\text{POL}}(V_1,V_2,C)=u\oint_C g(C)ds-\left(\int_{inside(C)}\ln\left(P(\boldsymbol{T}\mid V_1)\right)d\Omega+\int_{outside(C)}\ln\left(P(\boldsymbol{T}\mid V_2)\right)d\Omega\right), \tag{5.3}$$

where u is a non-negative parameter. When curve C is right at the edges between two regions, the energy in (5.3) converges to a global minimum.

First, we consider the region-based term, which is related to the speckle model of the polarimetric SAR images, i.e., $\ln(P(\boldsymbol{T}\mid \boldsymbol{V}))$. We know that a p-dimensional random complex vector $\vec{k}$ follows a joint Gaussian distribution corresponding to the one-look polarimetric image. Moreover, its $p\times p$ covariance matrix, averaged over N samples, is a positive semi-definite Hermitian matrix that follows a complex Wishart distribution corresponding to the multi-look image with N number of looks. Based on the complex Wishart/Gaussian distribution and ML criterion, the Wishart distance measure [5], which is an essential part of many approaches, is obtained as follows:

$$d_p(\boldsymbol{T},\boldsymbol{V})=-\ln P(\boldsymbol{T}|\boldsymbol{V})=N\left(\ln|\boldsymbol{V}|+\text{Tr}\left(\boldsymbol{V}^{-1}\boldsymbol{T}\right)\right)+const, \tag{5.4}$$

where $\boldsymbol{T}$ is the covariance matrix (or coherency matrix) of the backscattering coefficients, $\boldsymbol{V}$ is the ML estimation of $\boldsymbol{T}$, N is the number of looks, p is the matrix dimension, and $const$ is a constant that can be omitted. $|\cdot|$ denotes the determinant and $\text{Tr}(\bullet)$ denotes the trace of a matrix. When $N=1$, this equation measures the distance of a Gaussian distribution. For combined multi-band polarimetric SAR data, the distance measure formula in (5.4) can also be applied directly to measure the distance between an arbitrary pixel and its class center [5]. Equation (5.4) can be extended to many cases, such as in the combination use of multi-frequency, multi-polarization, and multi-temporal SAR data, as long as the employed images are co-registered. Given the multi-frequency data, we first arrange $\boldsymbol{T}_{i(i=1\ldots J)}$ and $\boldsymbol{V}_{i(i=1\ldots J)}$ in a block diagonal structure as

$$\boldsymbol{T}=\begin{bmatrix}\boldsymbol{T}_1 & 0 & 0\\ 0 & \ddots & 0\\ 0 & 0 & \boldsymbol{T}_J\end{bmatrix}_{p_1+\cdots+p_J},\boldsymbol{V}=\begin{bmatrix}\boldsymbol{V}_1 & 0 & 0\\ 0 & \ddots & 0\\ 0 & 0 & \boldsymbol{V}_J\end{bmatrix}_{p_1+\cdots+p_J},$$

where J is the total number of bands for one scene, and $\boldsymbol{T}_i$ is the covariance matrix from the ith band data. A simplified equivalent likelihood distance measure can then be obtained by assuming that all bands have the same number of looks, and that the speckle is statistically independent between frequency bands [5], as shown in the following equation:

$$d(\boldsymbol{T},\boldsymbol{V})=-\ln P(\boldsymbol{T}|\boldsymbol{V})=\sum_{i=1}^{J}d_{p_i}(\boldsymbol{T}_i,\boldsymbol{V}_i)=\ln|\boldsymbol{V}|+\mathrm{Tr}\left(\boldsymbol{V}^{-1}\boldsymbol{T}\right). \tag{5.5}$$

This distance measure can also be applied to any dimension of SAR data, e.g., $p=1$ for intensity data, $p=2$ for compact or dual polarimetric data, and $p=6$ for polarimetric and interferometric data.

Then, we consider the implementation of the curve evolution. Curve C can be represented implicitly by the zero-level set of a level set function $\phi: \rightarrow \mathrm{R}$ [19], which allows an automatic change in topology. For $(x,y)\in\Omega$, C is defined on the boundary of an open set w as $C=\{(x,y)|\ \phi(x,y)=0\}$, where $w=inside(C)$ and $w=outside(C)$. For $(x,y)\in\Omega\backslash w$, $\phi(x,y)>0$; and for $(x,y)\in\Omega\backslash w$, $\phi(x,y)<0$. Therefore, evolving curve C is equivalent to solving a differential equation with respect to $\phi(x,y)$. By using the Heaviside function $H(\phi(x,y))$, which is equal to 1 if $\phi(x,y)\geq 0$ and to 0 if $\phi(x,y)<0$, and the one-dimensional Dirac measure $\delta(\phi(x,y))$, the energy functional $E_{\mathrm{POL}}(\boldsymbol{V}_1,\boldsymbol{V}_2,C)$ can be expressed in the following level set formulation:

$$\begin{aligned}E_{\mathrm{POL}}(\boldsymbol{V}_1,\boldsymbol{V}_2,\phi(x,y))&=u\int_{\Omega}\delta(\phi(x,y))g(x,y)|\nabla\phi(x,y)|dxdy\\&+\left(\begin{aligned}&\int_{\Omega}\left(\ln|\boldsymbol{V}_1|+\mathrm{Tr}\left(\boldsymbol{V}_1^{-1}\boldsymbol{T}(x,y)\right)\right)H(\phi(x,y))dxdy+\\&\int_{\Omega}\left(\ln|\boldsymbol{V}_2|+\mathrm{Tr}\left(\boldsymbol{V}_2^{-1}\boldsymbol{T}(x,y)\right)\right)\left(1-H(\phi(x,y))\right)dxdy\end{aligned}\right).\end{aligned} \tag{5.6}$$

Parameter u, playing as a scaling role, is used to weight the different terms in the energy functional, i.e., the boundary length term g and the likelihood term. Both terms are affected by the speckle and make different contributions to the curve evolution. In [15,16,23], and [27], u was chosen for different images; however, these studies did not clearly explain how u was set. In Section 5.3, we discuss the effect of parameter u on the segmentation results.

5.2.2 Numerical Implementation

A dynamic curve evolution scheme is associated with the Euler-Lagrange equations to minimize the energy functional in (5.6) with respect to ϕ. In the following part, (x, y) is omitted for convenience. The scheme can be obtained by parameterizing an artificial time to the decent equation implemented via PDE. The minimization procedure for the two-region case is described as follows.

1. Calculate the SAR edge information R by using the CFAR edge detector introduced in [11], and the edge indicator g by using (5.2).
2. Initialize the level set function ϕ_i, where i is the iteration number. Let $i = 0$ be the initial value.
3. Keep the level set function ϕ_i fixed, and minimize the energy $E_{\text{POL}}(\boldsymbol{V}_1, \boldsymbol{V}_2, \phi_i)$ with respect to the covariance matrices $\boldsymbol{V}_1$ and $\boldsymbol{V}_2$. The minimization of $E_{\text{POL}}(\boldsymbol{V}_1, \boldsymbol{V}_2, \phi_i)$ is equivalent to finding the ML estimates of $\boldsymbol{V}_1$ and $\boldsymbol{V}_2$, which are the empirical means of the covariance matrices, given by

$$\boldsymbol{V}_1 = \frac{\int_\Omega \boldsymbol{T}(x, y) \bullet H(\phi_i(x, y))\,dxdy}{\int_\Omega H(\phi_i(x, y))\,dxdy},$$

$$\boldsymbol{V}_2 = \frac{\int_\Omega \boldsymbol{T}(x, y) \bullet \left(1 - H(\phi_i(x, y))\right)dxdy}{\int_\Omega \left(1 - H(\phi_i(x, y))\right)dxdy}. \tag{5.7}$$

4. Keep the covariance matrices $\boldsymbol{V}_1$ and $\boldsymbol{V}_2$ fixed, and minimize $E_{\text{POL}}(\boldsymbol{V}_1, \boldsymbol{V}_2, \phi_i)$ with respect to ϕ_i. Using the associated Euler-Lagrange equation for ϕ_i, the level set evolution equation is obtained as follows:

$$\frac{\partial \phi_i}{\partial t} = \delta(\phi_i)\left(\begin{array}{c} u\,\text{div}\left(g\dfrac{\nabla \phi_i}{|\nabla \phi_i|}\right) \\ \hline -\left(\left(\ln|\boldsymbol{V}_1| + \text{Tr}\left(\boldsymbol{V}_1^{-1}\boldsymbol{T}\right)\right) - \left(\ln|\boldsymbol{V}_2| + \text{Tr}\left(\boldsymbol{V}_2^{-1}\boldsymbol{T}\right)\right)\right) \end{array}\right), \tag{5.8}$$

where $\mathrm{div}(\bullet)$ is a divergence operator, and the corresponding term is the curvature of the normal curve. Then, ϕ_{i+1} is updated by $\phi_{i+1} = \phi_i + dt \times \partial\phi_i / \partial t$, where dt is the time step.

5. If the number of pixels switching between classes is smaller than a predetermined threshold or if a prespecified number of iterations is reached, then stop the iteration. Otherwise, let $i = i + 1$ and repeat steps (3)–(5).

In the evolution of ϕ_i in (5.8), we replace the common Dirac factor $\delta(\phi_i)$ by $|\nabla\phi_i|$ [29] to speed up the convergence.

5.2.3 Multi-phase Segmentation

An initial curve produces a binary partition (i.e., a two-region problem) in the level set method for image segmentation, whereas more curves are required for multi-phase representation. In [15], the authors proposed a multi-phase approach by using N level set functions to obtain $N+1$ segments, i.e., N segments are represented by N curves and the background excluded by all other curves is the last segment. This multi-phase extension is robust to the initial conditions. In [27], research was devoted to multi-phase segmentation with fewer initial curves, i.e., N phases can be represented by $\log_2 N$ curves. The multi-phase formulation presented in [27] was developed by using the Mumford and Shah model, which is generalized into two cases, namely, piecewise constant and piecewise smooth. The piecewise constant considers that the homogeneous area can be reasonably represented by a constant estimated by the ML criterion. Therefore, in our multi-phase extension, the piecewise constant model is combined with the proposed model for segmentation of polarimetric SAR images. In the experiments, the proposed method is compared with the method presented in [15]. Both multi-phase methods are described briefly in this section. In the description, the present model (5.8) is embedded into the dynamic schemes instead of the original active contour models in [15] (i.e., a Wishart distribution-based model) and in [27] (i.e., an active contour model without edge [23]).

5.2.3.1 Segmentation Using the Multi-phase Scheme

The multi-phase method in [15] is based on the fact that a pixel is competed between different regions, which are not necessarily spatially adjacent. Assume that Ω is partitioned into N+1 regions, which are denoted as $R_i^t|_{i=1\cdots N+1}$, by a set of level set functions $\phi_i^t|_{i=1\cdots N}$ at iteration t. Let $R_i^t|_{i\neq N+1} = \{(x,y)|\phi_i^t > 0\}$ and $R_{N+1}^t = \Omega - \cup_{i=1}^N R_i^t$. The zero-level sets of the level set functions are disjointed. The partition procedure is under a constraint, i.e., if a pixel $(x,y) \in R_i^t$ and it leaves R_i^t, then it must move to only one other region R_j^{t+1} where $j \neq i, i \in [1\cdots N+1], j \in [1\cdots N+1]$. Thus for any given pixel, which is only involved in the variation of region $R_i^t \cup R_j^t$, two level set curve evolution equations, i.e., $\frac{\partial\phi_i}{\partial t}$ and $\frac{\partial\phi_j}{\partial t}$, are required at most to be calculated.

In this way, the multi-phase segmentation is reduced to a two-region problem in the domain $R_i^t \cup R_j^t$. Note that i and j are not simultaneously equal to $N+1$. If $i \neq N+1$ and $j \neq N+1$, both ϕ_i^{t+1} and ϕ_j^{t+1} are updated. If $i(\text{or } j) = N+1$, then only one level set function ϕ_j^{t+1} (or ϕ_i^{t+1}) needs to be updated. The multi-phase minimization procedure is described as follows:

1. Initialize N level set functions $\phi_i^0|_{i=1\cdots N}$ for $N+1$ initial regions $R_i^0|_{i=1\cdots N+1}$, and let $t=0$.
2. For $(x,y) \in \Omega$ and $\forall i \in [1\cdots N+1]$, check the index of the region that contains pixel (x,y), assuming that $(x,y) \in R_i^t$. Then, find another region $R_j^t, j \neq i$, which is the most competitive region compared to R_i^t for this given pixel. R_j is determined by the following criterion:

$$j = \arg \min_{\{j0 \in [1\cdots N+1], (x,y) \notin R_{j0}\}} \{d(\boldsymbol{T}, \boldsymbol{V}_{j0}) - d(\boldsymbol{T}, \boldsymbol{V}_i)\} \tag{5.9}$$

where $d(\boldsymbol{T}, \boldsymbol{V}_{j0})$ is the Wishart distance measure in (5.5), $\boldsymbol{T}$ is the covariance matrix, and $\boldsymbol{V}_{j0}$ is the ML estimate in region R_{j0}. Since (x,y) is involved in only two level sets, the multi-phase curve evolution equations are derived as follows:

$$\text{If } i \neq N+1, \text{ then } \frac{\partial \phi_i^t}{\partial t} = |\nabla \phi_i^t| \left(u \operatorname{div}\left(g \frac{\nabla \phi_i^t}{|\nabla \phi_i^t|} \right) - \left(d(\boldsymbol{T}, \boldsymbol{V}_i^t) - d(\boldsymbol{T}, \boldsymbol{V}_j^t) \right) \right). \tag{5.10}$$

$$\text{If } j \neq N+1, \text{ then } \frac{\partial \phi_j^t}{\partial t} = |\nabla \phi_j^t| \left(u \operatorname{div}\left(g \frac{\nabla \phi_j^t}{|\nabla \phi_j^t|} \right) - \left(d(\boldsymbol{T}, \boldsymbol{V}_j^t) - d(\boldsymbol{T}, \boldsymbol{V}_i^t) \right) \right). \tag{5.11}$$

3. Update ϕ_j^{t+1} (if $j \neq N+1$) and ϕ_i^{t+1} (if $i \neq N+1$), and check if the termination condition is satisfied, e.g., a predetermined number of iterations is achieved. If not, then $t=t+1$ and return to step (2).

5.2.3.2 Segmentation Using the Piecewise Constant Model in [27]

The piecewise constant multi-phase method is an extension of the two-phase method presented in [23]. The essence of this method is that a pixel is competed between spatial adjacent regions. $m = \log_2 N$ level sets are sufficient to represent N phases. Given the m curves, which are represented by the zero-level sets of $\phi_i|_{i=1\cdots m}$, the image domain Ω can then be partitioned into N phases by the intersection of the closed curves. We denote the phases (or segments) as $R_{b_1\cdots b_m}|_{b_1,\cdots,b_m \in [0\,1]}$, where $b_1,\cdots,b_m$ are logical phase numbers defined through the following conditions. If $\phi_i > 0, i \in [1\cdots m]$, then

$b_i = 1$; otherwise, $b_i = 0$. Take a three-curve region R_{101} as an example. This region is formed by the set $\{(x,y)\,|\phi_1(x,y) > 0 \cap \phi_2(x,y) < 0 \cap \phi_3(x,y) > 0\}$. Based on the aforementioned definition, the image domain is expressed as $\cup_{b_i \in [0\,1], i=1\cdots m} R_{b_1\cdots b_m} \cup C$, where C is the set of zero-level sets. For this multi-phase problem, the energy functional shown in (5.6) can be generalized as

$$\begin{aligned} E_{\mathrm{POL}}(\boldsymbol{V}, \phi_1, \cdots, \phi_m) = u \sum_{i=1\cdots m} \int_\Omega \delta(\phi_i(x,y))\, g(x,y) \left|\nabla \phi_i(x,y)\right| dxdy \\ + \sum_{b_i \in [0\,1], i=1\cdots m} \int_{R_{b_1\cdots b_m}} d\left(\boldsymbol{T}(x,y), \boldsymbol{V}_{b_1\cdots b_m}\right) dxdy, \end{aligned} \tag{5.12}$$

where $\boldsymbol{V}_{b_1\cdots b_m}$ is a constant matrix approximating to the data in region $R_{b_1\cdots b_m}$. By minimizing (5.12) with respect to variations of $\boldsymbol{V}_{b_1\ldots b_m}$ and ϕ_i, we obtain the associated Euler-Lagrange equations, embedded in a dynamic scheme for all level sets $\phi_i\,|_{i=1\cdots m}$ at iteration t, as follows.

1. For $\forall i \in [1\cdots m], b_i \in [01]$, calculate the average covariance matrix for region $R^t_{b_1\cdots b_m}$.

$$\boldsymbol{V}^t_{b_1\cdots b_m} = \mathrm{mean}\left(\boldsymbol{T}(x,y)\right) \quad \text{in} \quad \text{region } R^t_{b_1\cdots b_m}, \tag{5.13}$$

   where mean(•) indicates the ML estimation.

2. For $\forall i \in [1\cdots m]$, calculate the level set evolution equations.

$$\begin{aligned} \frac{\partial \phi_i^t}{\partial t} = \left|\nabla \phi_i^t\right| \Bigg(u\,\mathrm{div}\left(g \frac{\nabla \phi_i^t}{\left|\nabla \phi_i^t\right|} \right) + \sum_{b_j \in [0\,1], j=1\cdots m, j\neq i} \left(\left(-d\left(\boldsymbol{T}, \boldsymbol{V}^t_{b_1\cdots b_m | b_i = 1}\right) + d\left(\boldsymbol{T}, \boldsymbol{V}^t_{b_1\cdots b_m | b_i = 0}\right) \right) \right. \\ \left. \left(\prod_{k=1, k\neq i}^{m} \left(b_k H(\phi_k^t) + (1 - b_k)\left(1 - H(\phi_k^t)\right) \right) \right) \right) \Bigg). \end{aligned} \tag{5.14}$$

The formulation in (5.14) is complicated compared with those in (5.10, 5.11). In practice, however, this formulation does not have a significant additional computational cost. Assuming that an image is partitioned into $N = 2^m$ phases, then $N-1$ initial curves are necessary with the method in [15], and m initial curves are needed in the piecewise constant model. At each iteration for a single pixel, the method in [15] requires the calculation of N Wishart distances, two to four additions, and one or two curvature operations. Meanwhile the piecewise constant model requires the calculation of N Wishart distances, mN additions, and m curvature operations. We test the computation time for an eight-phase segmentation problem, where $N = 8$ and $m = 3$, via MATLAB performed on a 3.4 GHz CPU with 8 GB RAM. The computation time of the piecewise constant model is approximately 1.006–1.010 times that of the Ben Ayed's method [15] at each iteration.

5.3 Experimentation

We test the proposed method on several polarimetric data sets, including RADARSAT-2 data, synthetic data generated from real backscattering coefficients, and multi-band NASA/JPL AIRSAR data acquired over Altona, Canada and Flevoland, the Netherlands, etc. We show several representative results of the experiments to illustrate (1) the effect of edge indicator g on edge location and total segmentation accuracy (TSA), (2) the effectiveness of the proposed method for multi-phase segmentation, (3) the number of iterations, and (4) the improvement for agriculture field discrimination by incorporating multi-band data into the level set framework.

We evaluate the segmentation performance and compare it with the Ben Ayed's method in [15] and the classic Wishart classifier in [5]. For convenience, we refer to the multiphase extension described in Section II-C-C1 as AP, whereas the method described in Section II-C-C2 is referred to as VP. Our model is incorporated in AP and VP. Both the Ben Ayed's method and AP require $N-1$ initial curves to represent N phases, whereas VP needs m initial curves for $N = 2^m$ phases. The piecewise constant model, which is employed in VP, cannot realize an arbitrary number of partitions; thus, a Wishart distribution-based cluster merging criterion [3] is adopted after the segmentation to merge the phases with the lowest degree of separation until a fixed number of classes is obtained. The cluster merging measure is defined as:

$$D_{ij} = 0.5\left(\ln\left|\boldsymbol{V}_i\right| + \ln\left|\boldsymbol{V}_j\right| + \mathrm{Tr}\left(\boldsymbol{V}_i^{-1}\boldsymbol{V}_j + \boldsymbol{V}_j^{-1}\boldsymbol{V}_i\right)\right) \tag{5.15}$$

where $\boldsymbol{V}_i$ and $\boldsymbol{V}_j$ denote the cluster centers. The two clusters with the shortest distance are merged. When this step is added after the segmentation of VP, the image can also be partitioned into an arbitrary number of regions, just as the Ben Ayed's method and AP do.

The data used for validation are AIRSAR C-, L-, and P-band polarimetric data from the Flevoland test site acquired on July 3, 1991, as shown in Figure 5.1. The multi-band polarimetric synthetic data, which are generated by using a complex Wishart distribution with four looks and the real covariance matrices obtained by averaging over homogeneous regions in Figure 5.1. Figure 5.2 shows the reference map and the span image of the synthesized data. All parameters, except

Figure 5.1 Span image (the total backscattering power of the C-band, L-band, and P-band data) of the test site.

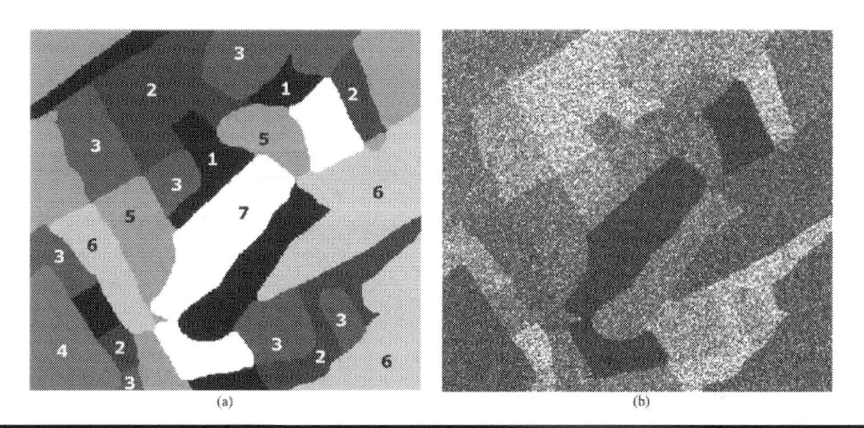

Figure 5.2 Synthetic data. (a) Synthetic reference map that contains seven classes (class 1, class 2, ..., class 7). (b) Span image of the synthetic C-band data with four looks.

u, are set as follows: $dt = 0.5, k = 9$. The edge detection filter configuration [11] $K_f = \{9,3,1,\pi/4\}$ and a false alarm probability $P_f = 10\%$ are used to calculate the edge indicator g.

5.3.1 Parameter Setting and Synthetic Data

To demonstrate the contribution of edge information on image segmentation, Table 5.1 provides the variation of TSA with the mean curvature parameter u using the VP method and C-band synthetic polarimetric data. u should

Table 5.1 Variations in TSA with Parameter u Obtained by Using VP and the C-Band Synthetic Data

u	0	0.05	0.10	0.15	0.20	0.25	0.30	0.35	0.40
TSA	67.5	86.5	85.2	85.9	95.8	90.1	87.9	81.3	84.7
	4%	3%	9%	1%	6%	9%	3%	8%	6%

be chosen according to the applied images [23,27]. Table 5.1 implies that an appropriate u should be set to obtain good results. We have tested on many polarimetric data sets and found that segmentation is improved when a certain proportion between $u\sum_{\Omega_b} g(x,y)$ and $\sum_{\Omega_b} \mathrm{Tr}\left(\boldsymbol{V}^{-1}\boldsymbol{T}(x,y)\right)$ occurs, wherein $(x,y)\in\Omega_b$ is a homogeneous region. We use an empirical value to relate both terms, i.e., let $v_e = E\left(u_{\max}\left(\sum_{\Omega_b} g(x,y)\right)/\left(\sum_{\Omega_b} \mathrm{Tr}\left(\boldsymbol{V}^{-1}\boldsymbol{T}(x,y)\right)\right)\right)$, where $u_{\max}$ corresponds to the value with the maximum TSA. The estimated approximation of v_e is 0.2; thus, we use the following empirical equation for the adaptive parameter setting of different data sets:

$$u = \frac{0.2\sum_{\Omega_b} \mathrm{Tr}\left(\boldsymbol{V}^{-1}\boldsymbol{T}(x,y)\right)}{\sum_{\Omega_b} g(x,y)}. \tag{5.16}$$

Note that empirical ratio v_e varies with parameter k, which is set to 10 in this study. u is calculated by (5.16) as 0.218, 0.191, 0.205, 0.528, and 0.577 for C-, L-, P-, L+C-, and L+C+P-band synthetic polarimetric data, respectively. These parameters are used in the following experiments.

Table 5.2 shows the performances of the Ben Ayed's method, AP, and VP using C-band synthetic data, and Figure 5.3 provides the final visual comparison. When the proposed method (VP) is used, TSA is obtained as 95.86% when $u = 0.2$ (Table 5.1); then the TSA improves to 96.95% when $u = 0.218$ (Table 5.2). Table 5.2 and Figure 5.3 show that the segmentation result of the Ben Ayed's method is inferior to those of AP and VP. Moreover, the VP algorithm converges much faster

Table 5.2 TSA versus the Iterations Obtained by Using the C-band Synthetic Data via Different Approaches

Number of Iterations	*Ben Ayed's Method*	*AP*	*VP*
50	77.62%	74.95%	94.74%
100	78.33%	81.64%	96.95%
200	79.33	83.19%	96.95%

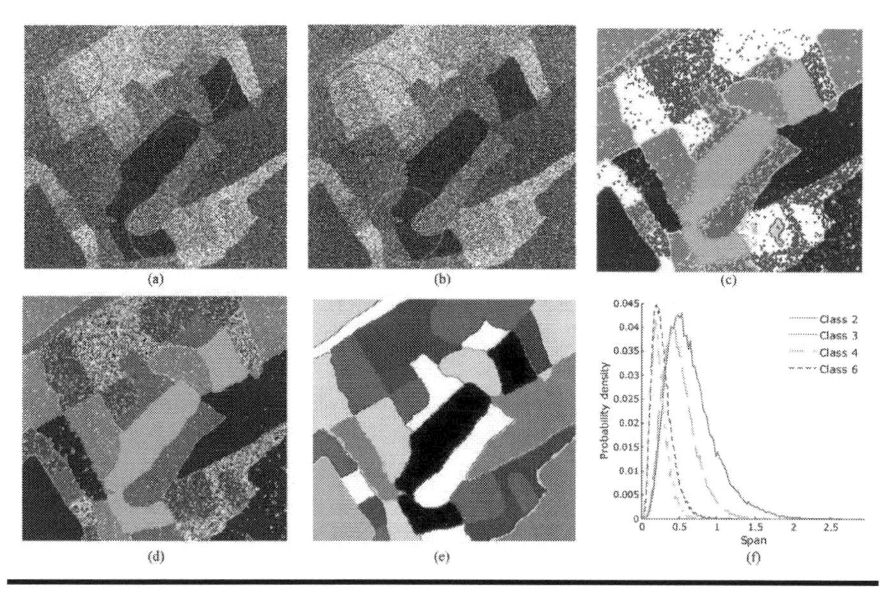

Figure 5.3 Comparisons of the final segmentation using the C-band synthetic data. (a) Initial contours for Ben Ayed's method and AP. (b) initial contours for VP. (c) Result and final curve position of Ben Ayed's method. (d) Result and final curve position of AP. (e) Result and final curve position VO. (f) Region distributions of the span in the C-band for classes 2, 3, 4, and 6, respectively.

than the Ben Ayed's method, i.e., fewer iterations are needed. Although the TSA of AP is improved by adding an edge indicator g, its TSA remains inferior to that of VP. The primary reason for this is that the Ben Ayed's method and AP involve all the level set regions for pixel competition at each iteration for a given pixel, thus resulting in the pixel shifting between nonadjacent regions. While with the VP method, a pixel is basically competed between two adjacent regions in each level set function, thus ensuring that the pixel only shifts between neighboring regions at each iteration. In Figure 5.3, the initial and the final curves are displayed in the same color for each method. It shows that both the Ben Ayed's method and AP cannot distinguish class 4 from class 6, and that the former cannot exhibit differences between classes 2 and 3. By contrast, these classes are identified correctly by VP and the segmentation result is consistent with the reference map, as shown in Figure 5.3e. Figure 5.3f illustrates the probability distribution of span for classes 2, 3, 4, and 6. We see that the classes that were barely distinguished by the Ben Ayed's method and AP have similar total backscattering powers.

Integrating multi-band polarimetric information can improve the application performance of SAR images [5,10]. Table 5.3 evaluates the performance of the L-band, P-band, and the combined multi-band polarimetric data in terms of TSA. Results show that multi-band data improve segmentation accuracy, particularly

Table 5.3 Evaluation in Terms of TSA for the Multi-brand Data

Frequency	*Ben Ayed's Method*	*AP*	*VP*
L-band	83.51%	93.39%	95.79%
P-band	76.64%	88.04%	88.82%
C+L-band	95.09%	95.08%	97.01%
C+L+P-band	95.51%	96.54%	98.95%

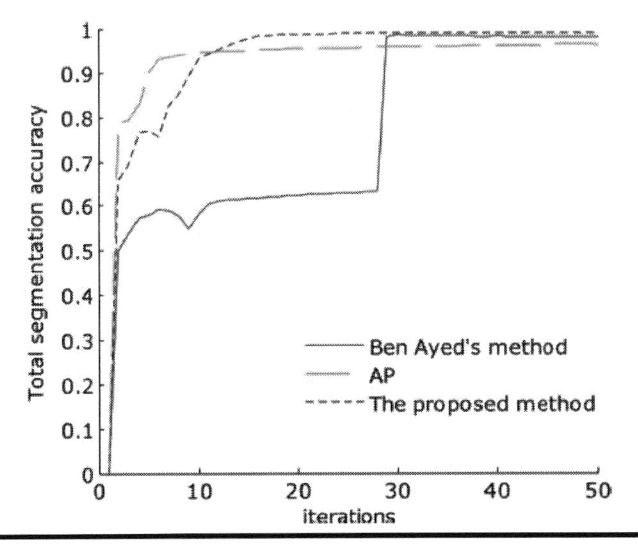

Figure 5.4 TSA versus the iteration number obtained by using the combined C+L+P-band data.

for the Ben Ayed's method. Moreover, the converging speed significantly increases when the combined multi-band polarimetric SAR data are used (Figure 5.4). The three approaches converge steadily after approximately 30 iterations.

5.3.2 Real Polarimetric Data

Figure 5.5 shows the results of real multi-band polarimetric data. Based on the empirical parameter setting equation, u is set to 0.060, 0.061, 0.066, 1.071, and 1.603, respectively, for the C-, L-, P-, L+C-, and L+C+P-band real polarimetric SAR images. Figure 5.5a is a subset from Figures 5.1, and 5.5b is a manually established segmentation map based on the ground truth map in [10] and visual inspection. The segmentation results obtained with the Ben Ayed's method, AP, and VP for each single-band data and the combined multi-band data are shown in

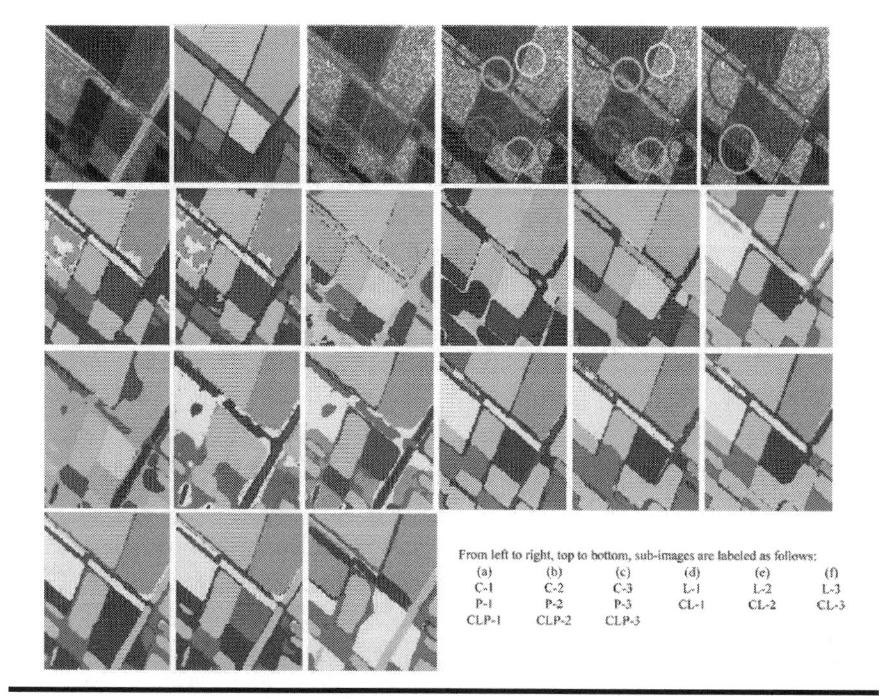

Figure 5.5 Segmentation results. (a) Composite image with the C-band in red, the L-band in green, and the P-band in blue. (b) Manual segmentation map for reference. (c) Manual boundaries in the span image. (d)–(f) Initial conditions for Ben Ayed's method, AP, and VP, respectively. The subimages from the second row are labeled as follows: C, L, and P denote the C-band, L-band, and P-band data, respectively: 1, 2, and 3 denote the applied methods, with 1 for Ben Ayed's method, 2 for AP, and 3 for VP. For example, a subimage labeled CLP-3 is the result obtained by using the combined C+L+P-band data and VP.

Figure 5(C-1)-5(CLP-3). In single-band segmentation, the L-band data results are superior to those of the other two bands. The multi-band segmentation obtained from C+L+P-band data is highly desirable because it has the least single points in each segmented region. Figure 5.5 also shows that data at different bands provide different levels of information. For example, if the combined data contain P-band information, then the corresponding result will detect a clear road because a bright road is observed in the P-band original image. The changing trends in the obtained results show that the level set performance is significantly improved by using the combined multi-band data. Compared with the Ben Ayed's method and AP, VP performs better in C-band and P-band data by exhibiting more regular boundaries and segmented regions.

The main technique of the Wishart distribution-based level set methods is the classical Wishart distance. The Wishart classifier [5] uses a priori knowledge of

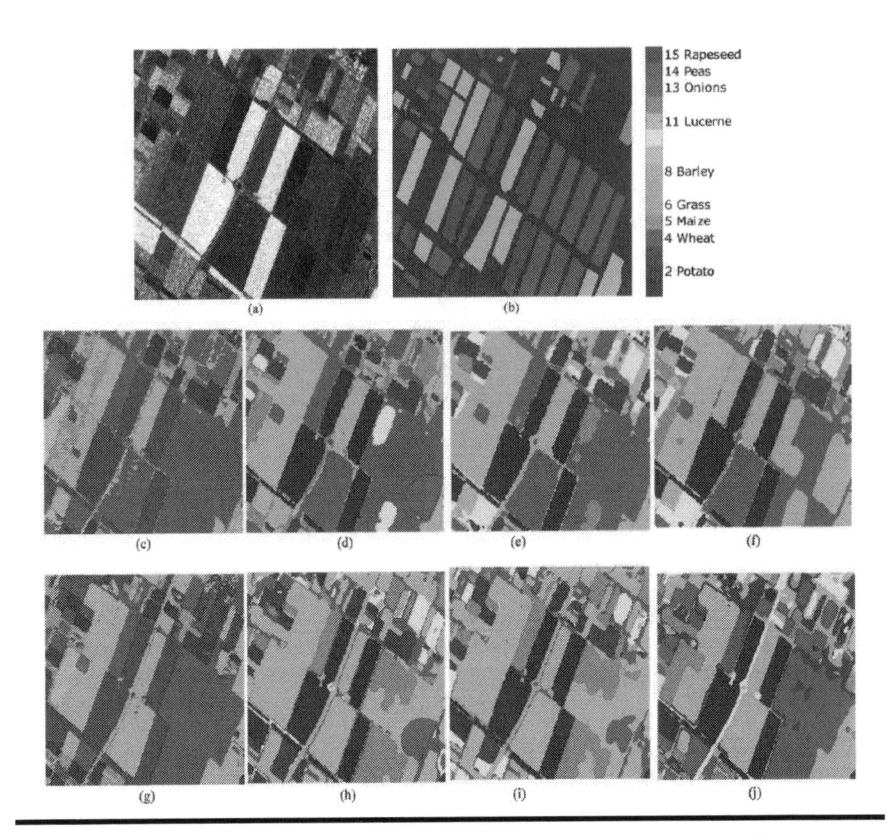

Figure 5.6 (a) Composite image with the C-band data in red, the L-band data in green, and the P-band data in blue. (b) Ground truth map. (c)–(f) Results obtained by using the Wishart classifier, Ben Ayed's method, AP, and VP, respectively, for the C-band data. (g)–(j) Results obtained by Wishart classifier, Ben Ayed's method, AP, and VP, respectively, for the C+L+P-band data.

each class to train the classification process; hence the supervised Wishart classifier generally provides good classification accuracy. We consider the Wishart classification result as a reference. Figure 5.6 shows the composite image of the C-, L-, and P-band data, the crop type map which consists of nine types of fields, as well as the classification and segmentation results for C-band and combined C+L+P-band data by using the Wishart classifier and the level set methods. The ground truth map over the entire scene is not available; thus, the results are not evaluated in terms of TSA. The results in Figure 5.6c–f show that for all methods the pieces of barley (crop label 8) are not labeled as a single class at C-band, whereas the pieces are labeled correctly when the combined C+L+P-band data are used, as shown in Figure 5.6g–j. In the results obtained by using C+L+P-band data, the fields of barley (crop label 8) and lucerne (crop label 11) are segmented as the same class by the Ben Ayed's method and AP, whereas the two fields are clearly distinguished by the Wishart classifier and VP. In addition, the Ben Ayed's method and AP are easily trapped in a local minimum, and their performances in detecting wheat fields are slightly inferior to those of the Wishart classifier and VP.

5.4 Conclusions

In this study, we proposed a multi-phase level set method for segmentation of multi-band and polarimetric SAR data. A CFAR edge indicator was incorporated into an active contour model to detect field boundaries accurately and accelerate curve evolution. The proposed active contour model was then embedded into a multi-phase level set framework, in which a piecewise constant approximation approach was adopted to represent the image. Both synthetic and real multi-band polarimetric SAR data were used for verification and evaluation. An empirical parameter setting criterion was developed in the experiments to ensure that the components of the energy functional are proportional. The proposed method requires fewer iterations and is more efficient in separating classes with similar total backscattering powers compared with the Wishart/Gaussian distribution-based level set method presented in [15]. We also showed that level set methods can be applied directly to process combined multi-band data, in which case segmentation performance is improved. Moreover, the curve evolving speed increases when multi-band data are used. The experimental results showed the potential of our method for polarimetric SAR image segmentation.

An edge indicator was introduced in this study to improve the active contour model. However, the indicator which is used to extract boundaries is not limited to the form used here. The edge indicator can be constructed as long as it is a monotonically decreasing function that efficiently accounts for image edges. This work also suggests that further improvements can be expected by incorporating more image features (e.g., textural information) and other information sources (e.g., polarimetric and interferometric SAR data, as well as optical data) into the level set framework.

Acknowledgment

The authors are grateful to the anonymous reviewers for their valuable comments and suggestions. This work was supported in part by the Nation Natural Science Foundation of China under Grant 41171317, by the State Key Program of the Natural Science Foundation of China under Grant 61132008, and by the Research Foundation of Tsinghua University.

References

1. J.-S. Lee, M. R. Grunes, T. L. Anisworth, L.-J. Du, D. L. Schuler, and S. R. Cloude, "Unsupervised classification using polarimetric decomposition and the complex Wishart classifier," *IEEE Trans. Geos. Remote Sens.*, vol. 37, no. 5, pp. 2249–2258, 1999.
2. L. Ferro-Famil, E. Pottier, and J.-S. Lee, "Unsupervised classification of multifrequency and fully polarimetric SAR images based on the H/A/Alpha-Wishart classifier," *IEEE Trans. Geos. Remote Sens.*, vol. 39, no. 11, pp. 2332–2342, 2001.
3. J.-S. Lee, M. R. Grunes, E. Pottier, and L. Ferro-Famil, "Unsupervised terrain classification preserving polarimetric scattering characteristics", *IEEE Trans. Geos. Remote Sens.*, vol. 42, no. 4, pp. 722–731, 2004.
4. J.-S. Lee, M. R. Grunes, and G. De Grandi, "Polarimetric SAR speckle filtering and its implication for classification," *IEEE Trans. Geos. Remote Sens.*, vol. 37, no. 5, pp. 2363–2373, 1999.
5. J.-S. Lee, M. R. Grunes, and E. Pottier, "Quantitative comparison of classification capability: fully polarimetric versus dual and single-polarization SAR," *IEEE Trans. Geos. Remote Sens.*, vol. 39, no. 11, pp. 2343–2351, 2001.
6. K. Ersahin, I. G. Cumming, and R. K. Ward, "Segmentation and classification of polarimetric SAR data using spectral graph partitioning," *IEEE Trans. Geos. Remote Sens.*, vol. 48, no. 1, pp. 164–174, 2010.
7. J. Morio, F. Goudail, X. Dupuis, P. C. Dubois-Fernandez, and P. Réfrégier, "Polarimetric and interferometric SAR image partition into statistically homogeneous regions based on the minimization of the stochastic complexity," *IEEE Trans. Geos. Remote Sens.*, vol. 45, no. 11, pp. 3599–3609, 2007.
8. E. A. Lehmann, P. A. Caccetta, Z.-S. Zhou, S. J. McNeill, X. Wu, and A. L. Mitchell, "Joint processing of Landsat and ALOS-PALSAR data for forest mapping and monitoring," *IEEE Trans. Geos. Remote Sens.*, vol. 50, no. 1, pp. 55–67, 2012.
9. M. Marghany and M. Hashim, "Discrimination between oil spill and look-alike using fractal dimension algorithm from RADARSAT-1 SAR and AIRSAR/POLSAR data," *Int. J. Phys. Sci.*, vol. 6, no. 7, pp. 1711–1719, 2011.
10. D. H. Hoekman, and M. M. Vissers, "A new polarimetric classification approach evaluated for agricultural crops," *IEEE Trans. Geosci. Remote Sens.*, vol. 41, no. 12, pp. 2881–2889, 2003.
11. J. Schou, H. Skriver, A. A. Nielsen, and K. Conradsen, "CFAR edge detector for polarimetric SAR images," *IEEE Trans. Geos. Remote Sens.*, vol. 41, no. 1, pp. 20–32, 2003.
12. K. Conradsen, A. A. Nielsen, J. Schou, and H. Skriver, "A test statistic in the complex Wishart distribution and its application to change detection in polarimetric SAR data", *IEEE Trans. Geos. Remote Sens.*, vol. 41, no. 1, pp. 4–19, 2003.
13. S. N. Anfinsen, T. Eltoft, and A. P. Doulgeris, "A relaxed Wishart model for polarimetric SAR data," in *Proceedings of the 4th International Workshop on Science and Applications POLinSAR*, Frascati, Italy, April 2009, vol. ESA SP-668.
14. L. Bombrun, G. Vasile, M. Gay, and F. Totir, "Hierarchical segmentation of polarimetric SAR images using heterogeneous clutter models," *IEEE Trans. Geos. Remote Sens.*, vol. 49, no. 2, pp. 726–737, 2011.
15. I. Ben Ayed, A. Mitiche, and Z. Beihadj, "Polarimetric image segmentation via maximum-likelihood approximation and efficient multiphase level-sets", *IEEE Trans. Pattern Anal. Mach. Intell.*, vol. 28, no. 9, pp. 1493–1500, 2006.

16. I. Ben Ayed, A. Mitiche, and Z. Belhadj, "Multiregion level-set partitioning of synthetic aperture radar images" *IEEE Trans. Pattern Anal. Mach. Intell.*, vol. 27, no. 5, pp. 793-800, 2005.
17. R. P. Marques, F. N. Sombra de Medeiros, and D. M. Ushizima, "Target detection in SAR images based on a level set approach," *IEEE Trans. Syst. Man. Cybern. C Appl. Rev.*, vol. 39, no. 2, pp. 214–222, 2009.
18. R. R. Ganta, S. Zaheeruddin, N. Baddiri, and R. Rameshwar Rao, "Segmentation of oil spill images with illumination-reflectiance based adaptive level set model," *IEEE J. Sel. Topics Appl. Earth Observ. Remote Sens.*, vol. 5, no. 5, pp. 1394–1402, 2012.
19. S. Osher and J. A. Sethian, "Fronts propagating with curvature-dependent speed: Algorithms based on Hamilton-Jacobi formulations," *J. Comput. Phys.*, vol. 79, pp. 12–49, 1988.
20. V. Caselles, F. Catté, T. Coll, and F. Dibos, "A geometric model for active contours in image processing," *Numer. Math.*, vol. 66, pp. 1–31, 1993.
21. V. Caselles, R. Kimmel, and G. Sapiro, "Geodesic active contours," *Int. J. Comput. Vis.*, vol. 22, no. 1, pp. 61–79, 1997.
22. D. Mumford and J. Shah, "Optimal approximations by piecewise smooth functions and associated variational problems," *Commun. Pure Appl. Math.*, vol. 42, pp. 577–685, 1989.
23. T. F. Chan and L. A. Vese, "Active contours without edges," *IEEE Trans. Image Process.*, vol. 10, no. 2, pp. 266–277, 2001.
24. T. F. Chan, B. Yezrielev Sandberg, and L. A. Vese, "Active contours without edges for vector-value images," *J. Vis. Commun. Image Represent.*, vol. 11, pp. 130–141, 2000.
25. R. Touzi, A. Lopès, and P. Bousquet, "A statistical and geometric edge detector for SAR images," *IEEE Trans. Geosci. Remote Sens.*, vol. 26, pp. 764–773, 1988.
26. G. D. Grandi, J.-S. Lee, D. Schuler, and E. Nezry, "Texture and speckle statistics in polarimetric SAR synthesized images," *IEEE Trans. Geosci. Remote Sens.*, vol. 41, no. 9, pp. 2070–2088, 2003.
27. L. A. Vese and T. F. Chan, "A multiphase level set framework for image segmentation using the Mumford and Shah model," *Int. J. Comput. Vis.*, vol. 50, no. 3, pp. 271–293, 2002.
28. G. Aubert and J.-F. Aujol, "A variational approach to remove multiplicative noise," *SIAM J. Appl. Math.*, vol. 68, no. 4, pp. 925–946, 2008.
29. H. K. Zhao, T. Chan, B. Merriman, and S. Osher, "A variational level set approach to multiphase motion," *J. Comput. Phys.*, vol. 127, pp. 179–195, 1996.

Chapter 6

Smart Perception System for Subsurface Robot Mapping: From Simulation to Actual System Realization

Ioannis Kostavelis, Dimitrios Giakoumis, Evangelos Skartados, Andreas Kargakos, and Dimitrios Tzovaras

Contents

6.1 Introduction

A vast number of applications focus on the assessment of dense underground utilities in urban areas (e.g., electricity/communication cables, construction of pipelines, water and waste network), on the evaluation of the subsurface for energy and mineral production operations, as well as on the detection of buried objects for search and rescue applications at disaster sites. These applications require the modeling of the shallow (up to 5 m) subsurface terrain, which is typically performed with specifically designed sensors, namely, Ground Penetrating Radar (GPR) [1]. It is evident that technological achievements in the GPR imaging sensors bloomed over the past decades [2,3], yet the existence of unified applications that allow smart and automatic representation of the subsurface area which can be commonly apprehended by humans and robots remains an open issue [1,4].

Even if the biggest volume of GPR data processing has already been automated, still the experts' effort is required for further annotation to refine the initial findings, a factor that increases labor costs and holds the analysis of large-scale data back [5]. This relies on the fact that the acquired GRP data, i.e., radar-grams, are typically studied as isolated images for the detection of hyperbolic and linear patterns, which indicate the existence of an object, without the combination of multiple radar-grams with their spatiotemporal extrapolation into the 3D space, where more comprehensive patterns can be revealed. Apparently, the lack of simulation environments that will facilitate the development of such methodologies without the need to have access to expensive GPR antennas and the absence of physically integrated subsurface scanning sensors with surface operating robots prohibits automated subsurface terrain modeling with cyber-physical systems.

Towards this direction, the goal of this chapter is twofold. First, it aims to introduce an integrated perception system in a simulation environment which is expected to offer roboticists with a valuable tool to perform simulations on subsurface areas. To this end, the generated subsurface data obtained from the simulated perception system closely resemble the data obtained with real GPR systems, allowing further integration and processing of the information regarding the buried objects in the subsurface.

Second, it documents a novel smart 3D underground mapping framework based on the integration of a real GPR antenna with a surface operating rover, suitable for subsurface cyber-physical applications in robotics domains. This book chapter is grounded on our previous work on GPR simulation [6] and subsurface utility mapping [7], and it has been extended to present more implementation details on the simulation environment, an exhaustive discussion of the radar-gram preprocessing steps, as well as more evaluation results both in simulation and in a real environment where the integrated smart perception system has been tested on a custom test field.

6.2 Related Work

6.2.1 GPR Simulation Tools

Several tools such as the gprMax, the Reflexw, the GPRSim, and others that are less common have been developed over the last years for the modeling and simulation of GPR. Reflexw covers the complete range of wave data such as seismic, GPR, and ultrasound, and the different geometry assemblies involving surface reflection and refraction, borehole crosshole and tomography, and combination of borehole and surface measurements [8]. GPRSIM is interactive 2D forward modeling software designed specifically for GPR and it can predict the full waveform of microwaves that are reflected, transmitted, refracted, and attenuated across model ground structures [9]. The gprMax simulation tool, introduced by Warren et al. [10], is the most prevalent simulation tool in the GPR community and comprises open source software that contains a set of electromagnetic wave simulation tools based on Finite-Difference Time Domain numerical methods that offer many advanced features such as anisotropic and dispersive material modeling, realistic soil modeling, modeling of heterogeneous objects, modeling of objects with rough surfaces, and modeling of GPR antennas. One of the biggest drawbacks, however, of the aforementioned simulation tools is that they are very costly both processing-wise and time-wise for the construction of a simulated environment of the required specifications. Moreover, they cannot be used for online simulations and neither can they be integrated with other systems for joint simulation operations.

6.2.2 GPR Data Pre-processing and Hyperbola Detection

Authors in [11] presented a work for an image analysis technique capable of locating the position of objects in the subsurface by identifying the produced patterns on the GPR image. They grounded their technique on Hough Transforms and developed a method based on calculation of three parameters, for each hyperbola found in the image. They were mostly focused on the modeling of the velocity propagation of the electromagnetic pulse in the material above the scattering object. This formatted the data to be analyzed on the field, allowing the scan to be repeated immediately when erratic results were obtained. The method has been applied on both synthetic and real data and revealed promising results. In another effort concentrated on the removal of GPR data noise, the authors in [12] proposed a method to remove ringing noise that appeared as nearly horizontal and periodic events from GPR images. Specifically, the approach included a background removal with f-k filtering, predictive deconvolution with filtering in wavenumber domain, and filtering by Radon transform. It has also been shown that ringing can be successfully removed by the eigenimage filtering method, where the GPR image is decomposed into eigenimages by singular value decomposition. Finally, it has been proven that these de-noising methods are more effective when compared with the simple methods for ringing noise removal, using realistic yet a limited number of realistic images. Torrione et al. [13] proposed a method for landmine detection with GPR data, and they firstly proposed a pre-processing step using a computationally inexpensive algorithm that flags potential locations of interest. According to the authors, these flagged locations are then passed to a feature-based processer who further discriminates target-like anomalies from naturally occurring clutter. Specifically, the pre-processing step involved data aligning, ground-bounce removal and time clipping, media filtering to remove any GPS inference of the device, and data depth-segmentation. The proposed method was applied on real data and allowed approximately 90% detection of buried utilities.

The first step towards underground mapping includes processing of the acquired GPR data for the detection of specific patterns such as hyperbolic or linear segments. The problem of hyperbola detection has been tackled by several approaches during recent years, the majority of which treat the problem with classical computer vision methods [14–16]. Specifically, among the most common techniques for hyperbola detection is the utilization of Hough transform [17,18], which takes advantage of the geometric characteristics of the primitive shapes that constitute a hyperbola signature. Yet, accurate capturing of the hyperbola's parameters with generalized Hough transform requires great discretization of its parameters, which significantly increases the computational time. A. Simi et al. [19] utilized Randomized Hough Transform while applying a threshold to candidate hyperbola apexes in order to extract hyperbola detections. A 2D map is produced by projecting the apex detections on a plane. Apart from hyperbolic patterns, Dell Acqua et al. [20] developed a method for detection of linear objects (pipes) on GPR data based on Hough-Radon transform. The proposed algorithm was able to further analyze the data set in a local fashion, in order to eliminate spurious targets from the set of lines of maximum consensus. It has been evaluated on real data and proved adequate to detect pipes with an angular deviation in orientation of linear segments less than 10°. As an extension of the Hough-Transform method, Borgioli et al. [21] introduced a weighting factor depending on the differentials of the unknown parameters with respect to the experimental errors, namely, the probe position error and the time-of-light error. This feature enabled optimally placed sets of data pairs to be given greater weight than ill-conditioned sets, as, for example, when all data pairs lie near one end of the arc.

The result is a decrease in the background amplitude with respect to the maximum of the peaks in the Hough accumulator space. It is shown that this improvement persists even when many arcs are present. Authors in [21] exploited a combination of Hough-Transform with Kirchho Migration to embed results from both techniques into a supervised framework to perform GPR data analysis. The evaluation was performed on 19 radar-grams and revealed accuracy in the detection of hyperbolic patterns above 90%.

6.2.3 Integration of GPR with Surface Operating Rovers

The existing technological background is focused mostly on the processing of 2D radar-grams (products of GPR imaging) in a pixel-wise manner [22], while limited progress has been achieved in the construction of a globally consistent 3D map of the subsurface environment. Moreover, even if the largest amount of GPR data processing can be automated to an extent, the opinion of experts on data annotation is required to reinforce the initial findings, a parameter that introduces extra labor costs and prohibits the large-scale analysis of acquired data [5]. This is mainly due to the fact that the acquired radar-grams are mostly examined as isolated images for the detection of hyperbolic and linear patterns that indicate the existence of an object, without the combination of multiple scans with their spatiotemporal extrapolation into the 3D space, where more comprehensive patterns can be revealed. Synchronous arrays of GPR antennas can provide massive subsurface data collection capabilities, and in order to achieve analogous large-scale processing, the automation in structured acquisition procedures is imperative. The automatic data acquisition and the consistent processing of the all of the acquired GPR readings is made feasible by incorporating the motion of the GPR antenna into the processing loop. The latter necessitates GPR integration with a robotic carrier that would allow structured GPR motion modeling through the rigid body transformations of the robot. Such a topology has been realized in the work described in [23], where the authors developed a novel robotic system integrated with a GPR for automated bridge inspection. The collected GPR data were then analyzed for the inspection of rebar used for subsurface bridge construction. Although the developed method proved capable of detecting defective spots in the subsurface of a bridge, the mobile robot was utilized only as a way to carry the GPR antenna for the collection of the data while the robot's locomotion data were not considered during the process. The authors in [24,25] demonstrated an integrated robotic system that consisted of an all-terrain mobile robotic platform integrated with a GPR antenna and RGB cameras to collect GPR measurements and that was intended to be utilized for surface and subsurface inspection of a bridge. In another application, the authors in [26] employed an all-terrain mobile platform to carry a GPR antenna, a system specifically hardened to operate in the extreme temperatures of the South Pole station of Antarctica. The objective of the mission was to gather subsurface data with the GPR for off-line inspection of ice sheets. It is revealed that a common characteristic among the aforementioned works is that the robotic topologies were designed to operate in terrain where instantaneous changes of robot attitude were absent. Specific attempts have been proposed to develop integrated robotic systems for subsurface inspection in uneven terrain such as the ExoMars mission, which involved the development of the WISDOM Radar to be mounted on the ExoMars rover with the aim of inspecting the Mars subsurface and identifying the best locations for drilling during its travels. The designed radar should provide information about the nature of the shallow subsurface over depths ranging from 3 to 10 m [27]. The interpretation of GPR data depends greatly on knowledge of the GPR sensor's spatial orientation and relation to surface features; thus, it is essential that any autonomous GPR study have such a capability. Several advances in the automation of GPR data acquisition have used Differential GPS (DGPS) [28,29], a theodolite based on laser, or proprioception to track the pose of the GPR during data collection. Barfoot et al. answered to the above limitations by integrating for the first time a GPR antenna with a robotic platform through visual odometry (VO)[30]. The resulting system was capable of providing a 3D, photorealistic surface model coupled with a ribbon of GPR data, and a 2D topography corrected GPR radargram with the surface topography plotted above on it. The outcome was an autonomously generated coupled surface/subsurface representation; however, a 3D metric map of the subsurface was not provided by that method.

6.3 GPR Imaging

To achieve large-scale automated data acquisition of subsurface data, the GPR sensor is typically integrated with wheeled mobile vehicles. In our approach we assumed the existence of a GPR antenna that is an array of GPR sensors placed on specific rigid topology. Moreover, the GPR antenna is towed by a wheeled mobile vehicle to allow coverage of long distances and, thus, to facilitate large subsurface perception capacity. The working principal of GPR relies on the transmission of electromagnetic pulses into the ground at frequencies usually in the range of 10–4000 MHz, depending on the design of the device and the target application [1]. While the signal is traveling in the subsurface, when it encounters an interface between layers of differing permittivity, part of the energy is reflected back to the surface while the remainder is diffracted from the subjacent medium. The reflection/diffraction process continues until the signal has weakened completely or the amount of time that the GPR receiver is programmed to search for a return signal (design principal of GPR device) has passed.

6.3.1 Perception with the Simulation Tool

As mentioned in the previous sections, several tools such as gprMax, Reflexw, and GPRSim have been developed over the last years for modeling and simulating GPR.

One of the biggest drawbacks, however, of the aforementioned simulation tools is that they are very costly both processing-wise and time-wise for the construction of a simulated environment of the required specifications. Moreover, they cannot be used for online simulations, nor can they be integrated with other systems for joint simulation operations.

The proposed solution for real-time simulation of GPR involves the utilization of sonar sensors. The operation of sonars is closely related to the operation of FPR antennas, with the main difference being that sonars rely on sonic wave propagation in free space, while GPR relies on electromagnetic wave propagation in the medium (ground). In robotics, simple low cost sonar sensors are widely employed to detect obstacles in the working environment of the robot. These sensors emit directed ultrasonic pulses that propagate in free space and record the time that the first reflection is received. This recorded time is then used to calculate the distance of the sensor to the closest object-obstacle that reflected the signal. Similarly, GPR antennas emit electromagnetic pulses that propagate in the subsurface. When these pulses meet a buried object or boundaries between materials of different permittivities, they can be reflected back to the surface where a receiving antenna records them for a fixed time window, resulting in a signal known as A-Scan. The appearance of a pulse in the A-Scan that closely resembles the emitted pulse indicates the existence of an object or material boundary, the distance to which can be calculated provided the velocity in the propagation medium. Based on the above descriptions, it is apparent that sonars can be utilized for the approximate simulation of GPR antennas, with the assumption that the simulated subsurface environment is modeled as free space with various objects that will act as targets to be detected. The approach followed herein involves the utilization of an array of GPR sensors simulated as sonars directed towards the ground and configured with minimum sensor range that surpasses the ground as shown in Figure 6.1a. At the same time by exploiting a simulated world in which the ground is modeled as a plane with negligible depth and mostly empty space underneath, the sonar can sense whatever lies underground given that it is within its range. Due to the limitations of the utilized 3D simulator Gazebo1, the sonar sensors are simulated using a number of laser rays that form a 2D cone2. Then, the desired range or the distance to the closest object in the ground is estimated by using ray casting for all rays of a sonar sensor and keeping the minimum resulting distance, as depicted in Figure 6.1b.

6.3.2 Real Smart Perception System

The real smart perception system consists of a commercially available surface operating rover and a GPR antenna. The selected rover is the Summit XL HL skid steering mobile robot platform with payload capacity up to 65 kg, suitable for navigation in uneven terrain and the towing of the GPR antenna. The utilized GPR is the Stream-C array provided by IDS GeoRadar. The central operation frequency of the antenna is about 600 MHz and its typical depth range reaches 1.5 m, providing

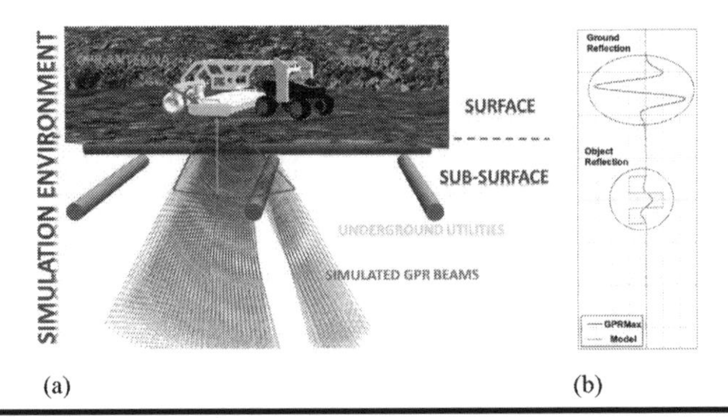

Figure 6.1 Demonstration of simulated GPR Model. The range is extracted from ray casting all rays of the sensor and keeping the minimum range as depicted in (a) by the green dimension line. Sample A-Scans from gprMax and the proposed GPR model are displayed in (b).

an in-range resolution of approximately 5 cm. The system collects up to 32 radar profiles, having the antenna box a length of about 1.2 m and a weight around 20 kg. The Stream-C with the Summit XL HL communicates with TCP/IP communication protocol for data transmission, which can be transmitted to any personalized device, thus enabling cyber-physical access to the system. Data acquisition and triggering from the GPR is performed through a programmable encoder wheel which has been mechanically integrated[1,2] with the left-back wheel of the rover so the measurements can be obtained only when the robot is on the move. The sampling rate of the GPR encoder has been set to 3 cm, i.e., when the robot traverses 3 cm, a trigger is activated and synchronous measurements from all the channels of the GPR are acquired. The electromechanically integrated surface rover is graphically illustrated in Figure 6.2.

6.3.3 B-Scan Formulation

Assuming that the robot travels on straight routes, each A-Scan corresponds to subsurface representation for a specific robot-traversed distance, i.e., 3 cm in our case. A single measurement from the GPR (single A-Scan) can provide information about the distance to the closest object that falls within the field of view of the sensor. However, this information is not enough for the estimation of the position of buried objects. This problem can be solved by migrating from one dimension to two dimensions which can be accomplished by taking multiple measurements along the robot's direction. This operation results in the formulation of a B-Scan or a sequence of concatenated A-Scans, which means that by concatenating

[1] http://gazebosim.org/

[2] http://wiki.ros.org/hector_gazebo_plugins

Figure 6.2 The perception system constituted from the Summit XL HL Rover and Stream-C GPR antenna.

continuously obtained A-Scans, a B-Scan is progressively built. Each B-Scan corresponds to a vertical slice of the ground above which the GPR has passed, and is typically represented as an image, where the pixel intensities on the B-Scan correspond to the amplitude values of the A-Scan.

For each sensor existing in the Stream-C GPR array or each sonar sensor in the simulation GPR tool, a separate B-Scan is constructed during robot motion. An illustrative representation of this procedure is described in Figure 6.3a. The formulated B-Scans, also known as radar-grams, are then further processed for the detection of buried utilities. The existence of an object, e.g., pipe, beneath the trajectory of the GPR results in the formulation of a down facing hyperbola in the resulting B-Scan and by employing simple geometric analysis it can be derived that the apex of the hyperbola corresponds to the actual depth of the buried object. Figure 6.3b illustrates

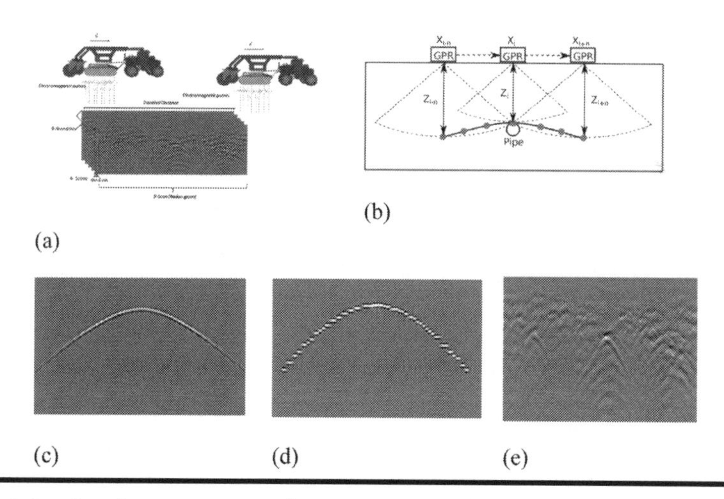

Figure 6.3 On the upper row the B-Scan assembly is represented (a) and the hyperbola formulation given a traversal scanning of a pipe is illustrated (b). On the bottom row B-Scan samples with three different data acquisition sources are illustrated. From left to right, (c) B-Scan from gprMax, (d) B-Scan from proposed simulation GPR Model, and (e) B-Scan with the a real GPR antenna corresponding to a real subsurface environment.

how hyperbolas are formed given the aggregated data (B-Scans) during the robot's motion in specific direction. Note that X_{i-n}, X_i, and X_{i+n}, represent the rover's position in distinct time instances and Z_{i-n}, Z_i, and Z_{i+n} correspond to the respective closest depths recorded by the signal reflection.

6.3.4 Hyperbola Detection in Simulated B-Scans

The hyperbola signature created from the simulated GPR (see Figure 6.3d) tool is clear and noise-free mainly due to the fact that the subsurface modeled area is empty and there are no artifacts from the medium transmission of the emitted signal. Thus, for the detection of its apex a geometrical fitting method proved to be adequate. To this end, a simple hyperbola detection algorithm is applied, one that is suitable for the GPR data generated using the proposed sonar-based simulated model. Specifically, the hyperbola detection algorithm considers a B-Scan and converts it to a normalized image. A preprocessing thresholding step aims to remove all pixels that do not belong to the hyperbolas. By applying the Hough transform for line detection, the algorithm isolates and later removes all the detected straight lines that originate from pipes parallel to the direction of motion of the GPR. In the next step, the method applies a closing morphological transform [31], which is basically dilation followed by an erosion operation that fills the gaps and completes the hyperbolic curves. The next step involves the vertical averaging of the pixels to get a thinning of the hyperbolic curves, which are then fed to the well-known DBSCAN [32] density-based clustering algorithm in order to segment the capability of segmenting the hyperbolas. The final step of the method comprises a smoothing via linear interpolation based on which the apexes of the hyperbolas can be isolated by simply finding the global maxima for each segmented hyperbola.

6.3.5 Hyperbola Detection in Real B-Scans

Detection of hyperbola signatures in real B-Scans (see Figure 6.3e) is a more challenging task, necessitating specific preprocessing steps in order to remove the noise and the ground bounce revealed from the alternation of the propagation medium (air-soil).

6.4 Preprocessing Steps of Real GPR Data

Considering the necessity of the preprocessing steps, a raw A-Scan captured from a GPR device typically suffers from two factors that negatively affect any further interpretation: DC bias and the "wow" effect. The first term describes a signal that has a mean value larger than zero, while the second one refers to a low-frequency trend in a recorded trace. Both of them are known to inherently exist in real GPR data, owing to the phenomenon of signal saturation by early arrivals, such as the ground/air wave, as well as inductive underground coupling effects. As a result, the spectrum of the recorded data is distorted and the performance of any technique based on spectral analysis deteriorates. Thus, a dewowing filtering is applied in accordance to which the DC component is removed by calculating the mean value of the single A-Scan trace and subtracting it from the signal values. Then, the removal of the low frequency component is applied by utilizing either a low-cut filter or equivalently a median filter.

Another preprocessing step essential for the collation of A-Scans during antenna traversing is the Time Zero Correction because the exact time that the transmitted signal meets the ground varies even among consecutively captured measurements, and thus, cannot be predetermined since it is affected by a number of factors, including thermal drift, electronic instability and most importantly the spatial distance between the antenna and the ground. Therefore, the procedure of stitching together consecutive, individual A-Scans in order to formulate a B-Scan signal introduces a factor that could possibly lead to poor data quality. Through B-Scan generation we aim to extract an "image" of the underground and it only makes sense that consecutive samples that form this image should have a common origin that defines the point zero of the considered coordinate system. Since this common origin cannot be explicitly determined beforehand in the time axis, it is necessary to define it through the recorded values. In order to achieve this uniformity in the constructed B-Scans, for all captured A-Scans the peak of the recorded signal which corresponds to the same event in time is detected and utilized to align those scans. All later events depicted in the assembly of the A-Scans will be correctly expressed with respect to a common origin. In Figure 6.4a on the left image the peaks of adjacent A-Scans forming a B-Scan are annotated with red color. The misalignment of those peaks introduces further artifacts on the time sequence of later events. On the middle image the Time Zero is adjusted for all Scans and artifacts are reduced. Finally, on the right image all values before Time Zero are discarded and the peak value is translated to the $t = 0$ time sample.

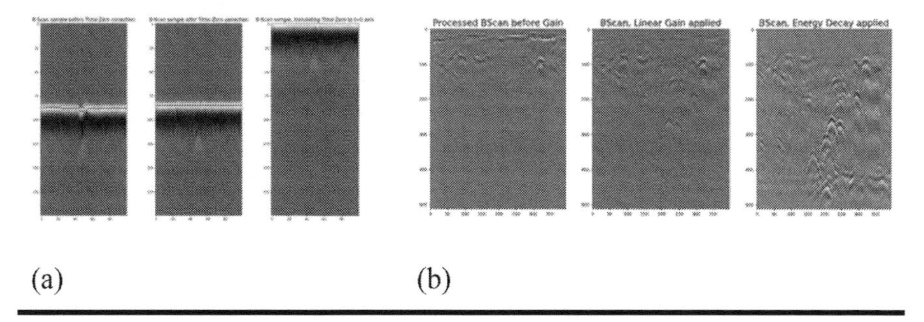

Figure 6.4 (a) An illustrative example of the time-zero correction preprocessing step and (b) an example of the gain function filtering step in a B-Scan image.

Having formulated the B-Scan, the next step is filtering its content. The nature of the transmitted wavelet, which is prone to attenuation and dispersion effects, combined with the complex, cluttered and heterogeneous environments that are usually dealt with, the inherent system noise and finally the noise introduced from other outer sources (e.g., surrounding mobile and WiFi networks) make GPR data processing and interpretation a rather challenging task. Noise filtering is therefore a necessary preprocessing step towards gaining automatic understanding from GPR data. Temporal/frequency filtering refers to the filtering of individual A-Scans in the time/frequency domain. One of the most important parameters characterizing a scanning procedure and dictating in particular the denoising procedure is the frequency of the transmitted pulse. The most appropriate type of filtering that should be applied on the individual GPR traces, for the purpose of rejecting out parts of the signal corresponding to irrelevant frequencies, is a bandpass filter and, thus, a Butterworth filter is utilized to take advantage of its properties in the bandpass zone. Spatial filtering refers to the denoising techniques applied along the space axis (i.e., across the recorded values of all the A-Scan traces at a specific time). For the task of hyperbola detection the most appropriate spatial filtering, due to its properties, is Background Removal. The mean of the recorded amplitude is calculated across all A-Scans for each time value and is subtracted by them. In that way the removal of the ground-bounce is achieved and the effects of highly attenuating ground types (e.g., wet soil creating vertical signatures) are reduced. At the same time the hyperbola patterns are amplified. The last preprocessing step of the B-Scan is the Gain function which improves the visual representation of the information available in the processed GPR data. The gain function is achieved by multiplying all signal values with appropriate time varying factors. The calculation of those factors may take the physical process of the wave propagation into consideration. The energy decay cost function considers the wave losses to be connected to the travelled distance d in a $1 = d2$ manner and calculates coefficients based on the squared distance from the antenna. In fact, a linear, a polynomial, an exponential, or any kind of function connecting the traveled distance with some multiplication coefficients performing some kind of equalization can be utilized as a gain function. The results of a linear gain function and an energy decay function on a processed B-Scan are illustrated Figure 6.4b.

6.5 Hyperbola Detection on Real GPR Data

Preprocessed A-Scans consist of consecutive positive and negative pulses, oscillating around a mean zero value. The hyperbola traces, which may indicate the existence of buried infrastructure, are expected to be shaped by either the positive or the negative pulses of consecutive A-Scans. The necessary positive-negative segmentation is performed by isolating sign changes on the A-Scan values around zero crossing. A zero crossing isolation step is applied to all A-Scans recorded in a scanning operation and a negative-positive separation on B-Scan is produced. The isolation step is accompanied by a key point extraction method which is the location on the B-Scan image of the peak values of segmented pulses (max and min values for positive and negative pulses respectively). This procedure produces the key-points which are nominal apexes of the existing hyperbolas in the entire radar-gram. The detected key-points are further utilized to produce 2D segmentations on the B-Scan. Specifically, each key-point constitutes a candidate apex, and segmentation favoring hyperbolic shapes is performed around it. Two segmentation approaches are applied, both of which utilize data driven parameters regarding the maximum expected size of a single hyperbolic signature. The first segmentation merges into a hyperbola candidate all those pulses in the neighboring A-Scans of the candidate apex that have key-points that occur at the same or a later time as the candidate one. The second segmentation step imposes a much stricter criterion that forces each new pulse to have a key-point value at a time strictly larger than the previous one. The first step is highly susceptible to noise pulses around the actual hyperbolic signature; however, it generates candidates with slow increase of reception time amongst consecutive scans. The second step demands an increasing slope of at least 45 degrees asking from the reception time to constantly increase amongst consecutive scans distancing from the candidate apex. Consequently, the first segmentation produces better separation close to the hyperbola apex regions while the second segmentation performs better when distancing from the apex as the hyperbola's slope converges to its asymptote's slope.

The next step comprises a feature extraction procedure based on the Histogram of Oriented Gaussians (HoG), which instead of a fixed grid on the image plane, a grid with varying size is applied to each candidate apex on the produced segmentation. The applied patch size is related to the expected size of the hyperbola signature and is initially considered to be 30×50 pixels. On that patch a 6×5 cell grid composed of 5×10 cells is applied. For each cell the histogram of the gradients of the cell pixels contains 9 bins. The resulting feature vector length is equal to *number-of-cells* $\times$ *binsize* $= 270$. The basic advantage of the adopted solution is that each hyperbola is adaptively described by the feature vector depending on its size in the B-Scan. The extracted feature vectors are used to train a four class SVM classifier on which three classes are referred as positive ones that contain hyperbola traces and the negative class is referred to patches containing noise. The hyperbola detection considered as a classification task has big intra-class variability due to the varying curvature that affects the shape and the final feature representation. Three separate positive classes of hyperbolas have been defined, according to the asymptote's slope, namely, 22.5°, 45°, and 67.5°. During training of SVMs with a one-vs-one approach, hyperbolic segments are clustered into the three positive classes, while noisy segments from real GPR images were used to define negative classes. During testing, comparisons are performed between all positive and negative classes and the one receiving the majority of votes is assigned to the segment under question. The classification step defines segments on the B-Scan positively identified as hyperbolas. The key-point that produced the specific feature vector is not always a sufficiently good location estimation on the radar-gram of the actual hyperbola apex and, thus, a hyperbola fitting step is performed after classification, where a gradient descent is applied to define the exact apex and curvature of the key-points of each detected patch that corresponds to a candidate hyperbola positively classified in the SVM. A hard threshold on the Least Square Error criterion applied on the fitting is used to further reject false positive hyperbolas.

6.6 Subsurface Mapping

After the detection of the hyperbola, apexes comprise the construction of the subsurface map, which is common both for the simulated as well as the real GPR images. To achieve this, localization information of the motion of the GPR antenna is required and, since the GPR antenna is towered by a surface operating rover, equipped with vision sensors, the robot's motion estimation is exploited. The GPR-rover topology is known and, thus, the surface rover motion estimation is inherited to the GPR antenna. As a result, the detected apexes are expressed in global coordinates through the construction of a subsurface map, endorsing the smart perception system with autonomy and large-subsurface mapping capacity.

6.6.1 *Surface Rover Localization*

For the robot motion estimation, a visual odometry algorithm has been implemented that is suitable to operate in outdoor environments. In particular, a stereo camera mounted on the surface rover to perform incremental motion estimation based on visual features tracking has been utilized. In each iteration loop a disparity image is computed through a stereo correspondence algorithm based on local block matching accompanied by global disparity space optimization. The calculated disparity image is utilized to obtain the depth value $z(x; y)$ coordinates calculated through triangulation for each pixel $(x; y)$ of the left camera image and kept as reference frame as follows:

$$z(x,y) = \frac{f}{disp(x,y)}$$

where f is the camera focal length, B is the stereo camera baseline, and $disp(x, y)$ is the respective disparity value. By applying the same procedure on all the pixels of a stereo pair a dense 3D point cloud of the scene is obtained. However, for rough motion estimation between the consecutive frames, only a subset of the initial point cloud is required. In particular, among the potential detectors suitable for localization, the proposed motion estimation system employs Speed Up Robust Features (SURF), which detects and matches the most prominent 2D points within two consecutive frames. The main reason for the utilization of SURF is its fast computation time compared to the existing methods. By evaluating the depth information at the respective 2D images, we obtain a set of point-wise 3D correspondences among the consequent frames. Let us assume that the robot observes a specific point P_t in the 3D space, such as $P_t = [x_t, y_t, z_t]^T$. In the next time instance $t + 1$ the robot undergoes a specific motion with rotation matrix R_{t+1}^t and translation vector $T_{t+1}^t = [T_x, T_y, T_z]^T$ so the corresponding point P_t in now observed as $P_{t+1} = [x_{t+1}, y_{t+1}; z_{t+1}]^T$. The transformation from point P_t to P_{t+1} is as follows:

$$P^t = R_{t+1}^t \cdot P^{t+1} + T_{t+1}^t$$

Considering 3D registration of all the detected SURF points P, a rigid body transformation could be found that expresses the overall camera (and thus robot) motion estimation in each execution loop. The incremental required rigid body transformation typically should conform with a sum of quadratic differences minimization criterion, resulting in a singular value decomposition (SVD) optimization problem. However, considering that errors are introduced mainly stemming from erroneous SURF feature matching, the depth estimation of the stereo correspondence algorithm and the native camera re-projection error obtained from the stereo pair calibration, an additional outlier rejection method is required to produce refined motion estimations. To this end, a RANSAC outlier detection step has been applied to retain only a subset of inlier points from the set of points P that satisfy maximum inliers criterion of a plane detection procedure. The retained inlier points are used along the SVD to compute the rover's motion estimation. In the next step, the rover's poses and transformations are stored as nodes and edges in the graph, respectively, representing the robot's trajectory. This graph is further enhanced by registering the generated dense point clouds with respect to the robot's pose, as well as by associating the observed features in each node. Having expressed the rover's location estimations as a graph of nodes, a global graph optimization step is applied through g2o optimization when the robot revisits the same location, i.e., observes the same SURF features. The outcome of this procedure is a globally consistent robot trajectory which applies the stored 3D point clouds and a surface metric map is produced.

6.6.2 3D Reconstruction of Underground Environment

Subsurface mapping includes the 3D registration of the detected hyperbolas from the GPR radar-grams to the robot's trajectory. To associate obtained underground data from the GPR measurements with robot localization, the

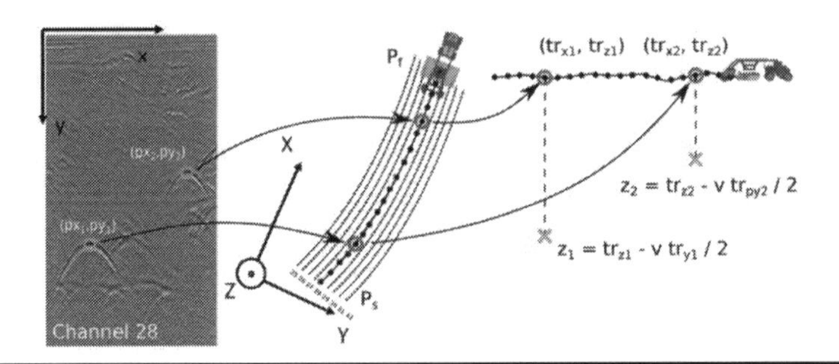

Figure 6.5 Transition from the 2D radar-gram frame (B-Scan) to robot coordinate frame.

robot motion estimation is taken into consideration. During the robot's motion, all the A-Scans gathered from the GPR antenna are progressively stored and proportionally distributed to the generated nodes of the graph, assuming constant robot velocity. Each A-Scan is thus anchored to a specific node and, as such, it inherits the node's information, i.e., pose, with respect the robot's coordinate frame (see Figure 6.5).

At this step it should be mentioned that given the fact that a B-Scan can be formulated when the GPR antenna performs straight routes, the surface rover's motion estimation is utilized as a criterion for the cut-off and a completion of each radar-gram in accordance to traveled route. Thus, deviations (e.g., >10°) in the robot's yaw angle indicate that the robot stopped its straight route and thus all the anchored A-Scans to the pose graph are recalled and concatenated to create a B-Scan. On the constructed B-Scan the aforementioned preprocessing and hyperbola detection procedure is applied to detect the candidate apexes of the buried utilities. From the hyperbola detection algorithm the apex (px_i, py_i) is computed into the radar-gram where the value py_i in the ordinate (y-axis) denotes the reception time that corresponds to the hyperbola apex in the time window of the recorded signal for an A-Scan, while the value px_i in the abscissa (x-axis) denotes the GPR-antenna covered distance. Therefore, the value py_i should be corrected to indicate the underground depth on which the hyperbola apex belongs and this is performed with the following equation:

$$pz_i \frac{t_{pyi} \cdot u}{2}$$

where pz_i is the actual depth of the apex, t_{pyi} is the reception time and u is the propagation velocity of the medium as illustrated in Figure 6.6.

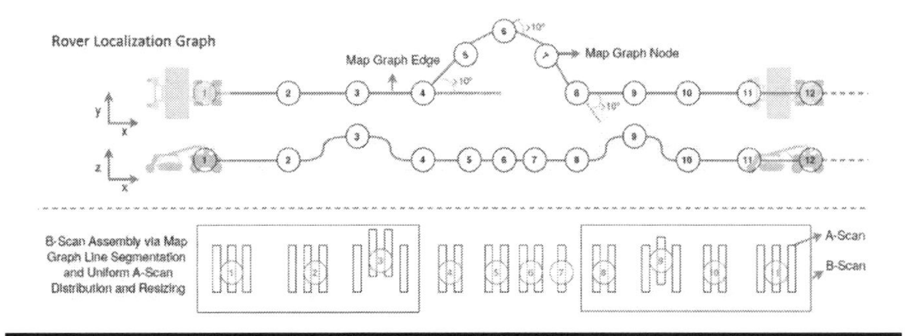

Figure 6.6 The pose graph that associates the robot's localization and the recorded A-Scans during the robot's motion. In the graph it is highlighted how the A-Scan aggregation is performed and the criterion utilized for the B-Scan isolation with respect to the localization graph during the rover's travel. Note that node IDs correspond to the aggregated A-Scans and each formulated B-Scan corresponds to the straight line covered by the rover.

6.7 Perception System Assessment

The evaluation of the smart perception system has been performed both in a simulation as well as in a real environment. In both cases both the hyperbola detection module on its own, as well as the integrated subsurface mapping tool, have been evaluated.

6.7.1 Evaluation in Gazebo Simulation

The performance of the proposed methodology for subsurface mapping has been evaluated through a simulated experiment in the Gazebo 3D robot simulator, the model of which is illustrated Figure 6.7a. A specially designed world was created that, in terms of the surface, consists mostly of terrain surrounded on three sides by obstacles, which in combination with a rocky ground texture, offers plenty of features for the visual odometry algorithm. Regarding the subsurface part of the world, five 20-cm-diameter pipes were added to be used by the subsurface mapping module. In order to enable sonar-based simulated GPR model operation, the space below the ground and between the pipes was left empty. Figure 6.7 demonstrates the operation of the proposed subsurface mapping system. The existing subsurface utilities, i.e., pipes to be detected, are displayed in the visualization of the robot workspace as dark grey cylinders for reference. As depicted in Figure 6.7b, the robot starts with no information about its environment and gradually constructs a metric representation of it in the form of a point cloud. At the same time, via the simultaneous operation of the subsurface mapping module,

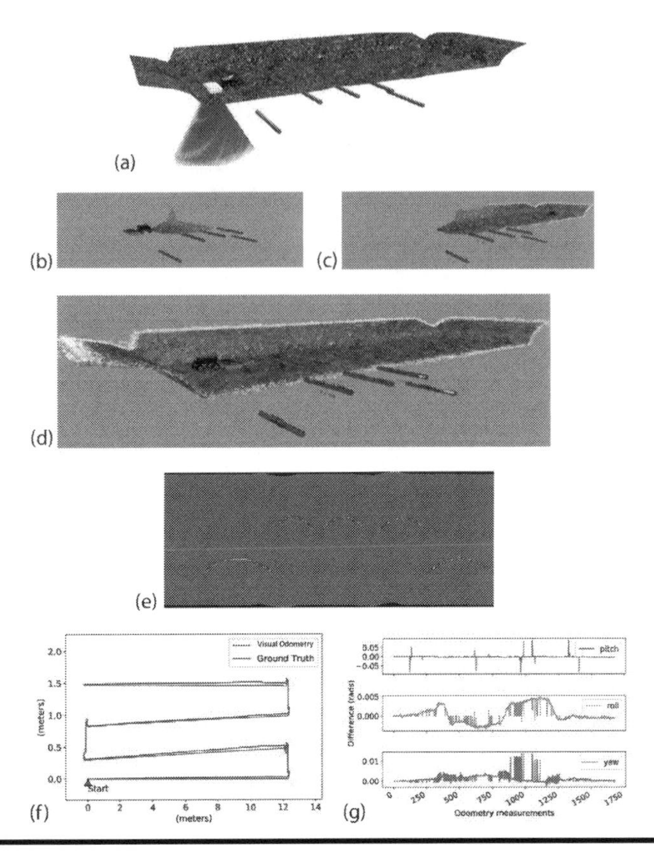

Figure 6.7 The second and third rows exhibit subsurface mapping at different moments from start to finish. In (d), the full constructed subsurface map is illustrated, where the red dots correspond to the detected pipes and the yellow-colored pipes correspond to the ground-truth. The last row refers to the visual odometry error when compared to the Gazebo simulation measurements; (f) exhibits the robot's trajectory along with the ground-truth, and (g) illustrates the orientation deviation of Euler angles.

the subsurface pipes are detected and visualized through a red point cloud. This point cloud corresponds to the apexes of the detected hyperbolas on the B-Scans generated after every straight line as described previously. The detected hyperbola apexes (see Figure 6.7e) are then processed by the utility mapping module to filter outliers and detect lines corresponding to the pipes. Figure 6.7f demonstrates the trajectory followed by the robot as estimated by the visual odometry module in blue, while the ground-truth provided by Gazebo simulation is exhibited with red color. In addition, Figure 6.7g demonstrates the Euler orientation error of the robot using the Euler angle's roll, pitch and yaw. The accuracy of the subsurface mapping depends on the accuracy of the robot's localization. The errors in both figures are deemed within acceptable bounds for the accurate 3D registration of the detected hyperbolas, which validates the proposed methodology. However, it should be mentioned that by implementing a different localization algorithm the results could be vary accordingly.

6.7.2 Evaluation in Real Test Field

The evaluation of the real system has been performed in a specifically designed and constructed test site. In total, 4 pipes have been placed on the subsurface and among them 3 are metallic and 1 is plastic (PVC) material. The pipes have been placed at various depths. This multi-variable set-up allowed evaluation of the different aspects of the developed solutions. The two sides of the test field specific area were kept free of buried utilities to allow surface rover maneuvring since during the curved motion, the acquired A-Scans are not considered for the construction of the B-Scans. The entire field has been initially measured and the terrain was attended, so as to allow as smooth as possible antenna operation on the surface of it. The annotation of the buried utilities performed on the fly during their installation in order to keep track of the type/size and position of the buried pipes. Thus ground-truth data were kept; however, their nominal error is calculated as less than 0.02 cm, which has been introduced due to soil displacement effect during the burring phase.

Firstly, the hyperbola detection assessment has been performed on the custom developed test site. The detection percentage of the hyperbolas that are actually correct is 90.1%, yet the recall, i.e., the percentage of all annotated hyperbolas that are successfully detected, is lower, specifically 75%. The accuracy of the 3D subsurface map is tightly related to the accuracy of the surface rover localization since the data acquired from the GPR antenna are registered to the localization pose graph of the surface rover. Therefore, it is essential to firstly quantify the localization error of the surface rover. An experiment was performed to test the efficiency and accuracy of the implemented modules. To this end, an experiment was set up in the field-like environment by exploiting pattern specific AprilTags at positions to be detected by the stereo camera and thus used as ground-truth estimations. When the rover stands in front of an AprilTag, a custom detector is executed, which provides a ground-truth estimation of the pose (position and orientation) of the rover. The ground-truth is then compared to the visual odometry provided by rover localization and an Euclidean distance error is computed, as well as an orientation difference error. Those errors are further examined after the rover detects loop closures, by revisiting areas, and optimizing the localization pose graph. Since the point clouds that formulate the map inherit the poses of the localization graph, the error of the optimized map is the overall error of the surface rover localization. The overall positioning error is calculated by considering the Euclidean distance of the position of the visual odometry and the ground-truth and found to be approximately 0.2 m, while the orientation error is calculated by considering the shortest angular distance of the Euler angles (roll, pitch and yaw) of the compared visual odometry and the ground-truth and found to be 0.02 degrees.

The accuracy of the constructed surface/subsurface map depends mostly on the robot's localization accuracy which means that the ability of the system to correctly register the detected utilities on the subsurface map relies on the error of the robot's motion estimation. Considering the depth estimation of the buried utilities, there is an uncertainty introduced from the GPR resolution (A-Scan) of the utilized Stream-C GPR antenna, which is 5 cm. More precisely, in the large-scale experiment, the total traveled distance of the robot was 60 m. The error in the localization concerning the displacement of the robot after the scanning of the entire field is approximately 0.40 m which is less than 0.7% of the total traveled distance. The biggest amount of this deviation is introduced in the XY plane, i.e., the robot's motion plane, and less deviation has been measured on the Z axis. The error on the robot's orientation was negligible and measured to be less than 1°. The next step of the evaluation comprises the ability of the developed framework to correctly locate the buried pipes. Figure 6.8 graphically illustrates the 3D subsurface map

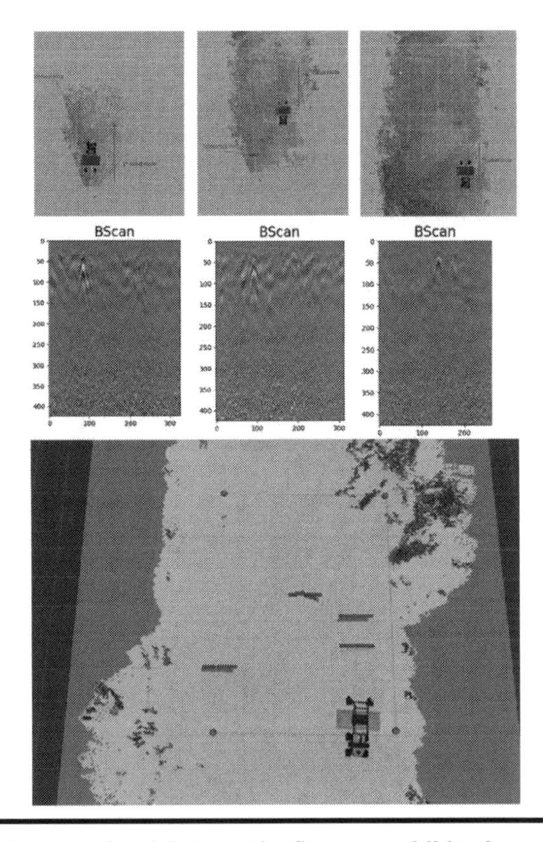

Figure 6.8 Evaluation of real dataset; the first row exhibits the progressively built subsurface map, the middle row illustrates the detected hyperbola apexes in three robot passes and the last row presents the constructed subsurface map with the detected pipes.

with the ground-truth. Specifically, it is revealed that all the buried pipes in the test site have been successfully mapped in the reconstructed environment. The second row of Figure 6.8 presents hyperbola detection on indicative B-Scans along the robot's traversal route. The resulting map has undergone a further outlier detection and DBSCAN step which retained only the most compact descriptions and discarded further erroneous detected apexes from the hyperbola detection step on the B-Scans. It should be noted that the position of the detected pipes closely resembles the position of the ground-truth with small deviations. The final result shown in Figure 6.8 closely matches the actual annotated pipes resulting in more than 90% coverage of the scanned utility network, which means that the 90% of the buried infrastructures is correctly detected and annotated with this method.

6.8 Conclusions

Summarizing, in this book chapter, a perception system for subsurface mapping using a surface rover and a GPR antenna has been presented. Firstly, a simulation tool for the perception of buried utilities has been developed and has been integrated in the Gazebo environment to be suitable for robotic applications. Then, a utilities detection method on the formulated radar-grams from GPR imaging has been constructed. The detection method has been tailored both for the simulation as well as for the real-world scenario. Considering the simulation environment image processing and geometrical fitting methods have been used since the acquired data are noise free, while for the real-world environment an in-depth data preprocessing has been firstly introduced and, then, a method based on HoG features, SVM classification, and final fitting approach has been developed to tackle the readings from the GPR sensor. The perception system both in simulation as well as in the real scenario has been integrated with a surface operating rover where the rover self-localization schema has been integrated with the GPR processing step to create structured subsurface maps, where buried utilities such as pipes are represented in terms of point cloud. The smart perception system has been evaluated both in simulation as well as in real scenario and exhibited promising performance since it was proven adequate to construct subsurface maps both in simple as well as in complex real life environments. To this end, the chapter presented a smart application by integrating a real GPR antenna with a surface rover based on technology fusion from the robotics navigation domain combined with radar imaging common in geoscience applications, to provide a perception output for large-scale environments facilitating autonomous buried utility detection.

Acknowledgment

This work has been supported by the EU Horizon 2020 funded project: "RoBot for Autonomous unDerGround trenchless opERations, mapping and navigation (BADGER)" under grant agreement no: 731968.

References

1. Degenhardt, J.J., Giardino, J.R.: Subsurface investigation of a rock glacier using ground-penetrating radar: Implications for locating stored water on mars. *Journal of Geophysical Research: Planets* 108(E4) (2003).
2. De Jongh, R., Ligthart, L., Kaploun, I., Schukin, A., Yarovoy, A.: Design and analysis of new GPR antenna concepts. *Tijdschrift-Nederlands Elektronica En Radiogenootschap* 64 (1999) 26–32.
3. Feng, X., Sato, M., Zhang, Y., Liu, C., Shi, F., Zhao, Y.: CMP antenna array GPR and signal-to-clutter ratio improvement. *IEEE Geoscience and Remote Sensing Letters* 6(1) (2009) 23–27.
4. Kaliampakos, D., Benardos, A.: Underground space development: Setting modern strategies. *WIT Transactions on the Built Environment* 102 (2008) 1–10.
5. Aly, M.: Real time detection of lane markers in urban streets. In: *Intelligent Vehicles Symposium, 2008 IEEE*, IEEE (2008) 7–12.
6. Kouros, G., Psarras, C., Kostavelis, I., Giakoumis, D., Tzovaras, D.: Surface/subsurface mapping with an integrated rover-GPR system: A simulation approach. In: *Simulation, Modeling, and Programming for Autonomous Robots (SIMPAR), 2018 IEEE International Conference on*, IEEE (2018) 15–22.
7. Kouros, G., Kostavelis, I., Skartados, E., Giakoumis, D., Tzovaras, D.: 3D underground mapping with a mobile robot and a GPR antenna. In: *IEEE/RSJ International Conference on Intelligent Robots and Systems (IROS)*, IEEE (2018) 3218–3224.
8. Sandmeier, K.: Reflexw 3.0 manual. Sandmeier Software, *Zipser Strabe* 1 (2002).
9. Xie, L.L., Jiang, F.Y., Chang, W.K.: Forward simulation of the underwater sand based on gprsim software. *Geophysical and Geochemical Exploration* 6 (2015) 26.
10. Warren, C., Giannopoulos, A., Giannakis, I.: gprMax: Open source software to simulate electromagnetic wave propagation for ground penetrating radar. *Computer Physics Communications* 209 (2016) 163–170.
11. Annan, A.: GPR—History, trends, and future developments. *Subsurface Sensing Technologies and Applications* 3(4) (2002) 253–270.
12. Kim, J.H., Cho, S.J., Yi, M.J.: Removal of ringing noise in GPR data by signal processing. *Geosciences Journal* 11(1) (2007) 75–81
13. Torrione, P.A., Throckmorton, C.S., Collins, L.M.: Performance of an adaptive feature-based processor for a wideband ground penetrating radar system. *IEEE Transactions on Aerospace and Electronic Systems* 42(2) (2006) 644–658.
14. Janning, R., Busche, A., Horváth, T., Schmidt-Thieme, L.: Buried pipe localization using an iterative geometric clustering on GPR data. *Artificial Intelligence Review* 42(3) (2014) 403–425.
15. Mertens, L., Persico, R., Matera, L., Lambot, S.: Automated detection of reflection hyperbolas in complex GPR images with no a priori knowledge on the medium. *IEEE Transactions on Geoscience and Remote Sensing* 54(1) (2016) 580–596.
16. Pasolli, E., Melgani, F., Donelli, M.: Automatic analysis of GPR images: A pattern-recognition approach. *IEEE Transactions on Geoscience and Remote Sensing* 47(7) (2009) 2206–2217.
17. Illingworth, J., Kittler, J.: A survey of the Hough transform. *Computer Vision, Graphics, and Image Processing* 44(1) (1988) 87–116.

18. Falorni, P., Capineri, L., Masotti, L., Pinelli, G.: 3-D radar imaging of buried utilities by features estimation of hyperbolic diffraction patterns in radar scans. In: *Ground Penetrating Radar, 2004. GPR 2004. Proceedings of the Tenth International Conference on*, Volume 1, IEEE (2004) 403–406.
19. Simi, A., Bracciali, S., Manacorda, G.: Hough transform based automatic pipe detection for array GPR: Algorithm development and on-site tests. In: *Radar Conference*, IEEE (2008) 1–6.
20. Dell'Acqua, A., Sarti, A., Tubaro, S., Zanzi, L.: Detection of linear objects in GPR data. *Signal Processing* 84(4) (2004) 785–799.
21. Borgioli, G., Capineri, L., Falorni, P., Matucci, S., Windsor, C.G.: The detection of buried pipes from time-of-flight radar data. *IEEE Transactions on Geoscience and Remote Sensing* 46(8) (2008) 2254–2266.
22. Jol, H.M.: *Ground Penetrating Radar Theory and Applications.* Amsterdam, the Netherlands: Elsevier (2008).
23. Kaur, P., Dana, K.J., Romero, F.A., Gucunski, N.: Automated GPR rebar analysis for robotic bridge deck evaluation. *IEEE Transactions on Cybernetics* 46(10) (2016) 2265–2276.
24. La, H.M., Lim, R.S., Basily, B., Gucunski, N., Yi, J., Maher, A., Romero, F.A., Parvardeh, H.: Autonomous robotic system for high-efficiency non- destructive bridge deck inspection and evaluation. In: *2013 IEEE International Conference on Automation Science and Engineering (CASE)*, IEEE (2013) 1053–1058.
25. Le, T., Gibb, S., Pham, N., La, H., Falk, L., Berendsen, T.: Autonomous robotic system using non-destructive evaluation methods for bridge deck inspection *IEEE International Conference on Robotics and Automation (ICRA)*, IEEE (2017).
26. Williams, R.M., Ray, L.E., Lever, J.H.: Autonomous robotic ground penetrating radar surveys of ice sheets; using machine learning to identify hidden crevasses. In: *IEEE International Conference on Imaging Systems and Techniques Proceedings*, IEEE (2012) 7–12.
27. Ciarletti, V., Clifford, S., Plettemeier, D., Le Gall, A., Herve, Y., Dorizon, S., Quantin-Nataf, C. et al. The WISDOM radar: Unveiling the subsurface beneath the ExoMars Rover and identifying the best locations for drilling. *Astrobiology* 17(6–7) (2017) 565–584.
28. Rial, F.I., Pereira, M., Lorenzo, H., Arias, P.: Acquisition and synchronism of GPR and GPS data: Application on road evaluation. In: *Image and Signal Processing*, 5982, International Society for Optics and Photonics (2005).
29. Fong, T., Allan, M., Bouyssounouse, X., Bualat, M.G., Deans, M., Edwards, L., Fluckiger, L. et al.: Robotic site survey at Haughton Crater. In *Proceedings of the 9th International Symposium on Artificial Intelligence, Robotics and Automation in Space (iSAIRAS)*, Los Angeles, CA (2008).
30. Furgale, P., Barfoot, T.D., Ghafoor, N., Williams, K. and Osinski, G.: Field testing of an integrated surface/subsurface modeling technique for planetary exploration. *The International Journal of Robotics Research* 29(12) (2010) 1529–1549.
31. Sonka, M., Hlavac, V. and Boyle, R.: *Image Processing, Analysis, and Machine Vision.* Stamford, CT: Cengage Learning (2014).
32. Ester, M., Kriegel, H.P., Sander, J. and Xu, X.: A density-based algorithm for discovering clusters in large spatial databases with noise. *Kdd* 96(34) (1996) 226–231.

Chapter 7

Computational Intelligence through Human Machine Interaction in Cyber World

Muhammad Noman Malik and Ata Ullah

Contents

7.1 Introduction

Computational intelligence prevails over artificial intelligence (AI) in human–computer interaction (HCI). Although these are different fields, they have common ground [1]. Artificial intelligence has magnified some computation that clearly provides economical benefits for integration in HCI [2], such as suggestions for online stores, consumer preferences, guidance through visual maps, and analyzing and controlling big data. This computational intelligence has augmented human interaction with computers and software systems [3]. CI is making remarkable contributions towards researching news of interactions devices. In this regard, the last few decades have witnessed progressive development in the HCI landscape. Researchers have embraced developing new interaction devices and technologies to facilitate the interactions of human with machines. Even technology has raised computational power and intelligence through various interaction devices. In this regard, input devices have revolutionized computer interaction from classical keyboards to ergonomic keyboards, touch screens are getting smarter, hand gestures can input and control hardware, there is human voice under natural language processing (NLP), and others.

Computational intelligence has actually advanced the concept of soft computing. To provide computational intelligence, artificial intelligence becomes the main way to attain various industrial applications such as computer vision, deep learning, data mining and semantic analysis, analytics for different business sectors, big data computations [4], smart health, and ubiquitous and mobile computing in various fields. Such computations have also achieved notable results in education technologies with various innovations for distance and online learning, human health with innovative devices to automated computing health, agriculture science with various soil sensing facilities, business field with artificial intelligence to support decision making, and others.

The notable consideration is that researchers are constantly exploring new ways to provide ease to humans while interacting with machines. Moreover, research has moved the computational powers of traditional mainframe computers to laptops, intelligent and smart workstations, smart phones, and smart-embedded devices used in various fields. These computations have produced distinguished achievements and are redefining the ways we interact with machines. The rise of internet technology has generated cyber space; according to a recent survey, 4.21 billion people are internet users. This number is increasing day by day through as people use laptops as well as mobile and other technology gadgets. In [5], it is highlighted that a usability evaluation is critical to ensure the productive and constructive use of products in the cyber world. Moreover, HCI security and usable security are essential to ensure reliability and guard against malicious attacks from intruders who are looking to invade the normal routes of transactions. Usability patterns of different products and human behaviors should also be considered during design time. Abbas [6] has discussed laws and regulations for the future cyber world along with security requirements of the Internet of Things (IoT). This work considers both HCI and human factors to evaluate the capabilities and behavior of certain operations in the cyber world. It helps to identify criminal behavior against data in transit, especially in social interaction scenarios.

7.2 Computational Intelligence and HCI Conceptualization

Computational intelligence (CI) generally refers to computational paradigms based on theory, design and development of various biologic and linguistic industrial applications. It sometimes also refers to soft computing and usually describes the computer's capability to self-learn based on the events, tasks and data [7]. IEEE Computational Intelligence Society describes this as strongly connected to three major principles: fuzzy system, neural network, and evolutionary computation (Figure 7.1). Although it has been described with different constructs under CI, there is still no accepted definitions of this [8].

The fuzzy system is reasoning through measuring and modeling real complex problems. It works through the generalization theory of traditional logic to resolve uncertain problems. The neural network is related to the computer's self-paced learning from task, event, and data. This artificial neural network focuses on medial data and forensic investigational issues. It can help with face detection, malfunctions that lead to identification of fraud, pattern recognition, and other tasks. Evolutionary computation describes the biological processing required to solve complex real problems. It targets resolving optimization problems by considering generation, evaluation and modification of available prospective solutions.

The conceptualization of the human machine interactions (HMI) has different names such as human computer interaction (HCI), computer human interaction (CHI) and man machine interaction (MMI). The aim of this field is to consider how humans can conveniently interact with different computing devices. HCI is defined as "a multidisciplinary research area focused on interaction modalities between humans and computers; sometimes, the more general term human-machine interface (HMI) is used to refer to the user interface in a manufacturing or process-control system" [9].

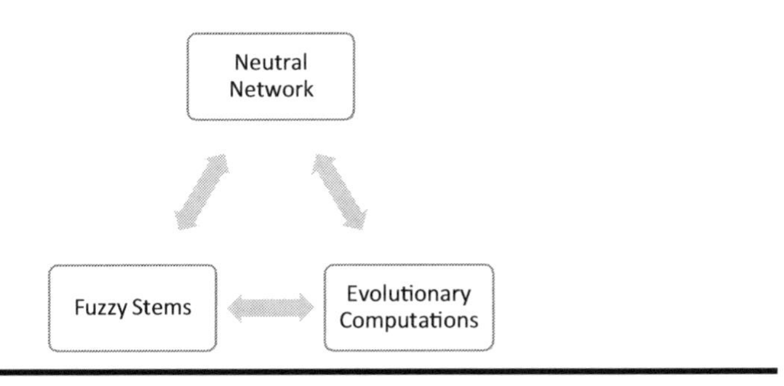

Figure 7.1 Three pillars of computational intelligence.

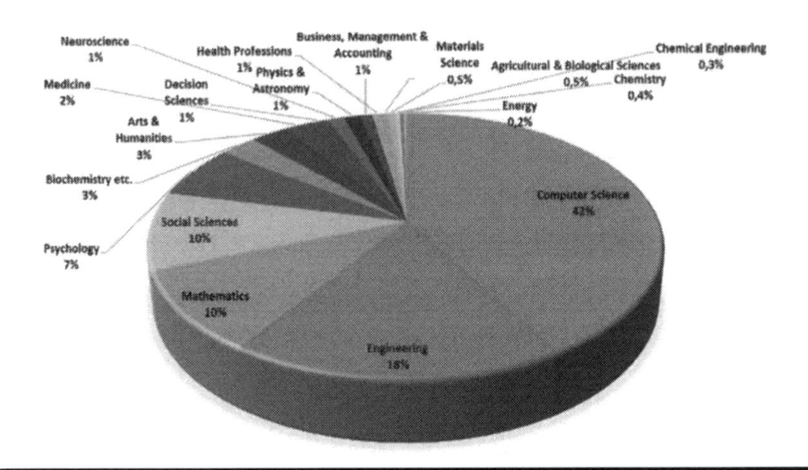

Figure 7.2 Major themes followed in the HCI field. (***Adapted from Koumaditis, K. and Hussain, T., Human-Computer Interaction. User Interface Design, Development and Multimodality, 10271, 23–37, 2017.***)

Researchers in this field focus on how humans interact with machines, as well as innovative design technologies that advance the convenience of human interactions. In addition researchers also focus on ergonomics related to the environment of interaction and examining potential harmful effects of using such technologies. Recently, this author has conducted a thorough literature review of HCI and highlighted major themes in the literature [3]. Figure 7.2 depicts major HCI themes; 42% of HCI studies are in the field of computer science and 18% are in the field of engineering.

7.3 Role of Computational Intelligence in the Cyber World

With the rise of the internet and cyber world, computational intelligence is gaining a strong toehold in the cyber world. CI has also produced the unique technology-based services of Chatbots, natural language processing (NLP) for companies to serve cyber users. CI has also become able to actively filter adult content on the web, capture terrorism preached on websites, monitor dark websites via automated intelligent systems, and provide new semantic analysis to monitor and track users networking on social media. The use of CI not only supports companies as they seek to reach users around the globe but also actively monitors them. CI has significantly addressed concerns and built capabilities in the cyber world in a revolutionary way. Some examples of how CI is penetrating the cyber world are discussed below.

CI is making remarkable contributions through natural language processing (NLP), has made revolutionized voice searching over the internet through Google, for example, via "best nearby hotel to stay," "what medication is required for a sore throat," and "top rated movie of the year." These features are commonly named Voice Control Assistant. These assistants are increasingly popular and can be seen in large companies' products such as Siri and Cortana.

In addition to these assistants, CI in the cyber world has been improvised through AI-powered Chatbots. These Chatbots helped take web interaction to the next technology level. Through these Chatbots, websites and web-based solutions interact with users through technology-based agents. Users feel that they are interacting with the companies' representatives, and take information and suggestions from them. Such technology-based interactions help companies, especially those engaged in e-commerce. Chatbots along with machine learning, AI and NLP help companies provide services like online sales agents, technical support, suggestions for finding better products and other help related to e-commerce. These intelligent technology agents, commonly known with Chatbots, are available on web-based platforms and mobile agents.

Not only does CI contribute to assisting and suggesting, it also helps monitor the whole network. As social media data is increasing, there is a strong need to monitor adult content, filter live streaming, and enable parental guidance of web use. So CI is taking this responsibility by providing all essential AI-based computational intelligence.

As social media data continue to significantly increase, it has become clear that big data and its analytics require CI filtering to ensure quality data. The number of users is increasing, and sometimes they post correct information, but mostly they post vague information that CI must filter out via AI and deep learning methodologies. Before information can be dispersed via social media, its quality and reliability must be ensured; therefore, many researchers are studying this area under the guise of various countries' defense and regulatory agencies.

Moreover, CI addresses major concerns in the cyber world, including terrorism. CI has taken a strong position to devise AI-based systems through which websites preaching terrorism, known as black websites, can be captured and monitored. Subsequently, regulatory agencies can block brutal acts of terrorism in the cyber world. CI analyses that consider the semantic meaning of terrorism preaching and multilingual text analytics are some current and futuristic approaches. National agencies now observe most criminal records through modern pattern analysis and biological computations.

Viruses are another pressing concern related to information security and privacy that always challenge cyber users. In this regard, an intelligent cyber defense system is needed for connecting the physical world with the cyber world. The system should detect and guard against various virus attacks including spam as well as active, passive, known and unknown attacks [10]. CI offers potential cyber security measures to tackle viruses along with information and privacy issues to provide dependable solutions.

Different applications of CI through the help of AI, deep learning and fuzzy systems are the core for its implementations in the cyber world. Computational intelligence in next-generation cyber-physical systems involves neural networks and brain computing. It helps to manage residual energy, mitigate faults and protect against cyberattacks [11]. The rapid development of the CI field has contributed to cyber space users' fight against cyber crime. Nevertheless, much research is needed to ensure the protection of cyber world users (see details in the following section).

7.4 Imperative Research Directions

The common goals of HCI and CI are blending to achieve synergy in various computing fields. They complement each other not only to produce innovative interactive technologies and devices, but also to produce environments where industry computations can benefit humans. These two core concepts impact medical sciences, space technologies, business, gaming, and engineering and computer science. Further, new innovations including holography, sixth sense, and 7d are also opening new ways of thinking for academia and industry. Some recent technologies and research are making remarkable contributions to industry. They are creating new ways of interaction and at the same time challenges to adoption in different settings. Figure 7.3 shows new CI and HCI trends.

The race of technology is creating innovations to increase human ease in dealing with life. For example, augmented reality and mixed reality are creating new human interactions in navigation, product finders, the tourism industry, computer games, and others. This augmentation towards real life and translating them into virtual and computer worlds is creating a sense of a blended environment without boundaries.

Holography is a relatively new technology that creates a sense of visualization through the holography lens. Although these lenses are expensive, industry has moved to benefit from them, such as harnessing holography technology to generate innovative marketing trends of their products outside malls and shops. Similarly, this technology is now used in communication and speech, showing your presence virtually when you actually physically exist in some other part of the world. M-S Kim [12] has explored hyper-connectivity to present the interaction between the cyber and physical worlds for data visualization and analysis by utilizing Geo-IoT concepts.

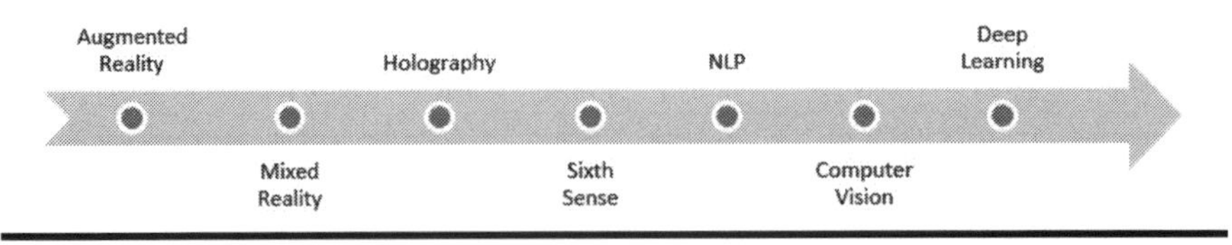

Figure 7.3 Trends in CI and CHI.

Sixth sense is related to the field of neurotechnology [13] that explores "what the user thinks." It should be interpreted through computational intelligence to open a cyber world of innovative application scenarios. For example, if the user of a mobile device wants to talk to his friend, the mobile device should dial his friend. This is done by sending a command to a computer through thoughts. This incredible technology is still under development; however, its use can be both positive and negative.

Another future use of CI is NLP, where user voice commands provide interaction with computing devices. The NLP paradigm is currently being used in Google assistance and Apple Siri systems. NLP have penetrated as a new interactive way out with computers, mobile devices, and other gadgets. Although its usage is already traced in industry, its challenging aspects related to syntax, grammar and voice quality are some of examples of areas of future research [14].

Computer vision can aid in understanding the context and content of all images. In this field, eye gaze technology, machine learning, and interaction through gestures aid not only typical users, but also users with disabilities and other special needs. It is quite beneficial in healthcare and ambient assisted living to monitor health activities and wellness in the real world, a capability which is not possible without the contribution made by deep learning and neural networks [15]. Detecting drivers' faults such as drowsiness and distraction, cahsierless retail stores, and hand gestures to operate computing devices are innovative areas where researchers and industry professionals need to do a lot of work. It is concluded that there is a long way to go in this competitive and continuously emerging world of technology. Researchers must be vigilant in cooperating with industry to yield maximum benefits when focusing on energy-efficient sustainable solutions. These sustainable solutions can eventually save our future.

References

1. J. Grudin, AI and HCI: Two fields divided by a common focus, *Ai Magazine*, 30, 48, 2009.
2. T. Winograd, Shifting viewpoints: Artificial intelligence and human-computer interaction, *Artificial Intelligence*, 170(18), 1256–1258, 2006.
3. K. Koumaditis and T. Hussain, *Human-Computer Interaction. User Interface Design, Development and Multimodality*, 10271, 23–37, 2017.
4. W. Pedrycz and S.-M. Chen, *Information Granularity, Big Data, and Computational Intelligence*, vol. 8. Springer, Cham, Switzerland, 2014.
5. J. Dykstra, Human-computer interaction and usable security. In: *Essential Cybersecurity Science*, O'Reilly Media, Sebastopol, CA, 2015.
6. A. Moallem, *Human-Computer Interaction and Cybersecurity Handbook*, CRC Press, Boca Raton, FL, 2018.
7. W. Duch, What is computational intelligence and what could it become, *Computational Intelligence, Methods and Applications Lecture Notes NTU*, Singapore, 2003.

8. W. Duch, What is Computational intelligence and where is it going? In: *Challenges for Computational Intelligence*, Springer, Berlin, Germany, 2007, pp. 1–13.
9. P. Montuschi, A. Sanna, F. Lamberti, and G. Paravati, Human-computer interaction: Present and future trends, *Computing Now*, 7(9), 2014.
10. S. Zhong, H. Zhong, X. Huang, P. Yang, J. Shi, L. Xie, and K. Wang, Connecting physical-world to cyber-world: Security and privacy issues in pervasive sensing. In: *Security and Privacy for Next-Generation Wireless Networks. Wireless Networks*, Springer, Cham, Switzerland, 2019.
11. C. Alippi, S. Ozawa, Computational intelligence in the time of cyber-physical systems and the Internet of Things. In: R. Kozma, C. Alippi, Y. Choe, and F. C. Morabito (Eds.), *Artificial Intelligence in the Age of Neural Networks and Brain Computing*, Academic Press, London, UK, 2019, pp. 245–263.
12. M.-S. Kim, Research issues and challenges related to Geo-IoT platform, *Spatial Information Research*, 26(1), 113–126, 2018.
13. P. R. Roelfsema, D. Denys, and P. C. Klink, Mind reading and writing: The future of neurotechnology, *Trends in Cognitive Sciences*, 22(7), 598–610, 2018.
14. H. Lu, Y. Li, M. Chen, H. Kim, and S. Serikawa, Brain intelligence: Go beyond artificial intelligence, *Mobile Networks and Applications*, 23(2), 368–375, 2018.
15. P. R. Roelfsema, D. Denys, and P. C. Klink, Computer vision for ambient assisted living: Monitoring systems for personalized healthcare and wellness. In: *Computer Vision for Assistive Healthcare*, Academic Press, London, UK, 2018, pp. 147–182.

Chapter 8

Multi-granular Activity Recognition within a Multiple Occupancy Environment

Darpan Triboan, Liming Chen, Feng Chen, and Zumin Wang

Contents

8.1 Introduction

Ambient assisted living (AAL) systems are being developed as a tool to assist a typical and growing aging population carry out activities of daily living (ADL) independently. As the technology evolves and becomes more ubiquitous, it is now possible to monitor human physiology and connect every object we interact with on a daily basis to the world wide web (WWW). With the knowledge of an inhabitant's context, intentions and past actions, the system can be trained to recognize human actions, learn, adapt and automate the tasks. However, human activity recognition (HAR) remains an important research challenge for a number of fields such as healthcare, security, automotive, and energy management, to name a few. Although extensive work has been carried out to recognize single (predominantly) and multi-occupancy activity recognition ($\mathcal{MAR}$), a number of challenges and limitations remain unresolved from technical, social and privacy perspectives. This chapter highlights some of the challenges and attempts to achieve fine-grained activity recognition (AR) performed by single and multiple occupants in a shared smart home environment.

The characteristics of a single occupant performing ADL is that one activity can be performed sequentially and in a composite manner (interleaving/concurrently) with other activities (two or more). The actions for each activity are generally performed in any order and can be assumed to be independent of previous/future actions. However, some dependencies between previous and future tasks can exist. A single occupant can also work in collaboration/cooperatively with other occupants in a shared space to complete one or more activities together or in parallel to each other [1]. In a collaborative AR context, the data associated with a specific occupant present one of the key challenges faced in shared occupant spaces [2]. Overall, an activity can be detected by inspecting each action at two granularity levels, coarse and fine-grained. In coarse-grained AR, general context, relations between ADL descriptions and occupant's actions are used to assume an activity unfolding, i.e., *cup, kettle, tea bag, milk, sugar* and *tap water* observations for *MakeTea* ADL. Therefore, the fine-grained AR method inspects more deeply on how each action of a specific ADL is performed and determines whether the intention of a given action is satisfied, for instance, detecting "*filling up*" kettle from the water tap, "*pouring*" water from the *kettle* into a *cup* and "*drinking*" from the *cup* when conducting *MakeTea* activity. Figure 8.1 depicts *MakeTea* ADL and describes key actions at two granularity levels along with *MakeToast* and *MakeBakedBeans* ADL.

The key challenges being focused in this chapter are to identify actions at coarse- and fine-grained level based on contextual factors and sensing parameters for a given ADL and a method for estimating AR confidence level ($\mathcal{ARCL}$) in real time. In addition, indicating a total number of occupants in the shared room to a caregiver if overcrowded and data association between multiple occupants conducting same or independent activities is a key challenge for giving personalized assistance.

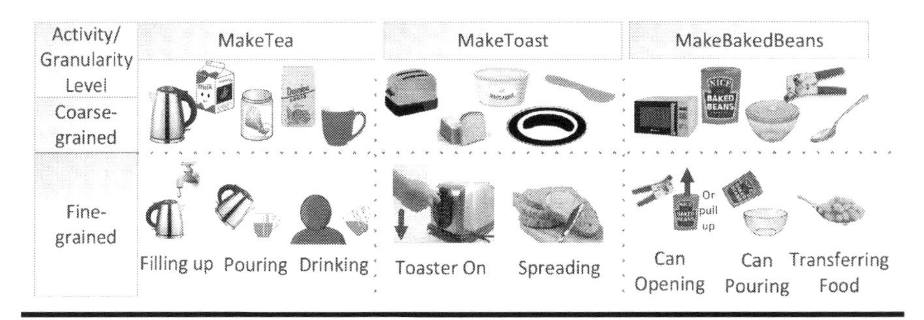

Figure 8.1 Coarse- and fine-grained granularity levels for three ADL.

In general, AR consists of three key parts: activity modeling, activity classification and learning, and data collection. Activity modeling tasks can be carried out by processing a large data set to create a trained model (data-driven approach) or conceptualizing domain expert(s) knowledge explicitly (knowledge-driven approach) [3,4]. Both of these approaches have advantages and limitations. The key advantage of the data-driven approach is that it can handle unseen activities and uncertainty in events more robustly in comparison to the knowledge-driven approach. However, the limitation of the data-driven approach is that it requires large data set processing time and computation to create a training model, hence creating a "cold start" problem. In addition, these models cannot be easily reused or applied to other occupants. On the other hand, the knowledge-driven approach requires no processing time due to the explicit description of facts with rich relationships (driven by formal and logical theories) defined by the domain experts in a form ontological model. The common issues with both of these approaches are that all the activities must be trained or modeled and they assume having complete descriptions of all possible human activities. Therefore, a hybrid approach [5] was introduced to take advantage of both of these approaches and use the ontological model as a "seed" to evolve and learn new activities over a period of time with the use of generative and discriminative classification approaches. The selection of activity classification and learning methods is informed by the activity modeling technique employed. Activity learning and discovery require detection of the occupant's activity patterns over a period of time and refining the initial activity model. More will be covered in our future work; however, this is out of the scope of this chapter.

The data collection methods are becoming ubiquitous and can be categorized as vision and sensor-based. Due to the higher computation requirement to extract feature points from an image and obtrusive nature of the vision-based approach to privacy in the personal area [6], the sensor-based approach is receiving more attention. The sensor-based approach can be categorized as ambient, dense or wearable sensing. The ambient sensing methods are used to monitor specific environmental parameters such as temperature and movement. The dense sensing method is applied by embedding sensors into everyday objects to evaluate where, what,

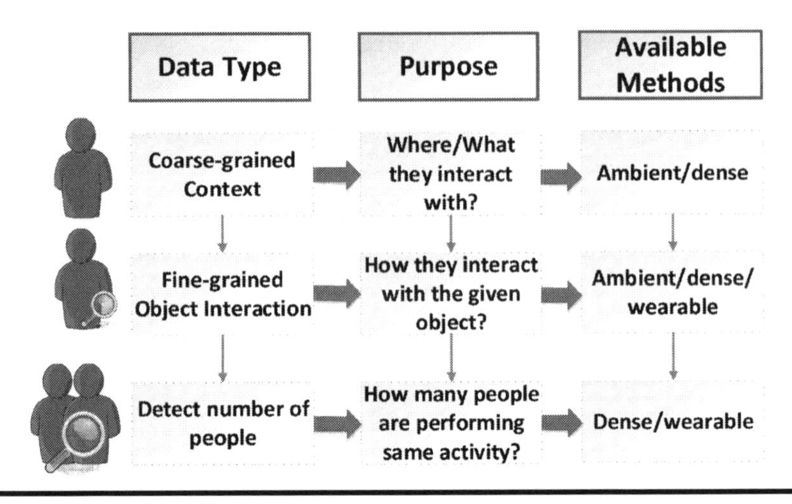

Figure 8.2 Fine-grained multi-occupant activity recognition data collection methods.

how and who interacts with these objects. Similarly, wearable sensing is performed to monitor user-specific physiological attributes (i.e., heart rate, movement sensors) by placing the sensor on the body or implanting into the body.

Figure 8.2 depicts what type of data can be retrieved, for what purpose, and the suitable sensor-based methods. The information gathered from the smart environment can be used to achieve both coarse- and fine-grained AR. Coarse-grained AR involves understanding the generic context of the user(s) such as where the activity is being performed, what objects they are interacting with and what ADL this action is related to. The ambient and dense sensing methods can provide such information.

For instance, an occupant enters the kitchen; opens the cupboard to take out a cup, sugar, and tea jar; and uses the kettle to heat the water. There can be a door or passive infrared sensor (PIR) to detect user location and embedded sensors such as capacitive touch sensor on the door handle. A given AR system can infer these actions are related to the making tea ADL; however, this information is limited and assume fine-grained tasks such as "*pouring*" hot water from the kettle to cup. In addition, the occupant could be "*tidying up*" the kitchen by putting the objects into their respective places or interleave these actions with another activity by using hot water from the kettle to make "*pasta*" or "*rice*."

To achieve fine-grained AR, how and when an occupant interacts with an individual object need to be analyzed with multi-modal data [7]. Previous studies have used inertial measure unit (IMU) position sensors (i.e., accelerometer and gyroscope sensor) either by positioning on the everyday object or using wearable devices with IMU sensors to analyze the position of the everyday objects to infer fine-grained actions such as "*pouring*," "*cleaning*," and "*washing-up*." Once the fine-grained AR is achieved from a set of sensor observations, the next challenge is distinguishing which occupant and how many people collaborated to conduct a particular activity in the shared space.

The remainder of the chapter is organized as follows. Section 8.2 covers related work in detecting coarse-/fine-grained and multiple occupants' activities. Section 8.3 proposes a novel approach to achieve this challenge with the algorithm details in Section 8.4. The approach is applied to a case study with multiple occupants performing kitchen activities in a composite manner in Section 8.5 and the conclusion and future work in Section 8.6.

8.2 Related Work

To achieve fine-grained single-occupant AR, work in [8] combined acceleration and acoustic and multi-sensor classifiers and evaluated it using popular machine learning algorithms, J48 decision tree, random forest, a Bayesian network, and support vector machine. The data were collected from a single off-the-shelf smartwatch and the result indicates that this combined approach achieved greater accuracy (91.5%) in comparison to individual classifiers in recognizing five daily activities: eating, vacuuming, sleeping, showering and watching TV. The key limitation of this approach is that training data is required for individual users and cannot be easily reused. Furthermore, an energy-constrained smartwatch must be worn at all times which creates practical challenges of frequent recharging of the smartwatch and hinderance of natural body movements. Therefore, the wearable sensors are now being integrated into our clothes and accessories to monitor attributes such as movement and posture-based items by unobtrusively placing sensors on a different part of the body. The study in [9] explores a multimodal and multi-positional sensing approach to detect fine-grained AR. Multiple wearable sensors were positioned on different parts of the body and Bluetooth-based beacons to perform AR using the conditional random field (CRF) and decision fusion classifiers. Similarly, work in [10] used inertial rings and bracelets to achieve fine-grained occupant AR based on the wrist and index finger gestures of eating, drinking and brushing actions with different types of objects. The key limitations for both of the wearable sensor-based fine-grained AR studies are the lack of semantic reasoning, adaptability, scalability, practical usability, and power consumption challenges. In contrary, work in [11] presents a hybrid method where ontology and Markov Logic Network (MLN) approaches are leveraged to enable semantic and probabilistic reasoning between activities, context data and sensing devices. The proposed unsupervised approach outperformed the standard supervised method using CASAS and SmartFaber datasets. However, it assumes that action observed by a sensor indicates an event (mostly binary) that has been completed successfully.

In the context of multi-occupancy AR, work in [12] adapted coupled hidden Markov models (CHMMs) by adding vertices to model single and collaborative activities. The CASAS Multi-occupancy dataset was used from Washington State University (WSU) with non-obtrusive sensors containing 15 ADL performed by two occupants. However, the approach assumes if two occupants are in the same region, then they are performing the collaborative activity and cannot distinguish which occupant is performing what actions and how. Another work, [13], predicts next activity in a multi-occupant smart space using natural language processing (NLP), long short-term memory (LSTM) network and k-means clustering to find a semantic relationship between multiple vectors. The study achieved an 85% success rate in recognizing activities in a smart meeting room using ambient sensors and actuators. The limitation of this approach is that it cannot detect a total number of occupants, fine-grained activities and when applying the approach in other silent/noisy shared space. In addition, higher window size and predicted activity candidates are required in order to achieve greater accuracy.

Work in [14] presented a method of identifying collaborative and group-based activities using a decentralized approach where wearable sensors and mobile phones were used to perform classification. The information passed from each occupant's mobile phone were exchanged and analyzed for detecting collaborative and independent Multi-occupancy activity. The approach further assesses the energy consumption and recognition accuracy using the decentralized method. The single occupant activity classification results from a smartphone were shared with other occupants in the environment in order to detect any collaborative/parallel activities. Similarly, work in [15] tackled challenges of recognizing fine-grained and collaborative activities performed by surgeons and support staff in a medical operating theater setting. The approach leveraged using the conditional random field (CRF) classification method and simulation data from wearable and dense sensors.

In recent studies, researchers have relied on wearable devices in the context of single AR and $\mathcal{MAR}$. However, they have recognized the need to use nonintrusive sensors to monitor occupants' behavior and develop real-world applications [2]. For instance, work in [16] identifies occupants by using a biometric signature from skull bone conduction using eyewear like google glass. Likewise, work in [6] leveraged wall-mounted radio frequency (RF) transceivers and IR sensors to fingerprint individual occupants and Gaussian Mixture Model (GMM) for classification. Three test subjects were used, 2 male and 1 female, to collect over 2300 labeled samples per subject over 5 days and achieved 83% and 98% accuracy, respectively. However, this approach was tested on a single occupant at a time and struggled to classify two people with a similar build in stature. In other domains, less intrusive sensors such as fingerprint sensors and voice recognition are commonly being used to identify and authenticate individuals, for instance, smartphone-based attendance and payroll-based systems for employees working remotely [17] and fingerprint sensor–based door access control in [18]. However, little has been explored using these sensors for association sensor observations to a given occupant for the goal of AR and service provisioning.

In this chapter, the use of knowledge-driven modeling and classification techniques for ADL is explored using sensor-based data collection methods to achieve coarse-/fine-grained and Multi-occupancy AR. In addition, for practical and real-world applications, a non-wearable sensing approach is presented using a general ambient and dense sensing method for this goal.

8.3 Multi-granular Activity Recognition within Multiple Occupancy Environments

An ontological-based activity modeling and reasoning approach is proposed to distinguish single and composite activities. The ontological-based AR approach utilizes conceptual descriptions of concepts, relationships and instances notion to formally define ADL with environmental objects that have sensors attached to them. Therefore, incoming sensor events are initially semantically evaluated and separated in a set of sensors based on the relationships with the ongoing ADL(s). The segmented sets of sensors for a given ADL are then evaluated at two granularity levels: coarse- and fine-grained. At the coarse level, three key context satisfactory criteria are evaluated from the sensor's relationship with a given ADL: location (L_r), key objects (KO_s) and time interval (TI_t). At the fine-grained granularity level, detection of key fine-grained actions (FA_i) with the sensor data is performed with a specific object and matched against thresholds.

The ontological-based AR approach by itself cannot distinguish who is performing the actions and how many people are collaboratively or independently performing activities in the shared space. Therefore, discriminative sensing approaches and pattern detection techniques are required that can identify collaborative activity occurring, determine individuals with their unique signatures and track their activities at the action level. Details of proposed multi-occupancy AR are provided in Section 8.3.3.

To conduct fine-grained single- and multi-occupant activity recognition tasks, a multilayered service-oriented architecture (SOA) system is proposed and graphically depicted in Figure 8.3. This approach enables AR tasks to be delegated between web service, client devices and sensing environment. The sensing data is centrally collated by the layered web service. The utility layer consists of dedicated classes and packages to collect sensor from multiple sources (*Sensing Utils*), store/manipulate data from the database (*TDBUtils*) and provide other knowledge reasoning utilities. The repository layer puts each sensor observation in the queue, semantically segments [19] the queue based on ADL unfolding and interacts with support classes in utility layer classes. The segmented set of actions based ongoing ADL and their descriptions are then used by the façade layer to perform single-occupancy

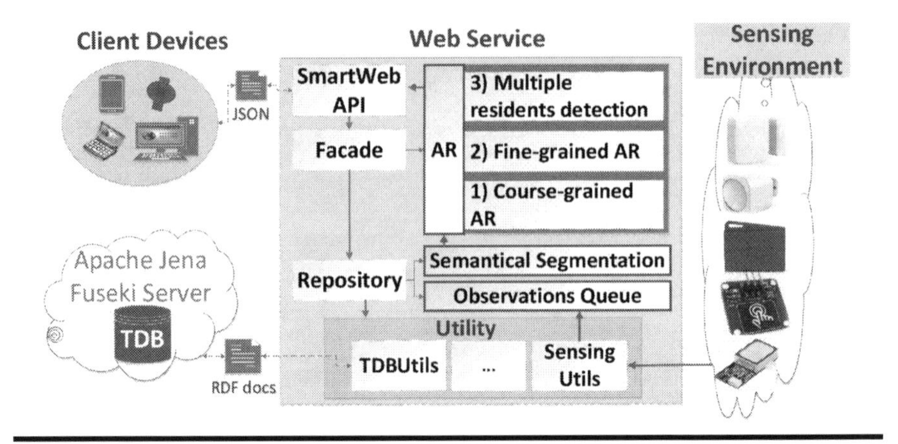

Figure 8.3 Fine-grained Multi-occupancy AR system architecture overview.

(coarse- and fine-grained) and multi-occupancy AR. All the AR results and sensor events log are stored in the graph-based database (Apache Jena Fuseki Server). The AR results, sensor events, and other requests made by client devices are made available via *SmartWebAPI* using RESTful communication protocol and in multiple formats, i.e., JavaScript Object Notation (JSON) and Extensible Markup Language (XML). More examples and details of multilayered SOA system and hardware sensing configuration can be seen in [20,21].

8.3.1 Single-Occupant Activity Recognition

8.3.1.1 Ontological Knowledge Representation

The ontological activity modelling approach allows the relationship between everyday objects within the living environment and generic ADLs to be logically representation. The factual knowledge has been conceptualized using formal theories and it allows expressive relationships to be defined between multiple entities. Description logic (DL) is a family of formal knowledge representation languages that are supported by OWL and RDF Schema vocabulary. DL enables the logical representation of conceptual structures and relationships using three main elements: concepts, roles and individuals. The concepts denote sets of individuals, and roles denote binary relationships between individuals. The individuals are instances of concepts. The vocabulary used for defining concepts and roles of an application domain is referred to as the terminology or the *TBox* in short. All named individuals are referred to as assertions about a real-world domain or the *ABox*. Hence, DL allows users to build complex descriptions of concepts and roles. Furthermore, DL-based reasoners can be used to automatically perform inferencing to derive facts that are not expressed explicitly in the ontological model. This process is known as T-Box reasoning.

The occupant-specific preferences are also described as instances of a specific ADL class and are stored in the graph-based database (triplestore). This process is known as assertion-box reasoning (A-Box). To avoid conflicts between instance checking and ADL class satisfiability for occupant's preferences, generic object relationship is used. SPARQL Protocol and RDF query language (SPARQL) are used to retrieve relevant occupant's preferences. Both generic and occupant-specific preferences knowledge are utilized to segment each sensor observation into a relevant set of activity queues and then perform further activity classification. The segmentation process is further described in Section 8.3.3.

8.3.1.2 Multigranularity ADL Description

The environmental objects, ADL, sensing network and their relationships are modeled using ontology editor (i.e., Protégé). Each ADL is further described with three coarse-grained parameters (L_r, KO_s and TI_t) and key fine-grain actions (FA_i) performed with a specific object. The coarse-grained parameters are selected to check if the key actions for the ADL are performed, at most, during the appropriate time of the day and place.

$$\mathcal{CCL} = \left(\frac{\sum_{r=1}^{x} L_r + \sum_{s=1}^{y} KO_s + \sum_{t=1}^{z} TI_t}{3} \right) \tag{8.1}$$

$$\mathcal{FCL} = \sum_{i=1}^{n} FA_i \tag{8.2}$$

$$\boldsymbol{\mathcal{ARCL}} = \left(\frac{\mathcal{FCL}*3 + \mathcal{CCL}}{4} \right) \tag{8.3}$$

The multi-granularly descriptions of ADL are given importance values defined by a domain expert's knowledge. Therefore, as the activity unfolds for a given ADL, their importance values are accumulated and averaged out with the number of parameters to calculate coarse-grained confidence level ($\mathcal{CCL}$) and fine-grained confidence level ($\mathcal{FCL}$). $\mathcal{CCL}$ takes L_r, KO_s and TI_t attributes from the sensor data and ADL description into consideration. Each parameter is given importance values (total of 100%) that are defined by domain experts in the ADL knowledge base for individual ADL. Hence, the sum of the importance values of three coarse-grain parameters are calculated and then averaged out to calculate $\mathcal{CCL}$; see equation (8.1). Similarly, $\mathcal{FCL}$ analyses sensor data of the individual object to detect key FA_i and add all respective importance values (total of 100%); see equation (8.2). The values are of $\mathcal{CCL}$ and $\mathcal{FCL}$ are combined and then averaged out to get an overall activity recognition confidence level ($\mathcal{ARCL}$) for a given ongoing activity. In addition, the assurance of detecting fine-grained action rather than assuming that a given action has taken place, the $\mathcal{FCL}$ value is given three times the importance of the $\mathcal{CCL}$ value, as shown in equation (8.3).

For example, to *Make Tea*, occupants can normally perform this task in the morning or afternoon by going into the kitchen, and they must interact with *KO* such as a *cup*, *kettle*, *water tap* and *tea bag/jar* to complete the activity. These *KO* are given an importance value to determine the level of completion of the activity. The importance values are derived depending on whether the actions between *KO* are shared and how significant it is in regards to a given activity for the action to be completed. For instance, the interaction between *TeaBag* and *Kettle* can be more important than *Cup* and *WaterTap* in order to determine the action of *Make Tea* activity. Similarly, other activities can be described as illustrated in Table 8.1. In the case where *L* and *TI* are shared for a given activity, the total importance values available (100%) are distributed as illustrated for *TakeMedicineDose* activity.

8.3.1.3 Sensing Attributes

The generic context can be obtained when an occupant opens *kitchen door* and interacts with *sugar jar, tea bag, cup, water tap* and *kettle*. Although these actions belong to the "*Make Tea*" ADL, it does not necessarily mean the occupant has complicated the action or they could be performing a more generic "*tidying*" activity. Therefore, to achieve fine-grained AR, each object's interactions and usage must be evaluated to detect key actions such as "*pouring*" hot water from the kettle into the cup. The advancement in sensing technology is becoming cheaper, smaller, wireless and energy efficient. However, collecting data from pre-installed sensing infrastructure remains costly and difficult to maintain (i.e., battery life), and the position of the sensors can be fixed or portable [8]. Hence, wearable sensors can be more appropriate to monitor vital physiological parts; however, this forces one to wear it at all times and creates practical challenges [2].

With this in consideration, a fusion of ambient and dense sensors data collection methods is proposed to detect actions at coarse- and fine-grained level. The ambient sensors will provide coarse-grained contextual information about the environment and the objects occupant is interact using sensors such as motion detector, magnetic door/window and capacitive touch sensors. In contrast, dense sensors such as TI SensorTags for object positioning and the liquid level sensing approach are proposed to be attached to relevant everyday objects for fine-grained object usage recognition. For instance, "*pouring*" water from the kettle to a cup can be determined if the correlation between the changing state of the water level and tilting position of the kettle and cup exceeds a given threshold. This threshold can vary depending on the initial quantity of the water, dimensions of the object and sensor placement on

Table 8.1 Spatio-temporal ADL Description for Multigranularity AR

	Coarse-Grained Parameters			
Activity	*Location (L)*[a]	*Key Objects (KO)*[a]	*Time Int. (TI)*[a]	*Fine-Grained Actions (FA)*[a]
Make Tea	Kitchen	TeaBag(50), Cup(10), Kettle(30), WaterTap(10)	6.30–11.30am, 3–6.30pm	Pouring(50), Drinking(20), Filling(30), WashingUp(10)
Make Baked Beans	Kitchen	BakedBeansCan(50), MicrowaveBowl(25), Microwave(25)	6.30am–2.30pm, 6–8.30pm	ToasterOn(70), MargarineSpread(30)
Make Toast	Kitchen	Toaster(50), BreadSlice(30), Margarine(10), EatingKnife(10)	6.30–11.30am, 3–6.30pm	CanOpening(60), CanPouring(20), TransferringFood (20)
Take Medicine Dose	Kitchen (50), Living room (50)	MedicineBox(80), WaterTap(10), Glass(10)	8–10am,1–2pm, 5–7pm, 10–11pm	Eating/Drinking Medicine (70), DrinkingWater(30)
Tidying	Any room/ Unspecified	Bin (25), Sink(25), Furniture(50)	Unspecified	MovingObject(40), PutIntoSink(20), CloseKitchen Furniture(20), PutInBin(20)
Washing Up	Kitchen	WashingSoap(30), HandGloves(5), EatingCutlery(20), CookingCutlery(20), WaterTap(25)	Unspecified	Wipe(35), CircularMotion(35), WashingLiquid(30)

[a] Total importance weighting of 100% per activity unless stated.

the everyday objects. Likewise, other fine-grained actions such as "*drinking*" from the cup can be detected with relevant sensors attached to the object. A heartbeat signal and liquid level information of a kettle, cup or other container can be sent to the web service at a regular interval or upon a change in water level detection threshold to reduce the sensor data transmission traffic and energy.

However, not all everyday objects would require water level sensing actions such as "*opening can*" for the *MakeBakedBeans* activity and "*transferring food*" to a plate. The fine-grained actions along with their belief weightings for the other ADL are listed in Table 8.1. The everyday object and action-specific thresholds can be defined as instances, stored and queried from the triplestore, or logical rules can be specified (i.e., using Semantic Web Rule Language (SWRL) and fuzzy rules [22,23]). However, with the complex semantic reasoning and computation requirement at the sensor segmentation stage, storing and retrieving threshold values based on individual objects in the triplestore would be efficient to reduce computational resources required for runtime rules-based reasoning. Moreover, to detect multi-occupants' activities, fingerprint sensors are embedded and strategically positioned on everyday objects. Figure 8.4 depicts the overall sensing parameters and data types required for coarse-/fine-grained and multi-occupancy AR.

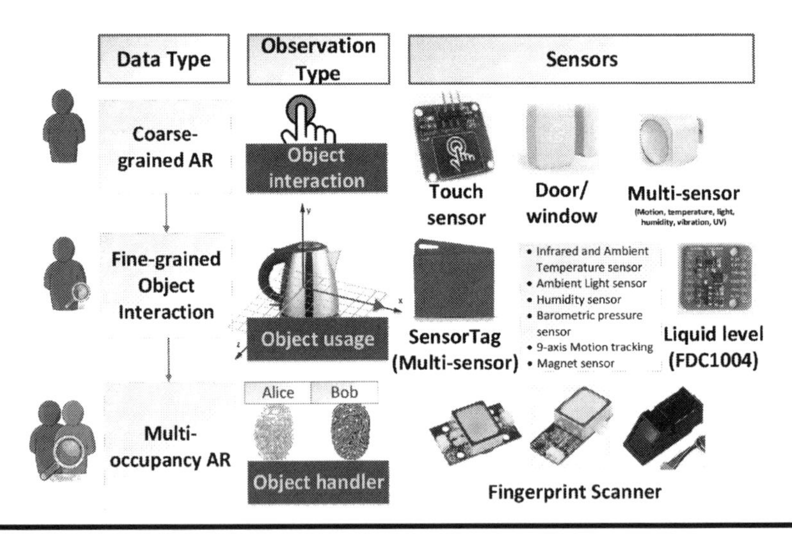

Figure 8.4 Proposed sensing parameters for single (coarse-/fine-grained) and multi-occupancy AR.

8.3.2 Multi-occupancy Activity Recognition

$\mathcal{MAR}$ analyses a segmented set of sensor observations of a given $\mathcal{ADL}_n$ to detect, identify and associate an occupant's (I_j) actions with everyday objects ($KO_s[FA_i]$), contextual and environment sensor data (i.e., L_r, TI_t) as described in equation (8.4).

$$\mathcal{MAR} = \left(\mathcal{ADL}_n\left[I_j\left[L_r, KO_s\left[FA_i\right], TI_t\right]\right]\right) \tag{8.4}$$

The detection of multi-occupancy actions is performed by using timestamp information from the number of objects simultaneously interacted in a given time interval and location. An occupant is assumed to interact or hold no more than two or three objects at the same time interval. For this, fix time windowing analysis is performed to detect potential multiple occupant-based activities. It is also assumed that a single occupant cannot be in two locations at the same time. Therefore, in a given fixed time window, if two motion or pressure sensors located in different areas are activated, multiple occupants are detected. However, both location and time windowing approach falls short in identifying how many occupants are in a location at the given time interval.

Although location and time windowing approach can detect multiple occupants in the same space, it is still unable to distinguish which occupants are interacting with the objects. Hence, a fingerprint sensor attached to everyday objects is proposed to distinguish which occupant in shared space interacted with the object. The fingerprint sensor can regularly scan for a fingerprint, automatically match against the enrolled/stored fingerprints in the sensor's database, and provide an identify (ID) number. Each fingerprint sensor can internally store fingerprint images (i.e., up to 3000 in GT-521F52) with a unique ID and perform image matching with a low error rate and delays. All of the occupants sharing the space are required to initially scan their fingers and thumbs on a fingerprint sensor that is synchronized with other fingerprint scanners. The unique IDs generated for each finger and the sensor are mapped together and associated occupant information is stored in the triplestore. Therefore, as the fingerprint sensor enters observation mode, the observed fingerprint image is matched using inbuilt recognition functionality and the ID matched is sent to the central system (i.e., web server).

Figure 8.5 presents an example of the $\mathcal{MAR}$ process during *make tea* (A1) and *make toast* (A2) activities with sensors (fingerprint(fp_n), sensor tag(st_m), and liquid (lq_o)) attached to the *kettle* (fs_1, st_1, lq_1), *cup* (fs_2, st_2, lq_2), *tea jar* ($fs_{3,}$ st_3), and *toaster* ($fs_{4,}$ st_4). The detection process initially counts 3 objects interactions for A1 and 1 object for A2 within a three-second (t_n) time window. The count of the objects' interaction for A1 exceeds the predefined threshold (i.e., <3) per person within a fixed three-second window. Therefore, the occupants, Alice and Bob, conducting actions for A1 are then identified using fp_n sensors data. Finally, the other sensors attached to 3 objects are associated with occupants.

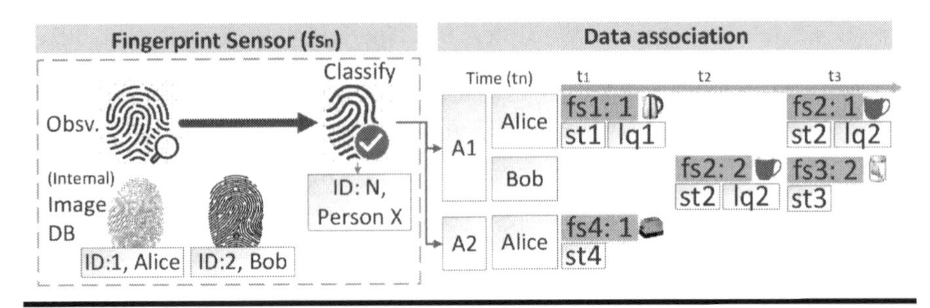

Figure 8.5 Multi-occupant identification and associated actions to detect collaborative or parallel activities.

8.3.3 Data Segmentation Process

To perform single occupant $\mathcal{ARCL}$ or $\mathcal{MAR}$, the incoming sensor events are initially segmented incrementally twofold. Firstly, T-box reasoning is performed to check if the given event is part of an ongoing ADL description in the ontology; otherwise, a new activity queue is created for the initial event. These checks consist of performing satisfiability, subsumption, and instance checking using an incremental Pellet reasoner. The second step is executed only if there are any conflicts identified by the Pellet reasoner in step one. In the second step, A-box reasoning is performed by querying the triplestore to find relevant ADL preferences specified by the occupant and checking if the sensor observation event is part of any preferences. In the event both steps find a discrepancy in ADL description and fail to find any association with other ongoing activities, the start of the new activity is assumed. For this purpose, the notion of multithreading is used, where each thread represents individual ongoing ADL and these ADL threads capture any sensor events based on semantic relevance to the activity independently. Comprehensive details on how the generic actions and preferences of occupants to conduct ADL are modeled and used for the semantic segmentation can be found in [19,24,25].

8.4 AR Confidence Level (ARCL) Algorithm

Table 8.2 presents the algorithm as a pseudo-code split into four sections to perform $\mathcal{CCL}$, $\mathcal{FCL}$, $\mathcal{ARCL}$ and $\mathcal{MAR}$. The algorithm takes in segmented sensors (*segmentedSensors*) as an input based on inferred ADL and iterates over each sensor to calculate AR confidence level and associated sensor events to the occupants. In addition, relevant parameters and importance values retrieved from the triplestore (TDB) are passed as an input for simplicity when calculating $\mathcal{CCL}$ (*cclKeyObjectsAndWeights*, *cclADLLocationsAndWeights*, *cclADLTIWeights*)

Table 8.2 Pseudo-code for Calculating $\mathcal{CCL}$, $\mathcal{FCL}$ and $\mathcal{MAR}$ Confidence

Input: *segmentedSensors, cclKeyObjectsAndWeights, cclADLLocationsAndWeights, cclADLTIWeights, fclSensorsAndWeights*
Output: *arResult*

```
1   for (Sensor s: segmentedSensors)
2      float cclResult, fclResult, arclResult = 0;
3     //1) course-grained AR and calculating CCL
4     if (cclKeyObjectsAndWeights.contains(s))
5       String location = getSensorLocationFromTDB(s);
6       cclResult += cclADLLocationsAndWeights.getWeight(location);
7       cclResult += cclKeyObjectsAndWeights.getWeight(s);
8       cclResult += cclADLTIWeights.getWeights(s.getTimeStamp());
9       arResult.updateCCLResult(cclResult/3); endif
10    //2) fine-grained AR and calculating FCL
11    if (fclSensorsAndWeights.contains(s))
12       Map w = fclSensorsAndWeights.get(s).getThresholdValues();
13       Map v = s.getDataValue();
14       String a = detectFineGrainedAction(w, v);
15    if(! a.isEmpty())
16          arResult.addFineGrainedActions(a);
17          fclResult += fclSensorsAndWeights.getWeight(a); endif
18       arResult.updateFCLResult(fclResult); endif
19    //3) overall ARCL value
20       arclResult = (fclResult*3) + cclResult/4;
21    //4) multi-occupancy AR (MAR)/data association
22    if (hasMultiOccupants(s)&!associateSensorWithOccupant
23     (s, arResult))
24          arResult.addDataAssociation(new Occupant("unknown"), s); endif
    endfor
```

and $\mathcal{FCL}$ (*fclSensorsAndWeights*). The algorithm outputs the AR results (*arResult*) containing $\mathcal{ARCL}$ and $\mathcal{MAR}$ containing data association between the occupant and everyday objects.

In the first section of the algorithm, lines 1–9 accumulatively calculates the $\mathcal{CCL}$ value (*cclResult*) by inspecting each sensor observation with the list of key objects, location and time interval passed (lines 5–9) as an input to retrieve relevant importance values. The sum of *cclResult* value is then divided by three, due to three parameters, accumulated by the previous *cclResult* and updated with the new $\mathcal{CCL}$ result (lines 9). Similarly, the second section calculates the $\mathcal{FCL}$ (*fclResult*) in lines 10–19 by detecting granular actions using the sensor data, predefined thresholds and the importance values for a given action to calculate $\mathcal{FCL}$.

The *detectFineGrainedAction()* function takes the thresholds related to a particular action and sensor type in order to compare the observed sensor values and return respective action (line 14). If the fine-grained action is detected, the action's importance is added to the *fclResult*, multiplied by three, due to the importance factor, added to the *cclResult* and the average is calculated. The *fclResult* is then accumulated and updated with the previous sensor's *fclResult* (lines 15–18). The overall $\mathcal{ARCL}$ value is calculated based on the *cclResult* and *fclResult* as a third step (lines 19–20).

The final part of the algorithm performs $\mathcal{MAR}$ by detecting and associating each sensor's events with the relevant occupant in lines 21–24. The *hasMultiOccupants()* function, on line 22, take sensor event and perform time windowing and location-based analysis to detect multiple occupants in the environment. If multiple occupants are detected, the *associateSensorWithOccupant()* function, on line 22, takes sensor event and *arResult* to identify and associate the action with the occupant. The data association function depends on the fingerprint sensor attached to a given everyday object and the predefined knowledge of other sensors attached to the same objects. In the case where there is no association found between the sensor and occupant, the sensor is added under a temporary "*unknown*" occupant for future analysis. The temporary occupants can be later identified and updated as feedback is received from the known occupants.

8.5 Use Case Study

An ADL scenario is described in Figure 8.6a, where three activities are carried out in a composite manner in the shared kitchen by two occupants, Bob and Alice. The actions for three activities, *MakeTea* (A1), *MakePasta* (A2) and *MakeToast* (A3), occurring between 10.00 am and 10.03 am are illustrated. The sensor observations

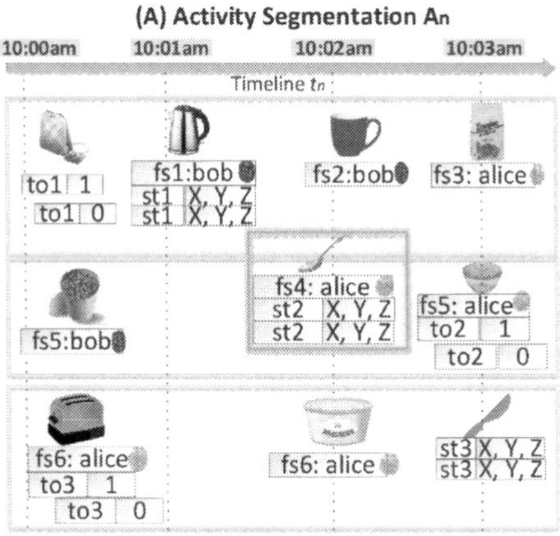

1) CCL	2) FCL	3) ARCL	4) MAR
A1: MakeTea 96.67%	st1=true (pouring) 50%	61.67%	alice (x1), bob (x2) Other (x2)
A2: MakeBaked Beans 91.67%	st2=true (transfer) 20%	37.92%	alice (x2), bob (x1)
A3: MakeToast 93.33%	st3=false (spreading) 0%	23.33%	alice (x2) other (x1)

Figure 8.6 (a) Three ADL semantically segmented sensor observations to be processed by the ARCL algorithm. (b) Four stage of multigranularly single and multi-occupancy activity detection result.

are collected by the respective event handler classes in the *SensingUtils* package of the web service and appended to the observations queue. Each sensor observation occurring at a given time (t_n) is then semantically segmented based on the object's relationship with a set of actions specified in the ADL description and appended to the activity (A_n) thread only if the observed action matches the ADL description.

The $\mathcal{ARCL}$ algorithm is performed in four stages by the individual activity thread and the sample results are depicted in Figure 8.6b. The first stage is to perform context analysis of each activity and calculate $\mathcal{CCL}$, i.e., identifying the location, key objects and time interval to calculate the confidence level of the activity occurring. The location information of the everyday object is predefined for fixed objects such as kettle, toaster and microwave. The key objects for each activity, location and time interval are mapped with the importance of a given activity which is stored and queried from the triplestore.

The second stage is to inspect sensor data to detect if the occupant has performed fine-grained actions such as "*pouring*" by inspecting accelerometer, gyroscope and liquid level sensor data. The threshold to detect "*pouring*" action vary depending on the dimensions of everyday objects and the quantity of content inside. Therefore, thresholds are predefined for when liquid quantity is low, medium, and high along the degree of rotation/tilt position for each object type. The associated importance values of both stages are used to calculate $\mathcal{CCL}$ and $\mathcal{FCL}$. The final stage is performing $\mathcal{MAR}$ using fingerprint sensors and associating sensor observations to the occupant identified. In addition, other sensors attached to the same object to the fingerprint sensor is grouped and associated with the occupant.

8.5.1 Discussion

One of the limitations of this approach is that each everyday object would require at least one fingerprint sensor in order to associate each sensor observation with a given occupant. In addition, the traditional capacitive fingerprint sensors can only cover the small area where an occupant's fingerprint can be scanned, hence, the position of the sensor is important. However, in the recent advancement in ultrasonic fingerprint technology can help overcome these limitations and reduce the cost of the sensors. Ultrasonic fingerprint sensor technology has been under investigation for more than a decade to overcome the poor performance of capacitive fingerprint sensors when fingers are oily, wet and it can easily be spoofed using printed or molded fingerprint images [26,27]. Recently, Qualcomm announced advance fingerprint scanning and authentication technology capable to cover a larger area of the display, thick glass and metal surface [28,29]. In addition, detection of directional gestures, heartbeat and blood flow even when immersed underwater can be used to add layers of authentication and identification of an occupant. Mobile phone manufacturer such as Vivo has already integrated this technology into their flagship phones and others such as Apple, Samsung, Xiaomi, and OnePlus 5 are expected to follow soon.

Despite the scalability and deployment challenges to attach a fingerprint sensor to each everyday object, this approach can identify individuals more discriminatively than passive identification (ID) broadcasting based approaches [30,31]. For instance, smart clothing with passive RFID tags [32] can be worn by another person or incorrectly assigned and Bluetooth based smart beacon deployed in the environment that are read by the smartphone belonging to another individual. However, RFID tags and beacon are very unobtrusive and passive sensing approach to detect the number of occupants and triangulated locations [33] in a shared environment and assume the link to a specific occupant.

Another limitation when adapting a dense sensing approach is that perishable and recyclable items such as soap, plastic bottles and other packaging materials pose scalability, reusability and integration challenges. In addition, the design of the everyday items and size dimensions parameters determine the sensor positions, hence, the varying threshold values.

8.6 Conclusion

This chapter developed course- and fine-grained activity recognition (AR) algorithms and estimates AR confidence level ($\mathcal{ARCL}$). The coarse-grained confidence level ($\mathcal{CCL}$) algorithm extracts location, time and key objects for a given activity along with their respective importance levels from the segmented sensor observations. Each key actions and parameters are given a predefined importance value based on the degree of belief for the action required to occur for calculating the confidence level. To recognize granular occupant actions using a given object, i.e., "pouring" water from the kettle to cup, the fine-grained confidence level ($\mathcal{FCL}$) algorithm is introduced which analysis the sensor observation against the thresholds values predefined with the importance level information. The sum of all fine-grained action's importance values is considered three times more important than the $\mathcal{CCL}$ value when calculating the overall $\mathcal{ARCL}$.

In addition, a Multi-occupancy AR ($\mathcal{MAR}$) algorithm is proposed which can detect, identify and associate actions of a number of occupants performing collaborative or parallel activities. The approach leverages a fix time windowing process to detect maximum object interactions with a predefined threshold and multi-location events. Moreover, fingerprint sensors attached to everyday objects are used to identify and associate sensor observations with occupants. However, the key limitation of this approach is the scalability and maintainability challenge to integrate fingerprint sensors in every object wirelessly. The layered service-oriented architecture (SOA) system and key sensors have been proposed to create a Multi-occupancy smart environment. The key sensors include ambient sensors (door/window and PIR) and dense sensors (inertial measurement unit (IMU), fingerprint, and liquid level sensors) for non-invasive and non-obstructive data collection. The approach is applied to a use case application scenario with composite kitchen activity with multiple occupants performing collaborative tasks.

Future work will involve implementing and evaluating the performance and accuracy of the proposed $\mathcal{ARCL}$ algorithms with $\mathcal{MAR}$, as well as optimizing semantic segmentation performance and investigating activity learning techniques to evolve ADL models.

References

1. M. Prossegger and A. Bouchachia, "Multi-resident activity recognition using incremental decision trees," in *Adaptive and Intelligent Systems*, Springer International Publishing, Cham, Switzerland, 2014, pp. 182–191.
2. A. Benmansour, A. Bouchachia, and M. Feham, "Multioccupant activity recognition in pervasive smart home environments," *ACM Computing Surveys*, vol. 48, no. 3, pp. 1–36, 2015.
3. L. Chen, G. Okeyo, H. Wang, R. Sterritt, and C. Nugent, "A systematic approach to adaptive activity modeling and discovery in smart homes," *Proceedings of the 4th International Conference Biomedical Engineering and Informatics, BMEI 2011*, vol. 4, pp. 2192–2196, 2011.
4. L. Chen, C. Nugent, and G. Okeyo, "An ontology-based hybrid approach to activity modeling for smart homes," *IEEE Transactions on Human-Machine Systems*, vol. 44, no. 1, pp. 92–105, 2014.
5. G. Okeyo, L. Chen, H. Wang, and R. Sterritt, "A hybrid ontological and temporal approach for composite activity modeling," *Proceedings of the 11th IEEE International Conference Trust, Security and Privacy in Computing and Communications*, pp. 1763–1770, 2012.
6. E. R. Schafermeyer et al., "Multi-resident identification using device-free IR and RF fingerprinting," *2015 37th Annual International Conference of the IEEE Engineering in Medicine and Biology Society (EMBC)*, pp. 5481–5484, 2015.
7. C. Lea, G. D. Hager, and R. Vidal, "An improved model for segmentation and recognition of fine-grained activities with application to surgical training tasks," in *Proceedings of the 2015 IEEE Winter Conference on Applications of Computer Vision, WACV 2015*, pp. 1123–1129, 2015.
8. H. Kim et al., "Collaborative classification for daily activity recognition with a smartwatch," in *2016 IEEE International Conference on Systems, Man, and Cybernetics, SMC 2016-Conference Proceedings*, pp. 3707–3712, 2017.
9. D. De, P. Bharti, S. K. Das, and S. Chellappan, "Multimodal wearable sensing for fine-grained activity recognition in healthcare," *IEEE Internet Computing*, vol. 19, no. 5, pp. 26–35, 2015.
10. A. Moschetti, L. Fiorini, D. Esposito, P. Dario, and F. Cavallo, "Daily activity recognition with inertial ring and bracelet: An unsupervised approach," in *Proceedings-IEEE International Conference on Robotics and Automation*, pp. 3250–3255, 2017.
11. D. Riboni, T. Sztyler, G. Civitarese, and H. Stuckenschmidt, "Unsupervised recognition of interleaved activities of daily living through ontological and probabilistic reasoning," in *ACM Ubiquitous Computing*, pp. 1–12, 2016.
12. Y.-T. Chiang, K.-C. Hsu, C.-H. Lu, L.-C. Fu, and J. Y.-J. Hsu, "Interaction models for multiple-resident activity recognition in a smart home," *IEEE/RSJ 2010 International Conference on Intelligent Robots and Systems IROS*, pp. 3753–3758, 2010.

13. Y. Kim, J. An, M. Lee, and Y. Lee, "An Activity-Embedding Approach for Next-Activity Prediction in a Multi-User Smart Space," *2017 IEEE International Conference on Smart Computing (SMARTCOMP)*, 2017.
14. D. Gordon, J.-H. Hanne, M. Berchtold, A. A. N. Shirehjini, and M. Beigl, "Towards collaborative group activity recognition using mobile devices," *Mobile Networks and Applications*, vol. 18, no. 3, pp. 326–340, 2012.
15. A. Doryab and J. Togelius, "Activity recognition in collaborative environments," *The 2012 International Joint Conference on Neural Networks (IJCNN)*, pp. 10–15, 2012.
16. S. Schneegass, "SkullConduct: Biometric User Identification on Eyewear Computers Using Bone Conduction Through the Skull," *Conference on Human Factors in Computing Systems*, pp. 1–6, 2016.
17. B. Soewito, F. L. Gaol, E. Simanjuntak, and F. E. Gunawan, "Smart mobile attendance system using voice recognition and fingerprint on smartphone," in *2016 International Seminar on Intelligent Technology and Its Application, ISITIA 2016: Recent Trends in Intelligent Computational Technologies for Sustainable Energy*, pp. 175–180, 2017.
18. R. Cahyaningtiyas, R. Arianto, and E. Yosrita, "Fingerprint for automatic door integrated with absence and user access," in *2016 International Symposium on Electronics and Smart Devices, ISESD 2016*, pp. 26–29, 2017.
19. D. Triboan, L. Chen, F. Chen, and Z. Wang, "Semantic segmentation of real-time sensor data stream for complex activity recognition," *Personal and Ubiquitous Computing*, pp. 1–15, 2017.
20. D. Triboan, L. Chen, and F. Chen, "Towards a mobile assistive system using service-oriented architecture," *2016 IEEE Symposium on Service-Oriented System Engineering SOSE 2016*, vol. 21, no. 6, pp. 581–597, 2016.
21. D. Triboan, L. Chen, F. Chen, and Z. Wang, "Towards a service-oriented architecture for a mobile assistive system with real-time environmental sensing," *Tsinghua Science and Technology*, vol. 21, no. 6, pp. 581–597, 2016.
22. F. Bobillo and U. Straccia, "The fuzzy ontology reasoner fuzzyDL," *Knowledge-Based Systems*, vol. 95, pp. 12–34, 2016.
23. D. Triboan, L. Chen, F. Chen, "Fuzzy-based fine-grained human activity recognition within smart environments," in *2019 IEEE Smart World Congress*, Leicester, UK, 19–23 August, 2019. (Conference paper – accepted)
24. D. Triboan, L. Chen, F. Chen, S. Fallmann, and I. Psychoula, "Real-time sensor observation segmentation for complex activity recognition within smart environments," in *2017 IEEE 14th International Conference on Ubiquitous Intelligence and Computing (UIC 2017)*, 2017.
25. D. Triboan, L. Chen, F. Chen, and Z. Wang, "A semantics-based approach to sensor data segmentation in real-time activity recognition," *Future Generation Computer Systems*, vol. 93, pp. 224–236, 2019.
26. X. Jiang et al., "Ultrasonic fingerprint sensor with transmit beamforming based on a PMUT array bonded to CMOS circuitry," *IEEE Transactions on Ultrasonics, Ferroelectrics, and Frequency Control*, vol. 3010, pp. 1–1, 2017.
27. J. C. Kuo, J. T. Hoople, M. Abdelmejeed, M. Abdel-Moneum, and A. Lal, "64-Pixel solid state CMOS compatible ultrasonic fingerprint reader," *Proceedings of the IEEE International Conference on Micro Electro Mechanical Systems*, pp. 9–12, 2017.

28. Qualcomm, "Qualcomm announces advanced fingerprint scanning and authentication technology|Qualcomm," *Mobile World Congress Shanghai 2017*, 2017. Available: https://www.qualcomm.com/news/releases/2017/06/28/qualcomm-announces-advanced-fingerprint-scanning-and-authentication. [Accessed: August 19, 2017].
29. QualComm, "Fingerprint sensors|Fingerprint scanner phone security|Qualcomm." Available: https://www.qualcomm.com/products/features/security/fingerprint-sensors. [Accessed: August, 2017].
30. Y. Jiang et al., "e-Textile embroidered wearable near-field communication RFID antennas," *IET Microwaves, Antennas Propagation*, vol. 13, no. 1, pp. 99–104, 2019.
31. P. Lukowicz et al., "Textile building blocks: Toward simple, modularized, and standardized smart textile," in *Smart Textiles: Fundamentals, Design, and Interaction*, Springer International Publishing, Cham, Switzerland, pp. 303–331, 2017.
32. M. Guibert et al., "Washing reliability of painted, embroidered, and electro-textile wearable RFID tags," in *2017 Progress in Electromagnetics Research Symposium-Fall (PIERS-FALL)*, pp. 828–831, 2017.
33. R. Kronberger, U. Dettmar, C. Hudasch, R. Lerche, M. Cremer, and A. Pervez, "A transmitter beamforming system for the localization of passive RFID tags," in *2016 IEEE Radio and Wireless Symposium (RWS)*, pp. 252–255, 2016.

Chapter 9

BCRAM: A Social-Network-Inspired Breast Cancer Risk Assessment Model

Ali Li, Rui Wang, Liyuan Liu, Lei Xu,
Fei Wang, Fei Chang, Lixiang Yu,
Yujuan Xiang, Fei Zhou, and Zhigang Yu

Contents

9.1 Introduction

Breast cancer has become a common threat to women's physical and mental health. The global incidence of breast cancer has been on the rise since the late 1970s [1]. China is one of the countries with the fastest growth in breast cancer incidence. Data obtained from the WHO show that in 2012, a total of 167.7 million women worldwide were diagnosed with breast cancer, while in the same year, China had approximately 18.7 million new cases (which is approximately 12.2% of the worldwide total), ranking second in the world [2]. Thus, the prevention and treatment of breast cancer are urgent tasks. Scientists are currently researching the causes, treatment methods and other aspects [3].

Although the incidence of breast cancer is high, with the increase in the level of breast cancer care, the mortality rate of breast cancer has been declining year by year. The data provided by the WHO's cancer report show that a third of all cancers can be avoided. In the prevention and control of breast cancer, early detection, early diagnosis and early treatment can reduce mortality. Early detection is the first step in the prevention and control of breast cancer. At present, the methods of early detection mainly include large-scale screening or census forms, and clinical examinations, mammography and ultrasonography are utilized to conduct preliminary inspections [4]. Although these methods can facilitate early detection, there are still some difficulties in their implementation. First, the equipment in most community hospitals has performance problems, so it is not possible to effectively perform breast cancer screening. Second, population-based screening is not financially worthwhile, especially for a populous country like China. In Guangzhou, the cost for each early detected breast cancer was RMB 90,000 to RMB 284,000, depending on the age group, which is equal to one to three times the real GDP per capita of Guangzhou in 2010 (RMB 88,000) [5]. Therefore, we must consider how to implement early detection under the existing economic and national conditions. Reducing the screening scope may be an option, which means that some people, but not all, will be selected for breast screening.

The prevention and control of breast cancer usually can adopt a hierarchical form. The hierarchical prevention and control mode for breast cancer is shown in Figure 9.1. In Figure 9.1, the survey population who are healthy are marked in blue. Patients who have been diagnosed with breast cancer are marked in orange. According to the data from the survey population and patient samples, the breast cancer risk assessment model can assign some people to the breast cancer high-risk group, another to the breast cancer low-risk group. Here, we need to emphasize that the people in the breast cancer high-risk group are at a high risk of developing breast cancer and need to undergo early screening; the people in this group have not suffered from breast cancer

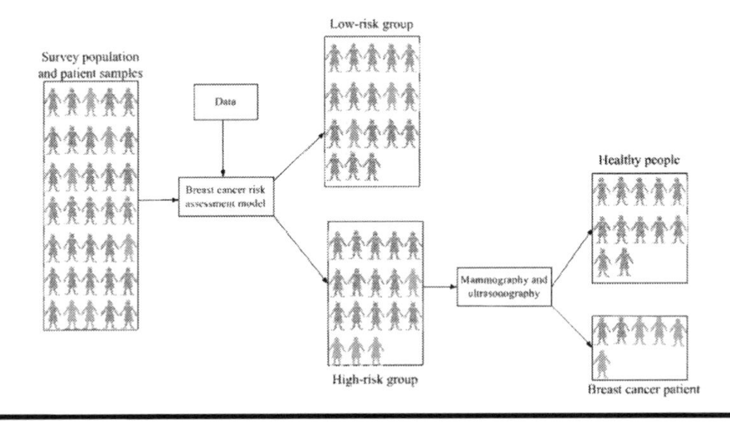

Figure 9.1 The hierarchical prevention and control mode for breast cancer.

previously. Thus, this high-risk group can also be called the early screening high-risk group. The people with high risk can undertake mammography and ultrasonography and then be confirmed as patients or not. If the people with high risk have not been confirmed as patients, they also can be given interventions and prevention. This breast cancer risk assessment model decreases the scope of screening, saves screening costs and contributes to the prevention and control of breast cancer. Therefore, researching the breast cancer risk assessment model is significant.

The contributions of the present paper are as follows: (1) a model based on medical social networks to assess breast cancer risk that is different from the existing model based on mathematical statistics method; (2) the unique design of the selection method for related risk factors of breast cancer that cause the model to have good generality and the ability to be generalized to other countries and regions; and (3) an experiment based on Chinese people indicates that the AUC and F-Measure of our model are better than those of various other models.

The paper is organized as follows. In Section 9.2, we review related works on existing risk assessment models and some emerging information technology for health and medicine. In Section 9.3, we introduce the idea of BCRAM and present the corresponding algorithm. In Section 9.4, we demonstrate the assessment value of BCRAM through experiments, present the results of a comparison with other models, and use follow-up data to show that a high proportion of people developing breast cancer were in the high-risk group, which means early warning has been given. Section 9.5 summarizes the paper.

9.2 Related Work

In this section, we will summarize the following related works: existing breast cancer risk assessment models and related information technology methods.

9.2.1 Existing Risk Assessment Models

In past decades, many empirical and statistical models have been developed to assess the lifetime risk of developing breast cancer. There are two types of model. One type is based on hereditary breast cancer and includes the Claus model, BRACPRO, BOADICEA, the Shattuck-Eidens model and breast cancer susceptibility gene (BRAC) analysis [6]. Another type is represented by the Gail model [7,8]; this type uses epidemiological factors to assess breast cancer risk. These models have proven to be effective for many women.

In China, breast cancer prevention started late, and there has not been an effective breast cancer prevention system. In our earlier research, we put forward a new model that is used to assess breast cancer risk [9,10], as well as the hierarchical prevention and control model for breast cancer. We also certified that the model has better assessment value than the Gail model for Chinese women. There are two other research models that are based on genetics [11,12]. Though screening efficacy has been improved because of the use of SNPs (mononucleotide polymorphisms), regional characteristics and genetic testing technology limit the application of these models at grassroots medical institutions, and the cost is high; therefore, these models do not meet the requirements of health economics. Therefore, these gene models cannot be widely used.

Gail, modified Gail [13], Tyrer-Cuzick [14] and our own earlier research use a statistical method and an equation to assess breast cancer risk. As in previous studies, mathematics modeling is a classic method. The mathematics modeling method is easy to realize. But this method also has shortcomings: (1) The essence of mathematical modeling is the data fitting, it is generally estimated and there is deviation, which may increase in the face of mass data. (2) The pathogenic factors of breast cancer are complex and diverse among different countries and regions. Living conditions and habits may be two of the risk factors that cause differences in breast cancer prevalence in different countries and regions. The fixed risk factors in the equation may lead to the poor generality of these models. Some researchers showed that the Gail model did not adapt well to world populations [15,16], including Chinese women. In the future, if the Gail model and other models are customized, they may gain good generality.

Therefore, a new model should consider solving the aforementioned basic problems, adopting a new method which can overcome some shortcomings of mathematical modeling, designing the selection method of related risk factor with breast cancer to make the model have good generality, and have better assessment value than existing risk assessment models.

9.2.2 Related Information Technology Methods

New information technologies have been developed, and people are trying to utilize these technologies to prevent and control diseases [17,18]. At present, research is being conducted on the big data of cancers, such as cancer data management and processing [19] and building an animated visualization tool to chart the association of cancers with other diseases over time [20]. However, existing methods for dealing with big data cannot be directly applied to breast cancer risk assessment.

In addition to medical image classification, in some research related to health, machine learning methods have been used, including supervised learning and unsupervised learning [21,22]. However, due to the complex causes of breast cancer, no specific standards are used to classify people into breast cancer high-risk and low-risk groups; therefore, traditional classification methods based on supervised learning are also not suitable for solving this problem.

The study of social networks originated in the early nineteenth century. The field of social networks studies how people are connected and the dynamics of their relationships within a specific community [23]. The concept of social networks has been applied to solve communication questions, e.g., mobile social networks and vehicular social networks; the concepts of community, game theory and other social characteristics have been widely applied. In addition, social networks have helped to solve some questions related to people's personal heath and public health [24–26]. In the research of social networks, scientists discovered that some social networks in the real world have community structure characteristics, e.g., the Karate club network. A community discovery algorithm can divide a social network into different groups based on connection strength. The connections among internal nodes in a community are relatively tight, but the connections between the various communities are relatively sparse [27]. The community structure reveals the common interests, hobbies or backgrounds of the social groups in the social network and serves as the inspiration for the proposed approach for breast cancer risk assessment.

In summary, at present, gene detection is expensive, and it is difficult to realize in a populous country such as China. The existing model based on epidemiological factors is not well adapted to Chinese women. Moreover, a model based on a new method which is different from the traffic mathematic method is urgently needed in our new big data era. Therefore, in the present paper, we put forward a new model, BCRAM, which is based on epidemiological factors. With the help of emerging information technologies, the model adopts a new method, one different from the traditional mathematical method, to construct a medical social network according to the similarities among people and discover the breast cancer high-risk group.

9.3 The Basic Idea and Algorithm of BCRAM

9.3.1 Basic Idea

Research shows that a woman who has a first-degree relative with a history of breast cancer has a high risk of developing breast cancer. Additionally, age at first parturition, menarche age, number of miscarriages, etc. are discovered to be related to breast cancer [28,29]. Researchers have used epidemiological factors to predict the risk of developing breast cancer in the future [9,30]. Here, we define each epidemiological factor related to breast cancer as a related risk factor (*rrf*). The set of all *rrf*s is represented as RRFo = (rrf_1, rrf_2, rrf_3, …, rrf_o), where o is the total number of *rrf*s.

In the medical field, some studies have discovered the role of similarity in disease [31]. Inspired by the idea, for epidemiological factors, we think that the greater the similarity in terms of *rrf* that a person may have with breast cancer patients, the higher that person's risk of developing the disease. All the people who have greater similarity with breast cancer patients form a high-risk group. The *rrf* similarity among people divides the people into different groups.

The idea of dividing people into groups according to similarity allows us to consider the community structure in a social network. The *rrf* of two people can be used to compute similarity; for example, if the age of two people is the same, the similarity value is high. Therefore, we can use the similarity values of people's *rrf* to construct the network. Here, the constructed network is called the medical social network to distinguish it from a traditional social network. The medical social network is built for the purposes of medicine and health analysis.

The medical social network is used to describe the similarity among people's *rrf*. It can be divided into different groups. The people who are located in a group with patients of breast cancer are identified as being at high risk, and they need to be screened early. The architecture of the model is shown in Figure 9.1. The first module is the data collection module, which is responsible for collecting data using many types of collection methods. The questionnaire is a common method and occupies an important position in early medical disease statistics. Today, with the development of wearable devices and body area networks, many types of medical data can be obtained easily [32,33]. The data can be obtained through inspection of hospital results and in other ways. The second module is the medical social network construction module. According to the collected data, the model computes the similarity of rrf_i, and then uses the similarity values to construct an unweighted or weighted medical social network. The third module is the group division module. The group division algorithm divides the medical social network into different groups and then discovers two groups, namely, the high-risk group and low-risk group, through some computing and applying the necessary threshold value.

9.3.2 BCRAM Algorithm

In the BCRAM realization algorithm, when different *rrf*s are used, the network construction and division methods are the same. The algorithm will iterate over many *rrf*s. In the beginning of the algorithm, the numbers of healthy people, breast cancer patients, and *rrf*s need to be initialized. In the iteration process, the input parameter initializations are different for each execution. The inputs of the *n*th execution will be the group division outputs of the ($n-1$)th execution. In the following pseudo-code description, we use only one rrf_m to describe the medical

Table 9.1 The Meanings of Symbols

Symbol	*Meaning*
M	The number of healthy people
P	The number of breast cancer patients
O	The total number of *rrfs*
GA	The group represented by the patients
GB	The group represented by the healthy people
$S_{rrf_m}(x,y)$	The rrf_m similarity of persons x and y
ΔQ_{GA}	The change in modularity (Q) that measures the quality of group division when node s is in GA

social network construction and group division method; later, we give an addition description of the realization process of BCRAM. The meanings of some symbols are shown in Table 9.1. Some symbols will be given more concrete interpretations later, e.g., Q and ΔQ.

Algorithm

Input: *M:* the number of healthy people, *P:* the number of breast cancer patients, $rrf_m \in$ RRFo (o represents the total number of *rrfs*)

Output: GA, GB

1: For $x = 1: (M + P)$
2: For $y = x = 1: (M + P)$
3: Compute $S_{rrfm}(x,y)$ $S_{rrfm}(x,y)$
4: *Endfor*
5: *Endfor*
6: Network G is built with S_{rrfm}
7: Group initialization, according to the rules, selects
8: two nodes p_i and M_j, $p_i \in GA, M_j \in GB$
9: For $s = 1$ to $(M + P)$
10: If $(s! = i$ and $s! = j)$
11: s moves to GA, compute ΔQ_{GA}, moves to
12: GB, compute ΔQ_{GB}
13: if $\Delta Q_{GA} > \Delta Q_{GB}$
14: s joins GA
15: Else

16: *s* joins GB
17: *Endif*
18: *Endif*
19: *Endif*

In steps 1–5, we compute the rrf_1 similarity between people. In step 6, the network based on rrf_1 is constructed. In steps 7–19, the network is divided into two intermediate groups. The division process will stop when all *rrf*s have been used, and many final groups will be generated. The flowchart of the algorithm is shown in Figure 9.2. According to the flow chat, the construction of medical social network and group division will be interpreted in detail.

9.3.2.1 The Construction of the Medical Social Network

The similarity value represents the closeness degree in terms of rrf_i between two people. Some approaches, such as Euclidean distance and cosine similarity measure, have been proposed to calculate the similarity of document data for recommendation systems. These methods are based on vectors, namely, they calculate the similarity between vectors. Here, rrf_i has only one value, so we use a simple method to calculate the similarity [34]: dividing the absolute difference between the two numbers by their maximum and subtracting this value from 1. For example, the rrf_i similarity between persons *x* and *y* can be expressed as (1). The value of $S_{rrf_i}(x,y)$ can be 0, 1 or $0 < S_{rrf_i}(x,y) < 1$.

$$S_{rrf_i}(x,y) = 1 - \frac{\text{abs}(x_{rrf_i} - y_{rrf_i})}{\max(x_{rrf_i}, y_{rrf_i})} \tag{9.1}$$

If rrf_i has only two values, i.e., 0 and 1 (in a real situation, it will be other values), according to equation (9.1), $S_{rrf_i}(x,y)$ is 0 or 1, and we can obtain an unweighted medical social network. For an unweighted medical social network, the people who

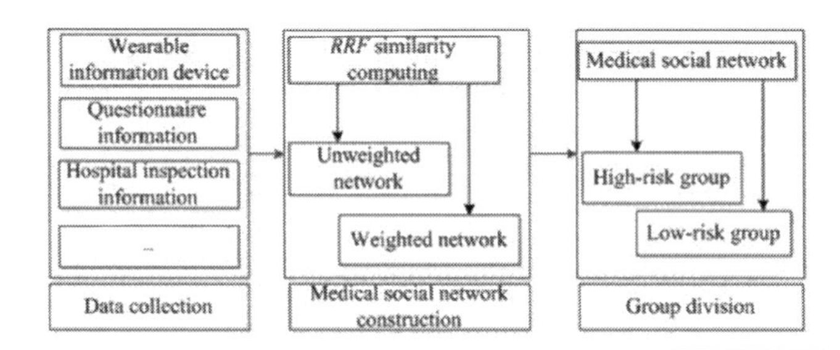

Figure 9.2 The architecture of BCRAM.

have the same value of rrf_i are in the same group. The network has two fully connected sub-graphs. For example, we construct a medical social network according to the family history of breast cancer. In our data source, the value for the family history of breast cancer is 1 or 2, which means that each person either has a family history of breast cancer or does not. Therefore, when two people each have a family history of breast cancer, $S_{rrf_i}(x, y) = 1$; this means that the two nodes are connected by an edge in the unweighted network. If the family histories of breast cancer are different for the two people, $S_{rrf_i}(x, y) = 0$; this means that the two nodes are not connected by an edge in the network.

If rrf_i includes more than two values, $Srrf_i\,(x,y) \in [0, 1]$, and we can obtain a weighted medical social network that can be represented as a matrix. The weights are the similarity values. The matrix and weighted network are shown schematically in Figure 9.3. In this schematic, $G = (5, 10)$. Based on a particular attribute rrf_i, $Srrf_i\,(0,1) = 0.9$, $Srrf_i\,(0,2) = 0.2$, $Srrf_i\,(0,3) = 0.2$ and $Srrf_i\,(0,4) = 0.9$. The network is undirected, so $Srrf_i\,(0,1) = Srrf_i\,(1,0) = 0.9$. Here, the value of S_{rrf} does not come from real data; the example is used only to interpret the structure of the weighted medical social network. When using real data, the value of S_{rrf} has more decimal places.

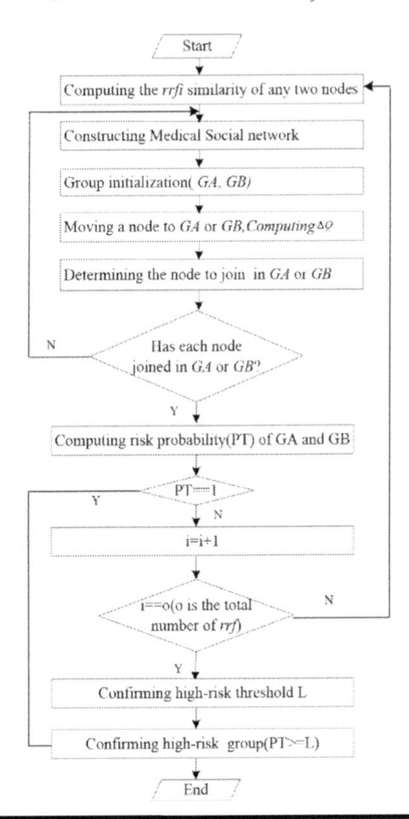

Figure 9.3 The flowchart of the BCRAM algorithm.

9.3.2.2 Group Division

For the constructed medical social network described above, we use a group division algorithm. According to the similarity, the group division algorithm will divide the medical social network into a high-risk group and low-risk group.

In the medical social network, there are breast cancer patients and healthy people. Here, the healthy people are the people whose breast cancer statuses have not been established through clinical diagnosis, whereas the patients are confirmed cases. All breast cancer patients belong to the set P. All healthy people belong to the set M. The breast cancer high-risk group is denoted as GA, and the low-risk group is denoted as GB. GA and GB need to be initialized. GA = {x| only one x is selected from P according to medical knowledge, that ensure P is a representative sample}. Here, the general method is referred to as the medical knowledge, which includes the patient's breast cancer family history and other pathological characteristics. Once the GA node is confirmed, GB can be expressed as (9.2). The minimum similarity indicates that x and y should be in different groups, namely, GA and GB.

$$\text{GB}= \{y \mid S_{rrf_i}(x, y) \text{ is minimum}, x \in \text{GA}, y \in M\} \tag{9.2}$$

First, through group initialization, GA or GB is a group, and each other node represents a group. A parameter needs to be used to measure the quality of group division. Q is the fraction of the edges that fall within the given groups minus the expected fraction if the edges were distributed at random. Q can be expressed as (9.3).

$$Q = \sum\nolimits_{i=1}^{c} (e_{ij} - a_i^2) \tag{9.3}$$

In equation (9.3), e_{ij} denotes the number of edges that connect groups i and j. a_i denotes the number of edges that connect group i.

Second, for all nodes except x and y, when a node i moves to the group GA or GB, the Q gain ΔQ is computed and can be expressed as (9.4).

$$\Delta Q = \left[\frac{\Sigma in + 2K_{i,in}}{2m} - \left(\frac{\Sigma tot + K_i}{2m}\right)^2\right] - \left[\frac{\Sigma in}{2m} - \left(\frac{\Sigma tot}{2m}\right)^2 - \left(\frac{K_i}{2m}\right)^2\right] \tag{9.4}$$

The first term is the Q value of a node moving into group z. z represents the group that node i will move to. Here, z is GA or GB. The second term is the Q value of a node being a group by itself, which means that it is not in group z. In this equation, Σin is the sum of the weights of the links inside group z, Σtot is the sum of the weights of the links incident to nodes in the group, k_i is the sum of the weights of the links incident to node i, $k_{i,in}$ is the sum of the weights of the links from node i to nodes in group z, and m is the sum of the weights of all the links in the network. The value of m can be expressed as (9.5).

$$m = \frac{1}{2}\sum_{ij} S_{sa}(i, j) \tag{9.5}$$

In equation (9.5), $S_{sa}(i, j)$ represents the weight of the edge between i and j. $\Sigma_{ij} S_{sa}(i, j)$ is the total weight of all links incident to node i. In an undirected graph, the weight of each link is computed twice. Therefore, the sum of the weights is half of $\Sigma_{ij} S_{sa}(i, j)$.

When the node moves to group GA, ΔQ is denoted as ΔQ_{GA}. When the node moves to group GB, ΔQ is denoted as ΔQ_{GA}. If $\Delta Q_{GA} > Q_{GB}$, the node joins group GA; otherwise, it joins group GB. Each node joins either GA or GB. In the entire model, GA and GB are only intermediate groups.

In GA or GB, by dividing the number of patients by the overall number of people, we can calculate the risk probability. The risk probability value is denoted as PT. Either the value of PT is 1 or the groups generated with rrf_o are called terminal groups. When the PT value of GA is equal to 1, GA is a terminal group, and only GB is considered as input and takes part in the next division; otherwise, both GA and GB will be used as inputs, and another *rrf* will be used to continue to divide the groups. The group division will continue until each *rrf* in RRF_0 has been used, and many terminal groups will be generated.

Finally, through the ROC curve (Receiver Operating Characteristic Curve), we can confirm the value of L as the high-risk probability threshold value. Therefore, if the PT value of a terminal group is equal to or greater than L, the terminal group is a high-risk group; otherwise, it is a low-risk group. Consequently, the breast cancer high-risk group is confirmed.

9.4 Implementation and Evaluation of BCRAM

To demonstrate the assessment value of BCRAM, we will use real data to perform experiments and analyze the experimental results. We set three tests. Test 1 will discover suitable RRF_0 to be used by BCRAM. Test 2 will compare the assessment value of BCRAM with that of some statistical models through the ROC curve and other assessment indexes. Test 3 will use follow-up data to further demonstrate the value of the model.

In the medical field, the sensitivity, specificity, FNR (False-negative rate, equals 1-sensitivity), FPR (false-positive rate, equals 1-specificity), F-measure, and ROC curve can be used to evaluate a risk assessment model.

When the sensitivity and specificity are used in a medical diagnosis, the sensitivity needs to be maximized, whereas the FNR needs to be minimized. The higher the sensitivity, the smaller the probability that actual breast cancer patients fail to be diagnosed. The specificity also needs to be as large as possible, which can guarantee that most healthy people are diagnosed properly. However, sensitivity and specificity are contradictory. Improving the sensitivity will decrease the specificity. Therefore, it is difficult to guarantee that all indexes are optimal. As we all know, the cost associated with the FNR is much higher than that associated with the FPR. Therefore, maximizing the sensitivity of the model is more important than maximizing its specificity. At the same time, for the breast cancer risk assessment model, if the value of specificity is very large (e.g., close to 1), the goal of discovering the high-risk group has not been realized. Of course, if the value is very small, all of the people are in the high-risk group, and most of the people are high risk. This is unreasonable, and the model has no meaning. Achieving a medium specificity value is appropriate. And the sensitivity should be as large as possible.

The ROC curve is a medical evaluation criterion based on sensitivity and specificity. The area under the ROC curve (AUC) is a popular measure for assessing the value of a model. The larger the AUC, the better the assessment value of the model. And the index is not influenced by no equilibrium data.

Here, because of our no equilibrium data, we will not use the accuracy index.

9.4.1 Data Source

We adopt real data that are collected through questionnaires. From questionnaire design to survey and data statistics, the entire process ensures data integrity and accuracy. The data collection is supported by a major project of the Ministry of Health medical clinical specialty.

Random samples were obtained through multi-stage stratified cluster sampling. The target population included 25- to 70-year-old females of the Han ethnic group with over two years of local residence and at least six months of local residence at the time of the survey. Long-term migrant workers, who left their hometowns for work, were excluded from this study. The provinces in eastern China where the Han ethnic group mainly resides, including Shandong, Jiangsu, Hebei and Tianjin, were selected as the survey provinces. Subsequently, counties or regions were randomly selected from each province. Finally, villages or communities were randomly selected from the sampled counties or regions, and women who met the study requirements were selected for the survey.

Data were collected through in-person interviews based on a self-designed structured questionnaire. The questionnaire included six aspects gathered from patient interviews: (1) demographic characteristics: age, marital status, education, occupation, household income, height, body weight, financial status and social status; (2) female physiological and reproductive factors: age at menarche, age at menopause, menstrual cycle history, childbearing history, breastfeeding methods, abortions or miscarriages, contraceptive methods and use of contraceptive medicine; (3) medical and family history: primarily breast-related diseases and family history of breast cancer; (4) dietary habits: frequency of the intake of various types of food; (5) lifestyle habits: smoking (including passive smoking), alcohol intake, tea intake, physical exercise and mental and psychological conditions (the items under psychological status were combined to calculate the overall life satisfaction and current life satisfaction scores); and (6) breast-cancer-related knowledge: risk factors for breast cancer and early signs and symptoms of the disease (the cumulative scores of the relevant items were counted as the related knowledge score and behavioral prevention score). The last component of the questionnaire was gathered from clinical breast exams and included the results from visual examinations, palpation and related diagnostic tests.

The investigation collected breast-health-related information from 124,758 women in the eastern part of our country, including three provinces, one city, nine counties/cities, 66 districts/towns and 373 villages/communities. These data are the initial data, and the collection was performed in 2008. Data on a total of 117,320 women were confirmed to use in the experiment, of which 320 were breast cancer patients. Later, in 2015, 14,652 people from Jiangsu province were followed up with, and 14,040 people are confirmed to use in the experiment.

9.4.2 Experiment Setting

Constructing a medical social network will require the storage of a large matrix. MATLAB, which has some advantages in terms of matrix operations, is used. When the number of people is very large, the scale of the medical social network is also very large. The CPU and memory demands will be high, and the processing speed may be slow. Therefore, the data can be divided into several groups. The running host is equipped with an 8-core Intel Xeon CPU running at 2.80 GHz and 8 GB of memory, and it is running the Windows Server 2008 OS.

Test 1: The test will determine the influences of different RRF_i (i is the total number of *rrf*) for BCRAM and discover a suitable RRF_0 to be used by BCRAM. Here, 5000 people are selected as one test group, in which there are 320 patients with breast cancer. A further 117,000 healthy people are divided into 25 test groups. Each group has 4680 healthy people and 320 patients.

We hope to select some *rrf*s and then use our method to discover a suitable RRF_0. The discovery of *rrf* is always in progress. Some *rrf*s have been certified in the medical field [30]. Breast cancer is related to biological factors and the family history of breast cancer; the research shows that women with first-degree relatives with breast cancer have a higher risk of breast cancer [28,29]. Personal history of benign breast disease increases the susceptibility to carcinogenic substances, and therefore there is a high risk of breast cancer in patients with benign breast disease [35]. Some research studies indicate that age at menarche, age of menopause, and other physiological factors are risk factors of breast cancer [36]. Moreover, age, age at first parturition, BMI, diabetes, miscarriage times, and current life satisfaction degree are risk factors for breast cancer [37–39]. In China, the breast cancer incidence rate in urban areas is higher than in rural areas, so residence is also a risk factor [40,41].

Therefore, these *rrfs* discovered in other research studies can be regarded as references for us and be used to confirm the candidate *rrfs* of the RRF_o. Lastly, the candidate factors are family history of breast cancer, personal history of benign breast disease, current life satisfaction degree, number of miscarriages, age at first parturition, BMI, age at menarche, age, diabetes, and residence.

Then, we set different RRF_i and discover suitable RRF_o that can make the model have the best assessment value. According to previous research, family history of breast cancer, personal history of benign breast disease, current life satisfaction degree and number of miscarriages have higher impacts on the disease than other *rrfs*, and therefore RRF4 uses these four factors. Then, we add other *rrfs* to acquire different choices of RRF_i, which are shown in Table 9.2.

Test 2: The test will compare the assessment values of the Gail, BCRAM, modified Gail and Tyrer-Cuzick models. The RRF_o will be selected according to the results of test 1. The test data are the same as in test 1.

Test 3: The test will evaluate the proportion of those identified for early warning that developed breast cancer in the follow-up data. In the initial data, there are 14,040 healthy people and 320 breast cancer patients. In the follow-up data, 35 people who are healthy in the initial data are confirmed to be breast cancer patients.

9.4.2.1 Test 1 Experimental Results and Evaluation

Test 1 discovers a suitable RRF_o to be used by BCRAM.

With different RRF_i, we use BCRAM to assess any of the 25 test data groups. Through the process of group division, many terminal groups are generated. In these groups, we use different threshold values to calculate the sensitivity and 1-specificity and draw the ROC curve. The ROC curve is shown in Figure 9.4. In Figure 9.4, when BCRAM is utilized with RRF4, the assessment result is the worst. However, the assessment result is the best with RRF8. These results indicate that adding factors can improve the assessment, e.g., the assessment result of RRF4 is obviously better than that of RRF5. In addition, the ROC curves with RRF9 and RRF10 are closer to that with RRF8 but do not improve with further factor addition. This indicates that constantly adding factors does not always improve the assessment results. The ROC curve indicates that RRF8 is the best selection for BCRAM.

Here, to certify the credibility of the result, we use the logistic method that is usually used in the medical field to acquire *rrfs* based on the same data. The specific process is: (1) using single-factor conditional logistic regression analysis to analyze all study variables with breast cancer one by one, and when $a = 0.02$, all statistically significant factors are analyzed; (2) on the basis of single-factor analysis, using multifactor conditional logistic regression analysis, and using stepwise regressive method to screen variables. Lastly, nine *rrfs* are discovered: age,

Table 9.2 The Selection of RRF_i

Symbol	*Concrete Related Risk Factors*
RRF4	Family history of breast cancer, personal history of benign breast disease, current life satisfaction degree, number of miscarriages
RRF5	Family history of breast cancer, personal history of benign breast disease, current life satisfaction degree, age at first parturition
RRF6	Family history of breast cancer, personal history of benign breast disease, current life satisfaction degree, number of miscarriages, age at first parturition, BMI
RRF7	Family history of breast cancer, personal history of benign breast disease, current life satisfaction degree, number of miscarriages, age at first parturition, BMI, age at menarche
RRF8	Family history of breast cancer, personal history of benign breast disease, current life satisfaction degree, number of miscarriages, age at first parturition, BMI, age at menarche, age
RRF9	Family history of breast cancer, personal history of benign breast disease, current life satisfaction degree, number of miscarriages, age at first parturition, BMI, age at menarche, age, diabetes
RRF10	Family history of breast cancer, personal history of benign breast disease, current life satisfaction degree, number of miscarriages, age at first parturition, BMI, age at menarche, age, diabetes, residence

family history of breast cancer, personal history of benign breast disease, current life satisfaction degree, number of miscarriages, diabetes mellitus, age at parturition, city/rural and BMI [9]. In two results, except age at menarche, the factors of RRF8 are included in the logistic result. This explains the credibility of RRF8. However, regarding which is better of the two results, a respective risk assessment will provide an answer.

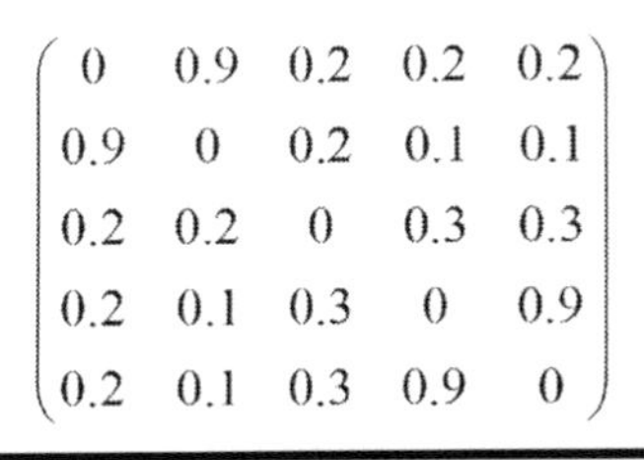

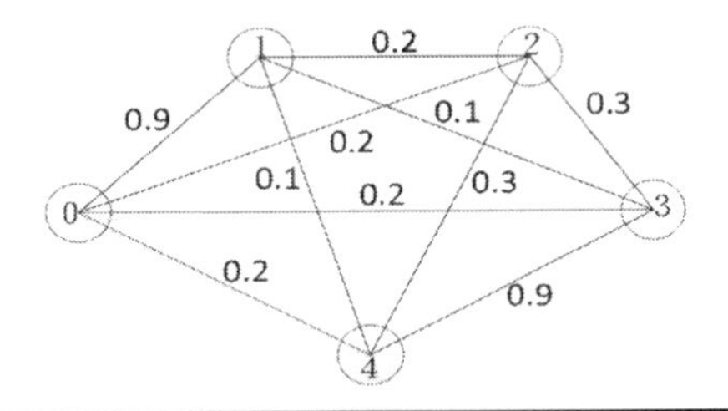

Figure 9.4 The weighted medical social network and matrix.

9.4.2.2 Test 2 Experimental Results and Evaluation

Test 2 compares the assessment value of some assessment models through the ROC curve and other assessment indexes.

We firstly give an introduction to the compared models. The Gail model uses age, age at menarche, age at first parturition, number of previous biopsies and number of first-degree relatives with breast cancer to assess breast cancer risk. The Gail model has been available for nearly 30 years and has been modified and applied to real patients. The model has reduced the mortality of breast cancer in the United States. In the medical field, the duration of use of the Gail model is long, and it is a classic model that has wide application. Many models have been put forward since the Gail model. Here, we select a modified version of the Gail model [13] and the Tyrer-Cuzick model for comparison with our model. The Tyrer-Cuzick model has been certified to have better assessment ability [42]. Compared with the Gail model, the modified model added three modifiable risk factors (alcohol consumption, leisure physical activity and body mass index). The analysis and data give perspective on the potential reductions in absolute breast cancer risk from preventative strategies based on lifestyle changes. The relative risk model (Rrm) uses the following *rrfs*: age at menarche, number of previous breast biopsies, number of first-degree female relatives with breast cancer, age at first live birth (Age1st), body mass index for women aged 50 years and older, body mass index for women younger than 50 years in age, alcohol consumption in three categories (never, current and former for women who stopped drinking at least 1 year before the interview), occupational physical activity at ages 30–39 years, leisure-time physical activity at ages 30–39 years, education level and age at interview. The Tyrer-Cuzick model incorporates the BRCA genes, a low penetrance gene and personal risk factors. The personal risk factors include age at menarche, age at menopause, age at first parturition, height, BMI, atypical hyperplasia and lobular carcinoma in situ. The last model is one we have put forward in earlier work [9,10]. Here, the model is marked as the Liu-Yu model.

The ROC curves of Gail, Rrm, BCRAM and Tyrer-Cuzick are shown in Figure 9.5. The ROC area (AUC) of Rrm is 0.694, the AUC of Gail is 0.574, the AUC of BCRAM is 0.785, the AUC of Tyrer-Cuzick is 0.694, and the AUC of Liu-Yu is 0.722. Therefore, the assessment value of BCRAM is the best. If the AUC value is between 0.7 and 0.9, then the model has high accuracy. The experimental results show that BCRAM is more adapted to Chinese women for breast cancer risk assessment and has certain assessment value.

In the ROC curve, the Youden index = sensitivity + specificity-1, and when the Youden index is largest, the assessment result of the model is best. The specificity, sensitivity, FPR, FNR and F-measure of each model are shown in Table 9.3 according to the node whose Youden index is largest in the ROC curve of each model. For BCRAM, we can see that the sensitivity and specificity values meet our goals. BCRAM can realize the largest sensitivity and smallest FNR. And the

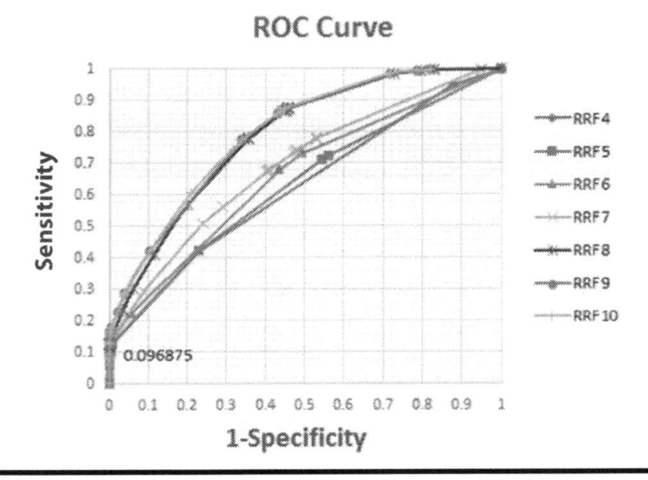

Figure 9.5 The ROC curves of different RRF_i.

Table 9.3 Other Indexes of the Five Models

Model	*FPR*	*FNR*	*Sensitivity*	*Specificity*	*F-Measure*
BCRAM	0.396	0.174	0.826	0.604	0.696
Gail	0.233	0.575	0.425	0.767	0.547
RRM	0.475	0.187	0.813	0.525	0.638
Tyrer-Cuzick	0.290	0.384	0.616	0.710	0.660
Liu-Yu	0.400	0.247	0.753	0.600	0.668

F-Measure index synthetically considers sensitivity and specificity, and therefore, the F-Measure value certifies that the BCRAM model has the best assessment value.

The value of specificity is 0.604, 1-specificity = 0.395. The result means that only 39.5% of healthy people need to undertake screening. The model decreases the screening scope and saves 60.4% cost. Therefore, the design of the model is significant.

Moreover, the AUC indicates BCRAM is more adaptive to Chinese women than other models. Therefore, the model is necessary for Chinese women.

9.4.2.3 Test 3 Experimental Results and Evaluation

Test 3 uses follow-up data to certify the early-warning value of the BCRAM model.

The tests use BCRAM to assess 14,040 healthy people and discover the high-risk group. The test uses 5000 people as a test group, which includes 4680 healthy people and 320 breast cancer patients. There are three test groups, and the result is the average of the three test groups. The ROC curves are shown in Figure 9.6.

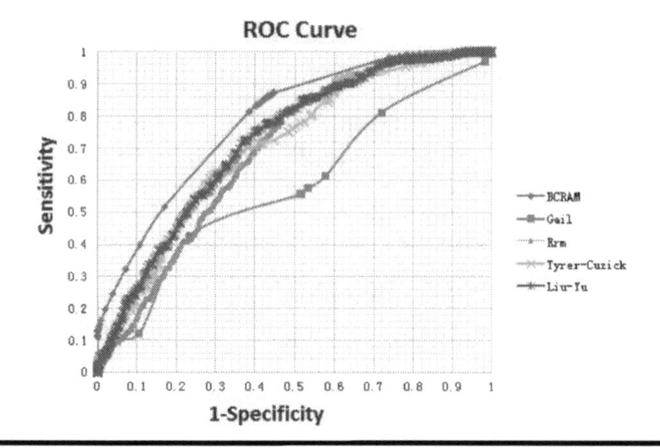

Figure 9.6 The ROC curves of Rrm, BCRAM, Gail and Tyrer-Cuzick.

In Figure 9.6, when sensitivity = 0.7125, 1-specificity = 0.2358, the Youden index is largest and the model has the best assessment value. Because the values of sensitivity and 1-specificity are acquired according to a certain threshold value L, L is 0.065 when the Youden index is largest.

In the follow-up data, 35 healthy people have been confirmed to be breast cancer patients. When we do not consider the accuracy of assessment of the initial data, we can use a different high-risk threshold value L to compute the high-risk group and identify the newly discovered patients in the high-risk group. The statistical results are shown in Figures 9.7 and 9.8.

Different values of L will result in different high-risk groups. When the value of L is smaller, more newly discovered patients are included in the high-risk group; of course, the number of people in the high-risk group is also larger. When $L = 0.065$, there are 1104 people in the high-risk group, and the model identifies 11 people who are newly discovered to be patients in the follow-up data. 31.43% of the newly discovered patients can be given early warning. Although $L = 0.065$, the assessment result is best, the value of early warning is not very high. Because of the need of early warning, we should choose a lower L value which will lead to a larger high-risk group. If we choose $L = 0.02676$, there are 2443 people in the high-risk group, and the model identifies 23 people who are newly discovered to be patients in the follow-up data. If we choose $L = 0.013$, there are 3414 people in the high-risk group, and the model identifies 30 people who are newly discovered to be patients in the follow-up data. In all, 85.71% of the newly discovered patients can be given early warning and sent for screening; at the same time, 27.05% of healthy people are identified as not needing to be screened, and the cost of screening them is saved. When we choose $L = 0.0076$, the model identifies 31 people who are newly discovered to be patients in the follow-up data. 88.57% of the newly discovered patients can be given early warning. If we choose $L = 0.0048$, more patients would

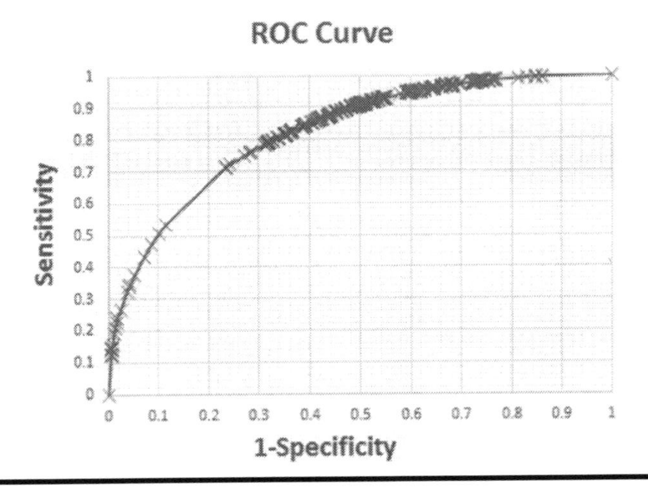

Figure 9.7 The ROC curve of gail and BCRAM based on 14,290 data points.

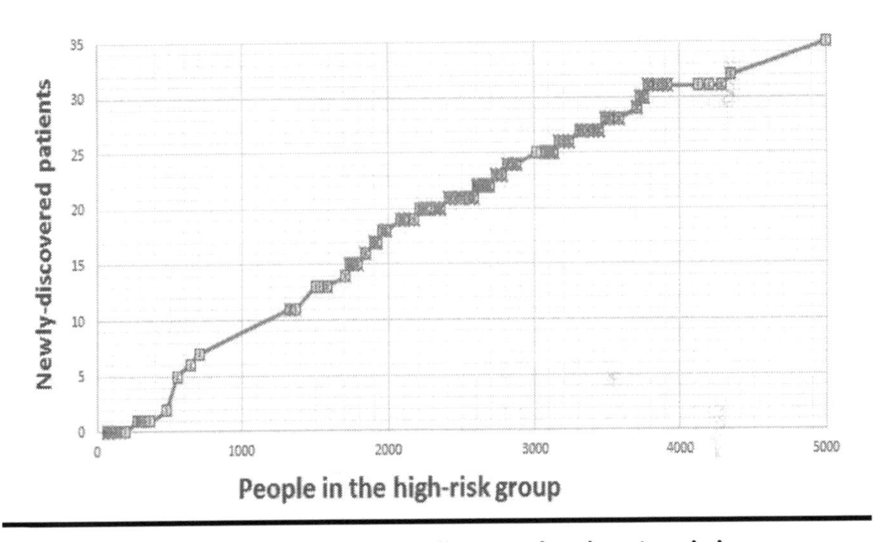

Figure 9.8 High-risk group and newly discovered patients' statistics.

receive early warning, there are 4030 people in the high-risk group, and the model identifies 32 people who are newly discovered to be patients in the follow-up data. In all, 91.4% of the newly discovered patients can be given early warning and sent for screening; at the same time, 13.89% of healthy people are identified as not needing to be screened, and the cost of screening them is saved. According to the result, when we choose $L = 0$, the high-risk group includes all healthy people and all 35 people who are newly discovered to be patients in the follow-up data. This means that all people will undergo breast screening, so BCRAM has no effect. If $L > 0$, not all 35 people who are newly discovered to be patients in the follow-up data can be included in the high-risk group; some people will be included in the low-risk group. That is, when we use BCRAM to assess breast cancer risk, the model cannot give 100% early warning to patients who are discovered to have breast cancer in the future. This is because not all patients have obvious risk factors. However, when we use the model to decrease the screening scope, through the low threshold *L*, the model can ensure early warning for a high proportion of newly discovered patients in the future.

All experimental results certify BCRAM is a meaningful approach in the prevention and control of breast cancer.

9.5 Conclusion

Scientists and doctors are working hard to realize "early detection, early diagnosis and early treatment," improve the survival rate of breast cancer and reduce the mortality. A breast cancer risk assessment model can assess whether a person is at high risk of developing breast cancer and construct a breast cancer high-risk group. The people who are in the high-risk group need to undergo further screening. Some existing risk assessment models have poor generality.

In this paper, we put forward BCRAM, which utilizes social network methods to assess breast cancer risk. BCRAM computes the similarity of *rrfs* and constructs a weighted or unweighted medical social network. Based on the constructed medical social network, a group division algorithm divides the network into two intermediate groups. After all *rrfs* in the RRF_0 are used, many terminal groups are generated. According to the high-risk probability value, all terminal groups are confirmed to be high-risk or low-risk groups. The people in the high-risk group have higher risk than those in the low-risk group. Lastly, we compare our model with the classic Gail model and Rrm model and demonstrate that the assessment value of BCRAM is better than that of the Gail, Rrm and Tyrer-Cuzick models.

BCRAM is used to discover the breast cancer high-risk group. The model has several advantages. (1) Risk factors are acquired through questionnaires, and the cost is low; therefore, it is suitable for use in developing countries. (2) It does not depend on fixed factors; the unique design of the method for selecting risk factors related to breast cancer provides the model with good generality, and it can be generalized to other countries and regions. (3) It can give early warning to a high proportion of patients who are discovered to have breast cancer in the future and is meaningful for the prevention and control of breast cancer.

In summary, the model realizes breast cancer risk assessment to discover breast cancer high-risk groups and helps to decrease the scope of screening. Therefore, BCRAM can contribute to the prevention and control of breast cancer.

References

1. J. Laurance, "Breast cancer cases rise 80% since seventies; Breast cancer," *The Independent*, 2006.
2. J. Ferlay, I. Soerjomataram, R. Dikshit, S. Eser, C. Mathers, M. Rebelo et al., "Cancer incidence and mortality worldwide: Sources, methods and major patterns in GLOBOCAN 2012," *International Journal of Cancer*, vol. 136, no. 5, pp. E359–E386, 2015.
3. C. Woolston, "Breast cancer: 4 big questions," *Nature*, vol. 527, no. 7578, pp. S120–S120, 2015.
4. K. Ganesan, U. R. Acharya, C. K. Chua, L. C. Min, K. T. Abraham, and K. H. Ng, "Computer-aided breast cancer detection using mammograms: A review," *IEEE Reviews in Biomedical Engineering*, vol. 6, pp. 77–98, 2013.
5. X. U. Juan, Q. Wang, M. A. Hong-Min, and J. H. Xia, "Primary efficacy of physical examination combined with ultragraphy and complemented with mammography for breast cancer screening," *Chinese Journal of Cancer Prevention & Treatment*, vol. 20, no. 17, pp. 1295–1299, 2013.
6. C. E. Jacobi, G. H. de Bock, B. Siegerink, and C. J. van Asperen, "Differences and similarities in breast cancer risk assessment models in clinical practice: which model to choose?" *Breast Cancer Res Treat*, vol. 115, no. 2, pp. 381–390, 2009.
7. M. H. Gail, L. A. Brinton, D. P. Byar, D. K. Corle, S. B. Green, C. Schairer et al., "Projecting individualized probabilities of developing breast cancer for white females who are being examined annually," *Journal of the National Cancer Institute*, vol. 81, no. 24, pp. 1879–1886, 1989.
8. J. P. Costantino, M. H. Gail, D. Pee, S. Anderson, C. K. Redmond, J. Benichou et al., "Validation studies for models projecting the risk of invasive and total breast cancer incidence," *Journal of the National Cancer Institute*, vol. 91, no. 18, pp. 1541–1548, 1999.
9. F. Wang and Z. G. Yu, "Current status of breast cancer prevention in China," *Chronic Diseases & Translational Medicine*, vol. 1, no. 1, pp. 2–8, 2015.
10. L. Liu, "A pilot study on risk factors and risk assessment score screening model for high-risk population of breast cancer," M.S thesis, School of Public Health, Shandong University, Jinan, China, 2010.
11. J. Dai, Z. Hu, Y. Jiang, H. Shen, J. Dong, H. Ma et al., "Breast cancer risk assessment with five independent genetic variants and two risk factors in Chinese women," *Breast Cancer Research: BCR*, vol. 14, no. 1, pp. R17(1–12), 2012.
12. W. Zheng, W. Wen, Y. T. Gao, S. Yu, Y. Zheng, J. Long et al., "Genetic and clinical predictors for breast cancer risk assessment and stratification among Chinese women," *Journal of the National Cancer Institute*, vol. 102, no. 13, pp. 972–981, 2010.
13. E. Petracci, A. Decarli, C. Schairer, R. M. Pfeiffer, D. Pee, G. Masala et al., "Risk factor modification and projections of absolute breast cancer risk," *Cancer Spectrum Knowledge Environment*, vol. 103, no. 103, pp. 1037–1048, 2011.
14. J. Tyrer, S. W. Duffy, and J. Cuzick, "A breast cancer prediction model incorporating familial and personal risk factors," *Statistics in Medicine*, vol. 23, no. 7, pp. 1111–1130, 2004.
15. R. K. Matsuno, J. P. Costantino, R. G. Ziegler, G. L. Anderson, H. Li, D. Pee et al., "Projecting individualized absolute invasive breast cancer risk in Asian and Pacific Islander American women," *Journal of the National Cancer Institute*, vol. 103, no. 12, pp. 951–961, 2011.

16. Y. C. Wen, W. S. Ong, P. H. Tan, N. Q. J. Leo, G. H. Ho, C. S. Wong et al., "Validation of the Gail model for predicting individual breast cancer risk in a prospective nationwide study of 28,104 Singapore women," *Breast Cancer Research*, vol. 14, no. 1, pp. 1–12, 2013.
17. G. Zheng, R. Shankaran, M. A. Orgun, L. Qiao, and K. Saleem, "Ideas and challenges for securing wireless implantable medical devices: A review," *IEEE Sensors Journal*, vol. 17, no. 3, pp. 562–576, 2017.
18. M. Piñol, R. Alves, I. Teixidó, J. Mateo, F. Solsona, and E. Vilaprinyó, "Rare disease discovery: An optimized disease ranking system," *IEEE Transactions on Industrial Informatics*, vol. 13, no. 3, pp. 1184–1192, 2017.
19. W. Xing, W. Jie, D. Tsoumakos, and M. Ghanem, "A network approach for managing and processing big cancer data in clouds," *Cluster Computing*, vol. 18, no. 3, pp. 1–10, 2015.
20. U. Iqbal, C. K. Hsu, P. A. Nguyen, D. L. Clinciu, R. Lu, S. Syedabdul et al., "Cancer-disease associations: A visualization and animation through medical big data," *Computer Methods & Programs in Biomedicine*, vol. 127, pp. 44–51, 2016.
21. P. Li, Y. Wang, Y. Tian, T. S. Zhou, and J. S. Li, "An automatic user-adapted physical activity classification method using smartphones," *IEEE Transactions on Biomedical Engineering*, vol. 64, no. 3, pp. 706–714, 2017.
22. S. Simons, D. Abasolo, and J. Escudero, "Classification of Alzheimer's disease from quadratic sample entropy of electroencephalogram," *Healthcare Technology Letters*, vol. 2, no. 3, pp. 70–73, 2015.
23. M. Fire, R. Goldschmidt, and Y. Elovici, "Online social networks: Threats and solutions," *IEEE Communications Surveys & Tutorials*, vol. 16, no. 4, pp. 2019–2036, 2013.
24. L. I. Besaleva and A. C. Weaver, "Applications of social networks and crowdsourcing for disaster management improvement," in *International Conference on Social Computing*, 2013, pp. 213–219.
25. J. Zhou, Z. Cao, X. Dong, X. Lin, and A. V. Vasilakos, "Securing m-healthcare social networks: challenges, countermeasures and future directions," *IEEE Wireless Communications*, vol. 20, no. 4, pp. 12–21, 2013.
26. H. Huang, T. Gong, N. Ye, R. Wang, and Y. Dou, "Private and secured medical data transmission and analysis for wireless sensing healthcare system," *IEEE Transactions on Industrial Informatics*, vol. 13, no. 3, pp. 1227–1237, 2017.
27. M. E. J. Newman, "Fast algorithm for detecting community structure in networks," *Physical Review E Statistical Nonlinear & Soft Matter Physics*, vol. 69, no. 6, pp. 066133–066133, 2004.
28. D. G. Evans, I. S. Fentiman, K. Mcpherson, D. Asbury, B. A. Ponder, and A. Howell, "Familial breast cancer," *Postgraduate Medical Journal*, vol. 64, no. 757, pp. 847–849, 1988.
29. K. Mcpherson, C. M. Steel, Dixon, and J. M, "Breast cancer—epidemiology, risk factors, and genetics risk factors for breast cancer," *BMJ*, vol. 321, no. 7261, pp. 624–628, 2000.
30. C. Meads, I. Ahmed, and R. D. Riley, "A systematic review of breast cancer incidence risk prediction models with meta-analysis of their performance," *Breast Cancer Research & Treatment*, vol. 132, no. 2, pp. 365–377, 2012.

31. K. Hu, J. B. Hu, J. Xiang, H. J. Li, Y. Zhang, S. Chen et al. Predicting disease-related genes by path-based similarity and community structure in protein-protein interaction network. Available: https://www.researchgate.net/publication/318652817_Predicting_disease-related_genes_by_path-based_similarity_and_community_structure_in_protein-protein_interaction_network.
32. S. C. Mukhopadhyay, "Wearable sensors for human activity monitoring: A review," *IEEE Sensors Journal*, vol. 15, no. 3, pp. 1321–1330, 2015.
33. T. Cruz, L. Rosa, J. Proença, L. Maglaras, M. Aubigny, L. Lev et al., "A cybersecurity detection framework for supervisory control and data acquisition systems," *IEEE Transactions on Industrial Informatics*, vol. 12, no. 6, pp. 2236–2246, 2016.
34. X. Chen, L. Zhang, and W. Li, "A network evolution model for Chinese traditional acquaintance networks," *IEEE Intelligent Systems*, vol. 29, no. 5, pp. 5–13, 2014.
35. W. Y. Chen, S. E. Hankinson, S. J. Schnitt, B. A. Rosner, M. D. Holmes, and G. A. Colditz, "Association of hormone replacement therapy to estrogen and progesterone receptor status in invasive breast carcinoma," *Cancer*, vol. 101, no. 7, pp. 1490–1500, 2004.
36. H. S. Feigelson, C. R. Jonas, L. R. Teras, M. J. Thun, and E. E. Calle, "Weight gain, body mass index, hormone replacement therapy, and postmenopausal breast cancer in a large prospective study," *Cancer Epidemiology and Prevention Biomarkers*, vol. 13, no. 2, pp. 220–224, 2004.
37. F. Resta, V. Triggiani, C. Sabbà, B. Licchelli, S. Ghiyasaldin, A. Liso et al., "The impact of body mass index and type 2 diabetes on breast cancer: Current therapeutic measures of prevention," *Current Drug Targets-Immune, Endocrine & Metabolic Disorders*, vol. 4, no. 4, pp. 327–333, 2004.
38. M. C. Pike, B. E. Henderson, J. T. Casagrande, I. Rosario, and G. E. Gray, "Oral contraceptive use and early abortion as risk factors for breast cancer in young women," *British Journal of Cancer*, vol. 43, no. 1, pp. 72–76, 1981.
39. Q. Zhang, L. Y. Liu, F. Wang, K. Mu, and Z. G. Yu, "The changes in female physical and childbearing characteristics in China and potential association with risk of breast cancer," *BMC Public Health*, vol. 12, no. 1, pp. 368(1–7), 2012.
40. L. Guixuan and J. Lichun, "Difference of clinical features of breast cancer between urban women and rural women in Yingkou area, Liaoning Province," *Chinese Journal of Cancer Prevention and Treatment*, vol. 11, no. 1, pp. 22–24, 2004.
41. L. Liandi, R. Keqin, and Z. Siwei, "Statistical analysis of data from 12 cancer registries in China, 1993–1997," *Bulletin of Chinese Cancer*, vol. 11, no. 9, pp. 497–507, 2002.
42. C. E. Jacobi, G. H. de Bock, B. Siegerink, and C. J. van Asperen, "Differences and similarities in breast cancer risk assessment models in clinical practice: Which model to choose?" *Breast Cancer Research & Treatment*, vol. 115, no. 2, pp. 381–390, 2009.

Chapter 10

Finite-Time Synchronization of Chaotic Memristive Multidirectional Associative Memory Neural Networks and Applications in Image Encryption

Weiping Wang, Xin Yu, Xiong Luo, and Jürgen Kurths

Contents

10.1 Introduction

Images play an important role in human life. With the rapid development of network communication, secure transfers of large amounts of image data have become a challenging task. Therefore, encryption technologies have become highly important tools. Recently, image encryption methods based on chaotic mapping have attracted the attention of many researchers in [1–4]. In [1], an encryption algorithm that uses the chaos-based S-BOX was developed for secure and speed image encryption. A visually meaningful image encryption scheme based on the lift wavelet transformation was proposed in [2]. In [3], a chaotic system–based image encryption scheme with identical encryption and decryption algorithm was analyzed. Meanwhile, the authors in [4] proposed a chaotic system for color image encryption by combining Logistic, Sine and Tent systems. Although the image encryption methods based on chaotic mapping have been widely developed, there are few studies of biological neural networks [5–12], especially for memristive neural networks (MNNs) [11,12]. The problem of image encryption based on chaotic neural networks was studied in [5–7] and the methods of image encryption based on the synchronization were showed in [8–10]. Meanwhile, the authors presented a novel image encryption scheme employing the memristive hyperchaotic system, cellular automata and DNA sequence operations in [11]. In [12], a new memristive chaotic system was presented, and its dynamical behaviors were analyzed. Therefore, an image encryption scheme based on memristive chaotic sequences is still a substantial topic.

Memristors have typical non-linear characteristics, and they are employed to replace the fixed-value resistors [13] in artificial neural networks to form MNNs [14–16]. In recent years, the dynamic behaviors of MNNs were analyzed in [17–19], where the dynamic behaviors have been widely applied to associative memory [20], medical image processing [21,22], etc. Meanwhile, memristive bidirectional associative memory neural networks (BAMNNs) have been extensively studied in [23–27]. In addition, as an extension of BAMNNs, MAMNNs are similar to BAMNNs in structure. MAMNNs were proposed by M. Hagiwara [28] and the dynamic behaviors of MAMNNs have attracted great attention of many researchers in [29–31]. The authors proposed a multi-valued exponential associative memory model in [29], and they analyzed the stability of this model. A discrete-time MAMNNs model with varying-time delays was formulated in [30], in which the global exponential stability of the system was analyzed. The authors devised a method in [31], which can accurately detect nodes able to exert strong influence over the multilayer networks. However, there exist few works in the literature about memristive MAMNNs. Thus, it is significant to study the dynamic behaviors of memristive MAMNNs.

It is generally known that time delays are inevitable in the hardware implementation of MNNs due to the switching of amplifiers. Various types of time delays, such as time-varying delays [32], distributed delays [33] and mixed delays [34], are often considered. Meanwhile, stability and synchronization of chaotic systems play an important role due to their potential applications to image encryption [5–12], secure communication [35], secure image transmission [36], intelligent data analysis [37], etc. However, in practical applications, it is desirable that a synchronization objective is realized in finite time. In recent years, some results on the synchronization of chaotic MNNs were obtained in [38–41], but there are few studies about the finite-time synchronization of memristive MAMNNs. Therefore, it is meaningful to analyze the finite-time synchronization of chaotic memristive MAMNNs.

Motivated by the above discussions, the main contributions of this paper can be summarized as follows:

1. We propose a novel memristive MAMNNs model with mixed time-varying delays. More precisely, the proposed model is investigated with time-varying delays and distributed delays.
2. We design two kinds of delay-independent and delay-dependent controllers to analyze the synchronization of the drive-response system.
3. Sufficient criteria guaranteeing the finite-time synchronization of the drive-response system are derived based on the drive-response concept and Lyapunov function.
4. With the removal of certain constraints on the weight parameters and discussion of the cases in detail, we obtain less conservative results for the synchronization of the drive-response system.
5. To illustrate the performance of the proposed criteria, an image encryption scheme based on chaotic memristive MAMNNs sequences is designed.

The rest of this paper is organized as follows. The proposed memeristive MAMNNs model with mixed delays is introduced with some preliminaries in Section 10.2. Sufficient criteria for ensuring finite-time synchronization of the drive-response system are described in Section 10.3. An image encryption method based on chaotic sequences of memristive MAMNNs is designed in Section 10.4. Numerical examples are discussed in Section 10.5, while Section 10.6 concludes this paper.

10.2 Model Description and Preliminaries

In this section, we introduce the following memristive MAMNNs with mixed delays:

$$\begin{aligned}\frac{dx_{ki}(t)}{dt} &= I_{ki} - d_{ki}\left(x_{ki}(t)\right)x_{ki}(t) + \sum_{p=1,p\neq k}^{m}\sum_{j=1}^{n_p} a_{pjki}\left(x_{ki}(t)\right)f_{pj}\left(x_{pj}(t)\right) \\ &+ \sum_{\substack{p=1,\\ p\neq k}}^{m}\sum_{j=1}^{n_p} b_{pjki}\left(x_{ki}(t)\right)f_{pj}\left(x_{pj}\left(t-\tau_{pjki}(t)\right)\right) \\ &+ \sum_{p=1,p\neq k}^{m}\sum_{j=1}^{n_p} c_{pjki}\left(x_{ki}(t)\right)\int_{t-\rho(t)}^{t} f_{pj}\left(x_{pj}(s)\right)ds,\end{aligned} \tag{10.1}$$

where $x_{ki}(t)$ denotes the voltage of the ith neuron in the field k, m is the total number of fields and n_p corresponds to the number of neurons in the field p. $d_{ki}\left(x_{ki}(t)\right)$, $a_{pjki}\left(x_{ki}(t)\right), b_{pjki}\left(x_{ki}(t)\right)$ and $c_{pjki}\left(x_{ki}(t)\right)$ denote the synptic connection weights. The time delays $\tau_{pjki}(t)$ and $\rho(t)$ are time-varying delays and distributed delay, respectively. $f_{ki}(x)$ is activation function. I_{ki} represents the external input constants of the ith neuron in the field k.

Throughout this paper, a column vector is defined as $col(x_{ki}) = (x_{11}, x_{12}, \cdots, x_{mn_m})^T$. $co[\underline{\xi}, \overline{\xi}]$ denotes the convex closure on $[\underline{\xi}, \overline{\xi}]$. In the Banach space, all sets of continuous functions are expressed as $C([-\tau, 0], R^n)$. Besides, the initial values of system (10.1) are given as follows: $\phi(s) = (\phi_{11}(s), \phi_{12}(s), \cdots, \phi_{mn_m}(s))^T \in C([-\tau, 0], R^n)$, in which $\tau = \max\limits_{1\leq p\leq m, p\neq k}\max\limits_{1\leq j\leq n_p}\{\tau_{pjki}(t), \rho(t)\}$.

Some notations are defined as follows:

$$\begin{gathered}\overline{d}_{ki} = \max\{\acute{d}_{ki}, \grave{d}_{ki}\},\ \underline{d}_{ki} = \min\{\acute{d}_{ki}, \grave{d}_{ki}\},\ \overline{a}_{pjki} = \max\{\acute{a}_{pjki}, \grave{a}_{pjki}\}, \\ \underline{a}_{pjki} = \min\{\acute{a}_{pjki}, \grave{a}_{pjki}\},\ \overline{b}_{pjki} = \max\{\acute{b}_{pjki}, \grave{b}_{pjki}\},\ \underline{b}_{pjki} = \min\{\acute{b}_{pjki}, \grave{b}_{pjki}\}, \\ \overline{c}_{pjki} = \max\{\acute{c}_{pjki}, \grave{c}_{pjki}\},\ \underline{c}_{pjki} = \min\{\acute{c}_{pjki}, \grave{c}_{pjki}\},\ 0 \leq \tau_{pjki}(t) \leq \tau_1,\ 0 \leq \rho(t) \leq \rho_1, \\ \dot{\tau}_{pjki}(t) \leq \tau_2 < 1.\end{gathered}$$

According to the features of memristors and the current-voltage characteristics, as well as the applied set-valued mapping theorem and the stochastic differential inclusion theorem, for convenience, we define:

$$co(d_{ki}(x_{ki}(t))) = \begin{cases} \acute{d}_{ki}, & |x_{ki}(t)| < \Gamma_{ki}, \\ co\{\acute{d}_{ki}, \grave{d}_{ki}\}, & |x_{ki}(t)| = \Gamma_{ki}, \\ \grave{d}_{ki}, & |x_{ki}(t)| > \Gamma_{ki}, \end{cases}$$

$$co(a_{pjki}(x_{ki}(t))) = \begin{cases} \acute{a}_{pjki}, & |x_{ki}(t)| < \Gamma_{ki}, \\ co\{\acute{a}_{pjki}, \grave{a}_{pjki}\}, & |x_{ki}(t)| = \Gamma_{ki}, \\ \grave{a}_{pjki}, & |x_{ki}(t)| > \Gamma_{ki}, \end{cases}$$

$$co(b_{pjki}(x_{ki}(t))) = \begin{cases} \acute{b}_{pjki}, & |x_{ki}(t)| < \Gamma_{ki}, \\ co\{\acute{b}_{pjki}, \grave{b}_{pjki}\}, & |x_{ki}(t)| = \Gamma_{ki}, \\ \grave{b}_{pjki}, & |x_{ki}(t)| > \Gamma_{ki}, \end{cases}$$

$$co(c_{pjki}(x_{ki}(t))) = \begin{cases} \acute{c}_{pjki}, & |x_{ki}(t)| < \Gamma_{ki}, \\ co\{\acute{c}_{pjki}, \grave{c}_{pjki}\}, & |x_{ki}(t)| = \Gamma_{ki}, \\ \grave{c}_{pjki}, & |x_{ki}(t)| > \Gamma_{ki}. \end{cases}$$

Obviously, $co\{\acute{d}_{ki}, \grave{d}_{ki}\} = [\underline{d}_{ki}, \overline{d}_{ki}]$, $co\{\acute{a}_{pjki}, \grave{a}_{pjki}\} = [\underline{a}_{pjki}, \overline{a}_{pjki}]$, $co\{\acute{b}_{pjki}, \grave{b}_{pjki}\} = [\underline{b}_{pjki}, \overline{b}_{pjki}]$ and $co\{\acute{c}_{pjki}, \grave{c}_{pjki}\} = [\underline{c}_{pjki}, \overline{c}_{pjki}]$, for $k, p = 1, 2, \cdots, m$, $p \neq k$, $i = 1, 2, \cdots, n_k$, $j = 1, 2, \cdots, n_p$. According to the above definitions, system (10.1) can be written as follows:

$$\begin{aligned} \frac{dx_{ki}(t)}{dt} \in {} & I_{ki} - co(d_{ki}(x_{ki}(t)))x_{ki}(t) + \sum_{\substack{p=1 \\ p \neq k}}^{m} \sum_{j=1}^{n_p} co\left(a_{pjki}\left(x_{ki}(t)\right)\right) f_{pj}\left(x_{pj}(t)\right) \\ & + \sum_{\substack{p=1 \\ p \neq k}}^{m} \sum_{j=1}^{n_p} co\left(b_{pjki}\left(x_{ki}(t)\right)\right) f_{pj}\left(x_{pj}\left(t - \tau_{pjki}(t)\right)\right) \\ & + \sum_{p=1, p \neq k}^{m} \sum_{j=1}^{n_p} \cos\left(c_{pjki}\left(x_{ki}(t)\right)\right) \int_{t-\rho(t)}^{t} f_{pj}\left(x_{pj}(s)\right) ds, \end{aligned} \tag{10.2}$$

or equivalently, there exist $\hat{d}_{ki}(x_{ki}(t)) \in co(d_{ki}(x_{ki}(t)))$, $\hat{a}_{pjki}(x_{ki}(t)) \in co(a_{pjki}(x_{ki}(t)))$, $\hat{b}_{pjki}(x_{ki}(t)) \in co(b_{pjki}(x_{ki}(t)))$ and $\hat{c}_{pjki}(x_{ki}(t)) \in co(c_{pjki}(x_{ki}(t)))$, such that

$$\begin{aligned} \frac{dx_{ki}(t)}{dt} = I_{ki} - \hat{d}_{ki}\left(x_{ki}(t)\right)x_{ki}(t) + \sum_{\substack{p=1,\\ p\neq k}}^{m}\sum_{j=1}^{n_p}\hat{a}_{pjki}\left(x_{ki}(t)\right)f_{pj}\left(x_{pj}(t)\right) \\ + \sum_{\substack{p=1,\\ p\neq k}}^{m}\sum_{j=1}^{n_p}\hat{b}_{pjki}\left(x_{ki}(t)\right)f_{pj}\left(x_{pj}\left(t-\tau_{pjki}(t)\right)\right) \\ + \sum_{\substack{p=1\\ p\neq k}}^{m}\sum_{j=1}^{n_p}\hat{c}_{pjki}\left(x_{ki}(t)\right)\int_{t-\rho(t)}^{t} f_{pj}\left(x_{pj}(s)\right)ds, \end{aligned} \tag{10.3}$$

In this paper, we consider system (10.2) or (10.3) as the drive system. Then the corresponding response system is described as follows:

$$\begin{aligned} \frac{dy_{ki}(t)}{dt} \in I_{ki} + \mu_{ki}(t) - \mathrm{co}\left(d_{ki}\left(y_{ki}(t)\right)\right)y_{ki}(t) \\ + \sum_{p=1,p\neq k}^{m}\sum_{j=1}^{n_p} co\left(a_{pjki}\left(y_{ki}(t)\right)\right)f_{pj}\left(y_{pj}(t)\right) \\ + \sum_{p=1,p\neq k}^{m}\sum_{j=1}^{n_p} co\left(b_{pjki}\left(y_{ki}(t)\right)\right)f_{pj}\left(y_{pj}\left(t-\tau_{pjki}(t)\right)\right) \\ + \sum_{p=1,p\neq k}^{m}\sum_{j=1}^{n_p} co\left(c_{pjki}\left(y_{ki}(t)\right)\right)\int_{t-\rho(t)}^{t} f_{pj}\left(y_{pj}(s)\right)ds, \end{aligned} \tag{10.4}$$

or equivalently, there exist $\hat{d}_{ki}(y_{ki}(t)) \in co(d_{ki}(y_{ki}(t)))$, $\hat{a}_{pjki}(y_{ki}(t)) \in co(a_{pjki}(y_{ki}(t)))$, $\hat{b}_{pjki}(y_{ki}(t)) \in co(b_{pjki}(y_{ki}(t)))$ and $\hat{c}_{pjki}(y_{ki}(t)) \in co(c_{pjki}(y_{ki}(t)))$, such that

$$\begin{aligned} \frac{dy_{ki}(t)}{dt} = I_{ki} + \mu_{ki}(t) - \hat{d}_{ki}\left(y_{ki}(t)\right)y_{ki}(t) \sum_{p=1,p\neq k}^{m}\sum_{j=1}^{n_p}\hat{a}_{pjki}\left(y_{ki}(t)\right)f_{pj}\left(y_{pj}(t)\right) \\ + \sum_{p=1,p\neq k}^{m}\sum_{j=1}^{n_p}\hat{b}_{pjki}\left(y_{ki}(t)\right)f_{pj}\left(y_{pj}\left(t-\tau_{pjki}(t)\right)\right) \\ + \sum_{p=1,p\neq k}^{m}\sum_{j=1}^{n_p}\hat{c}_{pjki}\left(y_{ki}(t)\right)\int_{t-\rho(t)}^{t} f_{pj}\left(y_{pj}(s)\right)ds, \end{aligned} \tag{10.5}$$

where $\mu_{ki}(t)$ represent the appropriate control inputs and

$$co(d_{ki}(y_{ki}(t))) = \begin{cases} \acute{d}_{ki}, & |y_{ki}(t)| < \Gamma_{ki}, \\ co\{\acute{d}_{ki}, \grave{d}_{ki}\}, & |y_{ki}(t)| = \Gamma_{ki}, \\ \grave{d}_{ki}, & |y_{ki}(t)| > \Gamma_{ki}, \end{cases}$$

$$co(a_{pjki}(y_{ki}(t))) = \begin{cases} \acute{a}_{pjki}, & |y_{ki}(t)| < \Gamma_{ki}, \\ co\{\acute{a}_{pjki}, \grave{a}_{pjki}\}, & |y_{ki}(t)| = \Gamma_{ki}, \\ \grave{a}_{pjki}, & |y_{ki}(t)| > \Gamma_{ki}, \end{cases}$$

$$co(b_{pjki}(y_{ki}(t))) = \begin{cases} \acute{b}_{pjki}, & |y_{ki}(t)| < \Gamma_{ki}, \\ co\{\acute{b}_{pjki}, \grave{b}_{pjki}\}, & |y_{ki}(t)| = \Gamma_{ki}, \\ \grave{b}_{pjki}, & |y_{ki}(t)| > \Gamma_{ki}, \end{cases}$$

$$co(c_{pjki}(y_{ki}(t))) = \begin{cases} \acute{c}_{pjki}, & |y_{ki}(t)| < \Gamma_{ki}, \\ co\{\acute{c}_{pjki}, \grave{c}_{pjki}\}, & |y_{ki}(t)| = \Gamma_{ki}, \\ \grave{c}_{pjki}, & |y_{ki}(t)| > \Gamma_{ki}. \end{cases}$$

The initial values of system (10.4) are given as follows: $\Phi(s)=(\Phi_{11}(s),\Phi_{12}(s),\cdots,\Phi_{mn_m}(s))^T \in C([-\tau,0],R^n)$ in which $\tau = \max\{\tau_1,\rho_1\}$.

We define the synchronization errors of the system as follows:

$$e_{ki}(t) = y_{ki}(t) - x_{ki}(t),$$

where the initial values are defined as follows: $\Psi(s)=\Phi(s)-\phi(s)=(\Psi_{11}(s),\Psi_{12}(s),\cdots,\Psi_{21}(s),\cdots,\Psi_{mn_m}(s))^T \in C([-\tau,0],R^n)$, in which $\tau = \max\{\tau_1,\rho_1\}$.

Assumption 10.1:

For $k = 1,2,\cdots,m$, $i = 1,2,\cdots,n_k$, $\forall s_1, s_2 \in R$ and $s_1 \neq s_2$, the activation function $f_{ki}(\cdot)$ is odd bounded and satisfies the Lipschitz condition.

$$|f_{ki}(s_1) - f_{ki}(s_2)| \leq L_{ki}|s_1 - s_2|, |f_{ki}(\cdot)| \leq F,$$

where L_{ki} and F are nonnegative constants.

Definition 10.1:

The response system is said to be synchronized with drive system in finite time, if under a suitable controller, there exists a constant $T>0$ such that $\lim_{t\to T} e_{ki}(t)=0$ and $e_{ki}(t)\equiv 0$, for $t\geq T$, where T is called the setting time.

Lemma 10.1:

(Chain Rule). Suppose that $V(x):R^n\to R$ is C-regular and $x(t):[0,+\infty)\to R$ is absolutely continuous on any compact subinterval of $[0,+\infty)$. Then $V(x(t)):[0,+\infty)\to R$ is differentiable for a.a.t $\in[0,+\infty)$, and we have

$$\frac{dV(x(t))}{dt}=\varpi(t)\dot{x}(t), \forall\varpi(t)\in\partial V(x(t)).$$

Lemma 10.2:

Assume that a continuous, positive-definite function $V(t)$ and real numbers $h>0$ and $0<\eta<1$, such that

$$\dot{V}(t)\leq -hV^{\eta}(t), t\geq t_0, V(t)\geq 0.$$

Then the synchronization error system is finite-time stable, i.e., $V(t)$ satisfies

$$V^{1-\eta}(t)\leq V^{1-\eta}(t_0)-h(1-\eta)(t-t_0),\quad t_0\leq t\leq T,$$

and $V(t)\equiv 0$ for $\forall t\geq T$, with the setting time T given by

$$T=t_0+\frac{V^{1-\eta}(t_0)}{h(1-\eta)}.$$

10.3 Main Results

In this section, some sufficient criteria guaranteeing the synchronization of the drive-response system are derived.

10.3.1 Delay-Independent Controller

In this subsection, we investigate the synchronization of the drive system (10.2) and the response system (10.4) with mixed delays. We design a delay-independent controller as follows:

$$\mu_{ki}(t) = -\delta_{ki}e_{ki}(t) - \theta_{ki}sign(e_{ki}(t)) - \frac{1}{2}sign(e_{ki}(t))h\,|\,e_{ki}(t)\,|^{\eta-1}, \tag{10.6}$$

where δ_{ki} and θ_{ki} are constants determined later, and the real numbers h and η satisfy $h > 0$ and $0 < \eta < 1$.

Theorem 10.1:

Suppose that Assumption 10.1 holds. Then under the control law (10.6), the response system (10.4) can synchronize with the drive system (10.2) in finite time

$$T = \frac{[V(0)]^{1-\eta}}{h(1-\eta)},$$

where

$$\delta_{ki} \geq \max\left\{\begin{array}{l} -\acute{d}_{ki} + \frac{1}{2}\sum_{p=1,p\neq k}^{m}\sum_{j=1}^{n_p}\left[\acute{a}^2_{pjki}L^2_{pj} + 1 + \acute{b}^2_{pjki}L^2_{pj} + \rho_1\acute{c}^2_{pjki}L^2_{pj} + \frac{1}{1-\tau_2} + \rho_1\right], \\ -\grave{d}_{ki} + \frac{1}{2}\sum_{p=1,p\neq k}^{m}\sum_{j=1}^{n_p}\left[\grave{a}^2_{pjki}L^2_{pj} + 1 + \grave{b}^2_{pjki}L^2_{pj} + \rho_1\grave{c}^2_{pjki}L^2_{pj} + \frac{1}{1-\tau_2} + \rho_1\right] \end{array}\right\},$$

$$\theta_{ki} \geq \left|\acute{d}_{ki} - \grave{d}_{ki}\right|\Gamma_{ki} + \sum_{p=1,p\neq k}^{m}\sum_{j=1}^{n_p}\left[\left|\acute{a}_{pjki} - \grave{a}_{pjki}\right|L_{pj}\Gamma_{pj} + \left|\acute{b}_{pjki} - \grave{b}_{pjki}\right|F + \left|\acute{c}_{pjki} - \grave{c}_{pjki}\right|\rho_1 F\right],$$

$$V(0) = e^2_{ki}(0) + \frac{1}{1-\tau_2}\sum_{p=1,p\neq k}^{m}\sum_{j=1}^{n_p}\left[\int_{-\tau_{pjki}(0)}^{0} e^2_{pj}(s)ds\right]$$
$$+\sum_{p=1,p\neq k}^{m}\sum_{j=1}^{n_p}\left[\int_{-\rho_1}^{0}\int_{s}^{0} e^2_{pj}dzds\right], h > 0, 0 < \eta < 1.$$

Proof 1:

Please see Appendix A.

Corollary 10.1:

Suppose that Assumption 10.1 holds. Then under the control law (10.6), the response system (10.4) can synchronize with the drive system (10.2) in finite time

$$T = \frac{[V(0)]^{1-\eta}}{h(1-\eta)},$$

where

$$\delta_{ki} \geq \max\left\{ \begin{array}{l} -\acute{d}_{ki} + \frac{1}{2}\sum_{p=1,p\neq k}^{m}\sum_{j=1}^{n_p}\left[\acute{a}_{pjki}^{2} L_{pj}^2 + 1 + \acute{b}_{pjki}^{2} L_{pj}^2 + \frac{1}{1-\tau_2}\right], \\ -\grave{d}_{ki} + \frac{1}{2}\sum_{p=1,p\neq k}^{m}\sum_{j=1}^{n_p}\left[\grave{a}_{pjki}^{2} L_{pj}^2 + 1 + \grave{b}_{pjki}^{2} L_{pj}^2 + \frac{1}{1-\tau_2}\right] \end{array} \right\},$$

$$\theta_{ki} \geq \left|\acute{d}_{ki} - \grave{d}_{ki}\right|\Gamma_{ki} + \sum_{p=1,p\neq k}^{m}\sum_{j=1}^{n_p}\left[\left|\acute{a}_{pjki} - \grave{a}_{pjki}\right| L_{pj}\Gamma_{pj} + \left|\acute{b}_{pjki} - \grave{b}_{pjki}\right| F\right],$$

$$V(0) = e_{ki}^2(0) + \frac{1}{1-\tau_2}\sum_{p=1,p\neq k}^{m}\sum_{j=1}^{n_p}\left[\int_{-\tau_{pjki}(0)}^{0} e_{pj}^2(s)ds\right], h > 0, 0 < \eta < 1.$$

Proof:

Please see Appendix A.

Let the distributed delay $\rho(t) = 0$. The process of the proof is similar to Theorem 10.1, so it is omitted here.

Remark 10.1:

There are some previous related works about synchronization of MNNs under the following conditions [42,43].

$$co[\underline{d}_{ki}, \bar{d}_{ki}]y_{pj}(t) - co[\underline{d}_{ki}, \bar{d}_{ki}]x_{pj}(t) \subseteq co[\underline{d}_{ki}, \bar{d}_{ki}](y_{pj}(t) - x_{pj}(t)),$$

$$co[\underline{a}_{pjki}, \bar{a}_{pjki}]f_{pj}(y_{pj}(t))$$
$$- co[\underline{a}_{pjki}, \bar{a}_{pjki}]f_{pj}(x_{pj}(t)) \subseteq co[\underline{a}_{pjki}, \bar{a}_{pjki}](f_{pj}(y_{pj}(t)) - f_{pj}(x_{pj}(t))),$$

$$co[\underline{b}_{pjki},\overline{b}_{pjki}]f_{pj}(y_{pj}(t-\tau_{pjki}(t)))-co[\underline{b}_{pjki},\overline{b}_{pjki}]f_{pj}(x_{pj}(t-\tau_{pjki}(t)))$$
$$\subseteq co[\underline{b}_{pjki},\overline{b}_{pjki}](f_{pj}(y_{pj}(t-\tau_{pjki}(t)))-f_{pj}(x_{pj}(t-\tau_{pjki}(t)))),$$
$$co[\underline{c}_{pjki},\overline{c}_{pjki}]\int_{t-\rho(t)}^{t}f_{pj}(y_{pj}(s))ds-co[\underline{c}_{pjki},\overline{c}_{pjki}]\int_{t-\rho(t)}^{t}f_{pj}(x_{pj}(s))ds$$
$$\subseteq co[\underline{c}_{pjki},\overline{c}_{pjki}](\int_{t-\rho(t)}^{t}f_{pj}(y_{pj}(s))ds-\int_{t-\rho(t)}^{t}f_{pj}(x_{pj}(s))ds).$$

It is easily checked that when $x_{ki}(t)$ and $y_{ki}(t)$ have same signs, or $x_{ki}(t)=0$ or $y_{ki}(t)=0$, the above conditions hold. Moreover, the results obtained in [42,43] are independent on the switching jumps Γ_{ki}. Hence, in this paper, with the removal of these strict conditions, the results we obtained are less conservative.

Remark 10.2:

In the controllers 6, the discontinuous terms $sign(e_{ki}(t))$ may be undesirable in some practical applications. In this case, the continuous terms $\frac{e_{ki}(t)}{|e_{ki}(t)|+a}$ can be chosen as approximations of $sign(e_{ki}(t))$, in which $a>0$ is sufficiently small.

10.3.2 Delay-Dependent Controller

In this subsection, we investigate the synchronization of the drive system (10.2) and the response system (10.2) with mixed delays. We design a delay-dependent controller as follows:

$$\begin{aligned}\mu_{ki}(t)=&-\delta_{ki}e_{ki}(t)-\theta_{ki}sign(e_{ki}(t))\left|e_{pj}(t-\tau_{pjki}(t))\right|\\&-\varepsilon_{ki}sign(e_{ki}(t))\left|\int_{t-\rho(t)}^{t}e_{pj}(s)ds\right|-sign(e_{ki}(t))(\gamma_{ki}+h\,|\,e_{ki}(t)|^{\eta}),\end{aligned}\tag{10.7}$$

where δ_{ki}, θ_{ki}, ε_{ki} and γ_{ki} are constants determined later, real numbers h and η satisfy $h>0$ and $0<\eta<1$.

Theorem 10.2:

Suppose that Assumption 10.1 holds. Then under the control law (10.7), the response system (10.4) can synchronize with the drive system (10.2) in finite time

$$T=\frac{[V(0)]^{1-\eta}}{h(1-\eta)},$$

where

$$\delta_{ki} \geq \max\left\{ \sum_{p=1, p\neq k}^{m} \sum_{j=1}^{n_p} \left[-\acute{d}_{ki} + \grave{a}_{pjki} L_{pj}, -\acute{d}_{ki} + \grave{a}_{pjki} L_{pj} \right] \right\},$$

$$\theta_{ki} \geq \max \sum_{p=1, p\neq k}^{m} \sum_{j=1}^{n_p} \left\{ \acute{b}_{pjki} L_{pj}, \grave{b}_{pjki} L_{pj} \right\}, \ \varepsilon_{ki} \geq \max \sum_{p=1, p\neq k}^{m} \sum_{j=1}^{n_p} \left\{ \acute{c}_{pjki} L_{pj}, \grave{c}_{pjki} L_{pj} \right\},$$

$$\gamma_{ki} > \left| \acute{d}_{ki} - \grave{d}_{ki} \right| \Gamma_{ki}$$

$$+ \sum_{p=1, p\neq k}^{m} \sum_{j=1}^{n_p} \left[\left| \acute{a}_{pjki} - \grave{a}_{pjki} \right| L_{pj} \Gamma_{pj} + \left| \acute{b}_{pjki} - \grave{b}_{pjki} \right| F + \left| \acute{c}_{pjki} - \grave{c}_{pjki} \right| \rho_1 F \right],$$

$$h > 0, 0 < \eta < 1, V(0) = sign(e_{ki}(0)) e_{ki}(0).$$

Proof:

Please see Appendix B.

Corollary 10.2:

Suppose that Assumption 10.1 holds. Then under the control law

$$\mu_{ki}(t) = -\delta_{ki} e_{ki}(t) - \theta_{ki} sign(e_{ki}(t)) \,|\, e_{pj}(t - \tau_{pjki}(t)) \,| - sign(e_{ki}(t))(\gamma_{ki} + h \,|\, e_{ki}(t) \,|^{\eta}),$$

the response system (10.4) can synchronize with the drive system (10.2) in finite time

$$T = \frac{[V(0)]^{1-\eta}}{h(1-\eta)},$$

where

$$\delta_{ki} \geq \max \sum_{p=1, p\neq k}^{m} \sum_{j=1}^{n_p} \left\{ -\acute{d}_{ki} + \acute{a}_{pjki} L_{pj}, -\grave{d}_{ki} + \grave{a}_{pjki} L_{pj} \right\},$$

$$\theta_{ki} \geq \max \sum_{p=1, p\neq k}^{m} \sum_{j=1}^{n_p} \left\{ \acute{b}_{pjki} L_{pj}, \grave{b}_{pjki} L_{pj} \right\},$$

$$\gamma_{ki} > \left| \acute{d}_{ki} - \grave{d}_{ki} \right| \Gamma_{ki} + \sum_{p=1,p\neq k}^{m} \sum_{j=1}^{n_p} \left[\left| \acute{a}_{pjki} - \grave{a}_{pjki} \right| L_{pj} \Gamma_{pj} + \left| \acute{b}_{pjki} - \grave{b}_{pjki} \right| F \right],$$

$$h > 0, 0 < \eta < 1, V(0) = sign(e_{ki}(0))e_{ki}(0).$$

Proof:

Let the distributed delay $\rho(t) = 0$. The process of the proof is similar to Theorem 10.2, so it is omitted here.

Remark 10.3:

Theorem 10.1 takes into account the influence of delay-independent controllers on system synchronization, while Theorem 10.2 considers the influence of delay-dependent controllers on system stability. The two theorems show the importance of controllers for the system synchronization.

Remark 10.4:

Due to the state of the neuron it is not only related to itself, but also the changes in the neuron associated with it will have an impact on it. Therefore, in Theorem 10.2, we consider the delay-dependent control strategy.

10.4 Image Encryption

Image encryption technologies play an important role in transmitting large amounts of image data. In this section, we propose an image encryption algorithm based on the chaotic memristive MAMNNs obtained in Main Results. The specific steps of the algorithm are as follows:

1. Read the original color image, its size is $m * n * 3$.
2. Use the Mchange and Nchange functions to perform row permutation and column permutation for the image, respectively.
3. Trichromatic separation.
   - The R, G and B components of the image are separated, and their respective matrices are $I_R = image(:,:,1)$, $I_G = image(:,:,2)$ and $I_B = image(:,:,3)$ respectively.
4. Generate three chaotic sequences.
   - According to the Corollary 10.1, we choose appropriate parameters and layers of the drive system, then we obtain three chaotic sequences $yint(1, m * n)$, $yint(2, m * n)$ and $yint(3, m * n)$ from different fields of memristive MAMNNs, respectively.

Table 10.1 Chaotic Sequence $yint(j,m*n)$

*Chaotic Sequence yint(j,m * n)*

x=zeros(3,m*n);
for j=1:3
  for i=1:m*n
    if round(10*yint(j, i))<10*yint(j, i)
      x(j, i)=mod(round(10⁸*(10*yint(j, i)-round(10*yint(j, i)))),256);
    else
      x(j, i)=mod(round(10⁸*(1-(10*yint(j, i)-round(10*yint(j, i))))),256);
    end
  End
End

- In order to make the numerical values of chaotic sequences between 0 and 255, the following operations are performed to the chaotic sequences $yint(j,m*n)$, where $j=1,2,3$. (See Table 10.1.)
- The three primary color matrices obtained in step 2 are converted into a one-dimensional matrix, respectively. Then we obtain three one-dimensional matrices $image_R = I_R(:)'$, $image_G = I_G(:)'$ and $image_B = I_B(:)'$.

5. Image encryption.
   - Perform the XOR operations on the three chaotic sequences $yint(j,m*n)(j=1,2,3)$ and image sequences. The encrypted image is found in Table 10.2.

Table 10.2 XOR Operation

XOR Operation

for i = 1:m*n
  $a(i) = bitxor(x(1,i),image_R(i));$
  $b(i) = bitxor(x(2,i),image_G(i));$
  $c(i) = bitxor(x(3,i),image_B(i));$
End

6. Trichromatic combination.
   - The three components R, G, B are combined and normalized by $image(:,:,1) = reshape(a,m,n)$, $image(:,:,2) = reshape(b,m,n)$, $image(:,:,3) = reshape(c,m,n)$ and $image = mat2gray(image)$.

10.5 Numerical Simulation

In this section, several numerical examples are given to illustrate the effectiveness of our proposed synchronization criteria.

Example 10.1:

We consider the following memristive MAMNNs with mixed delays. There are three fields and one neuron in each field.

$$\frac{dx_{k1}(t)}{dt} = I_{k1} - d_{k1}(x_{k1}(t))x_{k1}(t) + \sum_{p=1,p\neq k}^{3} a_{p1k1}(x_{k1}(t))f_{p1}(x_{p1}(t))$$
$$+ \sum_{p=1,p\neq k}^{3} b_{p1k1}(x_{k1}(t))f_{p1}(x_{p1}(t-\tau_{p1k1}(t)))$$
$$+ \sum_{p=1,p\neq k}^{3} c_{p1k1}(x_{k1}(t))\int_{t-\rho(t)}^{t} f_{p1}(x_{p1}(s))ds,$$

where

$$d_{11}(x_{11}(t)) = \begin{cases} 1.3, & |x_{11}| \leq \Gamma_{11}, \\ 1.4, & |x_{11}| > \Gamma_{11}, \end{cases} \quad d_{21}(x_{21}(t)) = \begin{cases} 0.1, & |x_{11}| \leq \Gamma_{21}, \\ 0.2, & |x_{11}| > \Gamma_{21}, \end{cases}$$

$$d_{31}(x_{31}(t)) = \begin{cases} 0.3, & |x_{31}| \leq \Gamma_{31}, \\ 0.4, & |x_{31}| > \Gamma_{31}, \end{cases} \quad a_{1121}(x_{21}(t)) = \begin{cases} -0.45, & |x_{21}(t)| \leq \Gamma_{21}, \\ 0.32, & |x_{21}(t)| > \Gamma_{21}, \end{cases}$$

$$a_{1131}(x_{31}(t)) = \begin{cases} 0.36, & |x_{31}(t)| \leq \Gamma_{31}, \\ 0.38, & |x_{31}(t)| > \Gamma_{31}, \end{cases} \quad a_{2111}(x_{11}(t)) = \begin{cases} -1.1, & |x_{11}(t)| \leq \Gamma_{11}, \\ 1.24, & |x_{11}(t)| > \Gamma_{11}, \end{cases}$$

$$a_{2131}(x_{31}(t)) = \begin{cases} 1.14, & |x_{31}(t)| \leq \Gamma_{31}, \\ 0.32, & |x_{31}(t)| > \Gamma_{31}, \end{cases} \quad a_{3111}(x_{11}(t)) = \begin{cases} 1.2, & |x_{11}(t)| \leq \Gamma_{11}, \\ 1.18, & |x_{11}(t)| > \Gamma_{11}, \end{cases}$$

$$a_{3121}(x_{21}(t)) = \begin{cases} -0.28, & |x_{21}(t)| \leq \Gamma_{21}, \\ 0.12, & |x_{21}(t)| > \Gamma_{21}, \end{cases} \quad b_{1121}(x_{21}(t)) = \begin{cases} 0.32, & |x_{21}(t)| \leq \Gamma_{21}, \\ 0.24, & |x_{21}(t)| > \Gamma_{21}, \end{cases}$$

$$b_{1131}(x_{31}(t)) = \begin{cases} -0.34, & |x_{31}(t)| \leq \Gamma_{31}, \\ 0.42, & |x_{31}(t)| > \Gamma_{31}, \end{cases} \quad b_{2111}(x_{11}(t)) = \begin{cases} 1.38, & |x_{11}(t)| \leq \Gamma_{11}, \\ 1.1, & |x_{11}(t)| > \Gamma_{11}, \end{cases}$$

$$b_{2131}(x_{31}(t)) = \begin{cases} 0.15, & |x_{31}(t)| \leq \Gamma_{31}, \\ -0.49, & |x_{31}(t)| > \Gamma_{31}, \end{cases} \quad b_{3111}(x_{11}(t)) = \begin{cases} -0.38, & |x_{11}(t)| \leq \Gamma_{11}, \\ -0.95, & |x_{11}(t)| > \Gamma_{11}, \end{cases}$$

$$b_{3121}(x_{21}(t))=\begin{cases}-0.45, & |x_{21}(t)|\leq\Gamma_{21},\\ -0.22, & |x_{21}(t)|>\Gamma_{21},\end{cases} \quad c_{1121}(x_{21}(t))=\begin{cases}-0.84, & |x_{21}(t)|\leq\Gamma_{21},\\ 0.18, & |x_{21}(t)|>\Gamma_{21},\end{cases}$$

$$c_{1131}(x_{31}(t))=\begin{cases}0.68, & |x_{31}(t)|\leq\Gamma_{31},\\ 0.42, & |x_{31}(t)|>\Gamma_{31},\end{cases} \quad c_{2111}(x_{11}(t))=\begin{cases}0.24, & |x_{11}(t)|\leq\Gamma_{11},\\ -0.58, & |x_{11}(t)|>\Gamma_{11},\end{cases}$$

$$c_{2131}(x_{31}(t))=\begin{cases}-0.62, & |x_{31}(t)|\leq\Gamma_{31},\\ -0.44, & |x_{31}(t)|>\Gamma_{31},\end{cases} \quad c_{3111}(x_{11}(t))=\begin{cases}-0.82, & |x_{11}(t)|\leq\Gamma_{11},\\ -0.84, & |x_{11}(t)|>\Gamma_{11},\end{cases}$$

$$c_{3121}(x_{21}(t))=\begin{cases}0.78, & |x_{21}(t)|\leq\Gamma_{21},\\ 0.19, & |x_{21}(t)|>\Gamma_{21}.\end{cases}$$

Let $\Gamma_{11}=\Gamma_{21}=\Gamma_{31}=1$. We set the action functions as $f_{ki}(x)=\tanh(x)$ The time-varying delays and distributed delays are $\tau_{pjki}(t)=0.5\cos(t)+0.5$ and $\rho(t)=0.5\sin(t)+0.5$, respectively. According to Assumption 10.1, we have $L_{ki}=L_{pj}=1$, $F=1$. By calculating, we get $\tau_1=1, \tau_2=0.5$ and $\rho_1=1$. The initial values are set as $[x_{11}(t),x_{21}(t),x_{31}(t)]=[1.05,0.25,-0.75]$, $[y_{11}(t),y_{21}(t),y_{31}(t)]=[-0.3,0.45,0.2]$.

Figure 10.1 represents the drive system (10.2) and the response system (10.2). They have chaotic attractors with the initial values given above. Figure 10.2 depicts the state trajectories of the drive system (10.2) and the response system (10.2). According to the conditions of Theorem 10.1, the delay-independent controllers are set as

$$\mu_{11}(t)=-4e_{11}(t)-5sign(e_{11}(t)),\ \mu_{21}(t)=-3e_{21}(t)-4sign(e_{21}(t))-\frac{1}{2}sign(e_{21}(t))|e_{21}(t)|^{-0.5},$$

$$\mu_{21}(t)=-3e_{21}(t)-4sign(e_{21}(t))-\frac{1}{2}sign(e_{21}(t))|e_{21}(t)|^{-0.5},$$

$$\mu_{31}(t)=-3e_{31}(t)-3sign(e_{31}(t))-\frac{1}{2}sign(e_{31}(t))|e_{31}(t)|^{-0.5}.$$

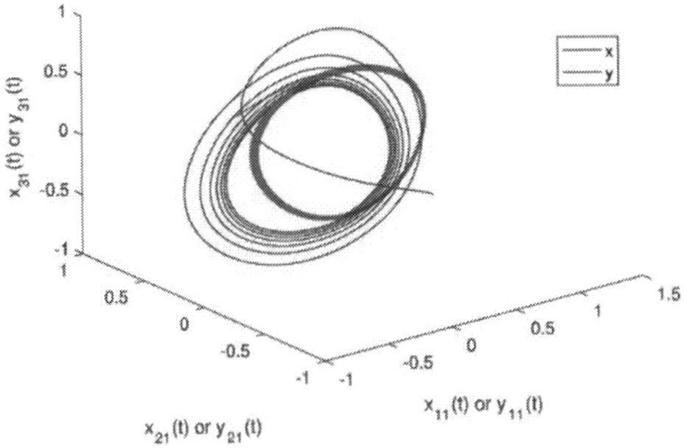

Figure 10.1 Phase trajectories of system (10.2) (corresponds to *x*) and system (10.4) (corresponds to *y*) without distributed delays.

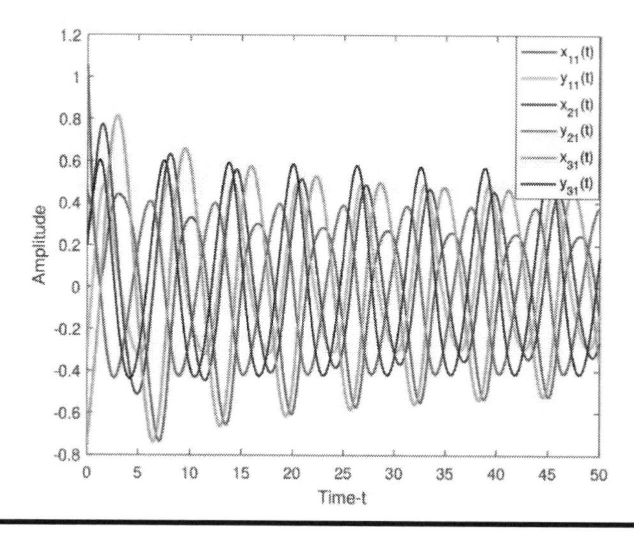

Figure 10.2 State trajectories of the drive system (10.2) (corresponds to *x*) and the response system (10.4) (corresponds to *y*) without distributed delays.

According to the conditions of Theorem 10.2, the delay-dependent controllers are set as

$$\mu_{11}(t) = -1.2e_{11}(t) - 1.2sign(e_{11}(t))\,|\,e_{pj}(t-\tau_{pj11}(t))\,| - 0.1sign(e_{11}(t)),$$

$$|\int_{t-\rho(t)}^{t} e_{pj}(s)ds\,| - sign(e_{11}(t))(5+|\,e_{11}(t)\,|^{0.5}),$$

$$\mu_{21}(t) = -0.5e_{21}(t) - 0.1sign(e_{21}(t))\,|\,e_{pj}(t-\tau_{pj21}(t))\,| - 0.5sign(e_{21}(t)),$$

$$|\int_{t-\rho(t)}^{t} e_{pj}(s)ds\,| - sign(e_{21}(t))(4+|\,e_{21}(t)\,|^{0.5}),$$

$$\mu_{31}(t) = -1.5e_{31}(t) - 0.1sign(e_{31}(t))\,|\,e_{pj}(t-\tau_{pj31}(t))\,| - 0.1sign(e_{31}(t)),$$

$$|\int_{t-\rho(t)}^{t} e_{pj}(s)ds\,| - sign(e_{31}(t))(3+|\,e_{31}(t)\,|^{0.5}).$$

Then (a–c) in Figure 10.3 describe the state trajectories of the errors system without controllers, with delay-independent and with delay-dependent controllers, respectively. It implies that the corresponding response system (10.4) can synchronize with the drive system (10.2) in finite time, in which the setting time according to Theorem 10.1 is $T_{11} \approx 2.7$, $T_{21} \approx 0.4$ and $T_{31} \approx 1.9$, the setting time according to Theorem 10.2 is $T_{21} \approx 2.3238$, $T_{22} \approx 0.8944$ and $T_{23} \approx 1.9494$.

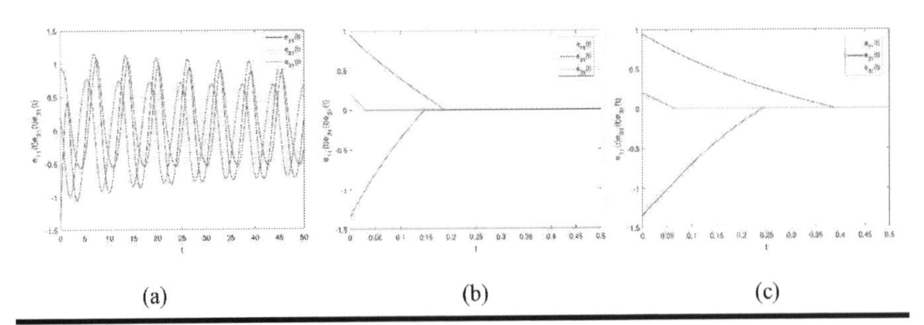

Figure 10.3 State trajectories of errors between the drive system (10.2) and the response system (10.4) without distributed delays, where (a) represents the errors without controllers; (b) represents the errors with delay-independent controllers; (c) represents the errors with delay-dependent controllers.

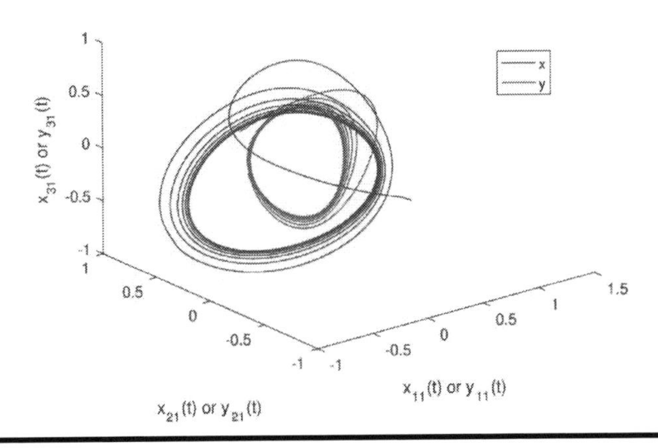

Figure 10.4 Phase trajectories of system (10.2) (corresponds to *x*) and system (10.4) (corresponds to *y*) with mixed delays.

Then we investigate system (10.2) and system (10.4) without distributed delays. Under the same parameters, Figure 10.4 represents the drive system (10.2) and the response system (10.4) without distributed delays. They have chaotic attractors with the initial values given above. Figure 10.5 depicts the state trajectories of system (10.2) and system (10.4). According to the conditions of Corollary 10.1, the delay-independent controllers are set as

$$\mu_{11}(t) = -3.5e_{11}(t) - 3.5sign(e_{11}(t)) - \frac{1}{2}sign(e_{11}(t))\,|\,e_{11}(t)\,|^{-0.5},$$

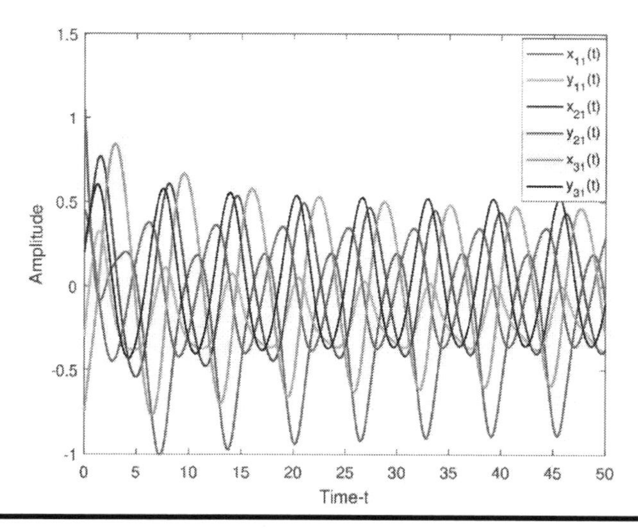

Figure 10.5 State trajectories of the drive system (10.2) (corresponds to *x*) and the response system (10.4) (corresponds to *y*) without distributed delays.

$$\mu_{21}(t) = -2.5e_{21}(t) - 2sign(e_{21}(t)) - \frac{1}{2}sign(e_{21}(t))\,|\,e_{21}(t)\,|^{-0.5},$$

$$\mu_{31}(t) = -2.5e_{31}(t) - 2.5sign(e_{31}(t)) - \frac{1}{2}sign(e_{31}(t))\,|\,e_{31}(t)\,|^{-0.5}.$$

According to the conditions of Corollary 10.2, the delay-dependent controllers are set as

$$\mu_{11}(t) = -1.2e_{11}(t) - 1.2sign(e_{11}(t))\,|\,e_{pj}(t - \tau_{pj11}(t))\,| - sign(e_{11}(t))(3.5 + |\,e_{11}(t)\,|^{0.5}),$$

$$\mu_{21}(t) = -0.5e_{21}(t) - 0.1sign(e_{21}(t))\,|\,e_{pj}(t - \tau_{pj21}(t))\,| - sign(e_{21}(t))(2 + |\,e_{21}(t)\,|^{0.5}),$$

$$\mu_{31}(t) = -1.5e_{31}(t) - 0.1sign(e_{31}(t))\,|\,e_{pj}(t - \tau_{pj31}(t))\,| - sign(e_{31}(t))(2.5 + |\,e_{31}(t)\,|^{0.5}).$$

Then (a–c) in Figure 10.6 describe the state trajectories of the errors system without controllers, with delay-independent and with delay-dependent controllers, respectively. It implies that the corresponding response system (10.4) can synchronize with the drive system (10.2) in finite time.

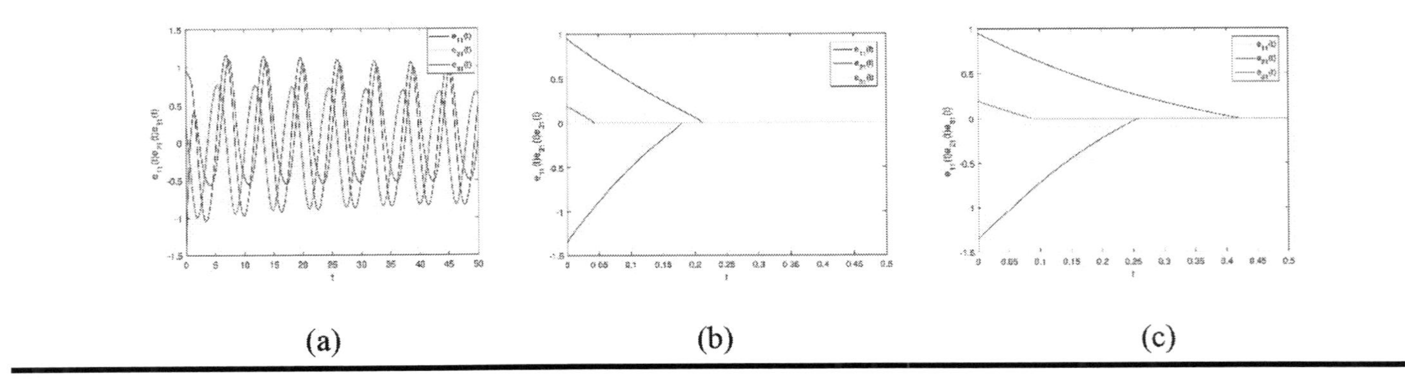

Figure 10.6 State trajectories of errors between system (10.2) and system (10.4) without distributed delays, where (a) represents the errors without controllers; (b) represents the errors with delay-independent controllers; (c) represents the errors with delay-dependent controllers.

Example 10.2:

We consider the following memristive MAMNNs without distributed delays. There are three fields and one neuron in each field.

$$\frac{dx_{k1}(t)}{dt} = I_{k1} - d_{k1}\left(x_{k1}(t)\right)x_{k1}(t) + \sum_{\substack{p=1 \\ p\neq k}}^{3} a_{p1k1}\left(x_{k1}(t)\right) f_{p1}\left(x_{p1}(t)\right)$$

$$+ \sum_{\substack{p=1 \\ p\neq k}}^{3} b_{p1k1}\left(x_{k1}(t)\right) f_{p1}\left(x_{p1}\left(t - \tau_{p1k1}(t)\right)\right),$$

where the parameters are the same as in Example 10.1. The initial values are set as $[x_{11}(t), x_{21}(t), x_{31}(t)] = [1.2, -0.3, 0.4]$, and Figure 10.7 represents system (10.2) without distributed delays. It has a chaotic attractor with the initial values.

Then we select a standard color image of the size of 512 * 512 to encrypt the image (lena.tif) based on the memristive MAMNNs without distributed delays. Figure 10.8 describes the process of encryption of the original image. It can be seen that the encrypted image has lost the original image feature based on the given encryption method.

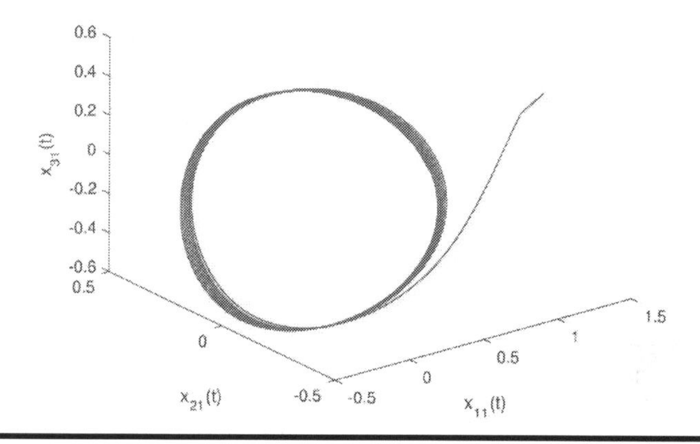

Figure 10.7 Phase trajectories of system (10.2) without distributed delays.

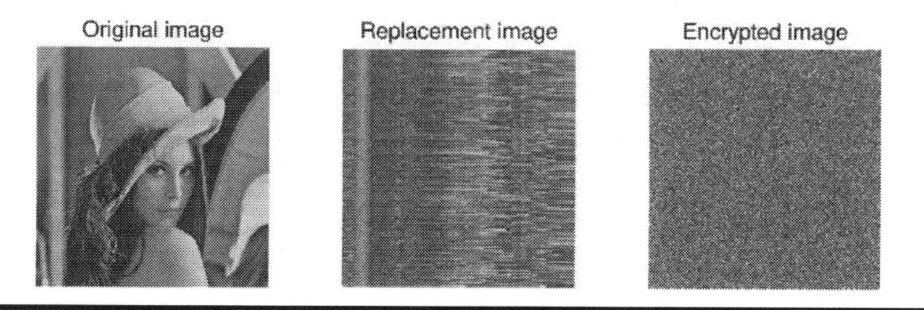

Figure 10.8 The process of encryption of an image.

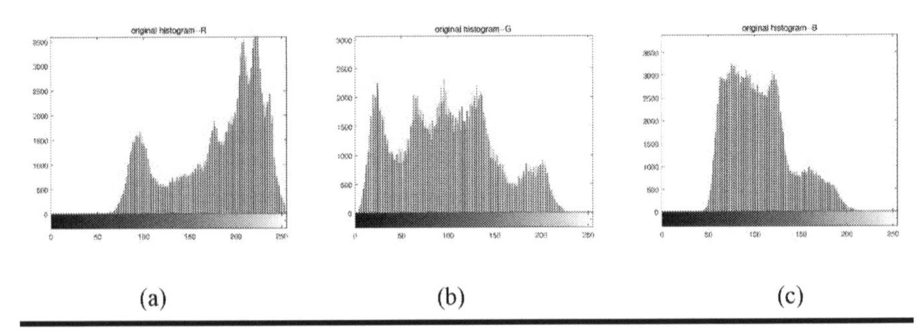

Figure 10.9 The histogram of the original image, where (a) represents the original image—R component; (b) represents the original image—G component; (c) represents the original image—B component.

The gray histogram is a powerful attribute to describe the statistical characteristics of the image. Figure 10.9 displays the gray histogram of the original image, and it can be seen that there exist distribution characteristics in the gray histogram of the three components. Figure 10.10 describes the gray histogram of the encrypted image. It can be seen that the gray histogram of the three components is uniformly distributed. This implies that our encryption method can effectively encrypt the image.

Correlation analysis of adjacent pixels is an important indicator to evaluate the encryption effect of an image. We randomly select 1000 pairs of pixel values, in which Figure 10.11 shows the correlation analysis of adjacent pixels of the original image; Figure 10.12 describes the correlation analysis of adjacent pixels of the encrypted image. The specific correlation is shown in Tables 10.3 and 10.4.

According to Table 10.3, we can see that the correlation coefficients of adjacent pixels of the original image are close to 1, i.e., it has a strong correlation.

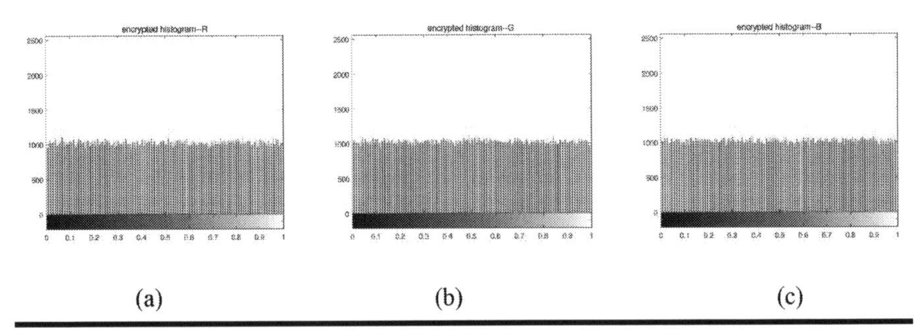

Figure 10.10 The histogram of the encrypted image, where (a) represents the encrypted image—R component; (b) represents the encrypted image—G component; (c) represents the encrypted image—B component.

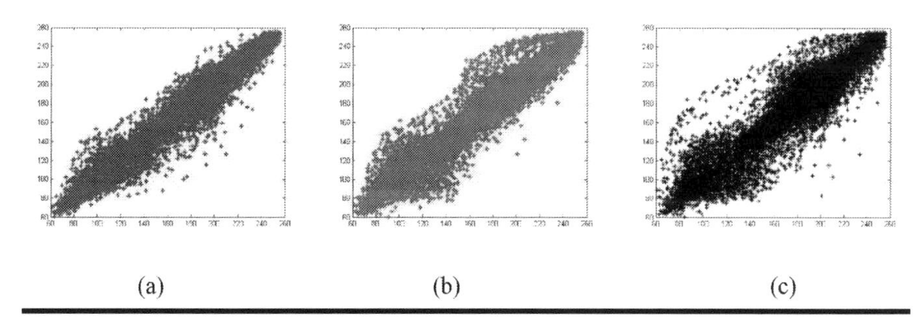

Figure 10.11 Correlation analysis of adjacent pixels of the original image, where (a) represents the horizontal direction; (b) represents the vertical direction; (c) represents the diagonal direction.

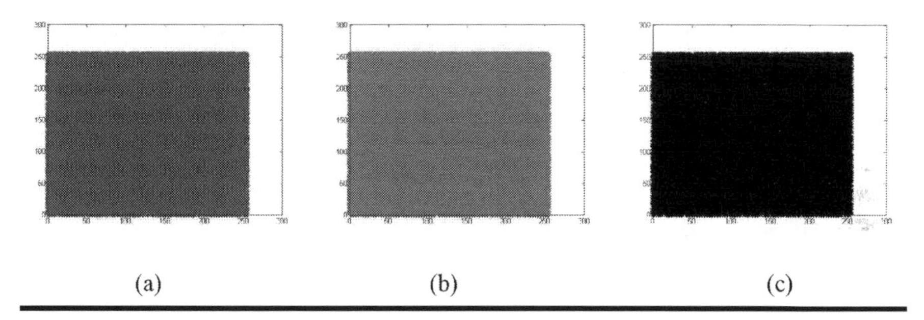

Figure 10.12 Correlation analysis of adjacent pixels of the encrypted image, where (a) represents the horizontal direction; (b) represents the vertical direction; (c) represents the diagonal direction.

Table 10.3 Correlation Analysis of Adjacent Pixel of the Original Image

	The Proposed	*Method in [44]*	*Replacement*	*Chaos*
Horizontal direction	0.9733	0.9663	0.9765	0.9717
Vertical direction	0.9843	0.9780	0.9812	0.9821
Diagonal direction	0.9623	0.9873	0.9644	0.9516

Table 10.4 Correlation Analysis of Adjacent Pixel of the Encrypted Image

	The Proposed	*Method in [44]*	*Replacement*	*Chaos*
Horizontal direction	−0.0175	0.0234	0.0810	0.0151
Vertical direction	0.0067	−0.0167	0.1816	−0.0155
Diagonal direction	0.0052	−0.0172	−0.0231	−0.0139

However, we can see that the correlation coefficients of adjacent pixels of the encrypted image are close to 0 in Table 10.4, i.e., they are almost irrelevant. This shows that our encryption method can effectively encrypt the image.

Compared with the results of literature [44], our proposed method has fewer correlation coefficients of adjacent pixels of the encrypted image, so it has better ability to encrypt images. At the same time, we combine the two encryption methods of replacement and chaos, which is more effective than using only one encryption method.

10.6 Conclusions

In this paper, we propose a novel memristive MAMNNs model, which includes time-varying delays and distributed time delays. Then the finite-time synchronization of our proposed model is analyzed by creating appropriate controllers. In the proposed approach, we obtain some less conservative results by removing certain strict conditions. By constructing a suitable Lyapunov function and using some inequality techniques, some sufficient criteria for guaranteeing the finite-time synchronization of the drive-response system are obtained. An image encryption scheme is designed based on the chaotic memristive MAMNNs. Furthermore, some numerical simulations are delivered to demonstrate the effectiveness of our proposed theories.

Appendix A: Proof of Theorem 10.1

Construct the following Lyapunov function:

$$\begin{aligned} V(t) = e_{ki}^2(t) + \frac{1}{1-\tau_2} \sum_{p=1,p\neq k}^{m} \sum_{j=1}^{n_p} \left[\int_{t-\tau_{pjki}(t)}^{t} e_{pj}^2(s)ds \right] \\ + \sum_{p=1,p\neq k}^{m} \sum_{j=1}^{n_p} \left[\int_{-\rho_1}^{0} \int_{t+s}^{t} e_{pj}^2(z)dzds \right]. \end{aligned} \tag{A10.1}$$

According to the differential inclusion theorem, Theorem 10.1 will be proved in nine cases.

1. $|x_{ki}(t)| < \Gamma_{ki}, |y_{ki}(t)| < \Gamma_{ki}$.

$$\frac{dx_{ki}(t)}{dt} = I_{ki} - \acute{d}_{ki}\, x_{ki}(t) + \sum_{p=1,p\neq k}^{m} \sum_{j=1}^{n_p} \acute{a}_{pjki}\, f_{pj}(x_{pj}(t))$$
$$+ \sum_{p=1,p\neq k}^{m} \sum_{j=1}^{n_p} \acute{b}_{pjki}\, f_{pj}(x_{pj}(t-\tau_{pjki}(t))) \tag{A10.2}$$
$$+ \sum_{p=1,p\neq k}^{m} \sum_{j=1}^{n_p} \acute{c}_{pjki} \int_{t-\rho(t)}^{t} f_{pj}(x_{pj}(s))ds.$$

The response system (4) can be written as follows:

$$\frac{dy_{ki}(t)}{dt} = I_{ki} - \acute{d}_{ki}\, y_{ki}(t) + \sum_{p=1,p\neq k}^{m} \sum_{j=1}^{n_p} \acute{a}_{pjki}\, f_{pj}(y_{pj}(t))$$
$$+ \sum_{p=1,p\neq k}^{m} \sum_{j=1}^{n_p} \acute{b}_{pjki}\, f_{pj}(y_{pj}(t-\tau_{pjki}(t))) \tag{A10.3}$$
$$+ \sum_{p=1,p\neq k}^{m} \sum_{j=1}^{n_p} \acute{c}_{pjki} \int_{t-\rho(t)}^{t} f_{pj}(y_{pj}(s))ds + \mu_{ki}(t).$$

Then the error system is obtained as follows:

$$\frac{de_{ki}(t)}{dt} = \mu_{ki}(t) - \acute{d}_{ki}\, e_{ki}(t) + \sum_{p=1,p\neq k}^{m} \sum_{j=1}^{n_p} \grave{a}_{pjki}\, \tilde{f}_{pj}(e_{pj}(t))$$
$$+ \sum_{p=1,p\neq k}^{m} \sum_{j=1}^{n_p} \acute{b}_{pjki}\, \tilde{f}_{pj}(e_{pj}(t-\tau_{pjki}(t))) \tag{A10.4}$$
$$+ \sum_{p=1,p\neq k}^{m} \sum_{j=1}^{n_p} \acute{c}_{pjki} \int_{t-\rho(t)}^{t} \tilde{f}_{pj}(e_{pj}(s))ds.$$

where

$$\tilde{f}_{pj}(e_{pj}(t)) = f_{pj}(y_{pj}(t)) - f_{pj}(x_{pj}(t)),$$

$$\tilde{f}_{pj}(e_{pj}(t-\tau_{pjki}(t))) = f_{pj}(y_{pj}(t-\tau_{pjki}(t))) - f_{pj}(x_{pj}(t-\tau_{pjki}(t))),$$

$$\int_{t-\rho(t)}^{t} \tilde{f}_{pj}(e_{pj}(s))ds = \int_{t-\rho(t)}^{t} f_{pj}(y_{pj}(s))ds - \int_{t-\rho(t)}^{t} f_{pj}(x_{pj}(s))ds.$$

Along the trajectory of system (11), we calculate the derivative as follows:

$$\dot{V}(t) = 2e_{ki}(t)\Big[-d'_{ki}\, e_{ki}(t) + \sum_{p=1,p\neq k}^{m}\sum_{j=1}^{n_p} a'_{pjki}\, \tilde{f}_{pj}(e_{pj}(t)) + \mu_{ki}(t)$$

$$+ \sum_{p=1,p\neq k}^{m}\sum_{j=1}^{n_p} b'_{pjki}\, \tilde{f}_{pj}(e_{pj}(t-\tau_{pjki}(t)))$$

$$+ \sum_{p=1,p\neq k}^{m}\sum_{j=1}^{n_p} c'_{pjki} \int_{t-\rho(t)}^{t} \tilde{f}_{pj}(e_{pj}(s))ds\Big] \tag{A10.5}$$

$$+ \frac{1}{1-\tau_2} \times \sum_{p=1,p\neq k}^{m}\sum_{j=1}^{n_p} e_{pj}^2(t) - \sum_{p=1,p\neq k}^{m}\sum_{j=1}^{n_p} e_{pj}^2(t-\tau_{pjki}(t))$$

$$+ \sum_{p=1,p\neq k}^{m}\sum_{j=1}^{n_p} \rho_1 e_{pj}^2(t) - \sum_{p=1,p\neq k}^{m}\sum_{j=1}^{n_p} \int_{t-\rho(t)}^{t} e_{pj}^2(s)ds.$$

According to Assumption 10.1, we obtain

$$\dot{V}(t) \leq -(2d'_{ki} + 2\delta_{ki})e_{ki}^2(t) - 2\theta_{ki}\,|e_{ki}(t)| - h\,|e_{ki}(t)|^{\eta}$$

$$+2|e_{ki}(t)| \sum_{p=1,p\neq k}^{m}\sum_{j=1}^{n_p} a'_{pjki}\, L_{pj}\, |e_{pj}(t)|$$

$$+2|e_{ki}(t)| \times \sum_{p=1,p\neq k}^{m}\sum_{j=1}^{n_p} b'_{pjki}\, L_{pj}\, |e_{pj}(t-\tau_{pjki}(t))|$$

$$+2|e_{ki}(t)| \times \sum_{p=1,p\neq k}^{m}\sum_{j=1}^{n_p} c'_{pjki}\, L_{pj} \int_{t-\rho(t)}^{t} |e_{pj}(s)|\,ds$$

$$+ \frac{1}{1-\tau_2} \times \sum_{p=1,p\neq k}^{m}\sum_{j=1}^{n_p} e_{pj}^2(t) - \sum_{p=1,p\neq k}^{m}\sum_{j=1}^{n_p} e_{pj}^2(t-\tau_{pjki}(t)) + \sum_{p=1,p\neq k}^{m}\sum_{j=1}^{n_p} \rho_1 e_{pj}^2(t)$$

$$- \sum_{p=1,p\neq k}^{m}\sum_{j=1}^{n_p} \int_{t-\rho(t)}^{t} e_{pj}^2(s)ds. \tag{A10.6}$$

By using the mean-value inequality, then we have

$$2\,|\,e_{ki}(t)\,|\,\acute{a}_{pjki}\,L_{pj}\,|\,e_{pj}(t)\,|\le \acute{a}^{2}_{pjki}\,L^{2}_{pj}e^{2}_{ki}(t)+e^{2}_{pj}(t),$$

$$2\,|\,e_{ki}(t)\,|\,\acute{b}_{pjki}\,L_{pj}\,|\,e_{pj}(t-\tau_{pjki}(t))\,|\le \acute{b}^{2}_{pjki}\,L^{2}_{pj}e^{2}_{ki}(t)+e^{2}_{pj}(t-\tau_{pjki}(t)),$$

$$2\,|\,e_{ki}(t)\,|\,\acute{c}_{pjki}\,L_{pj}\int_{t-\rho(t)}^{t}|e_{pj}(s)\,|\,ds\le \rho_1\,\acute{c}^{2}_{pjki}\,L^{2}_{pj}e^{2}_{ki}(t)+\int_{t-\rho(t)}^{t}e^{2}_{pj}(s)ds.$$

Then we get

$$\dot{V}(t)\le\Big[-2\acute{d}_{ki}-2\delta_{ki}+\sum_{p=1,p\neq k}^{m}\sum_{j=1}^{n_p}(\acute{a}^{2}_{pjki}\,L^{2}_{pj}+\acute{b}^{2}_{pjki}\,L^{2}_{pj}+\rho_1\,\acute{c}^{2}_{pjki}\,L^{2}_{pj}+1+\frac{1}{1-\tau_2}+\rho_1)\Big]e^{2}_{ki}(t)-2\theta_{ki}\left|e_{ki}(t)\right|-h\left|e_{ki}(t)\right|^{\eta}. \tag{A10.7}$$

Under the conditions of Theorem 10.1, we obtain

$$\dot{V}(t)\le -h\,|\,e_{ki}(t)\,|^{\eta}. \tag{A10.8}$$

Then, according to Lemma 10.2, the drive system (10.2) and the response system (10.4) are synchronized in the finite-time $T=t_0+\frac{V^{1-\eta}(t_0)}{h(1-\eta)}$. This implies the proof is completed.

2. $|\,x_{ki}(t)\,|>\Gamma_{ki},|\,y_{ki}(t)\,|>\Gamma_{ki}$.
   The drive system (10.2) can be written as follows:

$$\frac{dx_{ki}(t)}{dt}=I_{ki}-\acute{d}_{ki}\,x_{ki}(t)+\sum_{p=1,p\neq k}^{m}\sum_{j=1}^{n_p}\grave{a}_{pjki}\,f_{pj}(x_{pj}(t))+\sum_{p=1,p\neq k}^{m}\sum_{j=1}^{n_p}\acute{b}_{pjki}\,f_{pj}(x_{pj}(t-\tau_{pjki}(t)))+\sum_{p=1,p\neq k}^{m}\sum_{j=1}^{n_p}\grave{c}_{pjki}\int_{t-\rho(t)}^{t}f_{pj}(x_{pj}(s))ds. \tag{A10.9}$$

The response system (10.4) can be written as follows:

$$\frac{dy_{ki}(t)}{dt} = I_{ki} - \grave{d}_{ki}\, y_{ki}(t) + \sum_{p=1,p\neq k}^{m} \sum_{j=1}^{n_p} \grave{a}_{pjki}\, f_{pj}(y_{pj}(t))$$

$$+ \sum_{p=1,p\neq k}^{m} \sum_{j=1}^{n_p} \grave{b}_{pjki}\, f_{pj}(y_{pj}(t - \tau_{pjki}(t))) \qquad \text{(A10.10)}$$

$$+ \sum_{p=1,p\neq k}^{m} \sum_{j=1}^{n_p} \grave{c}_{pjki} \int_{t-\rho(t)}^{t} f_{pj}(y_{pj}(s))ds + \mu_{ki}(t).$$

Then the error system is obtained as follows:

$$\frac{de_{ki}(t)}{dt} = \mu_{ki}(t) - \grave{d}_{ki}\, e_{ki}(t) + \sum_{p=1,p\neq k}^{m} \sum_{j=1}^{n_p} \grave{a}_{pjki}\, \tilde{f}_{pj}(e_{pj}(t))$$

$$+ \sum_{p=1,p\neq k}^{m} \sum_{j=1}^{n_p} \grave{b}_{pjki}\, \tilde{f}_{pj}(e_{pj}(t - \tau_{pjki}(t))) \qquad \text{(A10.11)}$$

$$+ \sum_{p=1,p\neq k}^{m} \sum_{j=1}^{n_p} \grave{c}_{pjki} \int_{t-\rho(t)}^{t} \tilde{f}_{pj}(e_{pj}(s))ds.$$

The proof of the rest is similar to (10.1), so it is omitted here.

3. $|x_{ki}(t)| < \Gamma_{ki}, |y_{ki}(t)| > \Gamma_{ki}$.

   The drive system (10.2) can be written as system (A10.2), the response system (10.4) can be written as system (A10.10). Then the error system is obtained as follows:

$$\frac{de_{ki}(t)}{dt} = \mu_{ki}(t) - \grave{d}_{ki}\, e_{ki}(t) + \sum_{p=1,p\neq k}^{m} \sum_{j=1}^{n_p} \grave{a}_{pjki}\, \tilde{f}_{pj}(e_{pj}(t))$$

$$+ \sum_{p=1,p\neq k}^{m} \sum_{j=1}^{n_p} \grave{b}_{pjki}\, \tilde{f}_{pj}(e_{pj}(t - \tau_{pjki}(t))) + \sum_{p=1,p\neq k}^{m} \sum_{j=1}^{n_p} \grave{c}_{pjki} \int_{t-\rho(t)}^{t} \tilde{f}_{pj}(e_{pj}(s))ds$$

$$+(\acute{d}_{ki}-\grave{d}_{ki})x_{ki}(t)+\sum_{p=1,p\neq k}^{m}\sum_{j=1}^{n_p}(\grave{a}_{pjki}-\acute{a}_{pjki})f_{pj}(x_{pj}(t))$$

$$+\sum_{p=1,p\neq k}^{m}\sum_{j=1}^{n_p}(\grave{b}_{pjki}-\acute{b}_{pjki})f_{pj}(x_{pj}(t-\tau_{pjki}(t))) \tag{A10.12}$$

$$+\sum_{p=1,p\neq k}^{m}\sum_{j=1}^{n_p}(\grave{c}_{pjki}-\acute{c}_{pjki})\int_{t-\rho(t)}^{t} f_{pj}(x_{pj}(s))ds.$$

Along the trajectory of system (A10.12), we calculate the derivative as follows:

$$\dot{V}(t)\leq\Big[-2\grave{d}_{ki}-2\delta_{ki}+\sum_{p=1,p\neq k}^{m}\sum_{j=1}^{n_p}(\grave{a}_{pjki}^{2}L_{pj}^2+\grave{b}_{pjki}^{2}L_{pj}^2$$
$$+\rho_1\grave{c}_{pjki}^{2}L_{pj}^2+1+\frac{1}{1-\tau_2}+\rho_1)\Big]e_{ki}^2(t)$$
$$+2\{(\acute{d}_{ki}-\grave{d}_{ki})\Gamma_{ki}+\sum_{p=1,p\neq k}^{m}\sum_{j=1}^{n_p}(\grave{a}_{pjki}-\acute{a}_{pjki})L_{pj}\Gamma_{pj}$$
$$+\sum_{p=1,p\neq k}^{m}\sum_{j=1}^{n_p}\Big[\Big(\grave{b}_{pjki}-\acute{b}_{pjki}\Big)F+\Big(\grave{c}_{pjki}-\acute{c}_{pjki}\Big)\rho_1F\Big]-\theta_{ki}\}|e_{ki}(t)|-h|e_{ki}(t)|^{\eta}. \tag{A10.13}$$

Under the conditions of Theorem 10.1, we obtain

$$\dot{V}(t)\leq -h\,|\,e_{ki}(t)\,|^{\eta}. \tag{A10.14}$$

Then, according to Lemma 10.2, the drive system (10.2) and the response system (10.4) are synchronized in the finite-time $T=t_0+\frac{V^{1-\eta}(t_0)}{h(1-\eta)}$. This implies the proof is completed.

4. $|\,x_{ki}(t)\,|>\Gamma_{ki},|\,y_{ki}(t)\,|<\Gamma_{ki}$.
   The drive system (10.2) can be written as system (A10.9), the response system (10.4) can be written as system (A10.3). Then the error system is obtained as follows:

$$\frac{de_{ki}(t)}{dt} = \mu_{ki}(t) - \grave{d}_{ki}\, e_{ki}(t) + \sum_{\substack{p=1 \\ p\neq k}}^{m} \sum_{j=1}^{n_p} \grave{a}_{pjki} \tilde{f}_{pj}\left(e_{pj}(t)\right)$$

$$+ \sum_{p=1,p\neq k}^{m} \sum_{j=1}^{n_p} \grave{b}_{pjki} \tilde{f}_{pj}\left(e_{pj}\left(t - \tau_{pjki}(t)\right)\right)$$

$$+ \sum_{p=1,p\neq k}^{m} \sum_{j=1}^{n_p} \grave{c}_{pjki} \int_{t-\rho(t)}^{t} \tilde{f}_{pj}\left(e_{pj}(s)\right) ds + \left(\acute{d}_{ki} - \grave{d}_{ki} \right) y_{ki}(t)$$

$$+ \sum_{p=1,p\neq k}^{m} \sum_{j=1}^{n_p} (\acute{a}_{pjki} - \grave{a}_{pjki}) f_{pj}(y_{pj}(t)) \tag{A10.15}$$

$$+ \sum_{p=1,p\neq k}^{m} \sum_{j=1}^{n_p} (\acute{b}_{pjki} - \grave{b}_{pjki}) f_{pj}(y_{pj}(t - \tau_{pjki}(t)))$$

$$+ \sum_{\substack{p=1 \\ p\neq k}}^{m} \sum_{j=1}^{n_p} (\acute{c}_{pjki} - \grave{c}_{pjki}) \int_{t-\rho(t)}^{t} f_{pj}(y_{pj}(s)) ds.$$

The proof of the rest is similar to (10.3), so it is omitted here.

5. $|x_{ki}(t)| = \Gamma_{ki}, |y_{ki}(t)| = \Gamma_{ki}$.

The rest of five cases are similar to cases (10.3) and (10.4), and the process of proof is omitted here. To sum up, Theorem 10.1 is proved.

Appendix B: Proof of Theorem 10.2

Construct the following Lyapunov function:

$$V(t) = sign(e_{ki}(t))e_{ki}(t).$$

According to the differential inclusion theorem, Theorem 10.2 will be proved in nine cases.

1. $|x_{ki}(t)| < \Gamma_{ki}, |y_{ki}(t)| < \Gamma_{ki}$.
   The drive system (10.2) can be written as system (A10.2), the response system (10.4) can be written as system (A10.3). Then the error system can be written as system (A10.4).

Along the trajectory of system (10.11), we calculate the derivative as follows:

$$\dot{V}(t) \leq sign(e_{ki}(t))\Big[\mu_{ki}(t) - \acute{d}_{ki}\, e_{ki}(t) + \sum_{p=1, p\neq k}^{m} \sum_{j=1}^{n_p} \acute{a}_{pjki} \times \tilde{f}_{pj}(e_{pj}(t)) + \sum_{p=1, p\neq k}^{m} \sum_{j=1}^{n_p} \acute{b}_{pjki} \times \tilde{f}_{pj}(e_{pj}(t - \tau_{pjki}(t))) + \sum_{p=1, p\neq k}^{m} \sum_{j=1}^{n_p} \acute{c}_{pjki} \int_{t-\rho(t)}^{t} \tilde{f}_{pj}(e_{pj}(s))ds\Big]. \tag{B10.1}$$

Then we obtain

$$\begin{aligned} \dot{V}(t) \leq & -\acute{d}_{ki}\, |e_{ki}(t)| + \sum_{p=1, p\neq k}^{m} \sum_{j=1}^{n_p} |\acute{a}_{pjki}\, \tilde{f}_{pj}(e_{pj}(t))| \\ & + \sum_{p=1, p\neq k}^{m} \sum_{j=1}^{n_p} |\acute{b}_{pjki}\, \tilde{f}_{pj}(e_{pj}(t - \tau_{pjki}(t)))| \\ & + \sum_{p=1, p\neq k}^{m} \sum_{j=1}^{n_p} \left|\acute{c}_{pjki} \int_{t-\rho(t)}^{t} \tilde{f}_{pj}(e_{pj}(s))ds\right| - \delta_{ki}\left|e_{ki}(t)\right| - \theta_{ki}\left|e_{pj}(t - \tau_{pjki}(t))\right| \\ & -\varepsilon_{ki}\left|\int_{t-\rho(t)}^{t} e_{pj}(s)ds\right| - (\gamma_{ki} + h\left|e_{ki}(t)\right|^{\eta}). \end{aligned} \tag{B10.2}$$

According to Assumption 10.1, we have

$$\begin{aligned} \dot{V}(t) \leq & -(\acute{d}_{ki} + \delta_{ki})\,|e_{ki}(t)| + \sum_{p=1, p\neq k}^{m} \sum_{j=1}^{n_p} \left|\acute{a}_{pjki}\, L_{pj} e_{pj}(t)\right| \\ & + \sum_{p=1, p\neq k}^{m} \sum_{j=1}^{n_p} \left|\acute{b}_{pjki}\, L_{pj} e_{pj}(t - \tau_{pjki}(t))\right| + \sum_{p=1, p\neq k}^{m} \sum_{j=1}^{n_p} \left|\acute{c}_{pjki}\, L_{pj} \int_{t-\rho(t)}^{t} e_{pj}(s)ds\right| \\ & -\theta_{ki}\left|e_{pj}(t - \tau_{pjki}(t))\right| - \varepsilon_{ki}\left|\int_{t-\rho(t)}^{t} e_{pj}(s)ds\right| - (\gamma_{ki} + h\left|e_{ki}(t)\right|^{\eta}) \\ \leq & \sum_{p=1, p\neq k}^{m} \sum_{j=1}^{n_p} (-\acute{d}_{ki} + \acute{a}_{pjki}\, L_{pj} - \delta_{ki})\left|e_{ki}(t)\right| \\ & + \sum_{p=1, p\neq k}^{m} \sum_{j=1}^{n_p} (\acute{b}_{pjki}\, L_{pj} - \theta_{ki})\left|e_{pj}(t - \tau_{pjki}(t))\right| \\ & + \sum_{p=1, p\neq k}^{m} \sum_{j=1}^{n_p} (\acute{c}_{pjki}\, L_{pj} - \varepsilon_{ki})\left|\int_{t-\rho(t)}^{t} e_{pj}(s)ds\right| - h\left|e_{ki}(t)\right|^{\eta}. \end{aligned} \tag{B10.3}$$

Under the conditions of Theorem 10.2, we obtain

$$\dot{V}(t) \le -h\,|\,e_{ki}(t)\,|^{\eta}. \tag{B10.4}$$

Then, according to Lemma 10.2, the drive system (10.2) and the response system (10.4) are synchronized in the finite-time $T = t_0 + \frac{V^{1-\eta}(t_0)}{h(1-\eta)}$. This implies the proof is completed.

2. $|\,x_{ki}(t)\,| > \Gamma_{ki}, |\,y_{ki}(t)\,| > \Gamma_{ki}$.
   The drive system (10.2) can be written as system (A10.9), the response system (10.4) can be written as system (A10.10). Then the error system can be written as system (A10.11). The proof of the rest is similar to 1), so it is omitted here.
3. $|\,x_{ki}(t)\,| < \Gamma_{ki}, |\,y_{ki}(t)\,| > \Gamma_{ki}$.
   The drive system (10.2) can be written as system (A10.2), the response system (10.4) can be written as system (A10.10). Then the error system can be written as system (A10.12).
   Along the trajectory of system (A10.12), we calculate the derivative as follows:

$$\begin{aligned}
\dot{V}(t) \le & -\acute{d}_{ki}\,|\,e_{ki}(t)\,| + \sum_{p=1,p\neq k}^{m}\sum_{j=1}^{n_p}\left|\acute{a}_{pjki}\,\tilde{f}_{pj}(e_{pj}(t))\right| + \sum_{p=1,p\neq k}^{m}\sum_{j=1}^{n_p}\left|\acute{b}_{pjki}\,\tilde{f}_{pj}(e_{pj}(t-\tau_{pjki}(t)))\right| \\
& + \sum_{p=1,p\neq k}^{m}\sum_{j=1}^{n_p}\left|\acute{c}_{pjki}\int_{t-\rho(t)}^{t}\tilde{f}_{pj}(e_{pj}(s))ds\right| + sign(e_{ki}(t))(\acute{d}_{ki} - \grave{d}_{ki})x_{ki}(t) \\
& + sign(e_{ki}(t))\Big[\sum_{p=1,p\neq k}^{m}\sum_{j=1}^{n_p}(\grave{a}_{pjki} - \acute{a}_{pjki})f_{pj}(x_{pj}(t)) \\
& + \sum_{p=1,p\neq k}^{m}\sum_{j=1}^{n_p}(\grave{b}_{pjki} - \acute{b}_{pjki})f_{pj}(x_{pj}(t-\tau_{pjki}(t))) \\
& + \sum_{p=1,p\neq k}^{m}\sum_{j=1}^{n_p}(\grave{c}_{pjki} - \acute{c}_{pjki})\int_{t-\rho(t)}^{t}f_{pj}(x_{pj}(s))ds\Big] \\
& - \delta_{ki}\left|e_{ki}(t)\right| - \theta_{ki}\left|e_{pj}(t-\tau_{pjki}(t))\right| - \varepsilon_{ki}\left|\int_{t-\rho(t)}^{t}e_{pj}(s)ds\right| \\
& - (\gamma_{ki} + h\left|e_{ki}(t)\right|^{\eta}).
\end{aligned} \tag{B10.5}$$

According to Assumption 10.1, we have

$$\dot{V}(t) \leq \sum_{p=1,p\neq k}^{m} \sum_{j=1}^{n_p} (-\acute{d}_{ki} + \acute{a}_{pjki} L_{pj} - \delta_{ki}) |e_{ki}(t)|$$

$$+ \sum_{p=1,p\neq k}^{m} \sum_{j=1}^{n_p} (\acute{b}_{pjki} L_{pj} - \theta_{ki}) |e_{pj}(t - \tau_{pjki}(t))|$$

$$+ \sum_{p=1,p\neq k}^{m} \sum_{j=1}^{n_p} (\acute{c}_{pjki} L_{pj} - \varepsilon_{ki}) \left| \int_{t-\rho(t)}^{t} e_{pj}(s) ds \right| + \Big\{ \left| \acute{d}_{ki} - \grave{d}_{ki} \right| \Gamma_{ki} \tag{B10.6}$$

$$+ \sum_{p=1,p\neq k}^{m} \sum_{j=1}^{n_p} [| \grave{a}_{pjki} - \acute{a}_{pjki} | L_{pj} \Gamma_{pj} + | \grave{b}_{pjki} - \acute{b}_{pjki} | F + | \grave{c}_{pjki} - \acute{c}_{pjki} | \rho_1 F]$$

$$- \gamma_{ki} \Big\} - h |e_{ki}(t)|^{\eta}.$$

Under the conditions of Theorem 10.2, we obtain

$$\dot{V}(t) \leq -h \, | \, e_{ki}(t) \, |^{\eta}. \tag{B10.7}$$

Then, according to Lemma 10.2, the drive system (10.2) and the response system (10.4) are synchronized in the finite-time $T = t_0 + \frac{V^{1-\eta}(t_0)}{h(1-\eta)}$. This implies the proof is completed.

4. $| x_{ki}(t) | > \Gamma_{ki}, | y_{ki}(t) | < \Gamma_{ki}$.
   The drive system (10.2) can be written as system (A10.9), the response system (10.4) can be written as system (A10.3). Then the error system can be written as system (A10.15). The proof of the rest is similar to 3), so it is omitted here.
5. $| x_{ki}(t) | = \Gamma_{ki}, | y_{ki}(t) | = \Gamma_{ki}$.
   The rest of five cases are similar to cases (10.3) and (10.4), and the process of proof is omitted here. To sum up, Theorem 10.2 is proved.

Acknowledgments

This work was supported in part by the National Natural Science Foundation of China under Grants 61174103 and 61603032, in part by the National Key Research and Development Program of China under Grant 2017YFB0702300, in part by the University of Science and Technology Beijing—National Taipei University of Technology Joint Research Program under Grant TW201705, and in part by a FRD-IoT award and a graduate faculty travel award from Cleveland State University. And thanks to the authorization of IEEE Access.

References

1. Ü. Çavuşoğlua, S. Kaçar, I. Pehlivan and A. Zengin, "Secure image encryption algorithm design using a novel chaos based SBox," *Chaos, Solitons & Fractals*, vol. 95, pp. 92–101, 2017.
2. A. Kanso and M. Ghebleh, "An algorithm for encryption of secret images into meaningful image," *Optics and Lasers in Engineering*, vol. 90, pp. 196–208, 2017.
3. Y. Zhang, "A chaotic system based image encryption scheme with identical encryption and decryption algorithm," *Chinese Journal of Electronics*, vol. 26, pp. 1022–1031, 2017.
4. R. Parvaz and M. Zarebnia, "A combination chaotic system and application in color image encryption," *Optics and Laser Technology*, vol. 101, pp. 30–41, 2018.
5. N. Bigdeli, Y. Farid and K. Afshar, "A novel image encryption/decryption scheme based on chaotic neural networks," *Engineering Applications of Artificial Intelligence*, vol. 25, pp. 753–765, 2012.
6. K. Ratnavelu, M. Kalpana, P. Balasubramaniam, K. Wong and P. Raveendran, "Image encryption method based on chaotic fuzzy cellular neural networks," *Signal Processing*, vol. 140, pp. 87–96, 2017.
7. S.G. Zhou, "Image Encryption Technology Research Based on Neural Network," *Intelligent Transportation, Big Data and Smart City (ICITBS), 2015 International Conference on*, pp. 19–20, 2015.
8. M. Prakash, P. Balasubramaniam and S. Lakshmanan, "Synchronization of Markovian jumping inertial neural networks and its applications in image encryption," *Neural Networks*, vol. 83, pp. 86–93, 2016.
9. S.P. Wen, Z.G. Zeng, T.W. Huang, Q.G. Meng and W. Yao, "Lag synchronization of switched neural networks via neural activation function and applications in image encryption," *IEEE Transactions on Neural Networks and Learning Systems*, vol. 26, pp. 1493–1502, 2015.
10. X.M. Zhang, S.Y. Sheng, G.P. Lu and Y.F. Zheng, "Synchronization for arrays of coupled jumping delayed neural networks and its application to image encryption," *Decision and Control (CDC), 2017 IEEE 56th Annual Conference on*, pp. 12–15, 2017.
11. X. Chai, Z. Gan, K. Yang, Y. Chen and X. Liu, "An image encryption algorithm based on the memristive hyperchaotic system, cellular automata and DNA sequence operations," *Signal Processing: Image Communication*, vol. 52, pp. 6–19, 2017.
12. B. Wang F. Zou and J. Cheng, "A memristor-based chaotic system and its application in image encryption," *Optik*, vol. 154, pp. 538–544, 2018.
13. J.Q. Lu and D.W.C. Ho, "Stabilization of complex dynamical networks with noise disturbance under performance constraint," *Nonlinear Analysis Series B: Real World Applications*, vol. 12, pp. 1974–1984, 2011.
14. X. Huang, Y.J. Fan, J. Jia, Z. Wang and Y.X. Li, "Quasi-synchronization of fractional-order memristor-based neural networks with parameter mismatches," *IET Control Theory & Applications*, vol. 11, pp. 2317–2327,2017.
15. Y. Pershin and M. Ventra, "Experimental demonstration of associative memory with memristive neural networks," *Neural Networks*, vol. 23, pp. 881–886, 2010.
16. M. Itoh and L. Chua, "Memristor cellular automata and memristor discrete-time cellular neural networks," *International Journal of Bifurcation & Chaos*, vol. 19, pp. 3605–3656, 2009.

17. M.W. Zheng, L.X. Li, H.P. Peng, J.H. Xiao, Y.X. Yang, Y.P. Zhang and H. Zhao, "Finite-time stability and synchronization of memristor-based fractional-order fuzzy cellular neural networks," *Communications in Nonlinear Science and Numerical Simulation*, vol. 59, pp. 272–291, 2018.
18. J. Chen, C. Li, T. Huang and X. Yang, "Global stabilization of memristor-based fractional-order neural networks with delay via output feedback control," *Modern Physics Letters B*, vol. 31, pp. 1–19, 2017.
19. M. Yu, W. Wang, M. Yuan, X. Luo and L. Liu, "Exponential antisynchronization control of stochastic memristive neural networks with mixed time-varying delays based on novel delay-dependent or delay-independent adaptive controller," *Mathematical Problems in Engineering*, vol. 2017.
20. J. Yang, L. Wang, Y. Wang and T. Guo, "A novel memristive Hopfield neural network with application in associative memory," *Neurocomputing*, vol. 227, pp. 142–148, 2016.
21. S. Zhu, L. Wang and S. Duan, "Memristive pulse coupled neural network with applications in medical image processing," *Neurocomputing*, vol. 227, pp. 149–157, 2017.
22. X. Hu, G. Feng, S. Duan and L. Liu, "A memristive multilayer cellular neural network with applications to image processing," *IEEE Transactions on Neural Networks and Learning Systems*, vol. 28, pp. 1889–1901, 2016.
23. C. Chen, L.X. Li, H.P. Peng and Y.X. Yang, "Fixed-time synchronization of memristor-based BAM neural networks with time-varying discrete delay," *Neural Networks*, vol. 96, pp. 47–54, 2017.
24. M.W. Zheng, L.X. Li, H.P. Peng, J.H. Xiao, Y.X. Yang and Y.P. Zhang, "Fixed-time synchronization of memristive fuzzy BAM cellular neural networks with time-varying delays based on feedback controllers," *IEEE Access*, vol. 6, pp. 12085–12102, 2018.
25. R. Sakthivel, R. Anbuvithya, K. Mathiyalagan, Y.K. Ma and P. Prakash, "Reliable anti-synchronization conditions for BAM memristive neural networks with different memductance functions," *Applied Mathematics & Computation*, vol. 275, pp. 213–228, 2016.
26. W. Wang, M. Yu, X. Luo, L. Liu, M. Yuan and W. Zhao, "Synchronization of memristive BAM neural networks with leakage delay and additive time-varying delay components via sampled-data control," *Chaos, Solitons & Fractals*, vol. 104, pp. 84–97, 2017.
27. C. Chen, L.X. Li, H.P. Peng and Y.X. Yang, "Adaptive synchronization of memristor-based BAM neural networks with mixed delays," *Applied Mathematics and Computation*, vol. 322, pp. 100–110, 2018.
28. M. Hagiwara, "Multidirectional associative memory," *Proceedings of the International Joint Conference on Neural Network*, vol. 1, pp. 3–6, 1990.
29. S. Chen, "Multivalued exponential multidirectional associative memory," *Journal of Software*, vol. 9, pp. 397–400, 1998.
30. M. Wang, T. Zhou and X. Zhang, "Global exponential stability of discrete time multidirectional associative memory neural network with variable delays," *ISRN Discrete Mathematics*, vol. 2012, pp. 1–10, 2012.
31. P. Basaras, G. Iosifidis, D. Katsaros and L. Tassiulas, "Identifying influential spreaders in complex multilayer networks: A centrality perspective," *IEEE Transactions on Network Science and Engineering*, pp.1–15, 2017.
32. P. Jiang, Z. Zeng and J. Chen, "On the periodic dynamics of memristor-based neural networks with leakage and time-varying delays," *Neurocomputing*, vol. 219, pp. 163–173, 2017.

33. A. Wu and Z. Zeng, "Lagrange stability of memristive neural networks with discrete and distributed delays," *IEEE Transactions on Neural Networks and Learning Systems*, vol. 25, pp. 690–703, 2013.
34. W. Wang, L. Li, H. Peng, W. Wang, J. Kurths, J. Xiao and Y. Yang, "Anti-synchronization of coupled memristive neutral-type neural networks with mixed time-varying delays via randomly occurring control," *Nonlinear Dynamics*, vol. 83, pp. 2143–2155, 2016.
35. O. Kwon, J. Park and S. Lee, "Secure communication based on chaotic synchronization via interval time-varying delay feedback control," *Nonlinear Dynamics*, vol. 63, pp. 239–252, 2011.
36. H. Tirandaz and A. Karmi-Mollaee, "Modified function projective feedback control for time-delay chaotic Liu system synchronization and its application to secure image transmission," *Optik*, vol. 147, pp. 187–196, 2017.
37. X. Luo, J. Deng, J. Liu, W.P. Wang, X.J. Ban and Jenq-H. Wang, "A quantized kernel least mean square scheme with entropy-guided learning for intelligent data analysis," *China Communications*, vol. 14, pp. 127–136, 2017.
38. J. Chen, Z. Zeng and P. Jiang, "Global Mittag-Leffler stability and synchronization of memristor-based fractional-order neural networks," *Neural Networks*, vol. 51, pp. 1–8, 2014.
39. C. Chen, L. Li, H. Peng, Y. Yang and T. Li, "Finite-time synchronization of memristor-based neural networks with mixed delays," *Neurocomputing*, vol. 235, pp. 83–89, 2017.
40. Z. Cai, L. Huang, M. Zhu and D. Wang, "Finite-time stabilization control of memristor-based neural networks," *Nonlinear Analysis: Hybrid Systems*, vol. 20, pp. 37–54, 2016.
41. L. Wang, Q. Song, Y. Liu, Z. Zhao and F. Alsaadi, "Finite-time stability analysis of fractional-order complex-valued memristor-based neural networks with both leakage and time-varying delays," *Neurocomputing*, vol. 245, pp. 86–101, 2017.
42. A. Wu and Z. Zeng, "Anti-synchronization control of a class of memristive recurrent neural networks," *Communications in Nonlinear Science and Numerical Simulation*, vol. 18, pp. 373–385, 2013.
43. A. Wu, S. Wen and Z. Zeng, "Synchronization control of a class of memristor-based recurrent neural networks," *Information Sciences*, vol. 183, pp. 106–116, 2012.
44. X.Y. Niu, "Applications of image encryption under multiple chaotic sequences," MS thesis, Communication and information system, Heilongjiang University, Heilongjiang, China, 2014.

Chapter 11

Modalities for Decoding Human Brain Activity

Raheel Zafar and Ata Ullah

Contents

11.1 Introduction

Decoding of the human brain is one of the most complex, difficult but demanding research areas of the current era. The comprehensive meaning of brain decoding is to decode the thoughts, dreams and even the intentions of the person, e.g., to know a person's decision before she responds. Neuroscientists are able to understand how objects and features are represented inside the brain, although it is not fully achieved because of many limitations especially due to the unavailability of hardware which can measure all brain activities. Currently, functional magnetic resonance imaging (fMRI) is considered as the best modality which measures brain activity indirectly. Over the past few decades, there have been many developments in brain research especially in discriminating the patterns of brain activities starting from simple to complex experiments. In simple experiments, Kamitani et al. [1] decoded the behavior of the brain for orientation responses and Miyawaki et al. [2] decoded the activity patterns of the brain for alphabets. In complex experiments Naselaris et al. [3] decoded the human brain activity for grey scale natural images and Nishimoto et al. [4] decoded for movies. Although various groups are working on the brain across the world, this research is still open and there are a lot of opportunities for neuroscientists to reveal the secrets of the brain because in modern neuroscience this is the best time for a conceptual and technological revolution.

The research on brain study has a bright future, and hopefully better brain activations will be measured in the coming years. Due to the importance of this field, many developed and developing countries are establishing the brain centers and spending huge sums of money in this area of research. In 2013, President Obama announced a research grant of $100 million for brain exploration in the United States [5] and the European Union (EU) announced a grant of more than a billion euros for brain research in coming years [6]. Engineers and neuroscientists are conducting this research due to its applications in different fields such as developing a brain–computer interface which will be helpful in solving the problems of real world. An example of a real-world application is the development of a brain–machine interface to control prosthetic limbs. It is a basic application that could also be helpful in medical diagnoses, communication, and entertainment. In entertainment and advertising, it can be used to see the behavior of the brain related to different brand products, such as when a blind taste test was done between Pepsi and Coke [7] to see which one is better. Moreover, it is helpful in diagnosing different diseases like dementia, stroke, and vegetative states. It can also be used in stem cell therapy.

Brain decoding is helpful not only for advanced applications, but it can also be used in basic research related to cognitive neuroscience. For example, it is possible to test whether specific information is present in the brain by testing; it is possible to decode that information from brain activity. With the decoding of human brain activity, neuroscientists have hope that in the future two brains would communicate directly with each other, or one can read the mind of the other person. In a future cyber-enabled world, there could be a cyber brain to represent a person in the cyber world for automatically managing the tasks on behalf of a real person. There are many potential applications of brain decoding, for example, if such a decoding device would be available then it can be used in court cases, detective work, dream decoding, and diagnosis of diseases. It can also help to take a log of thoughts and ideas coming into the brain. In a similar vein, the brain of a patient who cannot speak due to dumbness or paralysis can also be read. After decoding these brain activities, a cyber-enabled real-time intelligent system can be developed to display the thoughts and reply accordingly, performing activities turning on a light, heater, or fan, or providing water, juice, or quick snacks.

11.2 Modalities for Brain Decoding

The modality of brain decoding is the mode in which the data of the brain is recorded. The primary goal of researchers in neuroscience is to understand the workings of the human brain. For this purpose human data is required. Different non-invasive functional neuroimaging techniques are used; the most common are functional magnetic resonance imaging (fMRI), electroencephalography (EEG), and magnetoencephalography (MEG). All these techniques are able to record concurrent brain activity directly or indirectly against the presented stimulus to the subjects. The underlying mental process can be extracted through a relation between the category of the stimulus and the pattern of recorded signal. There are different approaches to analyze the relationship between stimuli and brain activity, but the one based on predicting the stimulus from the concurrent brain recording is called brain decoding. Brain decoding started more than a decade ago [8], when a neuroscientist observed that there is a lot of untapped information during brain scanning. These brain scans were taken through fMRI. After that a large amount of research was done in fMRI and it became the best modality in this field as it has very good spatial resolution. However in recent years, other modalities like EEG and MEG are also used in this field.

11.2.1 Functional MRI

In fMRI, decoding of brain activity is quite mature and popular since most of the research groups related to decoding are working with fMRI. In fMRI, the pioneer work was done by Haxby [8]; after that there were many significant studies available in this area [1,9,10]. In fMRI, the neural activity is not measured directly; it measures the blood oxygen level dependent (BOLD) signal using an MRI scanner which is associated with the neural activity. Since there is a linear relationship between the BOLD signal and neural activity, the BOLD signal can give significant information during neural activity. The amplitude of the BOLD signal increases with neural activity and vice versa. The spatial resolution of fMRI makes it popular in neuroscience as exact localized information can be extracted which is enough to decode brain activity between different categories. In neuroscience, it is common to see the difference between the task and the baseline and in case of fMRI, different tools are available to see and extract the significant information. The common fMRI tools are statistical parametric mapping (SPM), FMRIB Software Library (FSL), FreeSurfer, AFNI, and Brain voyager. The most popular is SPM as it is freely available and Matlab based with a lot of available help. In SPM, the neural activity can directly be seen on a glass brain in SPM. The glass brain is a 3D brain visualization that displays source activity and connectivity. The sagittal, coronal, and transverse views are known as a glass brain that provides the visualization of analysis [11] as shown in Figure 11.1. Table 11.1 presents the degrees of freedom, full width

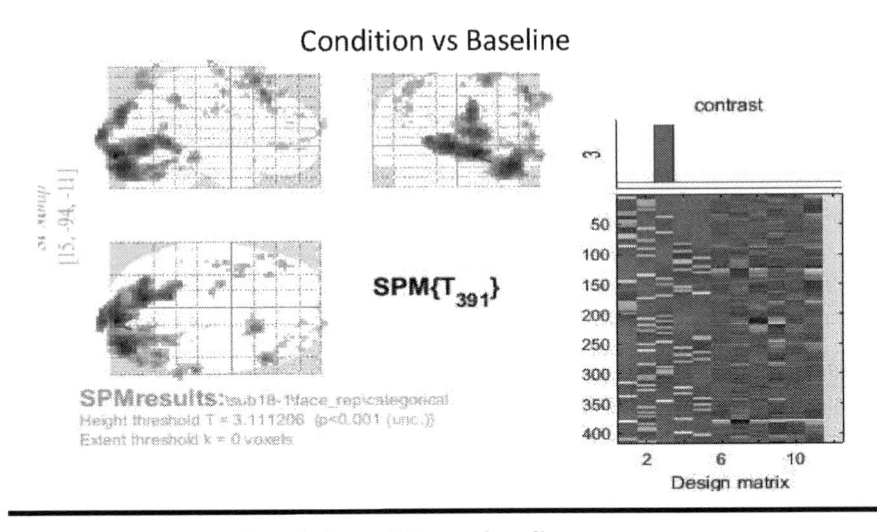

Figure 11.1 First-level analysis: Building vs baseline.

Table 11.1 Statistics Table for SPM

Statistics: *p-values adjusted for search volume*

set-level		cluster-level				peak-level					mm	mm	mm
p	c	$p_{FWE\text{-}corr}$	$q_{FDR\text{-}corr}$	k_E	p_{uncorr}	$p_{FWE\text{-}corr}$	$q_{FDR\text{-}corr}$	T	$(Z_{\equiv})$	p_{uncorr}			
0.006	43	0.000	0.000	1822	0.000	0.000	0.000	7.44	7.19	0.000	15	-94	-11
						0.000	0.000	6.43	6.26	0.000	39	-91	-23
						0.000	0.000	6.24	6.09	0.000	-6	-73	-2
		0.000	0.000	63	0.000	0.031	0.011	4.95	4.87	0.000	54	26	52
						0.422	0.068	4.38	4.32	0.000	57	29	43
						0.985	0.277	3.80	3.77	0.000	57	35	37
		0.000	0.000	92	0.000	0.166	0.041	4.59	4.52	0.000	24	17	67
						0.999	0.392	3.64	3.60	0.000	9	14	67
		0.016	0.004	31	0.001	0.195	0.041	4.55	4.49	0.000	66	-31	-14
		0.000	0.000	56	0.000	0.413	0.068	4.38	4.33	0.000	69	-46	49
						0.974	0.254	3.85	3.81	0.000	63	-43	40
		0.000	0.000	87	0.000	0.666	0.105	4.21	4.16	0.000	24	-76	64
						0.738	0.118	4.15	4.10	0.000	33	-76	73
		0.830	0.191	7	0.062	0.678	0.105	4.20	4.15	0.000	-12	-19	85
		0.487	0.078	11	0.023	0.791	0.131	4.11	4.06	0.000	-45	-7	55
		0.101	0.020	20	0.004	0.839	0.146	4.06	4.02	0.000	-21	-10	76
		0.144	0.023	18	0.005	0.933	0.193	3.94	3.90	0.000	-42	41	52
		0.902	0.195	6	0.082	0.933	0.193	3.94	3.90	0.000	-33	29	64
		1.000	0.468	1	0.468	0.983	0.277	3.81	3.78	0.000	18	17	-17
		0.026	0.006	28	0.001	0.985	0.277	3.80	3.77	0.000	-33	5	58
						0.997	0.345	3.70	3.67	0.000	-39	11	58

table shows 3 local maxima more than 8.0mm apart

Height threshold: T = 3.11, p = 0.001 (1.000)
Extent threshold: k = 0 voxels
Expected voxels per cluster, <k> = 2.012
Expected number of clusters, <c> = 28.41
FWEp: 4.846, FDRp: 4.552, FWEc: 28, FDRc: 18

Degrees of freedom = [1.0, 391.0]
FWHM = 7.7 7.9 7.6 mm mm mm; 2.6 2.6 2.5 {voxels}
Volume: 1481436 = 54868 voxels = 2846.7 resels
Voxel size: 3.0 3.0 3.0 mm mm mm; (resel = 17.29 voxels)
Page 1

at half maximum (FWHM), voxel size, position of voxels, *z*-values, number of clusters, number of significant voxels in each cluster, and the other information found during the analysis of the condition for SPM.

11.2.2 EEG and MEG

Decoding of brain activity using EEG and MEG is quite new as compared to fMRI, so extensive research work is required in this field for these two modalities. The advantage of using EEG and MEG is that unlike fMRI, they measure the brain activity directly and both have very high temporal resolution. The main limitation of EEG is its spatial resolution which is poor while MEG has good spatial resolution too on the order of millimeters. EEG is an old technique and has been used for brain studies for a long time [12]; however, in the field of decoding it is not mature and has been used in only a few recent studies [13]. Dingyi Pei et al. observed the hand kinematics using singular value decomposition and performed the neural decoding to identify the neural representation of kinematic synergies. After that these synergies are reconstructed for weighted linear combinations that are further utilized to extract the optimal weights by using linear estimations for optimal cases. In this scheme, EEG can successfully decode the synergy-based movements [14]. MEG is one of the best techniques to study brain activity since it has both good spatial and temporal resolution so it has been used often in recent studies for the application of decoding. Abdelkader et al. present a brain-Geminoid control system where two brain–computer interfaces were involved to perform four bimanual hand movements. It was set up to control a humanoid robot. A non-linear vector machine was utilized to classify the real-time hand movements along with 114 MEG sensors [15]. The current common available tools for the analysis of EEG data are EEGLAB, BESA, Net station, Brainstorm and SPM while MEG data can also be analyzed using the same tools, i.e., EEGLAB, BESA, Brainstorm, and SPM (Figure 11.2).

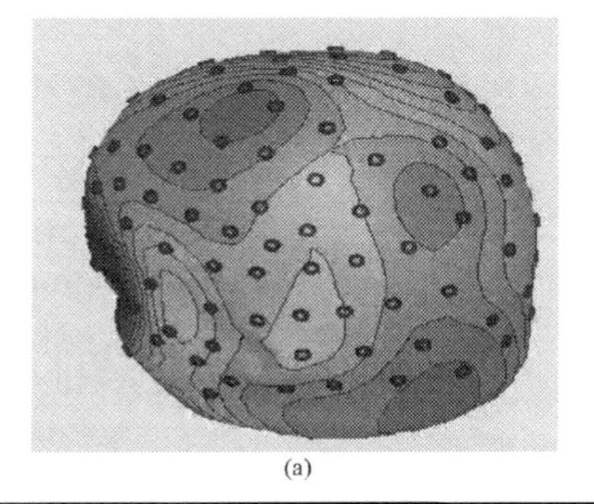

(a)

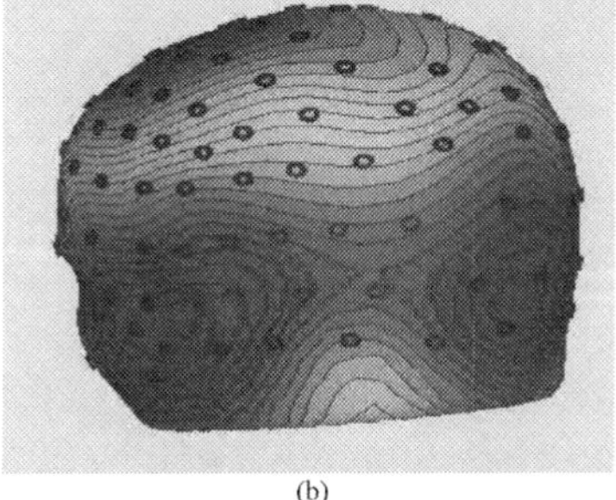

(b)

Figure 11.2 Activity of brain (a) before the task and (b) during the task.

11.3 Methods in Brain Decoding

In brain decoding, initially experiment design and data collection are the important parts which need a lot of attention. This is the reason different tools are used to clean the data or various pre-processing steps are done. In current studies, doctors and psychologists are also involved for better experiment design. After data collection and pre-processing the main part is the data analysis which has three main types: classification, identification, and reconstruction. In classification, we can determine one of the many possible brain states of the person. For example, we can differentiate different tasks or categories of images. During the identification procedure, the target is the identification of the specific image the person is seeing. The reconstruction procedure is the most complex one in which the purpose is to reconstruct the images based on the neuronal activities measured during different modalities. Each technique has its own pros and cons, but all these techniques are mostly dependent on statistical and mathematical techniques like the Bayesian model, correlation, convolutional neural network, and many others. In short, the purpose is to extract the maximum brain information using good experiment design, by removing noisy data through various pre-processing steps and using advanced statistical techniques and tools. In addition, data mining techniques are applied to extract patterns from large data sets, which involves machine learning, statistics, and database systems.

11.3.1 Analysis of Brain Data

Analysis of brain data is a complex procedure and consists of many steps, as the brain itself is quite complex. After collection of data, pre-processing is the initial step which itself has different methods and stages. After pre-processing, statistical analysis is the core stage which consists of feature extraction, feature selection, and classification. Feature extraction is the way to extract information from the brain. There are different ways to extract information like wavelet transform and time domain features; however, raw data can also be taken as features. Since the brain has a lot of data and only a small portion is significant, significant features are required from the data which is done using feature selection techniques. Different feature selection techniques are used for this purpose but the most common are t test, entropy, Bhattacharyya distance, and many others. Finally, classification is required to differentiate the different brain states which is done using various machine learning algorithms, for example, support vector machine, logistic regression, naïve Bayes, and others. There are different methods used in different studies for the purpose of feature extraction, selection, and classification [13,16] but the primary objective is to achieve increasing accuracy.

11.3.2 Convolutional Neural Network in Neuroimaging

Convolutional neural network (CNN) and deep learning (DL) have contributed a large set of application scenarios for intelligent learning and the classification of objects. CNN requires lower pre-processing computational costs as compared to other classification mechanisms for different types of images. It reduces human effort and eliminates the dependence on existing related knowledge. CNN is applicable in computer vision to efficiently maintain the parametric values for different shapes and measure the variations to predict and identify the matching objects [17]. It becomes quite challenging when the objects are speedily moving in a real-time environment. In these models, a set of "feature maps" are constructed by convolving the responses from different filters. It takes the image at various inputs to extract the parameters. Resulting parameters of convolution are further processed to reduce the sample count by applying pooling. CNN involves a large set of parameters that can be extracted for learning the features of images. For such computations, massive numbers of multilayer calculations are performed. In CNN there is no need for feature extraction, selection, and classification because the CNN model does everything by itself. The only thing is the input which we have to give to CNN model and at the final stage CNN give the output as final results. This makes the world easy but CNN also gives the best results compared to any other model. Although CNN is not mature in neuroimaging it has still been used in a couple of studies. Plis et al. [18] described deep learning for neuroimaging in which a model is described for neuroimaging applications. Moreover, few CNN studies [19,20] exist both for EEG and fMRI in which various models are designed for neuroscience applications. In addition to the above, CNN is also used with SVM means features extracted using CNN and classification is done with SVM instead of the CNN classifier, i.e., softmax. In short, although CNN is already used in neuroscience studies, it is immature in this field, since most existing models are not designed for neuroscience applications. This means CNN has a lot of potential in this field and in the future, CNN will be part of many neuroscience studies.

References

1. Y. Kamitani and F. Tong, "Decoding the visual and subjective contents of the human brain," *Nature Neuroscience*, vol. 8, pp. 679–685, 2005.
2. Y. Miyawaki, H. Uchida, O. Yamashita, M.-A. Sato, Y. Morito, H. C. Tanabe, N. Sadato, and Y. Kamitani, "Visual image reconstruction from human brain activity using a combination of multiscale local image decoders," *Neuron*, vol. 60, pp. 915–929, 2008.
3. T. Naselaris, R. J. Prenger, K. N. Kay, M. Oliver, and J. L. Gallant, "Bayesian reconstruction of natural images from human brain activity," *Neuron*, vol. 63, p. 902, 2009.

4. S. Nishimoto, A. T. Vu, T. Naselaris, Y. Benjamini, B. Yu, and J. L. Gallant, "Reconstructing visual experiences from brain activity evoked by natural movies," *Current Biology*, vol. 21, pp. 1641–1646, 2011.
5. A. Mooney, Obama seeks $100M to unlock mysteries of the brain. 2013. Available: http://www.cnn.com/2013/04/02/health/obama-brain-research [Accessed: February 18, 2019].
6. C. Ryan, Human brain project wins major EU funding. 2013. Available: http://www.ucl.ac.uk/news/news-articles/0113/130128-human-brain-project-wins-major-EU-funding [Accessed: February 16, 2019].
7. S. M. McClure, J. Li, D. Tomlin, K. S. Cypert, L. M. Montague, and P. R. Montague, "Neural correlates of behavioral preference for culturally familiar drinks," *Neuron*, vol. 44, pp. 379–387, 2004.
8. J. V. Haxby, M. I. Gobbini, M. L. Furey, A. Ishai, J. L. Schouten, and P. Pietrini, "Distributed and overlapping representations of faces and objects in ventral temporal cortex," *Science*, vol. 293, pp. 2425–2430, 2001.
9. K. N. Kay, T. Naselaris, R. J. Prenger, and J. L. Gallant, "Identifying natural images from human brain activity," *Nature*, vol. 452, pp. 352–355, 2008.
10. T. Horikawa, M. Tamaki, Y. Miyawaki, and Y. Kamitani, "Neural decoding of visual imagery during sleep," *Science*, vol. 340, pp. 639–642, 2013.
11. D. Bor and M. Brett, Graphical inspection of Results in SPM96: A step by step guide, 2013. Available: http://imaging.mrc-cbu.cam.ac.uk/imaging/SpmGraphical [Accessed: February 10, 2019].
12. S. Lee and M. Buchsbaum, "Topographic mapping of EEG artifacts," *Clinical EEG (Electroencephalography)*, vol. 18, pp. 61–67, 1987.
13. M. Taghizadeh-Sarabi, M. R. Daliri, and K. S. Niksirat, "Decoding objects of basic categories from electroencephalographic signals using wavelet transform and support vector machines," *Brain Topography*, vol. 28, pp. 33–46, 2015.
14. D. Pei, V. Patel, M. Burns, R. Chandramouli, and R. Vinjamuri, "Neural decoding of synergy-based hand movements using electroencephalography," *IEEE Access*, vol. 7, pp. 18155–18163, 2019.
15. A. N. Belkacem, H. Ishiguro, S. Nishio, M. Hirata, and T. Suzuki, "Real-time MEG-based brain-geminoid control using single-trial SVM classification," *2018 3rd International Conference on Advanced Robotics and Mechatronics (ICARM)*, Singapore, 2018, pp. 679–684.
16. K. N. Kay, J. Winawer, A. Mezer, and B. A. Wandell, "Compressive spatial summation in human visual cortex," *Journal of Neurophysiology*, vol. 110, pp. 481–494, 2013.
17. A. Krizhevsky, I. Sutskever, and G. E. Hinton, "Imagenet classification with deep convolutional neural networks," *Advances in Neural Information Processing Systems*, 2012, pp. 1097–1105.
18. S. M. Plis, D. R. Hjelm, R. Salakhutdinov, and V. D. Calhoun, "Deep learning for neuroimaging: A validation study," arXiv preprint arXiv:1312.5847, 2013.
19. X. Sun, C. Qian, Z. Chen, Z. Wu, B. Luo, and G. Pan, "Remembered or forgotten?—An EEG-based computational prediction approach," *PLoS One*, vol. 11, p. e0167497, 2016.
20. H. Cecotti and A. Graser, "Convolutional neural networks for P300 detection with application to brain-computer interfaces," *IEEE Transactions on Pattern Analysis and Machine Intelligence*, vol. 33, pp. 433–445, 2011.

Chapter 12

A Novel Human Activity Recognition Scheme for Smart Health Using Multilayer Extreme Learning Machine

Maojian Chen, Ying Li, Xiong Luo, Weiping Wang, Long Wang, and Wenbing Zhao

Contents

12.1 Introduction

More recently, wearable sensor has been identified as one of the effective tools used in a variety of smart health applications. Wearable sensors not only can be used to collect valuable health-related data of their users, they can be used in conjunction with other infrastructure-bound sensors, such as Microsoft Kinect sensor, to facilitate privacy-aware fine-grained activity tracking and real-time intervention [1]. This fusion of multi-modal data promises a new type of smart health applications that coach a user to live a healthier life style by monitoring the user in real time and reminding him or her when he or she engages in an unhealthy activity. In this article, we investigate how to achieve fine-grained activity recognition in the context of such an application.

This type of applications may have huge positive impact on our society. For example, in many industries, workers suffer from pervasive back injuries due to improper movements such as waist twisting, lifting, and pulling [2,3], which often lead to a huge loss of productivity. A previous study found that, if workers were able to follow appropriate guidelines, the risk of lumbar injuries could be reduced by a factor of 10.7 [2]. As another example, early detection of dementia could significantly improve the quality of life of dementia patients [4], which requires the detection of symptom of mild cognitive impairment and calling for intervention of caregivers when necessary [5].

Previously, a system was developed [6]. It consists of inexpensive programmable depth sensors, wearable devices, and smart phones. The wearable sensor behavior recognition system essentially captures the action signals by body movements through binding or wearing multiple sensor nodes on the body, and then performs preprocessing, feature extraction, and selection on these data. Finally, according to the selected features, an action recognition algorithm is used to classify and identify those actions. Furthermore, a novel system was proposed to track the activities of consented workers [1]. This system uses a smart watch to identify the user and to deliver a realtime alert to the user, and uses the Kinect sensor for fine-grained activity tracking. The system provides a valuable set of services for workers to increase compliance to the best practice in using proper body mechanics when doing pulling and lifting activities. In this system, it requires continuous observation of the workers' back movements and accurate identification of severe back bending activities.

In previous research works, some researchers focused on the detection of different kinds of human activities with apparent differences, such as walking, standing, and sitting [6]. Few people investigated how to differentiate activities with nuanced differences, such as hitting, kicking, pushing, throwing, which is critical in detecting symptoms of mild cognitive impairment and dementia.

In this article, we use Kinect sensors to take data from a series of actions taken by the elderly and then categorize this series of actions by using our proposed method, named as S-ELM-KRSL, through the combination of a novel multilayer neural network (NN) learning algorithm, called as stacked extreme learning machine (S-ELM), and a nonlinear and local similarity measure, namely kernel risk-sensitive loss (KRSL). And then, by identifying the current actions of the elderly, appropriate interventions can be applied to help them. For example, the elderly may have a series of actions before he or she becomes out of control. When activities such as hitting, kicking, pushing, and throwing are detected, it usually means the subject is in emotional distress and caregivers should be informed promptly.

Human action recognition has been studied for many years. Early studies are typically based on two-dimensional image data obtained from RGB videos. These data can be affected by many factors, such as the changes of the background, the intensity of lighting, and the changes in the location of the shot [7], which may make it difficult to accurately identify the various actions. With the availability of Microsoft Kinect, human activity recognition can be done with depth data or skeletal joint data [1].

In the past few years, the rapid development of machine learning has attracted the attention of many researchers. Among them, the NN-based extreme learning machine (ELM) algorithm is so popular [8–10]. The biggest advantage of the ELM algorithm is that it does not need to manually adjust the hidden node parameters in NN, which achieves particularly fast training speed. Through these years of development, the traditional ELM cannot meet a variety of practical problems. The ELM has been accordingly improved [11–14], which led to many different forms of ELM, and S-ELM is one of them [15]. Motivated by deep learning model, through the use of multilayer NN structure, S-ELM is more accurate than some traditional machine learning methods.

In addition to the ELM improvements mentioned above, another common issue is how to deal with noises or outliers in the training set [16]. In this case, the previous approaches used in traditional ELM processing, employ the mean square error (MSE) measure which may result in Gaussian distributed errors. However, in practical applications, many of the data are non-Gaussian, which makes the traditional ELM unsuitable [17,18]. Recently, the correntropy as a measure of local similarity has been proposed [19]. Correntropy uses the probability to evaluate the similarity of two variables [19]. It has the advantages of flexibility and easy implementation, hence it can be applied in many practices [20–22]. However, since the performance surface of correntropic loss (C-Loss) is non-convex, it is very flat when it is far away from the optimal solution, meanwhile, it is sharp around the optimal solution, resulting in poor accuracy and slow convergence [23]. Therefore, kernel risk-sensitive loss (KRSL) was proposed instead of correntropy [24]. KRSL is more convex than C-Loss, then the better convergence performance can be achieved in some applications [25].

Meanwhile, in our proposed scheme, some parameters need to be adjusted to achieve the best computational performance. Hence, Jaya as a popular algorithm-specific parameter-less optimization algorithm [26], is used to adjust those key parameters in our method, with the purpose of achieving a good generalization performance with minimal human intervention.

Therefore, our proposed scheme efficiently handles noises or outliers on large-scale and complex datasets. Compared with other ELM-related algorithms, the proposed algorithm S-ELM-KRSL can achieve higher classification accuracy, and reduce the workload of manually adjusting parameters of algorithm.

The rest of this article is organized as follows. Section 12.2 provides a brief review of ELM, S-ELM, KRSL, and Jaya. In Section 12.3, we detail our proposed scheme, including the algorithm S-ELM-KRSL used to classification for human actions. And the experiments are conducted to demonstrate the performance of the proposed scheme in Section 12.4. Finally, the conclusion is summarized in Section 12.5.

12.2 Related Work

This article uses an improved ELM with multilayer NN structure, i.e., S-ELM, to classify human actions, and then employs KRSL to handle outliers or noises. In this section, some related work in our scheme, including ELM, S-ELM, KRSL, and Jaya, are analyzed.

12.2.1 Extreme Learning Machine (ELM)

ELM is a learning algorithm for single-layer feed-forward NN with a fast training speed, where the NN is with only three layers, including the input layer, the hidden layer, and the output layer [8]. The characteristics of this algorithm are that the parameters of hidden layer nodes are selected at random, and no adjustment is needed during the training process. Only the number of hidden layer neurons needs to be set. The external power of this NN, i.e., the output weight, is the least-squares solution obtained by minimizing the square loss function. This NN parameter determination process does not need any iterative steps, thus greatly reducing the NN parameter adjustment time.

Given N arbitrary different samples $\{(x_i, y_i)|i = 1,\ldots, N\}$, where $x_i \in R^n$ is the input data vector, $y_i \in R^s$ is the corresponding target label of output for each sample. The output of the original ELM with L hidden nodes can be written as:

$$y_i = f_L(x_i) = \sum_{j=1}^{L} \beta_j g(w_j \cdot x_i + b_j), i = 1,\ldots,N, \tag{12.1}$$

where β_j is the output weight, $g(\cdot)$ is the activation function in hidden layer, $\mathbf{w}_j \in \mathbb{R}^n$ is the input weight vector connecting the input neuron and the j-th hidden neuron, and b_j is the deviation term of the j-th hidden neuron.

Here, (12.1) can be expressed in matrix form as:

$$\mathbf{H}\beta = \mathbf{Y}, \tag{12.2}$$

where $\beta = [\beta_1, \beta_2, \ldots, \beta_L]^T, \mathbf{Y} = [y_1, y_2, \ldots, y_N]^T$, $\mathbf{H}$ is the hidden layer output matrix, and it is defined as:

$$\mathbf{H} = \begin{bmatrix} h(\mathbf{x}_1) \\ \vdots \\ h(\mathbf{x}_N) \end{bmatrix} = \begin{bmatrix} h_1(\mathbf{x}_1) & \cdots & h_L(\mathbf{x}_1) \\ \vdots & \vdots & \vdots \\ h_1(\mathbf{x}_N) & \cdots & h_L(\mathbf{x}_N) \end{bmatrix}, \tag{12.3}$$

where $\mathrm{h}(\mathbf{x}_i) = [h_1(\mathbf{x}_i), \ldots, h_L(\mathbf{x}_i)](i = 1, \ldots, N)$.

The output weight β can be expressed as:

$$\beta = \mathbf{H}^{\dagger}\mathbf{Y}, \tag{12.4}$$

where $\mathbf{H}^{\dagger}$ is the Moore-Penrose generalized inverse of $\mathbf{H}$.

When $\mathbf{H}^{\mathrm{T}}\mathbf{H}$ is nonsingular, we can use the orthogonal projection method to compute $\mathbf{H}^{\dagger}$:

$$\mathbf{H}^{\dagger} = (\mathbf{H}^{\mathrm{T}}\mathbf{H})^{-1}\mathbf{H}^{\mathrm{T}}. \tag{12.5}$$

Then, β can be expressed as:

$$\beta = (\mathbf{H}^{\mathrm{T}}\mathbf{H})^{-1}\mathbf{H}^{\mathrm{T}}\mathbf{Y}. \tag{12.6}$$

Considering the noise in practical application, an ELM based on equality constrained optimization method was proposed to improve the generalization performance and stability of standard ELM [27]. The core idea of this approach is to minimize training errors and output weights.

It can be expressed as:

$$\text{Minimize} : \| \mathbf{H}\beta - \mathbf{Y} \|_{\mathrm{F}}^2 + \mu \| \beta \|_{\mathrm{F}}^2, \tag{12.7}$$

where $\| \cdot \|_F$ is the L_2 -norm, μ is a parameter that needs to be adjusted.

If the number of training samples is much larger than the number of hidden layers, that is $N \gg L$, the output weight vector can be displayed as:

$$\beta = \left(\frac{\mathbf{E}}{C} + \mathbf{H}^{\mathrm{T}}\mathbf{H} \right)^{-1} \mathbf{H}^{\mathrm{T}}\mathbf{Y}, \tag{12.8}$$

and the output of ELM is:

$$f(\mathbf{x}) = \mathbf{h}(\mathbf{x})\beta = \mathbf{h}(\mathbf{x}) \left(\frac{\mathbf{E}}{C} + \mathbf{H}^{\mathrm{T}}\mathbf{H} \right)^{-1} \mathbf{H}^{\mathrm{T}}\mathbf{Y}, \tag{12.9}$$

where $\mathbf{E}$ is an unit matrix, and C is a constant.

In another case, when the number of training samples is less than the number of hidden layers, that is $N < L$, the output weight vector can be displayed as:

$$\beta = \mathbf{H}^{\mathrm{T}} \left(\frac{\mathbf{E}}{C} + \mathbf{H}\mathbf{H}^{\mathrm{T}} \right)^{-1} \mathbf{Y}. \tag{12.10}$$

Then, the output of ELM can be written as:

$$f(\mathbf{x}) = \mathbf{h}(\mathbf{x})\beta = \mathbf{h}(\mathbf{x})\mathbf{H}^{\mathrm{T}} \left(\frac{\mathbf{E}}{C} + \mathbf{H}\mathbf{H}^{\mathrm{T}} \right)^{-1} \mathbf{Y}. \tag{12.11}$$

12.2.2 Stacked Extreme Learning Machine (S-ELM)

While addressing large-scale dataset, in order to achieve good generalization performance, we usually require many hidden nodes to train the learning model in multilayer NN. However, adding too many nodes may make the training network very complicated, and it may also cause some problems, such as the decrease of training speed decline and out-of-memory errors. In order to address these issues, the traditional ELM was improved and a new S-ELM was developed [15]. Motivated by multilayer NN learning structure, S-ELM is an NN with many hidden layers that can break down a large ELM into smaller ELMs and then connect these many smaller ELMs in series. The underlying hidden layer is exported, and several key components are extracted by principal component analysis (PCA) dimensionality reduction method and then transmitted to the upper layer [15].

We first fix L hidden layer nodes and then execute a traditional ELM network in the lower S-ELM to get the output matrix $\mathbf{H}$ of the hidden layer, where the output weight β can be obtained from formula (12.8) or formula (12.10). However, because the parameters of the hidden layer are random, the hidden layer and the output layer are not linearly related. Therefore, we perform a PCA method on β, such that the dimension of β decreases from L to L_1, where $L_1 < L$.

After dimensionality reduction via PCA, we can get some eigenvectors, which are arranged in decreasing order of eigenvalues. We take the first L_1 feature matrix as $\mathbf{P} \in \mathbb{R}^{L \times L_1}$, then the output weight after dimension reduction can be expressed as $\beta_1 = \beta^{\mathrm{T}}\mathbf{P}$. Similarly, the output of the hidden layer is obtained as follows:

$$\mathbf{H}_1 = \mathbf{HP}. \tag{12.12}$$

Then, in order to be able to represent all the information of the lower hidden layer, the newly obtained hidden layer output $\mathbf{H}_1$ is passed to the higher layer. For the next hidden layer in S-ELM, $(L - L_1)$ new hidden neurons are randomly generated, and then the output matrix $\mathbf{H}_{new}$ of these new nodes can be obtained as follows:

$$\mathbf{H}_{new} = \begin{bmatrix} h_{new}(\mathbf{x}_1) \\ \vdots \\ h_{new}(\mathbf{x}_N) \end{bmatrix} = \begin{bmatrix} h_1(\mathbf{x}_1) & \cdots & h_L(\mathbf{x}_1) \\ \vdots & \vdots & \vdots \\ h_1(\mathbf{x}_N) & \cdots & h_L(\mathbf{x}_N) \end{bmatrix}. \tag{12.13}$$

The hidden layer output of this layer is:

$$\mathbf{H} = [\mathbf{H}_1, \mathbf{H}_{new}]. \tag{12.14}$$

We repeat the above process in the hidden layer until the last hidden layer. The final output of the S-ELM network is formula (12.9) or formula (12.11). Then, we put together the output of each layer, and the following results are achieved as follows:

$$\begin{gathered} \mathbf{H} \to \mathbf{H}_1', \\ [\mathbf{H}_1', \mathbf{H}_{new2}] \to \mathbf{H}_2', \\ [\mathbf{H}_2', \mathbf{H}_{new3}] \to \mathbf{H}_3', \\ \cdots \\ [\mathbf{H}_{N-2}', \mathbf{H}_{new(N-1)}] \to \mathbf{H}_{N-1}', \\ [\mathbf{H}_{N-1}', \mathbf{H}_{newN}]. \end{gathered} \tag{12.15}$$

12.2.3 Kernel Risk-Sensitive Loss (KRSL)

KRSL is a metric based on correntropy, and it improves the calculation of the similarity between two variables [24]. Because of their insensitivity to noises, both correntropy and KRSL can effectively handle data with large outliers.

Let X and Y be two random variables, the correntropy of them can be written as:

$$\begin{aligned} V_\sigma(X,Y) &= \mathbb{E}\left[\kappa_\sigma(X-Y)\right] \\ &= \int \kappa_\sigma(x-y)\, dF_{XY}(x,y), \end{aligned} \tag{12.16}$$

where σ is the width of kernel band, $\mathbb{E}(\cdot)$ is the mathematical expectation operator, $\kappa_\sigma(\cdot)$ is the Mercer kernel function [19], and $F_{XY}(x,y)$ is the simultaneous distribution of (X,Y). For convenience, in this article, we only consider the Gaussian kernel, then the corresponding kernel function is written as:

$$\kappa_\sigma(x-y) = \frac{1}{\sqrt{2\pi}\sigma} \exp\left(-\frac{(x-y)^2}{2\sigma^2}\right). \tag{12.17}$$

However, since the performance surface of C-Loss is non-convex, it is very flat when the solution is sharp around it, leaving the optimal solution and resulting in poor accuracy and slow convergence. Therefore, KRSL was proposed instead of correntropy [24]. KRSL is more convex than C-Loss, then better convergence performance can be achieved [24].

KRSL is expressed as formula (12.18). And with a finite number of data samples $\{(x_i, y_i) \mid i = 1,\ldots,N\}$, empirical KRSL can be calculated as:

$$\begin{aligned} L_\lambda(X,Y) &= \frac{1}{\lambda}\mathbb{E}\left[\exp\left(\lambda\left(1-\kappa_\sigma(X-Y)\right)\right)\right] \\ &= \frac{1}{\lambda}\int \exp\left(\lambda\left(1-\kappa_\sigma(x-y)\right)\right) dF_{XY}(x,y), \end{aligned} \tag{12.18}$$

$$\hat{L}_\lambda(X,Y) = \frac{1}{N\lambda}\sum_{i=1}^{N} \exp\left(\lambda\left(1-\kappa_\sigma(x_i - y_i)\right)\right). \tag{12.19}$$

where $\lambda > 0$ is the risk-sensitive parameter.

Then, through formula (12.19), the empirical KRSL can measure the similarity between vector $\mathbf{X} = [x_1, x_2, \ldots, x_N]$ and vector $\mathbf{Y} = [y_1, y_2, \ldots, y_N]$.

12.2.4 Jaya Algorithm

Currently, there are some evolutionary algorithms (EAs), such as genetic algorithm (GA), evolution strategy (ES), evolution programming (EP), differential evolution (DE), and so on. Meanwhile, there are also some of the recognized swarm intelligence (SI) based algorithms, including particle swarm optimization (PSO), ant colony optimization (ACO), artificial bee colony (ABC), and so on [28]. Generally, the traditional EAs and SI based algorithms require common controlling parameters, including population size, number of generations, and many others. In addition to common control parameters, those algorithms also require their own algorithm-specific control parameters. For example, GA uses mutation probability, crossover probability, and selection operator. PSO uses inertia weight, and social and cognitive parameters. ABC uses the numbers of onlooker bees, employed bees, and scout bees.

The proper adjustment of algorithm-specific parameters is a very important task affecting the performance of the above algorithms. Improper algorithm-specific parameter adjustments may increase computational effort or generate local optimal solutions. Unlike those algorithms, Jaya is an algorithm-specific parameter-less algorithm. As a simple yet powerful optimization algorithm, it has been widely used recently [29].

Let $f(x)$ be the objective function we want to minimize or maximize. In any iteration i, we assume that there are m design variables $(j = 1,2,\ldots,m)$ and n candidate solutions (i.e., population size, $k = 1,2,\ldots,n$). Then, the best candidate gets the best $f(x)$ in the entire candidate solutions, and the worst candidate gets the worst $f(x)$ in the entire candidate solutions. If $v_{j,k,i}$ is the value of the j-th variable of the k-th candidate solution during the i-th iteration, the value is modified according to the following equation [26]:

$$\begin{aligned} v'_{j,k,i} = v_{j,k,i} + r_{1,j,i}\left(v_{j,best,i} - \left|v_{j,k,i}\right|\right) \\ - r_{2,j,i}\left(v_{j,worst,i} - \left|v_{j,k,i}\right|\right), \end{aligned} \tag{12.20}$$

where $v_{j,best,i}$ is the value of the variable j for the best candidate and $v_{j,worst,i}$ is the value of the variable j for the worst candidate. And $v'_{j,k,i}$ is the updated value of $v_{j,k,i}$. In addition, $r_{1,j,i}$ and $r_{2,j,i}$ are the two random numbers for the j -th variable during the i -th iteration in the range $[0,1]$, respectively. The term "$r_{1,j,i}\left(v_{j,best,i} - \left|v_{j,k,i}\right|\right)$" indicates the tendency of the solution to move closer to the best solution and the term "$-r_{2,j,i}\left(v_{j,worst,i} - \left|v_{j,k,i}\right|\right)$" indicates the tendency of the solution to avoid the worst solution. Moreover, $v'_{j,k,i}$ is accepted if it gives better function value. All the accepted function values at the end of iteration are maintained and these values become the input to the next iteration [26].

12.3 The Proposed Scheme

In this section, we will detail the scheme we propose. The ultimate goal of the scheme in this article is to be able to identify human activities and predict their next movements.

First, K-means clustering algorithm is used to select several key frames in each action sequence. These key frames can clearly represent the corresponding actions and extract the meaningful joint-based and body-part-based features of key frames.

Then, the motion sequence is expressed in terms of joint and body-based features, and our proposed algorithm S-ELM-KRSL is used to identify the motion.

12.3.1 Key Frames Selection Using K-Means

The classical K-means clustering algorithm is used in this article to extract a few cluster centers of similar data [30]. Then, the key frames are selected on the basis of these cluster centers.

We get 20 skeleton joints from the Kinect, and each joint is a 3-dimensional (3D) coordinate, which contains x-, y-, and z-axis position. In our proposed approach, we cluster the coordinates of skeleton 3D joints at each frame in an action sequence. Therefore, the 3D coordinates comprise a 60-dimensional vector at each time frame. Then, we can obtain several 60-dimensional central vectors after clustering. The details of K-means clustering algorithm are given below.

First, $\mathbf{X} = \{\mathbf{x}_1, \mathbf{x}_2, \ldots, \mathbf{x}_N\} \left(\mathbf{x}_i \in \mathbb{R}^d, i = 1, \ldots, N\right)$ is a set of N vectors to be clustered, where $\mathbf{x}_i$ is the i-th frame vector with d-dimension $(d = 60)$, N is the total number of frames in the action sequence. And $C = \{c_1, \ldots, c_K\} (K \leqslant N)$ is a set of K clusters. Subsequently, we can select K key frames of an action sequence as follows.

1. The initial K cluster centers are randomly selected as $\{\mathbf{z}_j \mid \mathbf{z}_j \in \mathbb{R}^d, j = 1, \ldots, K\}$.
2. The distance between sample $\mathbf{x}_i$ and each cluster center $\mathbf{z}_j$ is calculated, and then the sample is assigned to its nearest cluster center.
   The distance can be expressed:

$$\mathcal{D} = \arg\min_{j} \sum_{i=1}^{N} \sum_{j=1}^{K} \| \mathbf{x}_i - \mathbf{z}_j \|^2. \tag{12.21}$$

3. For each cluster j, the new cluster center is calculated again:

$$\mathbf{z}_j = \left(\sum_{i=1}^{N} r_{ij} \mathbf{x}_i \right) \cdot \left(\sum_{i=1}^{N} r_{ij} \right)^{-1}, \tag{12.22}$$

   where $r_{ij} = 1$ when the sample $\mathbf{x}_i$ belongs to the j-th cluster, otherwise $r_{ij} = 0$.
4. Steps (2) and (3) are repeated, until the cluster centers stay the same.
5. After extracting K cluster centers via K-means algorithm described above, we will select key frames of an action sequence. For each cluster center $\mathbf{z}_j (j = 1, \ldots, K)$, the Euclidean distance between each joint in $\mathbf{z}_j$ and the same joint at each frame is computed. Then, we can get a $N \times 20$ matrix $\mathbf{M}_j$ as:

$$\mathbf{M}_j = \begin{bmatrix} m_{1,1} & \cdots & m_{1,20} \\ \vdots & \vdots & \vdots \\ m_{N,1} & \cdots & m_{N,20} \end{bmatrix}, \quad (12.23)$$

where $m_{p,q}\left(p=1,\ldots,N;q=1,\ldots,20\right)$ represents the distance between the q-th joint at the p-th frame and the same joint in cluster center $\mathbf{z}_j$. Therefore, we will obtain K matrixes $\mathbf{M}_j\left(j=1,\ldots,K\right)$

6. For each matrix $\mathbf{M}_j$, we find the minimum of each column, then let it equal to 1 and others equal to 0, respectively.
7. All K matrixes $\mathbf{M}_j\left(j=1,\ldots,K\right)$ are combined, and then K frames which have the most number of value 1 are extracted. These frames are the key frames representing the corresponding action instance. Finally, they are rearranged in chronological order.

12.3.2 Feature Extraction

Feature extraction is a crucial procedure in action recognition, and distinct features may influence the final classification performance obviously. The Microsoft Kinect SDK provides 20 joints of the human skeleton. The skeleton structure and the distribution of joints captured from the Kinect sensor are illustrated in Figure 12.1 [31]. The coordinates of skeleton 3D joints can be treated as the features to be trained directly. However, in order to represent human actions

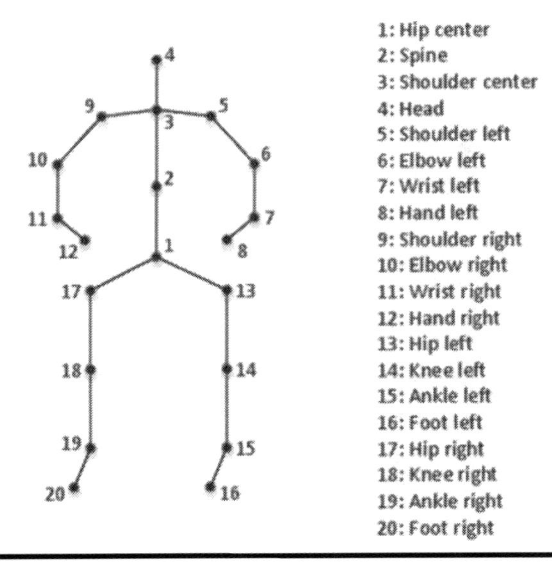

Figure 12.1 Skeleton joints captured by a Kinect sensor.

more accurately, our proposed approach extracts the distance features between a fixed human center point and other joints. Here, we choose the hip center as the center joint. Meanwhile, we compute the distances of each joint between its position at time t and its preliminary position at time t_0 with the purpose of describing spatiotemporal information of an action better. In addition, we incorporate the angles of critical joints between each two consecutive body parts as features [31]. These features can help us to understand the distinct importance of each body part in different actions, and to make it more accurate on action recognition.

Let $\mathbf{F}_t$ be the feature vector at time t for each key frame, and it can be expressed as:

$$\mathbf{F}_t = \left[\mathcal{D}_{HipCenter}, \theta\right], \tag{12.24}$$

where $\mathcal{D}_{HipCenter}$ is the distance between each joint and hip center, and θ denotes the angles of the important joints, which are shoulder, elbow, wrist, hip, knee and ankle in the left and right sides, respectively. We discard some joints' angles which do not change obviously during the action sequence, such as shoulder center, spine, hip center, and so on. Actually, these unconsidered joints will not influence the classification performance so significantly, and discarding them enables can the computational complexity to be reduced. As a consequence, we can achieve much faster training speed. Formally, these features can be represented as follows:

1. Let $P_i = \left(x_i, y_i, z_i\right)$ be the coordinates of the i-th skeleton 3D joint. The distance $\mathcal{D}_{HipCenter}$ between joint P_i and the hip center $P_c = \left(x_c, y_c, z_c\right)$ for each frame is calculated as [31]:

$$\mathcal{D}_{HipCenter} = \sqrt{\left(x_i - x_c\right)^2 + \left(y_i - y_c\right)^2 + \left(z_i - z_c\right)^2}, \tag{12.25}$$

2. We define each body part as a vector $\mathbf{V}$ formed by the 3D coordinates of two adjacent joints. For example, the upper arm can be represented with the shoulder joint and the elbow joint. The angle of a joint $\theta\left(\mathbf{V}_1, \mathbf{V}_2\right)$ between two body parts $\mathbf{V}_1$ and $\mathbf{V}_2$ can be computed using the variant of dot product as:

$$\theta\left(\mathbf{V}_1, \mathbf{V}_2\right) = \arccos\left(\left(\mathbf{V}_1 \cdot \mathbf{V}_2\right) \cdot \left(\left|\mathbf{V}_1\right| \cdot \left|\mathbf{V}_2\right|\right)^{-1}\right), \tag{12.26}$$

where $\theta\left(\mathbf{V}_1, \mathbf{V}_2\right)$ is the angle of joint P_i, and $\mathbf{V}_1$ is represented with joints P_i and P_j. Moreover, $\mathbf{V}_2$ is represented with joints P_i and P_k $\left(i \neq j \neq k\right)$. Here, $\mathbf{V}_1 \cdot \mathbf{V}_2$ represents the dot product between two 3D vector $\mathbf{V}_1$ and $\mathbf{V}_2$, meanwhile, $\left|\mathbf{V}_1\right|$ and $\left|\mathbf{V}_2\right|$ represent the norm of the vector $\mathbf{V}_1$ and $\mathbf{V}_2$, respectively.

As we mentioned earlier, the feature $\mathcal{D}_{HipCenter}$ has 19 elements (except the distance between the hip center and itself which equals to 0). At the same time, θ has 12 features for twelve important joints at each time frame. Hence, we have 31 features for each key frame in all.

12.3.3 Classification Using Our Proposed S-ELM-KRSL

Here, we provide the theoretical analysis of our proposed approach S-ELM-KRSL.

KRSL is used as a loss function of S-ELM instead of the objective function as follow:

$$\text{Minimize}: \| \mathbf{H}\beta - \mathbf{Y} \|_{\mathrm{F}}^{2}. \tag{12.27}$$

Our goal is to minimize the KRSL between the target output and the actual output in training. The new expression is:

$$\mathcal{J}(\beta) = min \sum_{i=1}^{N} L_{\lambda}\left(\mathbf{y}_i - \mathbf{t}_i\right), \tag{12.28}$$

where $\mathbf{y}_i$ is the target output of the sample $\mathbf{x}_i$, and $\mathbf{t}_i$ is the calculated output of $\mathbf{x}_i$. And $\mathbf{t}_i$ can be written as:

$$\mathbf{t}_i = \mathbf{h}_i \beta, \tag{12.29}$$

where $\mathbf{h}_i$ is the hidden layer output vector for $\mathbf{x}_i$, and β is the hidden layer output weight. We can get a new objective function as follows:

$$\mathcal{J}_{\mathrm{KRSL}}(\beta) = \underset{\beta}{min}\left[\frac{1}{N\lambda} \sum_{i=1}^{N} \exp\left(\lambda\left(1 - \kappa_{\sigma}\left(\mathbf{y}_i - \mathbf{h}_i\beta\right)\right)\right) + \eta \| \beta \|_{F}^{2}\right], \tag{12.30}$$

where λ is defined as formula (12.18), η is the regularization coefficient, and $\kappa_{\sigma}(\cdot)$ is defined as formula (12.17).

For the ℓ-th iteration, the optimal solution of formula (12.30) can be expressed as:

$$\beta^{\ell+1} = \left(\mathbf{H}^{\mathrm{T}}\mathbf{A}\mathbf{H} + \eta\mathbf{E}\right)^{-1} \mathbf{H}^{\mathrm{T}}\mathbf{A}\mathbf{Y}, \tag{12.31}$$

where $\mathbf{A}$ is a diagonal matrix in which the diagonal elements a_{ii} is:

$$a_{ii} = \frac{1}{N\sigma^2} \sum_{i=1}^{N} \exp\left(\lambda\left(1 - \kappa_{\sigma}\left(\mathbf{y}_i - \mathbf{h}_i\beta^{\ell}\right)\right)\right)\kappa_{\sigma}\left(\mathbf{y}_i - \mathbf{h}_i\beta^{\ell}\right). \tag{12.32}$$

12.3.4 Parameters Optimization Using Jaya

In consideration of the algorithm-specific parameter-less feature of Jaya, it is used to optimize those key parameters in our proposed S-ELM-KRSL, in an effort to achieve a good generalization performance with minimal human intervention.

Specifically, in order to minimize the objective loss function, we use Jaya algorithm to optimize the parameters of σ, η, and λ to achieve better results, where σ is the width of kernel band in the Mercer kernel function, η is the regularization coefficient, and λ is the risk-sensitive parameter.

12.4 Experimental Results and Discussion

In this section, we will show the experimental results of our proposed scheme. Specifically, we compare the algorithm S-ELM-KRSL proposed in this paper with other popular methods, including ELM, S-ELM, and S-ELM-Correntropy, to highlight the advantages of our algorithm in dealing with contaminated training data with outliers. Here, S-ELM-Correntropy is an enhanced ELM, where in the S-ELM architecture, the MSE criterion is replaced by correntropy in the same way as [20].

12.4.1 Experiment Description

The dataset used in this article was collected through Kinect sensors. This dataset called as Kintense contains the 3D coordinates of 20 skeleton joints with different actions, for a total of almost 13,000 actions sequences [32]. In this dataset, each action is normal, and each joint is visible. Specifically, if the joint is invisible due to ill posed position in smart health applications, this action is regarded as an invalid action and it could be also treated as an outlier.

Here, our experiments are conducted in the Matlab R2013a environment running on the computer with an Intel(R) Core(TM) i7-4710MQ CPU and a 4GB RAM.

12.4.2 Parameters Optimization Result

As mentioned above, the Jaya algorithm is employed to optimize $\sigma \in [0.7, 1.7]$, $\eta \in [0, 1]$, and $\lambda \in [5, 40]$. The final results show that the optimal values of σ, η, and λ are 1, 0.1, and 5, respectively.

Here, we should determine the size of the key frames. Considering that the more the number of layers, the larger size of the NN and the longer of the computational time, the number of layers is set to 3 as a trade-off. Through grid searching with cross-validation, the results are shown in Figure 12.2. Also considering the training time, we can find that when the number of key frames (i.e., the number of clusters mentioned in Section 12.3.1) is set to $K = 7$, the testing accuracy is best. Then, we accordingly divide the dataset into training sets and testing sets.

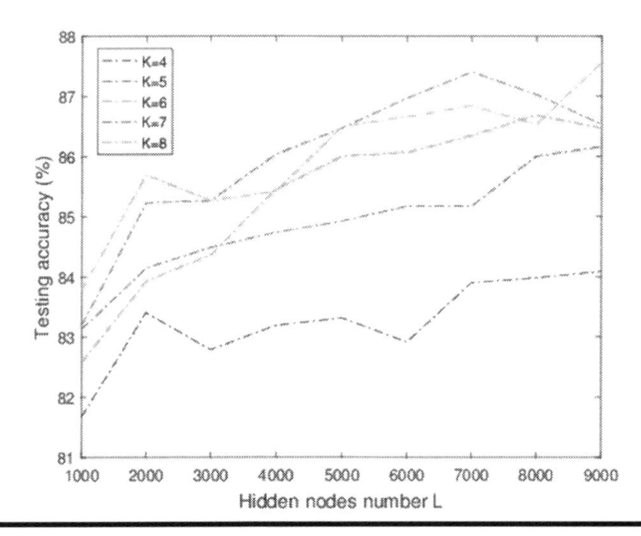

Figure 12.2 The relationship between testing accuracy and the number of hidden nodes while sing algorithm S-ELM-KRSL with different number of key frames.

12.4.3 Performance Comparison

In order to verify the superiority of our algorithm S-ELM-KRSL, we compare it with some other popular algorithms, including the traditional ELM, S-ELM, and S-ELM-Correntropy. These four algorithms all use the same sequence of actions and preprocessing methods.

Firstly, we adjust the number of hidden nodes L, and it is set within $\{1000, 2000, \ldots, 9000\}$ to choose the optimal value. The results of four different algorithms are shown in Figure 12.3.

In this figure, we can see that when the values of σ, η, and λ are fixed, the number of hidden nodes is changed to check the testing accuracy. While using S-ELM-KRSL, as the number of hidden nodes L, increases, the testing accuracy is also on the rise. When the value of L, is 7000, the test accuracy reaches the maximum value of 87.40%. Then, the accuracy decreases slowly as the number of hidden nodes increases.

Meanwhile, in Figure 12.3, when using ELM to perform activity recognition based on experimental dataset, we can find that in the beginning, the testing accuracy increases with the increase of the number of hidden nodes. When the number of hidden nodes is 2000, the test accuracy reaches the highest value of 81.40%. Subsequently, the test accuracy decreases as the number of hidden nodes increases.

For the S-ELM in this figure, we can also observe that the testing accuracy increases with the increase of the number of hidden nodes in the initial phase. As the number of hidden nodes is set as 3000, the test accuracy reaches the highest

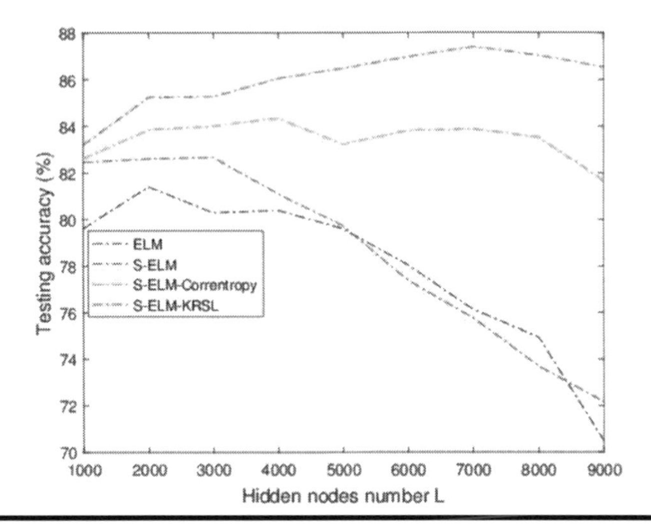

Figure 12.3 The relationship between testing accuracy and the number of hidden nodes while using four algorithms.

value of 82.67%. Then, the accuracy drops drastically when the number of hidden nodes increases.

Finally, by checking the S-ELM-Correntropy in Figure 12.3, we can easily find that when the number of hidden nodes is 4000, the test accuracy reaches the highest value of 84.34%. Subsequently, the test accuracy decreases as the number of hidden nodes increases.

Although we have achieved a relatively high accuracy through our scheme, there are still some action instances misclassified with others as shown in Table 12.1. We can find that 136 hitting samples are mistaken for the throwing action, and 155 throwing action samples are mistaken for the hitting action in the dataset Kintense. The misclassification of these action instances is due to the participation of the same body parts when performing some actions. For instance, the movement of the arm is involved with both the throwing action and the hitting action. Actually, it is a difficult and challenging issue to recognize various action samples with strong similarities.

Furthermore, to evaluate the computational complexity of those algorithms, we provide the comparison of training time, and the results are shown in Figure 12.4. And Table 12.2 visually shows the performance difference among the four algorithms. From Figure 12.4 and Table 12.2, we can easily find that the S-ELM-KRSL used in our scheme achieves higher accuracy, compared with some other competitive algorithms. However, among these four algorithms, it is implemented with the longest computational time, while the algorithm ELM is with the shortest training time.

Table 12.1 Confusion Matrix Obtained from the Dataset Kinect

	Hitting	*Kicking*	*Pushing*	*Throw*
Hitting	**716**	11	20	136
Kicking	13	**946**	2	7
Pushing	24	2	**492**	13
Throw	155	9	18	**667**

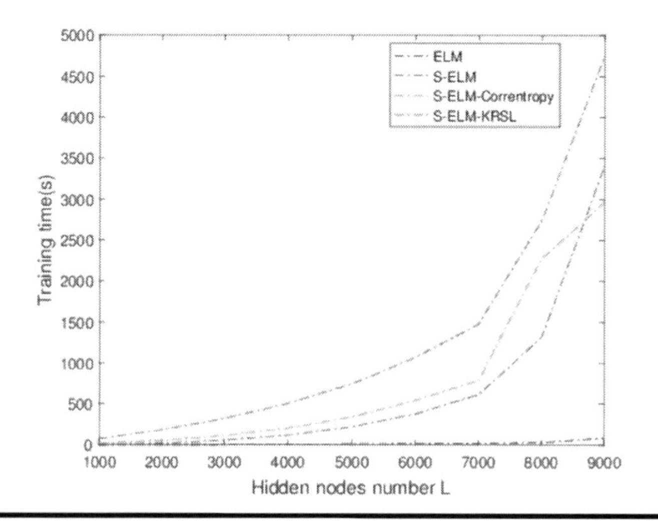

Figure 12.4 The relationship between training time and the number of hidden nodes while using four algorithms.

Table 12.2 Performance Comparison

Method	*ELM*	*S-ELM*	*S-ELM-Correntropy*	*S-ELM-KRSL*
Accuracy	81.40%	82.67%	84.34%	**87.40%**
#of hidden nodes	2000	3000	4000	**7000**

Obviously, motivated by deep learning model, our algorithm S-ELM-KRSL with the diffusion of the multilayer ELM architecture and the KRSL measure, can achieve satisfactory performance. Meanwhile, due to the multilayer NN architecture in which the KRSL is computed based on iterative strategy shown in formula (12.31), the computational effort increases while using S-ELM-KRSL.

However, considering the classification accuracy and the computational effort simultaneously, our proposed scheme may be a competitive choice.

12.5 Conclusion

This article aims at addressing an important issue on how to achieve fine-grained human activity recognition in the context of smart health application, through the fusion of data from wearable sensors. We propose a novel scheme in which the algorithm S-ELM-KRSL is developed to identify the motion sequence of body based on the skeleton data. In our algorithm, compared with the traditional measure used in ELM, the KRSL is less sensitive to noise or outliers, hence it can measure the actual output before the predicted output more effectively.

First, we select the key frames from each action sequence using the *K*-means clustering algorithm. These key frames represent the actions at this time. Then, we use the algorithm S-ELM-KRSL to represent these sequences of actions. We can see from the experimental results that the proposed scheme achieves a higher accuracy than some traditional methods, which verifies that the S-ELM-KRSL is more suitable for processing large-scale data with noises or outliers.

In our experiment, we show that our scheme can detect symptoms of mild cognitive impairment and dementia, including hitting, kicking, pushing, and throwing, with satisfactory accuracy.

In the future, we will integrate our scheme into a smart Internet of Things (IoT) system to monitor seniors who have mild cognitive impairment or dementia and provide intervention proactively based on the observed activities.

Acknowledgments

Manuscript received January 19, 2018; revised May 3, 2018; accepted June 21, 2018. Date of publication July 16, 2018; date of current version May 8, 2019. This work was supported in part by the National Natural Science Foundation of China under Grants 61174103 and 61603032, in part by the National Key Research and Development Program of China under Grant 2017YFB0702300, in part by the University of Science and Technology Beijing—National Taipei University of Technology Joint Research Program under Grant TW201705, and in part by a FRD-IoT award and a graduate faculty travel award from Cleveland State University. (Corresponding author: Xiong Luo.)

Thanks to the authorization of IEEE Internet of Things Journal.

References

1. W. Zhao, R. Lun, C. Gordon, A.-B. M. Fofana, D. D. Espy, M. A. Reinthal, B. Ekelman et al. "A human-centered activity tracking system: Toward a healthier workplace," *IEEE Trans. Hum. Mach. Syst.*, vol. 47, no. 3, pp. 343–355, 2017.
2. S. A. Ferguson, "The role of dynamic three-dimensional trunk motion in occupationally-related low back disorders," *Spine*, vol. 18, no. 5, pp. 617–628, 1993.
3. T. Gropelli and K. Corle, "Assessment of nurses' and therapists' occupational musculoskeletal injuries," *Medsurg. Nurs.*, vol. 20, no. 6, pp. 297–303, 2011.
4. J. A. Pillai and A. Bonner-Jackson, "Review of information and communication technology devices for monitoring functional and cognitive decline in Alzheimer's disease clinical trials," *J. Healthc. Eng.*, vol. 6, no. 1, pp. 71–83, 2015.
5. W. Zhao, J. A. Pillai, J. B. Leverenz, and X. Luo, "Technology-facilitated detection of mild cognitive impairment: A review," in *Proceedings of the IEEE International Conference on Electro Information Technology*, 2018.
6. J. Wang, Z. Liu, Y. Wu, and J. Yuan, "Mining actionlet ensemble for action recognition with depth cameras," in *Proceedings of the IEEE Computer Society Conference on Computer Vision and Pattern Recognition*, 2012, pp. 1290–1297.
7. R. Vemulapalli, F. Arrate, and R. Chellappa, "Human action recognition by representing 3d skeletons as points in a lie group," in *Proceedings of the IEEE Computer Society Conference on Computer Vision and Pattern Recognition*, 2014, pp. 588–595.
8. G.-B. Huang, Q.-Y. Zhu, and C.-K. Siew, "Extreme learning machine: Theory and applications," *Neurocomputing*, vol. 70, no. 1–3, pp. 489–501, 2006.
9. X. Luo, X. Chang, and X. Ban, "Regression and classification using extreme learning machine based on L1-norm and L2-norm," *Neurocomputing*, vol. 174, pp. 179–186, 2016
10. X. Luo, Y. Xu, W. Wang, M. Yuan, X. Ban, Y. Zhu, and W. Zhao, "Towards enhancing stacked extreme learning machine with sparse autoencoder by correntropy," *J. Franklin Inst.*, vol. 355, no. 4, pp. 1945–1966, 2018.
11. G.-B. Huang, Z. Bai, L. L. C. Kasun, and C. M. Vong, "Local receptive fields based extreme learning machine," *IEEE Comput. Intell. Mag.*, vol. 10, no. 2, pp. 18–29, 2015.
12. X. Luo and X. Chang, "A novel data fusion scheme using grey model and extreme learning machine in wireless sensor networks," *Int. J. Contr. Autom. Syst.*, vol. 13, no. 3, pp. 539–546, 2015.
13. P. A. Henríquez and G. A. Ruz, "Extreme learning machine with a deterministic assignment of hidden weights in two parallel layers," *Neurocomputing*, vol. 226, pp. 109–116, 2017.
14. X. Luo, C. Jiang, W. Wang, Y. Xu, J. H. Wang, and W. Zhao, "User behavior prediction in social networks using weighted extreme learning machine with distribution optimization," *Future Gener. Comput. Syst.*, vol. 93, pp. 1023–1035, 2019. doi:10.1016/j.future.2018.04.085.
15. H. Zhou, G.-B. Huang, Z. Lin, H. Wang, and Y. C. Soh, "Stacked extreme learning machines," *IEEE Trans. Cybern.*, vol. 45, no. 9, pp. 2013–2025, 2015.
16. X. Luo, J. Deng, J. Liu, W. Wang, X. Ban, and J. H. Wang, "A quantized kernel least mean square scheme with entropy-guided learning for intelligent data analysis," *China Commun.*, vol. 14, no. 7, pp. 127–136, 2017.

17. Y. Li, X. Luo, W. Wang, and W. Zhao, "Human action recognition with skeleton data using extreme learning machine," in *Proceedings of the Chinese Intelligent Automation Conference*, 2017, pp. 449–456.
18. X. Luo, D. Zhang, L. T. Yang, J. Liu, X. Chang, and H. Ning, "A kernel machine-based secure data sensing and fusion scheme in wireless sensor networks for the cyber-physical systems," *Future Gener. Comput. Syst.*, vol. 61, pp. 85–96, 2016.
19. W. Liu, P. P. Pokharel, and J. C. Príncipe, "Correntropy: Properties and applications in non-Gaussian signal processing," *IEEE Trans. Signal Process.*, vol. 55, no. 11, pp. 5286–5298, 2007.
20. Z. H. J. Xing and X. M. Wang, "Training extreme learning machine via regularized correntropy criterion," *Neural Comput. Appl.*, vol. 23, no. 7–8, pp. 1977–1986, 2013.
21. Y. Xu, X. Luo, W. Wang, and W. Zhao, "Efficient DV-Hop localization for wireless cyber-physical social sensing system: A correntropy-based neural network learning scheme," *Sensors*, vol. 17, no. 1, p. 135, 2017.
22. X. Luo, J. Sun, L. Wang, W. Wang, W. Zhao, J. Wu, J. H. Wang, and Z. Zhang, "Short-term wind speed forecasting via stacked extreme learning machine with generalized correntropy," *IEEE Trans. Ind. Inf.*, vol. 14, no. 11, pp. 4963–4971, 2018. doi:10.1109/TII.2018.2854549.
23. M. N. Syed, P. M. Pardalos, and J. C. Principe, "On the optimization properties of the correntropic loss function in data analysis," *Optim. Lett.*, vol. 8, no. 3, pp. 823–839, 2014.
24. B. Chen, L. Xing, B. Xu, H. Zhao, N. Zheng, and J. C. Principe, "Kernel risk-sensitive loss: Definition, properties and application to robust adaptive filtering," *IEEE Trans. Signal Process.*, vol. 65, no. 11, pp. 2888–2901, 2017.
25. X. Luo, J. Deng, W. Wang, J. H. Wang, and W. Zhao, "A quantized kernel learning algorithm using a minimum kernel risk-sensitive loss criterion and bilateral gradient technique," *Entropy*, vol. 19, no. 7, p. 365, 2017.
26. R. Rao, "Jaya: A simple and new optimization algorithm for solving constrained and unconstrained optimization problems," *Int. J. Ind. Eng. Comput.*, vol. 7, no. 1, pp. 19–34, 2016
27. G.-B. Huang, H. Zhou, X. Ding, and R. Zhang, "Extreme learning machine for regression and multiclass classification," *IEEE Trans. Syst. Man Cybern. Part B Cybern.*, vol. 42, no. 2, pp. 513–529, 2012.
28. A. P. Piotrowski, M. J. Napiorkowski, J. J. Napiorkowski, and P. M. Rowinski, "Swarm intelligence and evolutionary algorithms: Performance versus speed," *Inf. Sci.*, vol. 384, pp. 34–85, 2017.
29. C. Huang, L. Wang, R. S. Yeung, Z. Zhang, H. S. H. Chung, and A. Bensoussan, "A prediction model guided Jaya algorithm for the PV system maximum power point tracking," *IEEE Trans. Sustainable Energy*, vol. 9, no. 1, pp. 45–55, 2018.
30. A. K. Jain, "Data clustering: 50 years beyond K-means," *Pattern Recogn. Lett.*, vol. 31, no. 8, pp. 651–666, 2010.
31. B. Chikhaoui, B. Ye, and A. Mihailidis, "Feature-level combination of skeleton joints and body parts for accurate aggressive and agitated behavior recognition," *J. Ambient Intell. Humanized Comput.*, vol. 8, no. 6, pp. 957–976, 2017.
32. S. Nirjon, C. Greenwood, C. Torres, S. Zhou, J. A. Stankovic, H. J. Yoon, H.-K. Ra, C. Basaran, T. Park, and S. H. Son, "Kintense: A robust, accurate, real-time and evolving system for detecting aggressive actions from streaming 3D skeleton data," in *Proceeding of the IEEE International ConferencePervasive Computing and Communications*, 2014, pp. 2–10.

Chapter 13

A Physiological Signal-Based Method for Early Mental-Stress Detection

Likun Xia, Aamir Saeed Malik, and Ahmad Rauf Subhani

Contents

13.1 Introduction

Mental stress may be defined as the effect of an excessive workload under a time constraint to meet expectations [1–4]. It causes a person to become incapable of coping with a perceived threat to their physical, emotional, or psychological well-being. Stress and its related health conditions can pose a serious threat to the quality of life, and dysfunction in daily life can interfere with the social life and physical health of an individual. Stress is associated with a range of behavioral [5,6], cognitive [7], neurovascular [8], cardiovascular [9], and molecular effects [10].

The cognitive activation theory of stress (CATS) describes the association of the brain with mental stress [11]. There exists evidence of stress-related cognitive interference that lead to memory weakness [12] and the destruction of mental and physiological well-being [13]. Stress has been reported to be associated with the shrinkage of the hippocampus and prefrontal cortex [14] as well as the impairment of prefrontal networks [15]. In chronicity, stress can turn into stress-related diseases with serious impacts, including burnout, depression, and post-traumatic stress disorder [3,13].

Mental stress has been practically assessed through questionnaires such as the Perceived Stress Scale (PSS) [16], the Life Events and Coping Inventory (LECI) [17], and the Stress Response Inventory (SRI) [18]. Unfortunately, they only inspect stress symptoms after a person has become stressed and only provide subjective solutions, which delays treatment. Subjective feelings cannot indicate cognitive impairment. Moreover, they can be incorrectly evaluated owing to a person's unwillingness to admit that they are under stress. Therefore, to guarantee an accurate diagnosis, there is a requirement for objective assessment methods in order to quantify stress using neuroimaging modalities.

Electroencephalography (EEG) is a neuroimaging modality that is widely used to measure brain activity as it is non-invasive and comparatively low cost. Clinically, EEG has been used as a standard neuroimaging modality to observe the neural dynamics of the human brain. EEG signals reveal how information is processed in the brain. Recently, EEG recording ability has been improved owing to technological advances.

In laboratory settings of stress assessment using EEG, stress is first induced on known scales that lead to its assessment in stress versus control. Previous studies on the detection of mental stress can be mainly categorized into three categories: (1) the studies were related to concentration in a simulation environment, e.g., stress evaluation of drivers during driving [9,19]; (2) they included tasks of varying difficulty such that the mental or physical states could be identified and differentiated between the tasks [20,21]; and (3) they involved the assessment of stress using emotional methods [22–24] such that different emotional states could be identified. Recently, the Montreal Imaging Stress Task (MIST) has been validated as a paradigm for inducing stress in a functional magnetic resonance imaging environment [25]. Its suitability in an EEG environment is still unexplored. EEG has spatially and temporally abundant recording that makes it difficult to conclude a diagnosis only through a visual inspection of the recording. Therefore, optimum analysis techniques are essential for the detection of mental stress using EEG signals. Analyses exist for extracting the EEG features that represent the entire dataset. These techniques include time domain analyses such as the use of the Hjorth parameter [26]; entropy [27]; frequency domain analysis, which includes the analysis of power in different frequency bands [28]; and time–frequency analysis, which includes the use of the wavelet transform [29]. The obtained features are then fed to classifiers for classification or diagnosis. Classifiers such as the linear discriminant analysis (LDA) and quadratic discriminant analysis (QDA), support vector machine (SVM), regression analysis, multi-layer perceptron, and artificial neural networks [30] are commonly used [31].

Conventional EEG features lack the ability to represent the connectivity of various brain regions and to indicate how the regions communicate with each other under stress conditions. Recently, the quantitative EEG (qEEG) features have broadened the scope of application of EEG owing to their implication in some contemporary treatment techniques such as neurofeedback [32]. The qEEG features such as coherence [33], amplitude asymmetry [34], phase lag, relative power, and power ratios [35] are significantly useful in describing functional brain connectivity under mental stress conditions. Technically, only the features that can contribute to the assessment of stress are of significance with stress. Furthermore, some of the features are redundant as they can only increase the computational cost with minimal contribution to the result. Significance and redundancy can be tackled through feature selection and dimensionality reduction. The former provides the significance of a feature as compared with class variables, whereas in the latter, features are compared among each other in the feature space. If two features are similar, the one with the least contribution is discarded.

We aim to develop a methodology for detecting mental stress in the early stages by quantifying the stress into four levels. The subjects recruited should have a minimum prior stress such that we may inspect how stress affects a normal person. In order to induce a stress response, MIST is applied. qEEG-based features including relative power, power ratios, amplitude asymmetry, coherence, and phase lag are extracted from the EEG signals recorded during the experiment. The extracted features are optimized through normalisation, feature selection using the paired *t*-test, and dimensionality reduction with principal component analysis (PCA). A classifier model based on SVM using the radial basis function (RBF) kernel and sigmoid kernel is then applied to the optimized feature set.

13.2 Methodology

13.2.1 Experiment Design and Data Acquisition

13.2.1.1 Experiment Design

An experimental paradigm based on MIST [25] is designed, as shown in Figure 13.1, for inducing and evaluating mild psychological stress in terms of physiology and brain activation by using EEG. It is a computer-based tool that induces mild psychological stress in terms of physiology and brain activation [36,37] and is commonly used to explicitly evaluate responses in stress and control conditions. In this case, both the stress and control conditions were simulated in two separate sessions with at least a seven-day gap to reduce the learning effect on the performance and to minimize hypothalamic pituitary adrenal axis activation [38]. Each session consisted of four sequential blocks: habituation, rest, mental arithmetic task, and recovery.

In the habituation training block, signals were not recorded. This block was used to make the subject accustomed to the experimental environment. It was started with on-arrival rest and briefing of the experiment for 5 min. Subsequently, the subject was presented with sample questions of an arithmetic task. The answer to every question was a single-digit number (0–9). The subject was required to press the right key while looking at the screen to minimize eye movement.

The rest block was observed as the baseline for activations under each of the stress and control conditions. Physiological signals were recorded in the rest condition for 5 min. The subject was required to sit in a relaxed position with their hands lying on their thighs with open palms, their upper teeth separated from the lower teeth with the tongue floating inside the mouth, their feet touching the floor, and their legs not crossing each other. The subject was required to focus on a circle appearing on a computer screen in front of them. All these measures were taken to reduce the possibility of movement of the subject such that unwanted artifacts may be minimized.

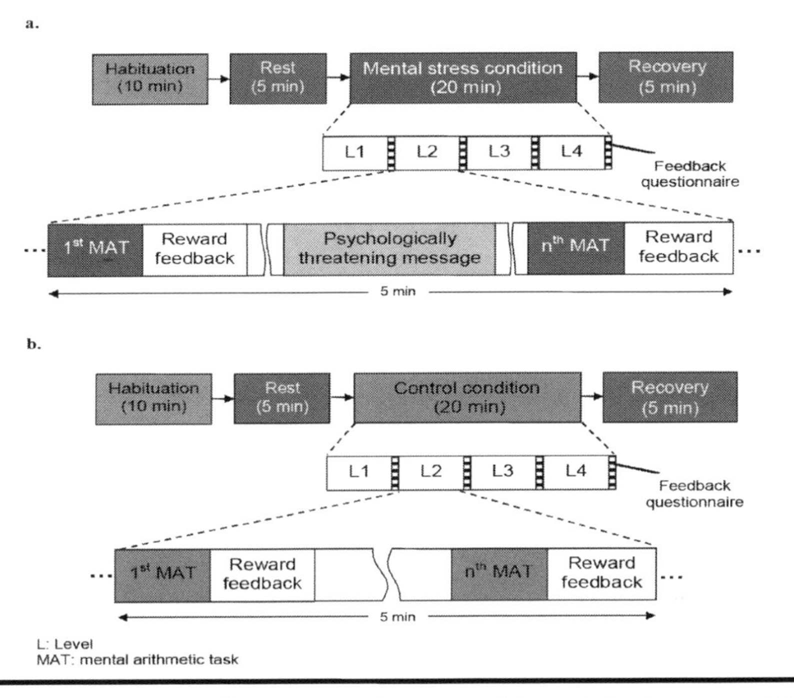

Figure 13.1 Experiment flow. (a) Mental stress condition and (b) Control condition.

The mental arithmetic task block was the core of the experiment design. The task was conducted differently in separate sessions under both stress and control conditions. Both conditions had similar arithmetic tasks. An arithmetic task included up to four numbers (maximum 99) using four operands (addition (+), subtraction (–), multiplication (×), and division (/)), e.g., $2 + (5 \times 25)/5$. It contained four levels (L1–L4). Level 1 involved the addition or subtraction between only two numbers, level 2 addition and subtraction between three numbers, level 3 multiplication along with addition and subtraction between four numbers, and level 4 any four operations between four numbers. The answer to every task was a one-digit number, and the subject was required to respond by pressing the correct key. There were four levels under each condition, each of which lasted 5 min. Under the stress condition, the subject performed mental arithmetic tasks on a computer with a time limit, i.e., the time for each task was limited such that the subject could not exceed an accuracy of 50%. Along with the time limit in each task, an extra text message ("delaying response text" and "speed up text") were displayed on the screen with stimuli aiming to distract the subject from the actual task and to induce additional stress in him/her. After each task, a feedback displaying the response time and correct/incorrect/no response based on the attempt appeared on the screen. Moreover, after certain trials, stressful feedback in terms of orders appeared on the screen. This feedback reveals the external pressures that a worker faces in a work environment parallel to the job. The procedure for the control condition was the same as the one for the stress condition but without a time restriction and stress-inducing feedbacks. The aim of the control condition was to compare any cerebral activation caused by the mental arithmetic aspects of the task. This would aid in declaring the activation caused by mental stress in stress conditions with greater accuracy. The feedback display ("correct" or "incorrect") remained after each task in the control condition. Finally, the recovery time was computed to determine the changes in terms of signals when the subject is again under the relaxed condition. In this case, details for both the ECG and EEG are recorded for 5 min.

13.2.1.2 Subject Selection and Data Acquisition

The experiment is accredited by the ethics commission in Hospital Universiti Sains Malaysia, Malaysia. Twenty-two healthy male subjects (mean age of 22.54 ± 1.53 years) were selected from Universiti Teknologi Petronas, Malaysia. They were selected based on the criterion that they had no severe perception of stress using the PSS [39]. The PSS quantises a person's perceived stress into four levels. Based on these levels, subjects who categorized in the first two levels of PSS were shortlisted. The subjects were instructed to avoid food and energy drinks for 2 h before the experiment. Owing to the cross-over design of the experiment, each subject had to participate in both the stress and control condition experiments. In order to minimize the effect of time on the subjects' cognitive ability, all subjects participated between 3 pm and 7 pm. The subjects signed an informed consent form, and they were rewarded with RM 40 to compensate their time.

The electrophysiological data acquisition was performed using a 128-EEG-sensor net with two ECG electrodes (shown in Figure 13.2a). The EEG was recorded using a Net Amps 300 amplifier (EGI, USA). All 128 sensors were referenced to the vertex (Cz) and their impedance was maintained below 50 KΩ. The threshold impedance was set based on the manufacturer's recommendation [40]. It was theoretically and experimentally proven that high skin-electrode impedance can be effectively used when the amplifier's input impedance is as high as ~200 MΩ [41] whereas our system's amplifier input impedance was 300 MΩ. A high skin-electrode impedance did not attenuate the signals and also prevented skin abrasion. An impedance of 5 kΩ was used to minimize the power line effect on the signals. This power line effect was minimal at a high impedance. Figure 13.2b shows the process of impedance correction. The green locations indicate that the impedance is below the threshold and the red locations indicate that the impedance is higher than the threshold and requires further preparation. For an ECG recording, two ECG electrodes were placed on each side of the bottom of the subject's neck (shown in Figure 13.2c). The data was acquired

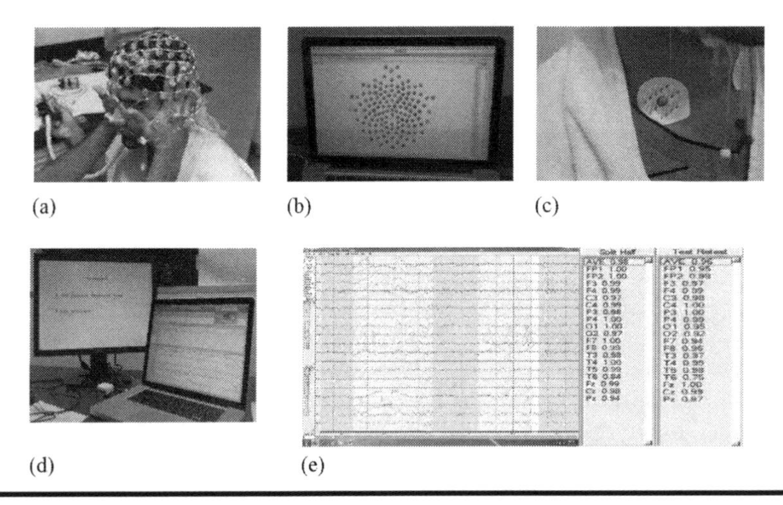

Figure 13.2 Data acquisition: (a) laying the net onto the subject's head (b) impedance checking (c) affixing the ECG electrodes at the bottom of the subject's neck (d) experiment recording, and (e) artifact removal by visual inspection.

at 500 samples/s. Subsequent to the recording, offline EEG signals were passed through a 0.1-Hz lowpass filter and 50-Hz notch filter to remove the DC artifacts and line noises (shown in Figure 13.2d) and down sampled to 128 samples/s. The EEG channels were then selected based on 10–20 montage (Fp1, Fp2, F3, F4, F7, F8, C3, C4, T3, T4, T5, T6, P3, P4, O1, O2, Fz, Cz, and Pz) with an average mastoid reference.

Finally, the EEG signals were cleaned in order to remove artifacts using manual selection in the Neuroguide software [42] (shown in Figure 13.2e; the red windows are manually selected portions of clean EEG). In the manual selection, the EEG recording was scanned, and artifact-free EEG portions were selected. During this process, the test–retest reliability and split-half reliability measures were observed to be greater than 0.95. The former is the ratio of variance between two halves of the selected EEG portions, where the split-half reliability is the ratio of the variance between even and odd seconds of the time series of the selected EEG portions.

13.2.2 Feature Extraction from EEG and ECG Signals

13.2.2.1 EEG Features

The cleaned EEG signals were analyzed for spectral analysis using the fast Fourier transform (FFT). An epoch length of 2 s, equivalent to a 0.5-Hz resolution, is used for auto-spectral and cross-spectral analysis over the frequency range of 0–30 Hz for every epoch. The epoch length is then analyzed by advancing a 0.5-s sliding window, i.e., 75% overlap between adjacent windows. The absolute power computed for all the frequency bands ((delta (0.5–4 Hz), theta (4–8 Hz), alpha (8–13 Hz), beta (13–29 Hz), and gamma (>29 Hz)) was used to extract features such as relative power, relative power ratio, coherence, phase lag, and amplitude asymmetry [43,44].

13.2.2.1.1 Relative Power

The relative power is derived from the absolute power of the frequency bands, i.e., as the power in a specific frequency band divided by the total power as shown in equation (13.1), relative power is computed for all five frequency bands across 19 electrodes giving rise to a total of 95 features (five frequency bands × 19 electrodes). These features are computed for every subject and at every level of the experiment.

$$\text{Relative power} = \frac{\text{Power in band}}{\text{Total power}} \times 100\% \tag{13.1}$$

13.2.2.1.2 Relative Power Ratio

The relative power ratio indicates the dominance of a frequency band over another. In this study, six ratios between the powers of four frequency bands, i.e., delta/theta, delta/alpha, delta/beta, theta/alpha, theta/beta, and alpha/beta, are calculated across every electrode. The ratios are restricted to the four most commonly studied frequency bands. In this manner, there are a total of 114 ratios (six relative power ratios × 19 electrodes) for every subject at any level of the experiment.

13.2.2.1.3 Coherence

The coherence is computed between 64 electrode pairs of intrahemispheric as well as homologous locations for each of the four frequency bands for individual subjects at every level of the experiment. It is a connectivity measure that describes the degree of association between two locations in the brain. It is defined as the ratio of cross-spectra ($|H_{uv}|^2$) to the product of the auto-spectra of two signals ($|H_u||H_v|$). This is an interpretation of the Pearson correlation coefficient for the variables in the frequency domain. Mathematically, it is represented as shown in equation (13.2):

$$\text{Coherence} = \frac{|H_{uv}|^2}{|H_u||H_v|} \tag{13.2}$$

13.2.2.1.4 Phase Difference

The phase difference (lag) is a brain connectivity measure that represents the delay between two EEG signals in different locations. It is computed for 64 pairs of intra-hemispheric as well as homologous locations for each band at every level. The phase of a particular signal is generally defined as shown in equation (13.3):

$$\text{Phase} = \text{Arc tan}\left(\frac{b}{a}\right) \tag{13.3}$$

where b represents the "imaginary" or "out-of-phase" component, and a represents the "real" or "in-phase" component of the signal. The real and imaginary components of the signals are computed using the FFT. The phase difference between the signals from two locations is then computed by subtracting their individual phases as shown in equation (13.4):

$$\text{Phase difference} = \text{Arc tan}\left(\frac{b_2}{a_2}\right) - \text{Arc tan}\left(\frac{b_1}{a_1}\right) \tag{13.4}$$

The phase difference is computed in radians and converted into degrees. The absolute phase delay is computed by squaring and then taking the square root of the squared difference. It is then computed by subtracting their individual phases.

13.2.2.1.5 Amplitude Asymmetry

The asymmetry is a connectivity measure that reflects the relative stimulation between two brain locations. It is determined by considering the difference between the amplitude of the signals that are normalized to the sum of their amplitudes, as shown in equation (13.5), where M and N are the instantaneous amplitudes of the given signals.

$$\text{Asymmetry} = \frac{M - N}{M + N} \tag{13.5}$$

13.2.2.2 ECG Features

In addition, from the ECG signals, the average heart rate (HR) and heart rate variability (HRV) are computed at every level under both conditions. The HR is derived from the R–R intervals of the ECG as the number of R peaks/min. The power spectral analysis of the R–R interval train using an autoregressive model (filter order 16) is performed in order to estimate the HRV. The power spectrum of the HRV is distributed into the very-low-frequency (VLF) (<0.015 Hz), low-frequency (LF) (0.04–0.15 Hz), and high-frequency (HF) (0.15–0.4 Hz) spectrums. The HF and LF components of the HRV are influenced by parasympathetic activity and sympathetic mediations, respectively [45]. The normalized powers of LF and HF (LFnu and HFnu) [46] are also calculated as shown in equation (13.6). LF/HF is presented as a ratio of the sympathetic to parasympathetic distribution or a reflection of the sympathetic attribution, as shown in equation (13.7). In this manner, a total of seven features are extracted to analyze cardiac variability in the experiment.

$$\text{LF/HFnu} = \frac{\text{LF/HF}}{\text{Total power} - \text{VLF}} \tag{13.6}$$

$$\text{Power ratio} = \frac{\text{LF}}{\text{HF}} \tag{13.7}$$

13.2.3 Feature Selection and Dimensionality Reduction

The extracted feature can have a very low correlation with the class variable such that it cannot be used to define two separate classes. The objective of the feature selection is to select a subset of features from the extracted features. The selected features can be used to distinguish between classes [47]. The feature selection before the classification of the EEG features supports the diagnosis of several neurological conditions such as Alzheimer disease [48]. Based on the involvement of the classifier, the feature selection methods can be divided into two types. The first type looks into the statistical information of features and does not incorporate the classifier. These features are Fisher's discriminant ratio FDR [29], minimum redundancy maximum relevance [49], and information gain. In the second type of method, feature selection is combined with the classifier, such as L1-SVM [50], and classifier performance is considered as the evaluation criteria.

In this paper, we used a paired *t*-test for the feature selection. The *t*-test has been used for feature selection in the case of several physiological signals based on studies that involve the use of EEG [51] and other modalities [52]. The *t*-test inspects the discriminatory power of a feature between classes by determining whether the mean of the feature between the classes is significantly different. If μ, σ, and n are the mean, standard deviation, and number of samples of a feature in one class, respectively, then the value of t is defined as

$$t = \frac{\mu_1 - \mu_2}{\sqrt{\frac{\sigma_1^2}{n_1} + \frac{\sigma_1^2}{n_2}}} \tag{13.8}$$

The computed value of t is compared with the critical value from the t distribution table. The critical value is determined according to the probability of the confidence interval (0.05) and the degree of freedom (n – 1) in the table. Any value of t greater than the critical value makes the feature capable of creating a significant separation between classes.

The selected features were then normalized using equation (13.8).

$$\text{Normalized data} = \frac{x_i - \mu}{\text{Range}} \tag{13.9}$$

where x_i is a sample in the feature vector, μ is the mean, and range indicates the difference between the maximum and minimum values of the feature vector.

Moreover, the extracted feature can be redundant because of a very high correlation with other features that can lead to the saturation of the classifier performance. The elimination of redundancy from the feature set is called dimensionality reduction. For dimensionality reduction, PCA was applied to the selected features. PCA has also been applied in several other studies [53]. It works by first transforming the original feature X set of one dimension into a new set [54]:

$$y = A^T x \tag{13.10}$$

Here A is the arrangement of eigenvectors that correspond to eigenvalues. The resultant components of y are mutually uncorrelated. The most significant of these components are then selected. PCA comprises the following steps:

1. From the feature matrix X, the covariance matrix S is estimated:

$$S = XX^T \tag{13.11}$$

2. Eigenvalue decomposition (EVD) is applied to S to compute l Eigenvalues and the corresponding Eigen vectors. Eigenvalues are sorted in the descending order. In addition, m largest eigenvalues are selected to incorporate 95% of the total energy. Corresponding eigenvectors are then stacked to compile the transformation matrix.

Furthermore, the first principal component (PC) from each level is selected for an overall representation in the experiment.

13.2.4 Detection of Mental Stress

Mental stress detection was performed by applying optimized features from the previous step to a machine learning classifier. A classifier utilizes features as its input to predict the related class to which a feature instance belongs. A classifier tunes its parameters in the training on few training instances of features. A trained classifier models the correspondence between the class variable and related features and is capable of recognizing new instances in an unforeseen testing dataset. For this purpose, we employed SVM [55] classifiers to determine the effectiveness of the proposed technique to detect mental stress.

The SVM is a supervised learning algorithm that operates with a kernel trick. Two kernels, RBF kernel ($C = 10000$ and gamma $= 0.5$) and sigmoid kernel [56] were used with the aim of assisting the input data to map into another space for further margin maximization [57]. The SVM identifies critical boundary examples (i.e., support vectors) from each class in the training dataset. For this paper, the classification was performed in the WEKA software.

13.2.5 Validation of Classifier Model

A fair evaluation of the designed classifier required the assessment of its performance over a range of selected features and classifier designs. To determine the classifier performance, we evaluated the classifier based on a 10-fold cross validation that splits the feature instances into 10 equal segments. During each iteration, 9 out of 10 segments were fed as a training subset to the classifier and 1 segment was used as the test subset. As every iteration resulted in different values of the confusion matrix, the final confusion matrix was averaged over the values of all the iterations. The performance metrics derived from the confusion matrix are given below:

$$\text{Accuracy} = \frac{\text{TP}+\text{TN}}{\text{positive} + \text{negative}} \times 100\% \tag{13.12}$$

$$\text{Recall} = \frac{\text{TP}}{\text{TP}+\text{FN}} \tag{13.13}$$

$$\text{Precision} = \frac{\text{TP}}{\text{TP}+\text{FP}} \tag{13.14}$$

where True positive (TP): stress classified as stress; True negative (TN): stress classified as controls; False positive (FP): controls classified as controls; False negative (FN): controls classified as stress.

13.3 Result

13.3.1 Validation of the Experimental Task

The experimental task was validated with the help of the subjective perception of time in order to solve a task at every level of the experiment. Each subject was required to validate individual perception in terms of time to solve a task in

Table 13.1 Rating of Time by Subjects for a Task at Every Level of Stress and Control Conditions with $P < 0.001$

	Stress		*Control*	
Level	μ	σ	μ	σ
1	5.68	2.18	9.14	1.46
2	4.41	2.10	8.59	1.78
3	3.77	2.29	8.55	1.75
4	3.18	2.12	7.86	1.82

the previous level. This was implemented using ratings from "1" to "10," with 10 being the maximum satisfaction time. The results in Table 13.1 show the subjective perception of the available time. The available time at every level of stress condition was significantly lower than that of control condition (*t*-test, $P < 0.001$). Other than the subjective perception of the available time, the experimental task was also validated based on the task performance, which was evaluated as a ratio of the number of correct responses to the total responses. The performance was compared between the stress and control conditions at each level using the paired *t*-test. The obtained results (shown in Figure 13.3) indicate that the performance under the stress condition was consistently lower than the optimum performance under the control condition. Moreover, the performance in the stress condition was significantly reduced as the difficulty level increased. Task performance was also considered as features at every level and applied to the classification in order to detect mental stress.

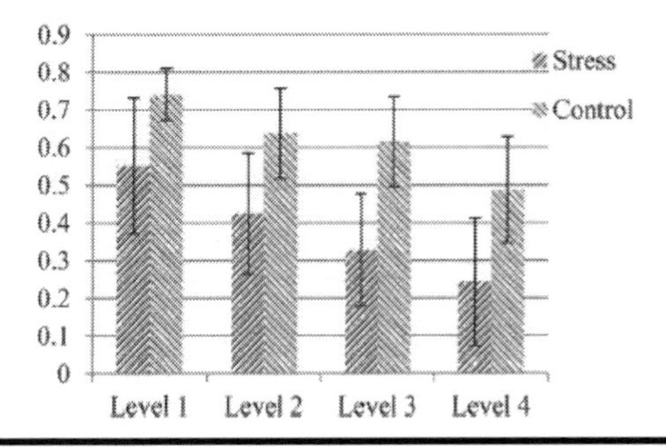

Figure 13.3 Task performance of stress and control at all levels with $P < 0.001$.

13.3.2 *Mental Stress Analysis*

The technique for recognizing significant quantitative variability between the stress and control conditions is developed using the paired *t*-test method. The method is applied on the features as follows.

13.3.2.1 *Relative Power*

The significant relative power ($P < 0.05$) between the stress and control conditions was illustrated in Figure 13.4 for all the analyzed frequencies. It was observed that the midline parietal lobe (Pz) is consistently significant in all frequency bands under the stress and control conditions. Other variations at lower frequency bands (delta, theta, and alpha) show minimal variations at levels 1 and 2 and significant variations at levels 3 and 4. At levels 3 and 4, the relative delta power is associated with cognition under the stress condition as it was found to be significant in anterior sources of the brain. The relative theta power is significant in the central and posterior sources at level 4, and the relative alpha power is significant in the left hemisphere at level 4.

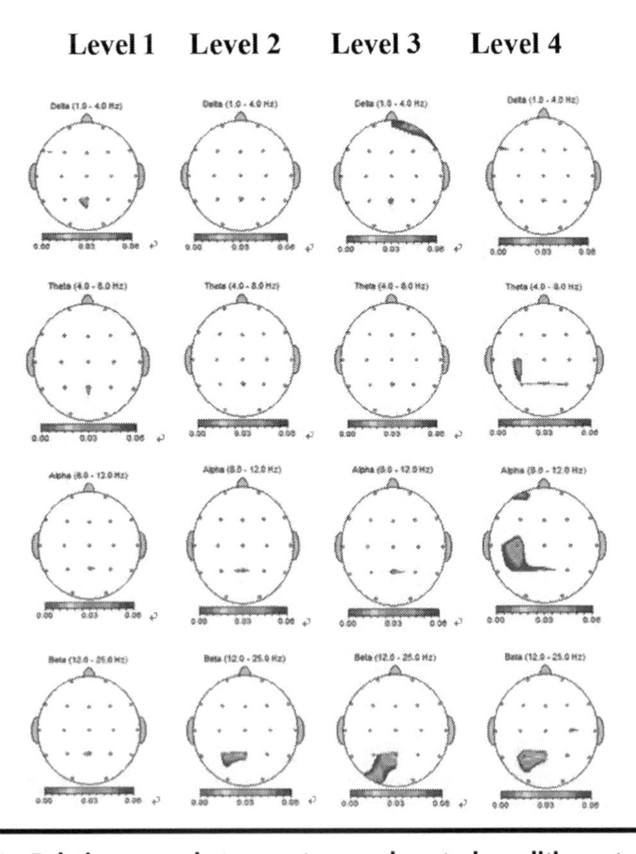

Figure 13.4 Relative power between stress and control conditions at every level.

Moreover, the relative beta power does not show variation at level 1 but spreads to the left parietal region at level 2 and then further extends towards the left central motor region (CMR) in high beta. Significance is also observed at the backward left position of Pz at level 3 and included the left temporal region in the relative high beta power. The same incremental trend in the parietal region can be found at level 4.

13.3.2.2 Relative Power Ratio

Figure 13.5 shows a significant relative power ratio ($P < 0.05$) between the stress and control conditions for all the frequencies. At level 1, the delta/theta, delta/alpha, and theta/alpha ratios are dominant locations of the midline and right posterior regions.

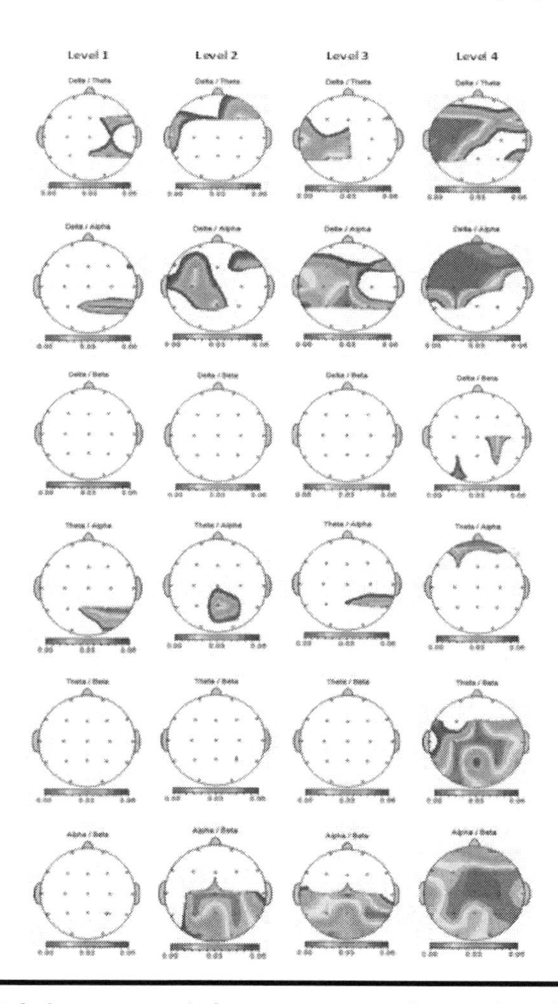

Figure 13.5 Relative power ratio between stress and control conditions at every level.

At level 2, the delta/theta and delta/alpha ratios can be observed to be significant in the frontal and left lateral locations. However, the theta/alpha ratio is significant only in the posterior regions. Moreover, at level 3, the delta/theta and delta/alpha ratios show significance in the left central and posterior region and delta/alpha and theta/alpha ratios in the right posterior regions. At level 4, the delta/theta and delta/alpha ratios are significant at the frontal, midline central, and left posterior regions and delta/alpha and theta/alpha ratios are significant in the prefrontal locations.

13.3.2.3 Coherence

Significant coherence ($P < 0.05$) between the stress and control conditions is presented in Figure 13.6 for all frequencies. It is observed that there are two colors of lines connecting locations: red and blue. The red color indicates a higher measure of stress than the control condition, whereas the blue color indicates the opposite. At level 1, all the frequency bands display significant coherence except for the beta band. The delta and theta bands are found to be strong coherent pairs between the bilateral sources of the prefrontal, frontal, and central lobes. This suggests that the subjects are initially less efficient at focusing their attention, forming expressions, and performing motor actions under stress conditions. A strong connection in the

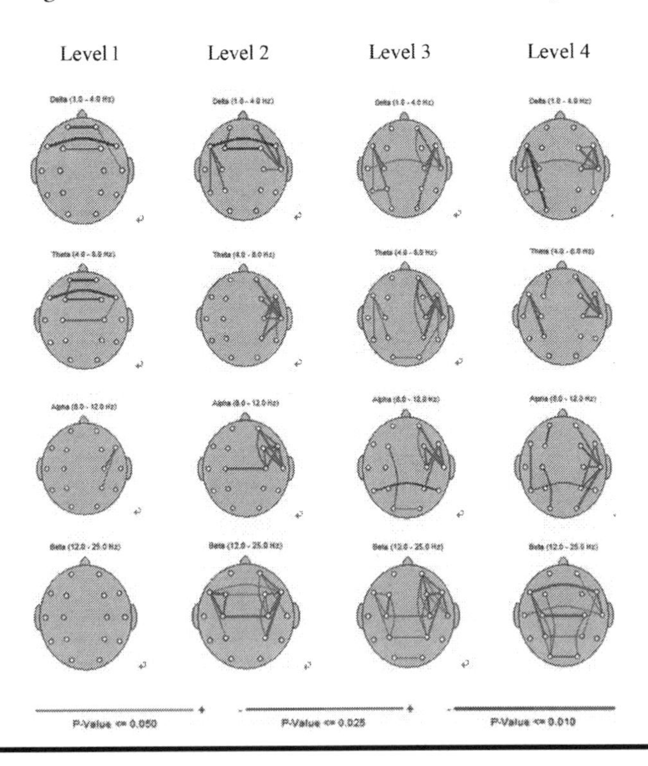

Figure 13.6 Coherence between stress and control condition at every level.

delta band can also be discovered at the prefrontal and temporal regions, and this phenomenon is observed in the next two levels. The frontal region is connected with the CMR for the theta and alpha bands. In addition, significant coherence is observed in the alpha band and at levels 3 and 4 of the frontoparietal lobe, where the coherence is lower under stress conditions than the control conditions, but the opposite appears to be the case between the lobes.

It is observed in levels 2 and 4 that the right temporal location actively pairs with other sources; in particular, the frontotemporal pairs at every frequency. Moreover, the left lateral frontal source shows a strong connection with the posterior sources for the delta and beta bands and bilateral central source pairs for the alpha and beta bands. A similar phenomenon can also be observed at level 3. Moreover, significant connections between the bilateral posterior locations are observed in the theta, alpha, and beta bands at levels 3 and 4. In addition, a significant coherence is observed at the left lateral frontal source pairing with other sources in the same hemisphere.

13.3.2.4 Phase Lag

Figure 13.7 presents the *t*-test results for significant pairs of the phase lag between the stress and control conditions at levels 1, 2, 3, and 4. The pairs connected with

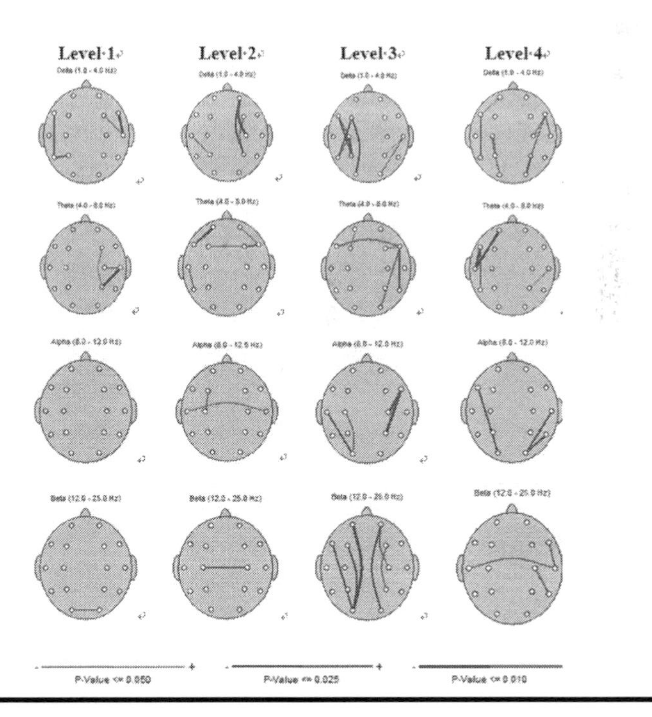

Figure 13.7 *t*-Test results of phase lag in levels 1–4 between stress and control conditions.

red lines indicate that the phase lag in the stress condition is higher than that in the control condition, whereas pairs connected with blue lines indicate that the phase lag in the stress condition is lower than that in the control condition.

13.3.2.5 Amplitude Asymmetry

Figure 13.8 shows the significant pairs of the amplitude asymmetry between the stress and control conditions. At level 1, only the alpha and beta bands showed amplitude asymmetry. In the alpha band, the asymmetry is found at the intrahemispheric sites. The notable locations that showed irregularities are the CMR, parietal and temporal on the left side (C3-P3 and C3-T5) and parietal, and the CMR and frontal on the right side (P4-F4 and P4-C4). In the beta band, the only pair that showed asymmetry is in the prefrontal region (FP1-FP2). All the asymmetries at level 1 are higher in the stress condition than the control condition.

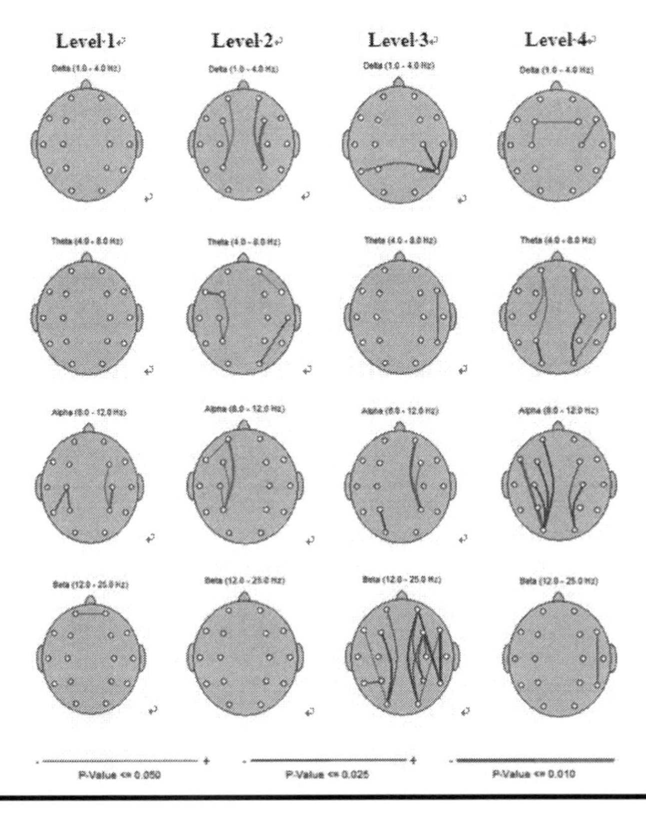

Figure 13.8 *t*-Test results of amplitude asymmetry at levels 1–4 between stress and control conditions.

At level 2, the most remarkable asymmetric pairs are from the frontoparietal region in the delta (FP1-P3, FP2-P4, F3-P3, and F4-P4), theta (F3-P3), and alpha bands (FP1-P3 and F3-P3). Moreover, asymmetric pairs are also significant within the frontal region as well as in the parietocentral region in the theta (F3-F7, FP2-F8, and C3-P3) and alpha bands (FP1-F7). One more asymmetric pair is significant between the occipital and temporal locations (O2-T4) in the theta band.

At level 3, the temporal location (T6) had asymmetric pairs with other temporal locations, CMR and parietal regions for the delta band (T5-T6, T4-T6, C4-T6, and P4-T6) and with the right lateral frontal region (F8-T6) for the theta band. These asymmetric pairs for the delta and theta bands had lower values for the stress condition than the control condition. In the alpha band, frontoparietal asymmetries (FP2-P4 and F4-P4) were higher for the stress condition than the control condition and parietooccipital asymmetry (P3-O1) is lower for the stress condition than the control condition. For the beta band, remarkable asymmetric pairs existed between the anterior and posterior regions of the brain. Notably, fronto-occipital (Fp1-O1, F3-O1, F7-O1, FP2-O2, F4-O2, and F8-O2), frontoparietal (FP-P4 and F4-P4), and frontotemporal pairs (FP2-T6, F8-T6) were found. Moreover, the frontal to motor region (F4-C4) and parietotemporal (P3-T5) asymmetries are also found in the beta band. These asymmetries in the amplitudes of the beta band were lower in the stress condition except for the case of the lateral frontal to occipital pairs (F7-O1 and F8-O2), which had higher asymmetries in the stress condition.

At level 4, the amplitude asymmetries in the delta power are found within the frontal or between the frontal and motor regions (F3-F4, F3-C3, and F8-C4). The lateral frontal to CMR pair (F8-C4) had a lower asymmetry in the stress condition while other the pairs had a higher asymmetry in the stress condition than the control condition. For the asymmetry in the theta power amplitude, the pairs are found within the frontal region, between the frontal and CMR or the frontoparietal region (FP1-C3, FP1-P3, FP2-F4, and FP2-C4). The central or parietal site further extended the asymmetric connections with the occipital sites (P3-O1 and C4-O2). The occipital region paired with the temporal region (O2-T4). Among these asymmetric pairs, the central and parietal pairs with occipital sites (P3-O1 and C4-O2) had lower asymmetry in the stress condition whereas all the other pairs had higher asymmetries in the stress condition than the control condition. In the asymmetry of the alpha power, the occipital locations were the most dominant while forming pairs in other brain regions (FP1-O1, F3-O1, F4-O2, F7-O1, C3-O1, C4-O2, and P3-O1). In these pairs, only the lateral to occipital pair exhibited a higher asymmetry in the stress condition whereas the asymmetry of all the other pairs was higher in the control condition than the stress condition. Beta power only exhibits asymmetry in the pairs between the frontotemporal regions (F8-T6), which have higher irregularity under the control condition than the stress condition.

Table 13.2 Results of HR and HRV During Stress and Control Conditions at Every Level (Paired *t*-Test, *P* < 0.05)

	Stress				*Control*			
	Level 1	*Level 2*	*Level 3*	*Level 4*	*Level 1*	*Level 2*	*Level 3*	*Level 4*
HR	81.2*	83.0*	82.4*	84.1*	74.4	76.7	75.3	75.5
VLF	1707.2	2605.7	1282.0	1203.1	1870.1	1081.2	1069.0	1306.2
LF	2577.8	4097.2	1896.1	2489.2	2126.7	1933.0	2097.1	1806.0
HF	9824.6	5298.2	2483.5	3439.2	2877.4	2530.0	2432.2	2185.5
LFnu	0.31	0.33	0.37	0.36	0.35	0.35	0.38	0.38
HFnu	0.38	0.38	0.37	0.37	0.39	0.39	0.38	0.36
LF/HF	0.96	0.91	1.13	1.01	1.07	0.95	1.10	1.19

* represents that the value in stress condition is significantly different (Paired *t*-Test, $P < 0.05$) with respect to control condition.

13.3.2.6 HR and HRV

Both the HR and HRV features were extracted from the ECG signals as shown in Table 13.2. It is observed that only the HR is found to be significantly higher at all four levels based on the *t*-test ($P < 0.05$) under both the stress and control conditions.

13.3.3 Dimensionality Reduction

The results obtained from the PCA for the dimensionality reduction of the feature set at every level are displayed in Table 13.3. The first PC at each level is selected for creating a feature set to represent the overall experimental condition. The feature sets of the individual levels as well as the overall experimental condition are applied to the classifier to detect mental stress.

13.3.4 Detection of Mental Stress

For the classification of the stress and control, in each level, the SVM realized maximum accuracies of 72.27% and 75% using the sigmoid and RBF kernels, respectively. The results indicate that the accuracy of the SVM with the sigmoid kernel remained greater than 70% for all four levels. Moreover, for the overall classification of the stress and control, in which the first PCs from the feature set of each level were combined, the SVM with the sigmoid kernel achieved a maximum accuracy of 79.54%.

Table 13.3 Number of Selected Features at Every Level After Performing the Paired *t*-Test

Features	*Number of Features at Each Level Before Paired t-Test*	*Number of Selected Features After Paired t-Test*			
		Level 1	*Level 2*	*Level 3*	*Level 4*
Relative power	95	5	8	12	20
Relative power ratio	114	14	24	33	62
Coherence	256	12	43	55	47
Phase lag	256	5	12	23	18
Amplitude asymmetry	256	5	13	21	18
HR and HRV	7	1	1	1	1
Total variables	984	42	101	145	166
Variables after applying PCA		18	23	26	26

This section presents the classification results obtained using the SVM classifier to discriminate the stress from the control at every level of the experiment as well in the overall experiment using the defined feature sets in Section 3.2. Table 13.4 highlights the classification performance at every level in terms of accuracy, TP rate, FP rate, precision, recall, and receiver operating characteristic (ROC) curve, respectively. Moreover, area under the curve (AUC) is measured and plotted in Figure 13.9. In level 1, the SVM with RBF kernel (SVM-RBF) exhibits a better performance than the sigmoid kernel (SVM-sigmoid). This indicates that the latter is more precise and predicts a lower FP, but its recall value is lower than that of the SVM-RBF, which indicates that its sensitivity in TP prediction is lower. In addition, the SVM-RBF has a larger ROC AUC than the SVM-sigmoid. At level 2, both the classifiers have the same performance. At level 3, the recall from both the classifiers is the same, whereas the SVM-sigmoid produces better results in terms of accuracy, FP rate, precision, and ROC AUC. At level 4, the results obtained from

Table 13.4 Classification Results of Levels 1–4

Level 1	*Level 2*	*Level 3*	*Level 4*
SVM-sigmoid			
A TP = 13 FP = 3 FN = 9 TN = 19 Accuracy = 72.72% TP rate = 59% FP rate = 13% Precision = 81% Recall = 61.9% ROC = 72%	B TP = 17 FP = 7 FN = 5 TN = 15 Accuracy = 72.72% TP rate = 77% FP rate = 31% Precision = 70% Recall = 77.27% ROC = 72%	C TP = 15 FP = 6 FN = 7 TN = 16 Accuracy = 70.45% TP rate = 68% FP rate = 27% Precision = 71% Recall = 68.18% ROC = 70%	D TP = 14 FP = 5 FN = 8 TN = 17 Accuracy = 70.45% TP rate = 63% FP rate = 22 % Precision = 73% Recall = 63.63% ROC = 70%
SVM-RBF			
E TP = 15 FP = 4 FN = 7 TN = 18 Accuracy = 75% TP rate = 68% FP rate = 18% Precision = 78% Recall = 68.18% ROC = 75%	F TP = 17 FP = 7 FN = 5 TN = 15 Accuracy = 72.72% TP rate = 77% FP rate = 31 % Precision = 70% Recall = 77.27% ROC = 72%	G TP = 15 FP = 8 FN = 7 TN = 14 Accuracy = 65.9% TP rate = 68% FP rate = 36 % Precision = 65% Recall = 68.18% ROC = 65%	H TP = 13 FP = 5 FN = 9 TN = 17 Accuracy = 68.18% TP rate = 59% FP rate = 22 % Precision = 72% Recall = 61.9% ROC = 68%

the SVM-sigmoid show that the detectability of stress is better at the beginning of the experiment, which reflects that physiological variations are more discriminant in the early levels of the experiment.

Table 13.5 presents the results obtained from SVM-RBF and SVM-sigmoid in the overall experiment in terms of accuracy, TP rate, FP rate, precision, recall, and ROC.

It is observed that the overall experiment results maximally discriminate between stress and control condition, which increase the detectability of mental stress. Moreover, SVM-sigmoid has a consistent accuracy of above 70% throughout the experiment. In a similar study [10,36], the achieved classification accuracy was above 80% when the MIST and recovery phases were concatenated. However, in the MIST phase alone, the accuracy was nearly 78%, which is almost equal to that in this study.

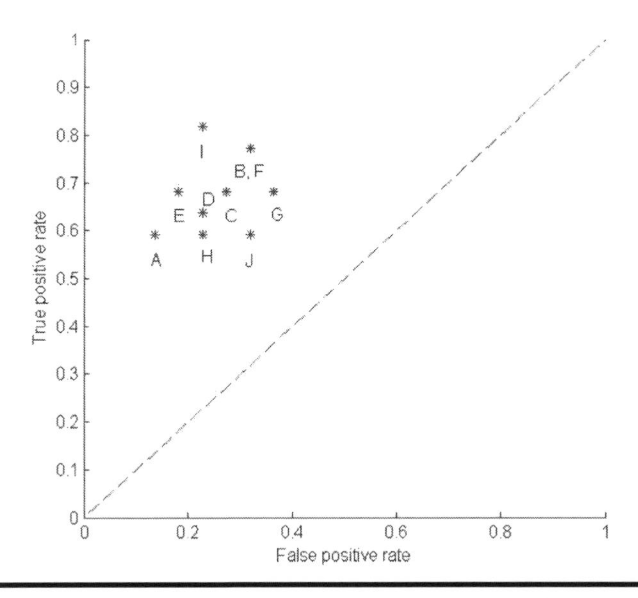

Figure 13.9 ROC AUC values. A, B, C, and D represent ROC AUC values of SVM-sigmoid at levels 1–4. E, F, G, and H represent ROC AUC values of SVM-RBF at levels 1–4. I and J represent ROC AUC values of SVM-sigmoid and SVM-RBF of the overall experiment.

Table 13.5 Classification Results of Overall Experiment

Overall Experiment	
SVM-sigmoid	*SVM-RBF*
I TP = 18 FP = 5 FN = 4 TN = 17 Accuracy = 79.54% TP rate = 81% FP rate = 22% Precision = 78% Recall = 81% ROC = 79%	J TP = 13 FP = 7 FN = 9 TN = 15 Accuracy = 63.63% TP rate = 59% FP rate = 31% Precision = 65% Recall = 59% ROC = 63%

13.4 Discussion

Regarding the clinical assessment of stress, several conventional methods rely on subjective treatment through stress inventories. These methods can potentially assist clinicians in identifying stress sources in a person's life. As the existence of stress affects the quality of our lives, there is a requirement to detect stress in its beginning stages. Moreover, there are chances that the response to these inventories comprise subjective biases if a person is unwilling to accept that they are experiencing mental stress. In this study, we develop a methodology for the objective analysis and detection of stress in its early stages. This method has been evaluated with subjects who had no severe stress in their individual lives; this method relies on the qEEG and ECG features during a mental stress task. The features were further shortlisted using the paired *t*-test and PCA for feature selection and dimensionality reduction, respectively. The former works by selecting those features that show a significant difference between two classes, whereas PCA reduces the dimensionality by discarding the redundant features in the feature sets.

Among the extracted features from the EEG, the relative power showed a significant difference between the stress and control conditions, especially in the last two levels of the experiment, i.e., levels 3 and 4. The most convincing physiological studies that identified the existence of mental stress have used processive stressors that do not generate an immediate threat to the homeostatic equilibrium. Less disturbing events such as nervousness due to performance and psychosocial pressures due to public speech, examinations, interpersonal relationships, and workplace environment can initiate physiological stress. The brain perceives stressors as a potential threat, and thus, psychological and psychosocial conditions can be interpreted through considerable cognitive processing.

Relative power positively correlates with mental stress in the parietal lobe (thought as association cortex [58]) throughout the experiment. The lobe does not process cognition but serves as a bridge between the sensory input and motor actions. In this regard, the results reflect a positive correlation between mental stress and increased activity of the association cortex. The overall results of the relative power ratio show that the sequence of higher power is beta > delta > theta > alpha as far as activation under the stress condition is concerned. However, the significance of the beta power is apparent only in the last level.

The EEG frequency measures are related to the network complexity and arousal as expected [59]. Higher activation of alpha under the stress condition represents a difficulty in learning, and the suppression of alpha under the stress condition in the posterior region is indicative of preferential attention to perceptual details, which has been observed in individuals with autism spectrum disorder [60].

The asymmetry results illustrate that the most significant asymmetric pairs can be found in the frontoparietal locations, especially at levels 3 and 4 of the task. Generally, the hemispheric asymmetries in the frontal regions are associated with stress and emotional regulation as well as major depressive disorder (MDD). A similar study [61] investigated frontal asymmetry in the alpha band as neurofeedback training and found improvement in the asymmetry as the training progressed. Another study [62] used frontal asymmetry in the beta band as neurofeedback on patients with MDD. Considerable reduction in the depressive symptoms correlated with the reduction in the frontal activity in the high beta band. Our results do not show any significant hemispheric asymmetry mainly because the arithmetic task under both conditions activates the same regions that do not show significance. This finding is in line with [63], where the efficacy of the neurofeedback is evaluated based on depressive symptoms. The training results show no difference in frontal hemispheric asymmetry in the alpha band in the pre- and post-training comparison when other findings show an improved effect of training on the depressive symptoms. Moreover, the anterior–posterior asymmetry in the beta band is significantly reduced under the stress condition (level 3). The asymmetry in the beta amplitude is very focal in individuals with dyslexia [64], where it is indicative of lexical decisions.

The possibility of the application of previous qEEG-based methods to clinical purposes is low owing to multiple factors including less efficient methods, small sample sizes that pose a hindrance to the generalization of the methods, and methodological differences incorporated by the heterogeneity of the sample populations. In contrast, the proposed method has presented positive efficiencies that indicate the feasibility of its clinical applicability. The advantage of employing the machine learning (ML) technique is the ability to incorporate objectivity in mental stress detection. According to the obtained results, EEG features such as relative power computation from the frequency bands—such as delta, theta, alpha, and beta bands—and asymmetry have shown their potential. The relatively simplistic EEG features present a low-cost solution for clinical applications and justify the feasibility of the proposed method as a potential CAD solution for predicting the mental-stress treatment efficacy.

The results have revealed that the HR is a useful feature from among the other features extracted from the ECG for classification. The HR can positively correlate with mental stress [65,66]. A higher HR during stress indicates more sympathetic arousal. Furthermore, HR, VLF, LF, HF, LFnu, HFnu, and LF/HF were extracted from the ECG. However, their discretization ability was not established in our work. This paper is primarily focused on the evaluation of qEEG features for the assessment of stress. The ECG features used in this case are considered as the margin to support the outcome. A detailed ECG analysis was not performed, but it would be a great contribution to the knowledge of stress assessment if the advancement of ECG is monitored and analyzed. A recent work combining ECG and photoplethysmography based on HR and blood pressure monitoring has been presented. It showed its robustness in health applications [67,68]. A similar approach may be undertaken to increase the robustness of our work.

13.5 Conclusions

EEG provides a low-cost solution that is feasible for remote applications in small clinics and healthcare facilities. In contrast, the existing clinical diagnostic approach involves well-structured questionnaires and interviews conducted with mental-stress subjects. Therefore, this study provides a quantitative solution for mental-stress detection and prediction. The selection of qEEG features and the proposed ML scheme (SVM classifier) have shown robustness and promising results with an accuracy of 79.45%, recall or TP rate of 81%, and specificity of 78% for the overall experiment representation. Moreover, the incorporation of ML techniques facilitates an automatic diagnosis process. This provides better performance at any level of the experiment, which indicates that the proposed method of detecting mental stress can be used in health applications.

In the future, the following work will be considered for improving the proposed method based on the potential limitations:

- The accuracy and robustness of the system is required to be further improved. The classifier used in this study has produced acceptable results, but it still cannot be confidently applied in clinics as only an accuracy of >90% is considered. Therefore, more participants/subjects from various races will be used to train our model in order to perfect the system in terms of robustness and accuracy.
- The system is sensitive to several individual conditions and states, for example, age gap, genders, tobacco smoking [69], and smoking abstinence [70]. Smoking might affect the spectral content of the EEG. In this study, participants are not asked to provide their smoking status, which might be a factor that potentially affects the reported results. Therefore, it is important to take each participant's condition into consideration, such as their habits, age, gender, and race, and thus, additional features will be considered for feature fusion in order to provide more information to the system.
- The number of participants can affect the accuracy of the classification. This had resulted in the issue of large age gaps and differences in gender between the stress and control conditions, which may be a potential limitation when age is considered as one of the features; in other words, the system may not be sufficiently trained for use in classification and prediction. Therefore, the new EEG phenomena (evoked theta, evoked delta, induced theta ERS, and gamma oscillation) of event-related potentials (ERPs) and event-related oscillations (EROs) may be candidates for assessing the treatment progress.
- A seven-day gap designed for data acquisition is suggested between the two tasks of the experiment, but the memory effect may still not be ruled out completely. Therefore, a longer gap will be considered on consulting clinicians and doctors in clinics such that the memory effect can be minimized, and the results can become more accurate.

Conflict-of-Interest Statement

The authors of this paper declare no conflicts of interest.

Acknowledgments

This work is supported by the National Natural Science Foundation of China (61572076, 61702348, 61772351, 61602326, 61602324), the Ministry of Education Malaysia through the Higher Institution Centre of Excellence (0153CA-005), Beijing Advanced Innovation Center for Imaging Technology, National Key R & D Plan (2017YFB1303000, 2017YFB1302800), the Project of the Beijing Municipal Science & Technology Commission (LJ201607), and Capacity Building for Sci-Tech Innovation-Fundamental Scientific Research Funds (025185305000).

References

1. A. Abbott, "Stress and the city: Urban decay," *Nature*, vol. 490, pp. 162–164, 2012.
2. F. Lederbogen, P. Kirsch, L. Haddad, F. Streit, H. Tost, P. Schuch et al., "City living and urban upbringing affect neural social stress processing in humans," *Nature*, vol. 474, pp. 498–501, 2011.
3. E. R. de Kloet, M. Joels, and F. Holsboer, "Stress and the brain: From adaptation to disease," *Nature Reviews Neuroscience*, vol. 6, pp. 463–475, 2005.
4. M. Kivimäki, P. Leino-Arjas, R. Luukkonen, H. Riihimäi, J. Vahtera, and J. Kirjonen, "Work stress and risk of cardiovascular mortality: prospective cohort study of industrial employees," *British Medical Journal*, vol. 325, 2002.
5. D. Carneiro, J. C. Castillo, P. Novais, A. Fernández-Caballero, and J. Neves, "Multimodal behavioral analysis for non-invasive stress detection," *Expert Systems with Applications*, vol. 39, pp. 13376–13389, 2012.
6. M. Gärtner, L. Rohde-Liebenau, S. Grimm, and M. Bajbouj, "Working memory-related frontal theta activity is decreased under acute stress," *Psychoneuroendocrinology*, vol. 43, pp. 105–113, 2014.
7. J. Lyle, E. Bourne, and R. A. Yaroush, "Stress and cognition: A cognitive psychological perspective," University of Colorado, Denver, CO, 2003.
8. G. Durantin, J. F. Gagnon, S. Tremblay, and F. Dehais, "Using near infrared spectroscopy and heart rate variability to detect mental overload," *Behavioural Brain Research*, vol. 259, pp. 16–23, 2014.
9. J. A. Healey and R. W. Picard, "Detecting stress during real-world driving tasks using physiological sensors," *IEEE Transactions on Intelligent Transportation Systems*, vol. 6, pp. 156–166, 2005.
10. A. Mariotti, "The effects of chronic stress on health: new insights into the molecular mechanisms of brain–body communication," *Future Science OA*, vol. 1, 2015.
11. H. Ursin and H. Eriksen, "The cognitive activation theory of stress," *Psychoneuroendocrinology*, vol. 29, pp. 567–592, 2004.
12. B. Roozendaal, B. S. McEwen, and S. Chattarji, "Stress, memory and the amygdala," *Nature Reviews Neuroscience*, vol. 10, pp. 423–433, 2009.

13. M.-F. Marin, C. Lord, J. Andrews, R.-P. Juster, S. Sindi, G. Arsenault-Lapierre et al., "Chronic stress, cognitive functioning and mental health," *Neurobiology of Learning and Memory*, vol. 96, pp. 583–595, 2011.
14. S. Chattarji, A. Tomar, A. Suvrathan, S. Ghosh, and M. M. Rahman, "Neighborhood matters: Divergent patterns of stress-induced plasticity across the brain," *Nature Neuroscience*, vol. 18, pp. 1364–1375, 2015.
15. A. F. T. Arnsten, "Stress weakens prefrontal networks: Molecular insults to higher cognition," *Nature Neuroscience*, vol. 18, pp. 1376–1385, 2015.
16. S. Cohen, D. A. J. Tyrrell, and A. P. Smith, "Negative life events, perceived stress, negative affect, and susceptibility to the common cold," *Journal of Personality and Social Psychology*, vol. 64, pp. 131–140, 1993.
17. J. E. Dise-Lewis, "The life events and coping inventory: An assessment of stress in children," *Psychosomatic Medicine*, vol. 50, pp. 484–499, 1988.
18. K. B. Koh, J. K. Park, C. H. Kim, and S. Cho, "Development of the stress response inventory and its application in clinical practice," *Psychosomatic Medicine*, vol. 63, pp. 668–678, 2001.
19. I. F. Chung, C. T. Lin, K. L. Lin, L. W. Ko, S. F. Liang, and B. C. Kuo, "Nonparametric single-trial EEG feature extraction and classification of driver's cognitive responses," *EURASIP Journal on Advances in Signal Processing*, vol. 2008, 2008.
20. G. F. Wilson, J. D. Lambert, and C. A. Russell, "Performance enhancement with real-time physiologically controlled adaptive aiding," in *Proceedings of the XIVth Triennial Congress of the International Ergonomics Association and 44th Annual Meeting of the Human Factors and Ergonomics Association, 'Ergonomics for the New Millennnium*, San Diego, CA, pp. 61–64, 2000.
21. C. L. Johnny and D. S. Tan, "Using a low-cost electroencephalograph for task classification in HCI research," in *UIST 2006 Proceeding of the 19th Annual ACM Symposium on User Interface Software and Technology*, Montreux, Switzerland, pp. 81–90, 2006.
22. K. Ishino and M. Hagiwara, "A feeling estimation system using a simple electroencephalograph," in *IEEE International Conference on Systems, Man and Cybernetics*, Washington, DC, pp. 4204–4209, 2003.
23. K. S. Rahnuma, A. Wahab, N. Kamaruddin, and H. Majid, "EEG analysis for understanding stress based on affective model basis function," in *15th IEEE International Symposium on Consumer Electronics, ISCE 2011*, Singapore, pp. 592–597, 2011.
24. R. S. Lewis, N. Y. Weekes, and T. H. Wang, "The effect of a naturalistic stressor on frontal EEG asymmetry, stress, and health," *Biological Psychology*, 75(3): 239–247, 2007.
25. K. Dedovic, R. Renwick, N. K. Mahani, V. Engert, S. J. Lupien, and J. C. Pruessner, "The montreal imaging stress task: Using functional imaging to investigate the effects of perceiving and processing psychosocial stress in the human brain," *Journal of Psychiatry and Neuroscience*, vol. 30, pp. 319–325, 2005.
26. C. Vidaurre, N. Krämer, B. Blankertz, and A. Schlögl, "Time domain parameters as a feature for EEG-based brain-computer interfaces," *Neural Networks*, vol. 22, pp. 1313–1319, 2009.
27. K. Kalimeri and C. Saitis, "Exploring multimodal biosignal features for stress detection during indoor mobility," in *Proceedings of the 18th ACM International Conference on Multimodal Interaction*, pp. 53–60, 2016.
28. J. F. Alonso, S. Romero, M. R. Ballester, R. M. Antonijoan, and M. A. Mañanas, "Stress assessment based on EEG univariate features and functional connectivity measures," *Physiological Measurement*, vol. 36, 2015.

29. H. U. Amin, W. Mumtaz, A. R. Subhani, M. N. M. Saad, and A. S. Malik, "Classification of EEG signals based on pattern recognition approach," *Frontiers in Computational Neuroscience*, vol. 11, 2017.
30. S. Russell and P. Norvig, *Artificial Intelligence: A Modern Approach*, 3 ed. Upper Saddle River, NJ: Prentice Hall, 2010.
31. W. Mumtaz, P. L. Vuong, L. Xia, A. S. Malik, and R. B. A. Rashid, "Automatic diagnosis of alcohol use disorder using EEG features," *Knowledge-Based Systems*, vol. 105, pp. 48–59, 2016.
32. A. R. Subhani, N. Kamel, M. N. Mohamad Saad, N. Nandagopal, K. Kang, and A. S. Malik, "Mitigation of stress: new treatment alternatives," *Cognitive Neurodynamics*, 2017.
33. A. R. Subhani, A. S. Malik, N. Kamil, and M. N. M. Saad, "Difference in brain dynamics during arithmetic task performed in stress and control conditions," in *Biomedical Engineering and Sciences (IECBES), 2016 IEEE EMBS Conference on*, pp. 695–698, 2016.
34. S. Norizam, "Determination and classification of human stress index using non-parametric analysis of EEG signals," Doctor of philosophy, Faculty of Electrical & Electronic Engineering, Universiti Teknologi Mara, http://umpir.ump.edu.my/16490/, 2015.
35. E. Santarnecchi, A. R. Khanna, C. S. Musaeus, C. S. Y. Benwell, P. Davila, F. Farzan et al., "EEG Microstate Correlates of Fluid Intelligence and Response to Cognitive Training," *Brain Topography*, pp. 1–19, 2017.
36. K. Dedovic, A. Duchesne, J. Andrews, V. Engert, and J. C. Pruessner, "The brain and the stress axis: The neural correlates of cortisol regulation in response to stress," *NeuroImage*, vol. 47, pp. 864–871, 2009.
37. J. C. Pruessner, K. Dedovic, M. Pruessner, C. Lord, C. Buss, L. Collins et al., "Stress regulation in the central nervous system: Evidence from structural and functional neuroimaging studies in human populations–2008 Curt Richter Award Winner," *Psychoneuroendocrinology*, vol. 35, pp. 179–191, 2010.
38. C. Setz, B. Arnrich, J. Schumm, R. La Marca, G. Tröster, and U. Ehlert, "Discriminating stress from cognitive load using a wearable EDA device," *IEEE Transactions on Information Technology in Biomedicine*, vol. 14, pp. 410–417, 2010.
39. S. Cohen, T. Kamarck, and R. Mermelstein, "A global measure of perceived stress," *Journal of Health and Social Behavior*, vol. 24, pp. 385–396, 1983.
40. Net Station Acquisition Technical Manual. Available: https://www.egi.com/knowledge-center.
41. T. C. Ferree, P. Luu, G. S. Russell, and D. M. Tucker, "Scalp electrode impedance, infection risk, and EEG data quality," *Clinical Neurophysiology*, vol. 112, pp. 536–544, 2001.
42. NeuroGuide Manuals and Documentation. Available: http://www.appliedneuroscience.com/Tutorials.htm.
43. P. L. Nunez, *Electrical Fields of the Brain*. New York: Oxford University Press, 1981.
44. P. L. Nunez, *Neocortical Dynamics and Human EEG Rhythms*. New York: Oxford University Press, 1994.
45. A. Malliani, M. Pagani, F. Lombardi, and S. Cerutti, "Cardiovascular neural regulation explored in the frequency domain," *Circulation*, vol. 84, pp. 482–492, 1991.
46. M. Malik, "Heart rate variability: Standards of measurement, physiological interpretation, and clinical use," *Circulation*, vol. 93, pp. 1043–1065, 1996.

47. S. Theodoridis and K. Koutroumbas, *Pattern Recognition*, 4th ed. Burlington, MA: Academic Press, 2008.
48. L. R. Trambaiolli, N. Spolaôr, A. C. Lorena, R. Anghinah, and J. R. Sato, "Feature selection before EEG classification supports the diagnosis of Alzheimer's disease," *Clinical Neurophysiology*, vol. 128, pp. 2058–2067, 2017.
49. A. R. Subhani, W. Mumtaz, N. Kamil, N. M. Saad, N. Nandagopal, and A. S. Malik, "MRMR based feature selection for the classification of stress using EEG," in *2017 Eleventh International Conference on Sensing Technology (ICST)*, pp. 1–4, 2017.
50. Z. Qingxue, Z. Dian, and Z. Xuan, "A novel machine learning-enabled framework for instantaneous heart rate monitoring from motion-artifact-corrupted electrocardiogram signals," *Physiological Measurement*, vol. 37, p. 1945, 2016.
51. C.-S. Ouyang, C.-T. Chiang, R.-C. Yang, R.-C. Wu, H.-C. Wu, and L.-C. Lin, "Quantitative EEG findings and response to treatment with antiepileptic medications in children with epilepsy," *Brain and Development*, vol. 40, pp. 26–35, 2018.
52. X. Ding, Y. Yang, E. A. Stein, and T. J. Ross, "Combining multiple resting-state fMRI features during classification: Optimized frameworks and their application to nicotine addiction," *Frontiers in Human Neuroscience*, vol. 11, 2017.
53. F. C. Cruz, E. F. Simas Filho, M. C. S. Albuquerque, I. C. Silva, C. T. T. Farias, and L. L. Gouvêa, "Efficient feature selection for neural network based detection of flaws in steel welded joints using ultrasound testing," *Ultrasonics*, vol. 73, pp. 1–8, 2017.
54. H. Abdi and L. J. Williams, "Principal component analysis," *Wiley Interdisciplinary Reviews: Computational Statistics*, vol. 2, pp. 433–459, 2010.
55. C. Corinna and V. Vapnik, "Support-Vector Networks," *Machine Learning*, vol. 20, 1995.
56. I. H. Witten, E. Frank, and M. A. Hall, *Data Mining: Practical Machine Learning Tools and Techniques*, 3rd ed. Amsterdam, the Netherlands: Elsevier, 2011.
57. F. Lotte, M. Congedo, A. Lécuyer, F. Lamarche, and B. Arnaldi, "A review of classification algorithms for EEG-based brain-computer interfaces," *Journal of Neural Engineering*, vol. 4, pp. R1–R13, 2007.
58. A. C. Guyton and J. E. Hall, *Textbook of Medical Physiology*, 11th ed. Amsterdam, the Netherlands: Elsevier, 2006.
59. R. W. Thatcher, D. North, and C. Biver, "EEG and intelligence: Relations between EEG coherence, EEG phase delay and power," *Clinical Neurophysiology*, vol. 116, pp. 2129–2141, 2005.
60. K. J. Mathewson, M. K. Jetha, I. E. Drmic, and S. E. Brayson, "Regional EEG alpha power, coherence, and behavioral symptomatology in autism spectrum disorder," *Clinical Neurophysiology*, vol. 123, pp. 1798–1809, 2012.
61. J. J. B. Allen, E. Harmon-Jones, and J. H. Cavender, "Manipulation of frontal EEG asymmetry through biofeedback alters self-reported emotional responses and facial EMG," *Psychophysiology*, vol. 38, pp. 685–693, 2001.
62. V. Paquette, M. Beauregard, and D. Beaulieu-Prévost, "Effect of a psychoneurotherapy on brain electromagnetic tomography in individuals with major depressive disorder," *Psychiatry Research: Neuroimaging*, vol. 174, pp. 231–239, 2016.
63. E. J. Cheon, B. H. Koo, and J. H. Choi, "The efficacy of neurofeedback in patients with major depressive disorder: An open labeled prospective study," *Applied Psychophysiology Biofeedback*, 2015.

64. R. Duncan Milne, J. P. Hamm, I. J. Kirk, and M. C. Corballis, "Anterior–posterior beta asymmetries in dyslexia during lexical decisions," *Brain and Language*, vol. 84, pp. 309–317, 2003.
65. A. R. Subhani, L. Xia, and A. Saeed Malik, "Association of autonomic nervous system and EEG scalp potential during playing 2D grand turismo 5," in *34th Annual International Conference of the IEEE Engineering in Medicine and Biology Society*, San Diego, CA, pp. 3420–3423, 2012.
66. A. R. Subhani, L. Xia, and A. S. Malik, "Quantification of physiological disparities and task performance in stress and control conditions," in *35th Annual International Conference of the IEEE Engineering in Medicine and Biology Society*, Osaka, Japan, 2013.
67. Q. Zhang, D. Zhou, and X. Zeng, "Highly wearable cuff-less blood pressure and heart rate monitoring with single-arm electrocardiogram and photoplethysmogram signals," *Biomedical Engineering Online*, vol. 16, p. 23, 2017.
68. Q. Zhang, X. Zeng, W. Hu, and D. Zhou, "A machine learning-empowered system for long-term motion-tolerant wearable monitoring of blood pressure and heart rate with ear-ECG/PPG," *IEEE Access*, vol. 5, pp. 10547–10561, 2017.
69. G.V. Tcheslavski, "Effects of tobacco smoking and schizotypal personality on spectral contents of spontaneous EEG," *International Journal of Psychophysiology*, vol. 70, pp. 88–93, 2008.
70. V. Teneggi, L. Squassante, S. Milleri, A. Polo, P. Lanteri, L. Ziviani, A. Bye, "EEG power spectra and auditory P300 during free smoking and enforced smoking abstinence," *Pharmacology Biochemistry and Behavior*, vol. 77, pp. 103–109, 2004.

Chapter 14

Efficient DV-HOP Localization for Wireless Cyber-Physical Social Sensing System: A Correntropy-Based Neural Network Learning Scheme

Yang Xu, Xiong Luo, Weiping Wang, and Wenbing Zhao

Contents

14.1 Introduction

In recent years, there has been an emerging interest in the field of socially-aware computing through integrating social computing and pervasive computing [1,2]. Then, the cyber-physical social system could deeply integrate the cyber world and the physical world, as well as the social world [3]. In addition, the social sensing is a novel application of the cyber-physical social system. Additionally, a new paradigm, named cyber-physical social sensing (CPSS), was developed, in which the perception processes allow humans to participate. The wireless sensor network (WSN) with a simple architecture and cost-saving performance, plays a critical role for the sensor process and provides some important information to serve as a social network in the CPSS [4,5], where those sensors are the primary entities replacing humanity in the traditional social network [6]. Various research regarding the WSN has been undertaken [7–11].

Generally, a critical step in constructing a sensor network is to precisely determine the node position through the process of localization. In other words, localization is an indispensable part of WSN [12]. With the purpose of locating sensor nodes precisely, we need effective localization techniques to improve the performance of WSN. Some traditional approaches of localization, i.e., the Global Positioning System (GPS)-based method [13], manual measurement and the calibration method, are unsatisfactory sometimes due to the high cost, especially for a large-scale sensor network.

Usually, all nodes in WSN are randomly distributed, and only a few nodes, called anchor nodes, equipped with GPS, could get their positions after being scattered. However, the other nodes, called unknown nodes, do not capture their own positions. The anchors usually help those unknown nodes by using connectivity between nodes and exchanging multiple hop routing information to locate themselves. The node localization methods of sensor networks could be grouped as range-based and range-free. The former depends on angle or range measurements between nodes, which could be obtained by the time-of-arrival (TOA) method or the received signal strength indication (RSSI) method [14], and special hardware equipment is necessary. RSSI is a preferable choice due to its relatively low cost [15], and RSSI has been widely used for device-free wireless localization [16–19]. Nevertheless, RSSI is sensitive to environmental noise [19] and may lead to a decrease of localization accuracy. Meanwhile, the latter relies only on connectivity, and it is naturally less expensive and simpler [20].

Among the available range-free localization schemes, some are heuristic and simple and could be carried out in a distributed environment. Additionally, the classic range-free localization algorithm, i.e., distance vector hop (DV-HOP) [21], is a good choice in a hardware support-limited environment because of its simplicity in implementation. However, the positioning accuracy will be greatly reduced when the node distribution is uneven. Consequently, some novel methods have been proposed on the basis of DV-HOP to enhance the accuracy of localization [22–24].

Taking advantage of both the range-free method and the range-based method, some algorithms were proposed by incorporating RSSI and DV-HOP to execute the localization for unknown nodes [25–28]. In this way, the localization error of the unknown and anchor nodes could be reduced effectively. Nevertheless, the calculation of the coordinate may still not be accurate in some cases [29].

Motivated by the scheme of neural network (NN)-based node localization with RSSI and hop counts [30], we present a novel DV-HOP localization scheme with RSSI and regularized correntropy criterion (RCC)-based ELM (ELM-RCC), named RHOP-ELM-RCC, to improve the performance of WSN in the CPSS. Compared with SNR (signal to noise ratio) parameters, the parameters of RSSI are more related to position [31]; RSSI may be accordingly more appropriate in our proposed scheme. We combine the DV-HOP and RSSI to reduce distance measurement error without additional hardware, in which RSSI estimates the distance utilizing the decreasing degree of the signals in the transfer process [32].

Since ELM is an effective NN learning algorithm with fast learning speed and minimal human intervention [33,34], it can be used to improve the performance of WSN [35,36]. In our previous work [37], we exploited the ELM-based single-hidden layer feedforward network (SLFN) to calculate the sub-anchor nodes. Moreover, RCC could be used to improve the ability of the anti-noise of ELM [38]. Here, we utilize the algorithm ELM-RCC to calculate the coordinates of unknown nodes in this article. Then, integrating the ELM-RCC into the DV-HOP localization algorithm with RSSI, the robustness for environmental noise and transport errors may be improved.

It should be indicated that RHOP-ELM-RCC is a general schema for wireless networks, e.g., IEEE 802.11, Scenario 4G/5G. Our work assumes a well-known transmission power. The case of unknown transmission power is out of the scope of the current article. This scenario is studied in [39]. In addition, the transmission power attenuation is directly proportional to the transmission distance.

The rest of this article is as follows. Preliminaries, including DV-HOP, RSSI, ELM, correntropy, and ELM-RCC, are analyzed in Section 14.2. The details of our proposed scheme are shown in Section 14.3, in which DV-HOP localizations with RSSI based on ELM or ELM-RCC are described, respectively. The simulation results and analysis are provided in Section 14.4. Additionally, a conclusion is drawn in Section 14.5.

14.2 Preliminaries

14.2.1 DV-HOP Algorithm

DV-HOP is a typical range-free localization algorithm. The key of the DV-HOP scheme is that the distance between the anchor nodes and the unknown nodes is gained through multiplying the average hop size by the hop count, and then, the coordinates of the unknown nodes are obtained using the maximum likelihood estimation method [40]. The anchor node estimates the average hop size using the minimum hop count and the distances, which are gained from itself to all other anchors, and then each unknown node determines its average hop size by selecting the minimum hop count to an anchor node [41]. Although the range measurement method of DV-HOP is unaffected by environmental factors, such as landscape and climate, the range measurement error is large if the sensor nodes are unevenly distributed in WSN. For example, in Figure 14.1, we assume that nodes A1, A2 and A3 are all anchor nodes, and the positions of the unknown nodes U1, U2, U3 and U4 are to be identified. The true distances of these anchor nodes are known, i.e., 30, 30, 40. Then, each anchor node obtains its average hop distance as follows:

$$\begin{aligned} &\mathrm{A1}:(30+40)\times(3+5)^{-1}=8.75,\\ &\mathrm{A2}:(30+40)\times(4+5)^{-1}=7.78,\\ &\mathrm{A3}:(30+30)\times(3+4)^{-1}=8.57. \end{aligned} \tag{14.1}$$

Then, each anchor node transfers its average hop distance by broadcasting in the form of flooding through the network, and the unknown node only receives the first value as its average hop size. Our flooding method could have a negative impact on battery-powered-only anchor nodes. Nevertheless, this aspect is out of scope of the current proposal. We take the unknown node U1 shown in Figure 14.1

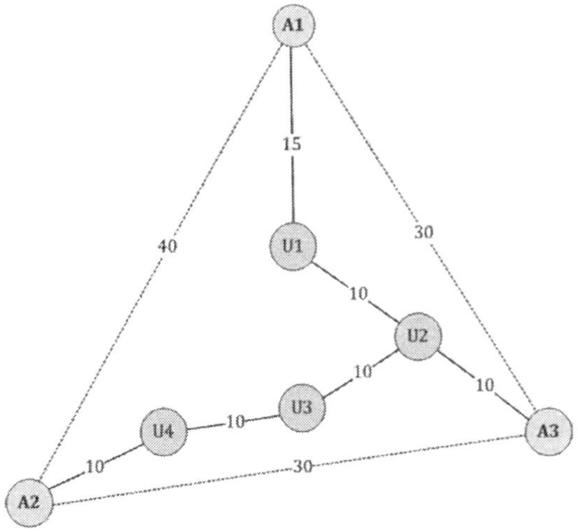

Figure 14.1 A diagram of the range measurement error for the distance vector hop (DV-HOP) algorithm.

as an example; the hop count from A1 to U1 is only one hop; thus, U1 just saves the average hop distance of A1, i.e., 8.75, as its average hop size. Then, U1 estimates the distances to all other anchors as follows:

$$\begin{aligned} &U1 \rightarrow A1: 8.75 \times 1 = 8.75, \\ &U1 \rightarrow A2: 8.75 \times 4 = 35, \\ &U1 \rightarrow A3: 8.75 \times 2 = 17.5. \end{aligned} \tag{14.2}$$

In Figure 14.1, it is obvious that the range measurement error is large with the DV-HOP scheme, where the actual range between A1 and U1 is 15, but not 8.75. Additionally, the large range error will make the final position error even greater by using the maximum likelihood estimation method or the triangular positioning algorithm.

14.2.2 Received Signal Strength Indication

Due to the lower implementation complexity without the need for additional hardware, RSSI becomes an attractive alternative in WSN [39]. However, RSSI is easily affected by noise and obstacles and may lead to significant estimation errors; moreover, two nodes may receive different RSSI originated from each other under an uncertain environment [30]. Currently, the signal propagation model of RSSI for WSN can be divided into three types, including the two-ray ground model, free space model and log-normal shadow model [42,43]. The first two models are applicable to some special occasions, while the last one describes the fading of signal strength and is appropriate for both outdoor and indoor environments, and it is a more general model of signal propagation. Then, the received signal power of nodes for the log-normal shadow model can be defined by [44]:

$$\mathrm{RSS}(d)(\mathrm{dBm}) = P_{tr} - P_{loss}(d_0) - 10\tau \log_{10} \frac{d}{d_0} + X_\sigma, \tag{14.3}$$

where d means the distance between the sending nodes and the receiving nodes, RSS(d) indicates the received signal power of nodes located at the distance of d, d_0 is the referenced distance, P_{tr} denotes the transmitting power, $P_{loss}(d_0)$ means the path loss for d_0, τ indicates loss exponent in the path and its value relies on the environment of propagation, and X_σ is the noise in RSSI, which is described as a Gaussian random variable with zero-mean and standard deviation σ.

14.2.3 Extreme Learning Machine

For P arbitrary different training samples $\{(x_i, t_i)_{i=1}^{P}\}$, where $t_i = (t_{i1}, t_{i2}, \ldots, t_{in}) \in \mathbb{R}^n$ and $x_i = (x_{i1}, x_{i2}, \ldots, x_{im}) \in \mathbb{R}^m$. In a WSN, t_i denotes the coordinate of node i, and x_i means the distances from the node i to all other m nodes. With a random input x, the corresponding output function of ELM could be specified as:

$$O(x) = \hbar(x)W, \tag{14.4}$$

$$W = \left(\frac{I}{C} + HH^{\mathrm{T}}\right)^{-1} H^{\mathrm{T}}T, \tag{14.5}$$

where W indicates the output weight in the connection of the hidden layer and the output in a *NN*, I denotes the identity matrix, C is the regularization parameter, $O_{P\times n} = (O_1, O_2, \ldots, O_P)^{\mathrm{T}}$, $T_{P\times n} = (T_1, T_2, \ldots, T_P)^{\mathrm{T}} = (t_1, t_2, \ldots, t_P)^{\mathrm{T}}$, $H_{P\times h} = (\hbar(x_1), \hbar(x_2), \ldots, \hbar(x_P))^{\mathrm{T}}$ represents the output of the hidden layer corresponding to the given training dataset and h indicates the amount of hidden nodes in the hidden layer. In addition, $\hbar(x_i) = (\hbar_1(x_i), \hbar_2(x_i), \ldots, \hbar_h(x_i)) \in \mathbb{R}^h$, where $i = 1, 2, \ldots, P$, and $\hbar(x_i)$ maps corresponding input x_i from m-dimensional space to the h-dimensional feature space of the hidden layer.

If the feature mapping function $\hbar(x)$ in the hidden layer is unclear to users, a kernel-based ELM was proposed in [33]. Then, the kernel matrix of ELM could be defined as:

$$\Omega_{\text{ELM}} = HH^{\text{T}} = \begin{bmatrix} \hbar(x_1) \\ \vdots \\ \hbar(x_P) \end{bmatrix} \begin{bmatrix} \hbar^{\text{T}}(x_1) & \cdots & \hbar^{\text{T}}(x_P) \end{bmatrix}$$

$$= \begin{bmatrix} \hbar(x_1)\hbar^{\text{T}}(x_1) & \cdots & \hbar(x_1)\hbar^{\text{T}}(x_P) \\ \vdots & \vdots & \vdots \\ \hbar(x_P)\hbar^{\text{T}}(x_1) & \cdots & \hbar(x_P)\hbar^{\text{T}}(x_P) \end{bmatrix} \tag{14.6}$$

$$= \begin{bmatrix} K(x_1,x_1) & \cdots & K(x_1,x_P) \\ \vdots & \vdots & \vdots \\ K(x_P,x_1) & \cdots & K(x_P,x_P) \end{bmatrix},$$

where the corresponding kernel function in Equation (14.6) could be denoted as:

$$K(a,b) = e^{-\gamma\|a-b\|^2}, \tag{14.7}$$

where γ is parameter of the kernel.

Then, the output function in Equation (14.4) could be rewritten as:

$$O(x) = \hbar(x)\left(\frac{I}{C} + \Omega_{\text{ELM}}\right)^{-1} H^{\text{T}}T. \tag{14.8}$$

In the above kernel implementation of ELM, it is not necessary to explicitly give the formula of the feature mapping function in the hidden layer, as well as the number of hidden nodes [45].

The weight connecting matrix W between the output layer and the hidden layer in Equation (14.4) is obtained by [38]:

$$\min_W\left(\| O - T \|_F^2\right) = \min_W\left(\| HW - T \|_F^2\right), \tag{14.9}$$

where $\|\cdot\|_F$ indicates the Frobenius norm. Usually, the minimum norm least square problem is sensitive to noises.

Equality-constrained optimization is used to enhance the stability and generalization of ELM [33]. Hence, Equation (14.9) could be converted as:

$$\min_W\left(\| HW - T \|_F^2 + \lambda \| W \|_F^2\right), \tag{14.10}$$

where $\|W\|_F^2 = \sum_{i=1}^{h} \|W_i\|_2^2$, in which the L_2-norm is used, and λ is the regularization parameter, usually, $\lambda = \frac{I}{C}$. Here, C and I are mentioned above.

Thus, the kernel-based ELM with regularization could be described as Algorithm 14.1.

Algorithm 14.1 The kernel-based ELM with regularization.

Input: training samples $\{(x_i, t_i) \mid x_i \in \mathbb{R}^m, t_i \in \mathbb{R}^n, i=1,\ldots,P\}$; the regularization parameter C; the kernel function $K(a,b)$; the input of a random testing sample x.

1. Calculate the kernel matrix Ω_{ELM} of the given P training samples based on Equation (14.6);
2. Calculate the output of the test sample O based on Equation (14.8).

Output: the test sample O.

14.2.4 Correntropy

Inspired by information theoretic learning (ITL) [46], the original correlation function of correntropy [47] is extended to the general case [48], while it is only used for a single random process before. Assume two arbitrary random variables S and J, of which the similarity could be measured by correntropy:

$$V_\delta(S,J) = E[\kappa_\delta(S-J)], \tag{14.11}$$

where κ_δ denotes the kernel function defined by Mercer's theorem [49] and the mathematical expectation denoted by E[·]. Then, the maximum of (14.11) is named the maximum correntropy criterion (MCC) [48,50].

Let P be the number of samples and it is finite, then the correntropy could be expressed as:

$$\hat{V}_\delta(S,J) = \frac{1}{P}\sum_{i=1}^{P}\kappa_\delta(s_i - j_i), \tag{14.12}$$

we omit the subscript δ in κ_δ for simplicity, and:

$$\kappa(s_i - j_i) = \kappa_\delta(s_i - j_i) = e^{-\frac{(s_i - j_i)^2}{2\delta^2}}. \tag{14.13}$$

Since correntropy is robust against outliers, it outperforms the traditional measure, i.e., mean squared error (MSE), when there exist outliers in the training data [48].

14.2.5 Regularization Correntropy Criterion-Based ELM

Another optimal solution of Equation (14.9) could be obtained by utilizing MCC [38], which is defined as:

$$\mathcal{F}(\widetilde{W}) = \max_{\widetilde{W}} \sum_{i=1}^{P} \kappa\left(T_i - O_i\right), \tag{14.14}$$

where the target vector, T_i, corresponds to the i-th input vector x_i, while O_i is obtained by [38]:

$$O_i = \sum_{j=1}^{h} W_j \hbar_j(x_i) + \omega_0,\ i = 1,2,\ldots,P, \tag{14.15}$$

where $W_j = (W_{j1}, W_{j2}, \ldots, W_{jn})^T \in \mathbb{R}^n$ and the bias vector $\omega_0 = (\omega_{01}, \omega_{02}, \ldots, \omega_{0n})^T \in \mathbb{R}^n$ represents the threshold of the output units.

For simplicity, we give a definition $\tilde{\hbar}(x_i) = (\tilde{\hbar}_1(x_i), \tilde{\hbar}_2(x_i), \ldots, \tilde{\hbar}_{h+1}(x_i)) = (1, \hbar_1(x_i), \hbar_2(x_i), \ldots, \hbar_h(x_i)) \in \mathbb{R}^{h+1}, i = 1,2,\ldots,P.$ Additionally, $\widetilde{H}_{P\times(h+1)} = (\tilde{\hbar}(x_1), \tilde{\hbar}(x_2), \ldots, \tilde{\hbar}(x_P))^T$. In addition, $\widetilde{W}_{(h+1)\times n} = (\widetilde{W}_1, \widetilde{W}_2, \ldots, \widetilde{W}_{h+1})^{\mathrm{T}} = (\omega_0, W_1, \ldots, W_h)^T$, where $\widetilde{W}_j = (\widetilde{W}_{j1}, \widetilde{W}_{j2}, \ldots, \widetilde{W}_{jn}) \in \mathbb{R}^n$, $j = 1,2,\ldots,(h+1)$. Then, Equation (14.15) could be updated as:

$$O_i = \sum_{j=1}^{h+1} \tilde{\hbar}_j(x_i) \widetilde{W}_j. \tag{14.16}$$

Then, we add L_2 regularization into Equation (14.14), named RCC, and it is revised as:

$$\mathcal{F}(\widetilde{W}) = \max_{\widetilde{W}} \left[\sum_{i=1}^{P} \kappa \left(T_i - \sum_{j=1}^{h+1} \tilde{\hbar}_j(x_i) \widetilde{W}_j \right) - \lambda \| \widetilde{W} \|_F^2 \right], \tag{14.17}$$

where λ still means the regularization parameter. Here, unlike the optimization in the kernel-based ELM with regularization using least square estimation (LSE), the half-quadratic optimization method [51] and the position rules of the convex conjugated function [52–54] are exploited to get the optimal solution [38]. With a fixed $\widetilde{W}$, Equation (14.17) is converted to:

$$\mathcal{F}(\widetilde{W})=\mathcal{F}(\widetilde{W},\theta)=\max_{\widetilde{W},\theta}\left[\sum_{i=1}^{P}\left(\theta_i\frac{\|T_i-\sum_{j=1}^{h+1}\tilde{\hbar}_j(x_i)\widetilde{W}_j\|_2^2}{2\delta^2}-\varphi(\theta_i)\right)-\lambda\|\widetilde{W}\|_F^2\right], \tag{14.18}$$

and in half-quadratic optimization, $\theta = (\theta_1,\theta_2,\ldots,\theta_P)$ represents the auxiliary variables.

Let D be a diagonal matrix, where the one in the i-th column and the i-th row is $D_{ii}=\theta_i^{r+1}$. Then, we have an iterative process as follows [38]:

$$\theta_i^{r+1}=-\kappa\left(T_i-\sum_{j=1}^{h+1}\tilde{\hbar}_i(x_j)\widetilde{W}_j^r\right), \tag{14.19}$$

$$\widetilde{W}^{r+1}=\underset{\widetilde{W}}{\operatorname{argmax}}\left[\operatorname{Tr}\left((T-\widetilde{H}\widetilde{W})^{\mathrm{T}}D(T-\widetilde{H}\widetilde{W})-\lambda\widetilde{W}^{\mathrm{T}}\widetilde{W}\right)\right], \tag{14.20}$$

where r means the r-th iteration and it is determined by:

$$|C_r-C_{r+1}|<\varepsilon. \tag{14.21}$$

Here, ε is a user-specified threshold, which controls the number of iterations indirectly. In addition, C is the correntropy of the target vector and the estimated output vector, and it is given as:

$$C=\frac{1}{P}\sum_{i=1}^{P}\kappa(T_i-O_i). \tag{14.22}$$

14.3 The Proposed Scheme

This section is to demonstrate the details of the novel scheme of DV-HOP localization with RSSI based on ELM-RCC, named RHOP-ELM-RCC. RSSI is used to improve the localization accuracy, and the accuracy could be further improved if the noise sensitivity of RSSI could be overcome. Moreover, when there exist outliers, the estimated coordinates, calculated by least squares (LS) [55] or ELM [37], will be affected to a certain extent. Then, the ELM-RCC mentioned above could decrease the effect of both noise and transport error. Meanwhile, for the sake of comparison, we also give a description of the DV-HOP localization algorithm with RSSI based on ELM, named RHOP-ELM.

14.3.1 DV-HOP Localization with RSSI Based on ELM-RCC

In the proposed scheme, we reduce distance measurement error by incorporating the DV-HOP and RSSI without additional hardware. After getting the distance from all of the anchor nodes to each unknown node, the coordinates of unknown nodes are calculated by the SLFN using ELM-RCC, which is of good nonlinear mapping capability and high learning speed, as well as it shows a powerful noise-resistant ability. Here, the localization scheme RHOP-ELM-RCC is presented as follows.

1. Each anchor node delivers a beacon detail and RSSI packet to all neighboring nodes through broadcasting. The beacon message includes the identity ID_i of the anchor node, location coordinates (x_i, y_i), hop count value hops_i initialized to zero and the accumulated distance DRSSI_i, which is initialized to zero, as well. Then, the format of the beacon message can be expressed as $\{\mathrm{ID}_i, (x_i, y_i), \mathrm{hops}_i, \mathrm{DRSSI}_i\}$. When each neighboring node receives the broadcast, it updates the values of hops_i and DRSSI_i through Equation (14.23) and then continues to broadcast the updated beacon message to other neighbor nodes.

$$\begin{cases} \mathrm{hops}_i = \mathrm{hops}_i + 1 \\ \mathrm{DRSSI}_i = \mathrm{DRSSI}_i + \mathrm{dis\_hop} \end{cases}, \tag{14.23}$$

where "dis_hop" is the estimated distance transformed by the RSSI value of this neighboring node [56]. Note that the increase of the number of RSSI samples could reduce the impact of noise on RSSI measurement. Thus, given a certain number of RSSI samples, we average all of the RSSI values in the same measurement. Then, "dis_hop" can be defined by:

$$\mathrm{dis\_hop} = 10^{\frac{P_{tr} - P_{loss}(d_0) - \overline{\mathrm{RSSI}}}{10\tau}} \times d_0, \tag{14.24}$$

where $\overline{\mathrm{RSSI}}$ is the average RSSI values of this neighboring node.

A node will compare the newly arriving hops_i with the existing hops_i once it receives a new packet of the same ID and will discard the new message of which the hop count is greater than the existing hop count. Otherwise, the new message would be adopted to replace the existing message of the same ID.

After this process, all nodes in the framework will get the minimal hop count and the corresponding accumulated RSSI distance to every anchor node.

2. Once the minimal hop count of one anchor and the corresponding accumulated RSSI distances from the anchor to other anchors are obtained, naturally, an average hop size and RSSI range of one hop could be estimated easily. The average hop size written as HOP_i and average RSSI distance written as DRSSAVG_i per hop are then estimated by anchor node i as:

$$\begin{cases} \text{HOP}_i = \left(\sum_{j \neq i}^{n} \sqrt{(x_i - x_j)^2 + (y_i - y_j)^2} \right) \cdot \left(\sum_{j \neq i}^{n} h_{ij} \right)^{-1} \\ \text{DRSSAVG}_i = \left(\sum_{j \neq i}^{n} \text{DRSSI}_{ij} \right) \cdot \left(\sum_{j \neq i}^{n} h_{ij} \right)^{-1} \end{cases}, \tag{14.25}$$

where (x_j, y_j) and (x_i, y_i) are the coordinates of anchor j and anchor i, respectively. Additionally, h_{ij} is the minimum hop count between anchor node i and anchor node j; DRSSI_{ij} is the RSSI accumulated distance between anchor i and anchor j. Here, the number of anchor nodes is n.

After obtaining the average hop size and the average hop RSSI distance, each anchor node transfers its hop size and average hop RSSI distance information. Once the unknown node gets the average hop RSSI range information from a certain anchor, as well as the hop size, it saves them as the average hop RSSI distance and the average hop size, then omits all of the subsequent information. Obviously, such a strategy guarantees that most of the unknown nodes will only receive the average hop size and average RSSI distance for one hop of the closest anchor nodes with the minimal hops.

3. The correction factor γ is estimated for the size of each hop through dividing the RSSI distance per hop, dis_hop, by average RSSI distance per hop. Then, the correction hop size can be updated by multiplying the correction factor by the average hop size. Let m be the hop count of unknown node j and anchor i. Then, the distance between the anchor i and unknown node j could be gained by:

$$\begin{aligned} d_{ji} &= \sum_{k=1}^{m} \gamma_k \times \text{HOP}_i = \sum_{k=1}^{m} \frac{\text{dis\_hop}_k}{\text{DRSSAVG}_i} \times \text{HOP}_i \\ &= \frac{\sum_{k=1}^{m} \text{dis\_hop}_k}{\text{DRSSAVG}_i} \times \text{HOP}_i = \frac{\text{DRSSI}_{ji}}{\text{DRSSAVG}_i} \times \text{HOP}_i, \end{aligned} \tag{14.26}$$

where $\gamma_k (k=1,\ldots,m)$ means the correction factor of the k-th hop from anchor i to unknown node j, dis_hop_k means the RSSI range of the k-th hop and $DRSSI_{ji}$ is the RSSI accumulated distance of anchor node i and unknown node j. From Equation (14.26), each unknown node could evaluate the distances to all anchor nodes on the basis of the stored information in packets, which include the accumulated RSSI distance to each anchor node, its own hop size and average RSSI distance per hop.

4. When the estimated distances from each anchor node to the unknown nodes are obtained, we will use the SLFN based on ELM-RCC to obtain the coordinates of these unknown nodes. The training samples for the SLFN using ELM-RCC are obtained from the virtual framework covering all cases [30]. If all nodes are deployed randomly in an $N \times N$ area, $N \times N$ training samples could be easily obtained. The inputs of these training datasets are the distances between every two coordinates from $(1,1),(1,2),\ldots,(1,N),\ldots,(N,1),(N,2),\ldots,(N,N)$, in the virtual complete topology to all anchor nodes, and the outputs of these samples are their corresponding coordinates. After getting the training samples, the SLFN using ELM-RCC is accordingly constructed and trained by using these $N \times N$ training samples and learning algorithm ELM-RCC, then the coordinate of the unknown node j could be estimated by exploiting the trained SLFN on the basis of input vector $d_j = (d_{jl})_{l=1}^{q}$, where q is the number of anchors, d_{jl} is the distance between unknown node j and anchor l, which could be obtained using Equation (14.26).

On the whole, the proposed DV-HOP localization scheme using RSSI and ELM-RCC could be concluded in Algorithm 14.2.

Algorithm 14.2 DV-HOP localization scheme with RSSI based on ELM-RCC (RHOP-ELM-RCC)

Input: the distance between anchor l and unknown node j: $d_{jl}(l=1,2,\ldots,q)$.

1. Obtain the hop count and RSSI distance by broadcasting the beacon messages and RSSI packets of each anchor nodes;
2. Average hop size and calculate the mean value of RSSI distance per hop based on Equation (14.25);
3. Compute the distances between anchor nodes and unknown nodes with the correction factor γ on the basis of Equation (14.26);
4. Use the distances obtained in Equation (14.26) as the input of ELM-RCC, and then, calculate the coordinate (x_j, y_j) for unknown node j using ELM-RCC.

Output: the coordinate of unknown node j.

14.3.2 DV-HOP Localization Scheme with RSSI Using Kernel-Based ELM

The DV-HOP localization scheme with RSSI using kernel-based ELM (RHOP-ELM) is also presented here to compare with RHOP-ELM-RCC. The only difference between them is whether RCC is exploited. The general steps of RHOP-ELM are similar to RHOP-ELM-RCC, and we could get RHOP-ELM by using the kernel-based ELM with regularization to replace the ELM-RCC in Step (4) of Algorithm 14.2.

14.4 The Performance Comparison and Analysis

14.4.1 Simulation Description

To test the performance of RHOP-ELM-RCC and RHOP-ELM in a WSN, some simulations are carried out. We measure the effectiveness of those schemes through localization error. Meanwhile, our performance comparisons are implemented among those schemes, including the DV-HOP scheme [24], DV-HOP utilizing RSSI (named RHOP) [29], a new DV-HOP (named One-HOP) [41], RHOP-ELM and RHOP-ELM-RCC. The MATLAB R2012a computing environment is applied to all simulations.

The training samples are obtained from the virtual framework including all cases. In this article, WSN is deployed in a two-dimensional area, and the actual data samples are randomly gathered from 50 nodes of the area of $50\text{ m} \times 50\text{ m}$ or 100 nodes from an area of $100\text{ m} \times 100\text{ m}$. Then, we proportionally select the anchor nodes from all nodes. It should be indicated that the node density of the area of $100\text{ m} \times 100\text{ m}$ with 100 nodes is 0.01, while the node density is 0.02 in the area of $50\text{ m} \times 50\text{ m}$ with 50 nodes. Additionally, it explains why in our simulations, the localization error in the area $100\text{ m} \times 100\text{ m}$ with 100 nodes is higher than that in the area $50\text{ m} \times 50\text{ m}$.

Moreover, the sensor nodes and anchor nodes could communicate freely, and they have the same communication capabilities. In the following simulations, we assume that 10% of the total nodes are anchor nodes, as shown in Figure 14.2. Additionally, every two nodes could communicate on the condition that the Euclidean distance between those two nodes is within the node transmission range R, which is the same as its maximum communication distance. Then, we run each algorithm 20 times in different areas and then calculate the average location error against R, ($R \in \{22, 24, 25, 28, 30\}$) shown in Figure 14.3; finally, we set $R = 25$. In the simulations of DV-HOP, RHOP and one-HOP, if there exist less than three anchor nodes that could communicate with an unknown node within the communication range R, then the coordinate of the unknown node cannot be obtained.

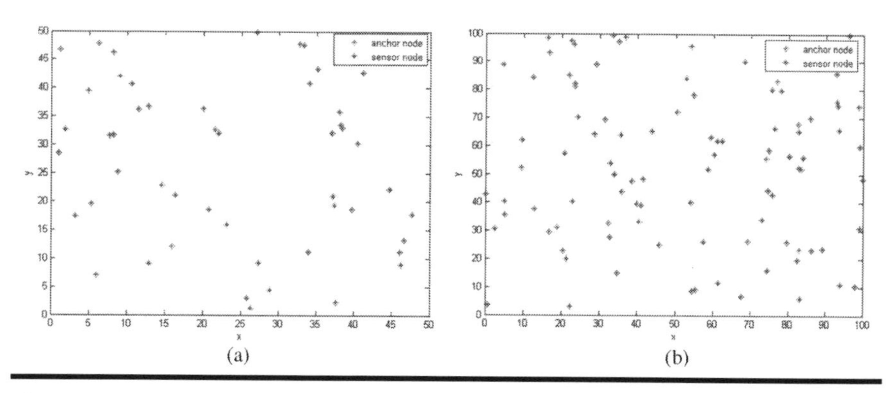

Figure 14.2 Different areas of node distribution. (a) There are 50 nodes in the area of 50 m × 50 m. (b) There are 100 nodes in the area of 100 m × 100 m.

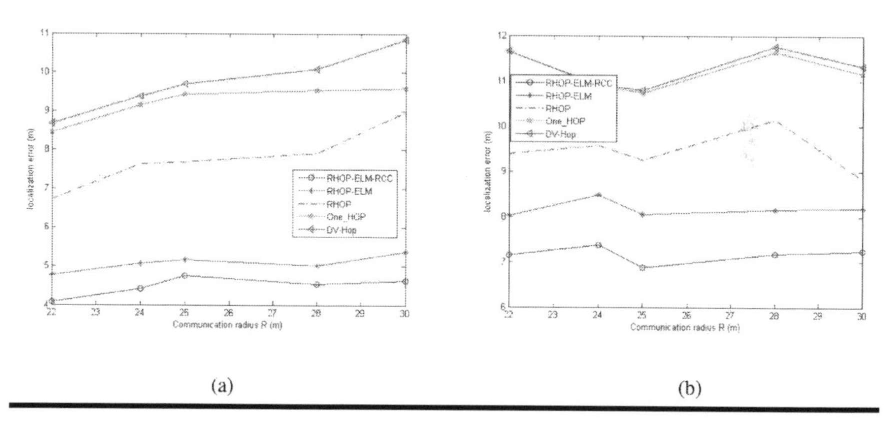

Figure 14.3 The impact of *R* in different areas. (a) The location error against *R* in the area of 50 m × 50 m; (b) The location error against *R* in the area of 100 m × 100 m.

Additionally, other simulation parameters for the algorithms in the network are shown in Table 14.1. The parameter ε of the proposed algorithm affects the location accuracy to a certain extent. We execute the proposed algorithm 20 times within different area; ε is set in $\{10^{-1}, 10^{-2}, 10^{-3}, 10^{-4}, 10^{-5}, 10^{-6}, 10^{-7}, 10^{-8}\}$, and the average value is shown in Figure 14.4. To obtain low location error, we accordingly set $\varepsilon = 10^{-3}$ in the area of $50\text{ m} \times 50\text{ m}$ and $\varepsilon = 10^{-4}$ in the area of $100\text{ m} \times 100\text{ m}$.

Here, the performance measurement is the localization error, which is inversely proportional with the localization accuracy. Then, the localization error is mathematically modeled as:

Table 14.1 Simulation Parameters

Item	*Value*
Area	$50\ \text{m} \times 50\ \text{m}, 100\ \text{m} \times 100\ \text{m}$
Transmission range, R	25 m
Path loss exponent, τ	4
Transmitting power, P_{tr}	0 dB
Path loss of the reference, $P_{loss}(d_0)$	$55\ \text{dB}(d_0 = 1\ \text{m})$
Numbers of total nodes	50, 100, 120
Ratios of anchors	10%, 20%, 30%, 40%, 50%
Numbers of nodes in hidden layer	Numbers of total nodes × ratio of anchors
Numbers of RSSI samples	1, 5, 10, 15, 20
Noise standard deviation	2, 5, 8, 11, 14
The proportion of outliers	0%, 3%, 6%, 9%, 12%, 15%, 18%
The threshold, ε	$10^{-3}, 10^{-4}$

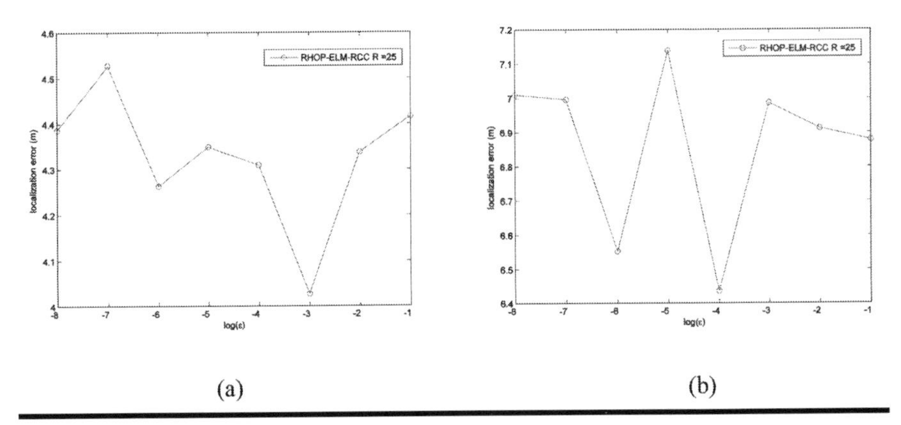

Figure 14.4 The impact of ε in different areas when R=25. (a) The average ε in the area of 50 m × 50 m when R=25; (b) The average ε in the area of 100 m × 100 m when R=25.

$$\text{Error} = \left(\frac{1}{m} \sum_{i=1}^{m} \left((x_i - x_i')^2 + (y_i - y_i')^2 \right) \right)^{\frac{1}{2}}, \tag{14.27}$$

where (x_i', y_i') and (x_i, y_i) are the estimated coordinate and real coordinate of unknown node i, respectively. Additionally, m means the number of the unknown nodes except those nodes whose coordinates cannot be obtained.

14.4.2 Localization Errors against the Number of Anchor Nodes

The system scenarios with pairs of the amount of nodes and node distribution area are (50, 50 m × 50 m) and (100, 100 m × 100 m), with the percentage of anchor nodes varying within {10%, 20%, 30%, 40%, 50%}. In addition, the RSSI samples and the noise standard deviation are set to 10 and 5, respectively.

Figure 14.5 demonstrates the comparison results of our scheme with other schemes under such a condition that the number of anchor nodes changes while the amount of total nodes remains unchanged. It is clear that the accuracy rate of the localization algorithm is closely correlated with the density of anchor nodes, and our scheme outperforms other schemes in localization error. Specifically, RHOP-ELM-RCC is superior to RHOP-ELM. When the localization errors of all schemes are large, the ratio of anchor nodes is very small; while increasing the ratio of anchor nodes, the localization error of each scheme decreases. The reason is that the growth of the percentage of anchor nodes will reduce the distance between unknown nodes and the anchor nodes, decrease the information loss and lead to a relatively high accuracy.

14.4.3 Localization Errors against the Number of RSSI Samples

Here, the WSN scenario is with a total of 50 nodes in 50 m × 50 m and 100 nodes in 100 m × 100 m. In addition, the anchor density is fixed to 20%, and the noise standard deviation is supposed to be five. Besides, the number of RSSI samples is described in Table 14.1.

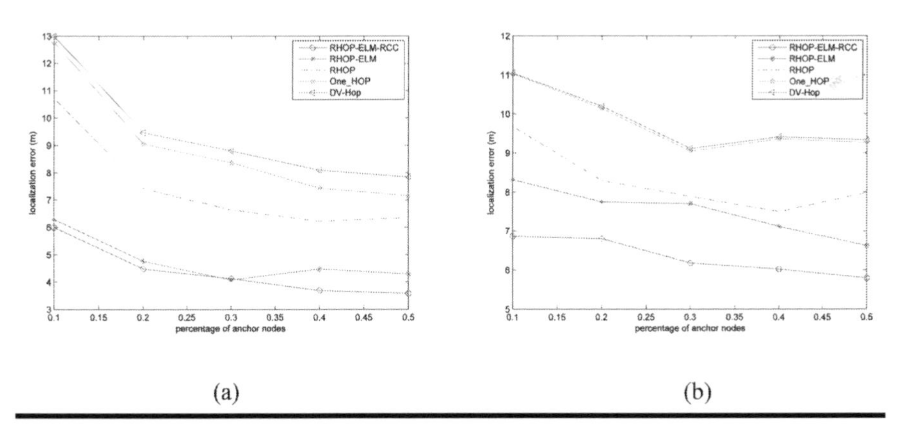

Figure 14.5 Localization errors against the amount of anchor nodes. (a) The case with 50 nodes in the area of 50 m × 50 m; (b) The case with 100 nodes in the area of 100 m × 100 m.

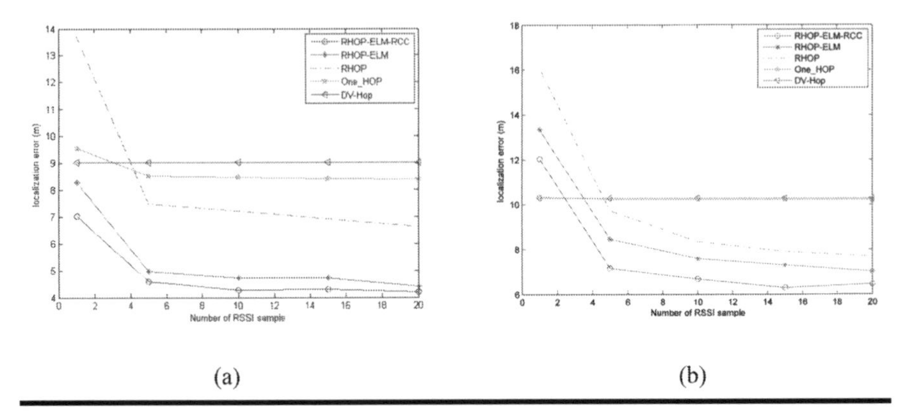

Figure 14.6 Localization errors against the amount of RSSI samples. (a) The case with 50 nodes in the area of 50 m × 50 m; (b) The case with 100 nodes in the area of 100 m × 100 m.

We observe that increasing RSSI samples is able to achieve an improvement in the distance estimation. Meanwhile, when the number of RSSI samples increases to 10 in Figure 14.6a and 15 in Figure 14.6b, the tendencies of localization error approach a steady state. These indicate that the number of RSSI samples is not a critical influencing factor in the positioning error along with the increase of this parameter. Additionally, the curves of DV-HOP and one-HOP are nearly horizontal, and the reason is that RSSI is not adopted in DV-HOP, which only utilizes hop count, while one-HOP does not exploit RSSI unless the hop count between the anchor node and the unknown node is just one. Besides, our proposed scheme is much better than others, and the performance of RHOP-ELM-RCC is also superior to that of RHOP-ELM.

14.4.4 Localization Errors against the Noise Standard Deviation

During this simulation, the density of anchors and the amount of RSSI sample are set to 20% and 10, respectively. Additionally, the dynamic standard deviation of noise could be found in Table 14.1. The simulation performs on two different topology areas with different total nodes, as well as different communication ranges, which are described in Section 14.4.1.

The localization errors against different noise standard deviations are shown in Figure 14.7. Obviously, DV-HOP and one-HOP are less affected by the noise. Because DV-HOP does not depend on the RSSI and RSSI is being used only when the hop count between the unknown node and an anchor node is right at one in the one-HOP scheme, when the hop count is over one, one-HOP works similarly to DV-HOP, which is unrelated to the RSSI. In addition, the other schemes are implemented by using RSSI through the whole process.

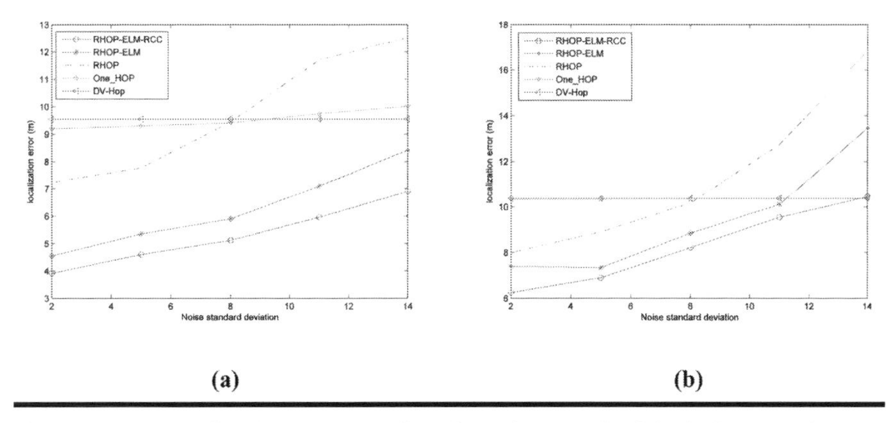

Figure 14.7 Localization errors against the noise standard deviation. (a) The case with 50 nodes in the area of 50 m × 50 m; (b) The case with 100 nodes in the area of 100 m × 100 m.

It should be indicated that the increase of noise standard deviation would lead to unstable fluctuating of RSSI in the log-normal shadow model during the calculation of the accuracy of the distance estimation. The localization errors of schemes related to RSSI all increase along with the increase of noise deviation. Comparing the performance of RHOP, RHOP-ELM, and RHOP-ELM-RCC, the contribution of ELM could help to reduce the localization error to a certain extent, and combining RCC with half-quadratic optimization could further improve anti-noise ability.

14.4.5 Localization Errors against the Outliers

In this part, we will demonstrate the robustness against outliers, caused by transmission error. In this simulation, the density of anchors is 20%; the number of RSSI samples is 10; the standard deviation of noise is five; and other initial parameters are shown in Table 14.1.

Since different algorithms have different ways to calculate the coordinates of unknown nodes, as well as the methods to generate outliers, to generate abnormal values for RHOP-ELM-RCC and RHOP-ELM, we randomly choose a proportion of outputs in the training samples, i.e., the coordinates of unknown nodes in the training samples, and change their coordinates. Meanwhile, for other schemes, i.e., DV-HOP, one-HOP and RHOP, we randomly select a proportion of sensor nodes as outliers, after the corresponding RSSI distances and hop counts are obtained, then change their coordinates. Additionally, the proportion of outliers is chosen from $\{0, 3\%, 6\%, 9\%, 12\%, 15\%, 18\%\}$.

Figure 14.8 illustrates that, except the location error of RHOP-ELM-RCC, the location errors of other schemes are influenced by the outliers, and the trends of

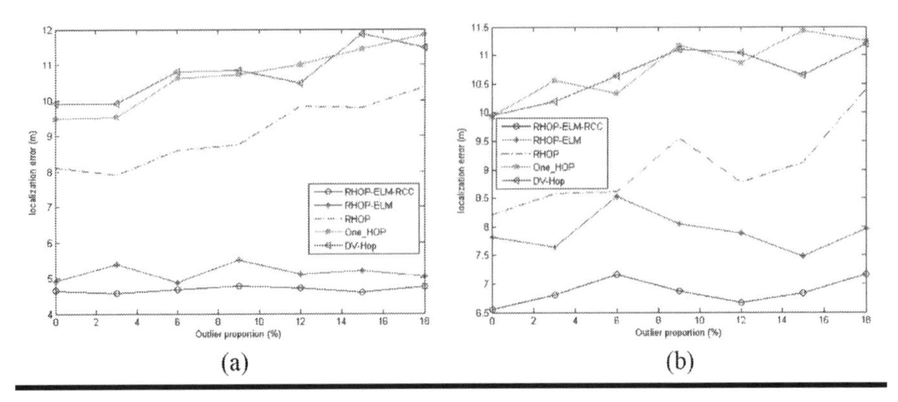

Figure 14.8 Localization errors against the outliers. (a) The case with 50 nodes in the area of 50 m × 50 m; (b) The case with 100 nodes in the area of 100 m × 100 m.

location error increase along with the increase of the proportion of outlier. Although there exist outliers, our proposed scheme outperforms others, due to the utilization of robust correntropy.

14.5 Conclusions

In the wireless CPSS system, the issue of sensor node localization plays a critical role in improving computational efforts. To improve the performance of WSN in wireless CPSS further, this article presents a novel NN learning scheme, named RHOP-ELM-RCC, through the combination of DV-HOP and RSSI using ELM-RCC. It is effective while calculating the coordinates of unknown nodes and decreasing the location error with no additional hardware consumption. During the localization process, we combine DV-HOP with RSSI to reduce the distance error. When the distances between anchor nodes and unknown nodes have been obtained, the SLFN based on ELM is adopted to compute the coordinates of unknown nodes. Since ELM has good abilities of nonlinear mapping and fast learning, the localization accuracy of RHOP-ELM is significantly improved. However, as the original ELM is implemented on the basis of the measure, i.e., MSE, which is sensitive to outliers, the ELM-RCC is accordingly employed using RCC, which is robust against noises, and the half-quadratic technique is utilized for the optimization. Through the simulation comparisons for the localization error, the results show the satisfactory performance of our proposed scheme. Furthermore, the performance of RHOP-ELM-RCC is better than that of RHOP-ELM and other traditional localization schemes.

This article only focuses on the optimization of the localization algorithm. In the future, to further improve the localization performance while using our scheme in the real world, we will discuss some issues, e.g., modeling the sleep/active functional modes of sensors to manage the battery efficiently, optimizing our scheme with unknown transmission power and many others.

Acknowledgments

This project is sponsored by the National Natural Science Foundation of China under Grants 61300074 and 61603032, the China Postdoctoral Science Foundation under Grant 2016M590048, the National Key Technologies R&D Program of China under Grant 2015BAK38B01, and the Fundamental Research Funds for the Central Universities under Grant 06500025.

Author Contributions

In this article, the initial idea was provided by Xiong Luo and Weiping Wang, who also revised the whole article; Yang Xu designed and implemented the experiments; the data and results were analyzed by Wenbing Zhao. All the participants have read and agreed to the final manuscript.

Conflicts of Interest

The authors declare no conflict of interest.

References

1. Pentland, A. Socially aware computation and communication. *Computer*, 38, 33–40, 2005.
2. Lazer, D., Pentland, A., Adamic, L. Computational social science. *Science*, 323, 721–723, 2009.
3. Zeng, J., Yang, L.T., Ma, J.H. A system-level modeling and design for cyber-physical-social systems. *ACM Trans. Embed. Comput. Syst.*, 15, 1–26, 2016.
4. Abbas, W., Laszka, A., Koutsoukos, X. Resilient wireless sensor networks for cyber-physical systems. In *Cyber-Physical System Design with Sensor Networking Technologies*, Zeadally, S., Jabeur, N., Eds., The Institution of Engineering and Technology: London, UK, 2016, pp. 239–267.
5. Luo, X., Zhang, D.D., Yang, L.T., Liu, J., Chang, X.H., Ning, H.S. A kernel machine-based secure data sensing and fusion scheme in wireless sensor networks for the cyber-physical systems. *Future Gener. Comput. Syst.*, 61, 85–96, 2016.
6. Zhao, H., Ma, X., Shi, C. Information interaction in wireless sensor networks based on socially aware computing. *Commun. Comput. Inf. Sci.*, 418, 71–81, 2014.

7. Ammar, A.B., Dziri, A., Terre, M., Youssef, H. Multi-hop LEACH based cross-layer design for large scale wireless sensor networks. In *Proceedings of the International Wireless Communications and Mobile Computing Conference*, Paphos, Cyprus, 5–9 September 2016, pp. 763–768.
8. Dong, M.X., Ota, K., Liu, A.F., Guo, M. Joint optimization of lifetime and transport delay under reliability constraint wireless sensor networks. *IEEE Trans. Parallel Distrib. Syst.*, 27, 225–236, 2016.
9. Liu, A.F., Liu, X., Long, J. A trust-based adaptive probability marking and storage traceback scheme for WSNs. *Sensors*, 16, 451, 2016.
10. Liu, A., Liu, X., Li, H., Long, J. MDMA: A multi-data and multi-ACK verified selective forwarding attack detection. *IEICE Trans. Inf. Syst.*, 99, 2010–2018, 2016.
11. Liu, A.F., Dong, M.X., Ota, K., Long, J. An efficient scheme for selective forwarding attack detecting in WSNs. *Sensors*, 15, 30942–30963, 2015.
12. Niewiadomska-Szynkiewicz, H. Localization in wireless sensor networks: Classification and evaluation of techniques. *Comput. Methods Appl. Mech. Eng.*, 22, 281–297, 2012.
13. Bulusu, N., Heidemann, J., Estrin, D. GPS-less low-cost outdoor localization for very small devices. *IEEE Pers. Commun.*, 7, 28–34, 2000.
14. Leung, C.S., Sum, J., So, H.C., Constrantinides, A.G., Chan, K.W. Lagrange programming neural networks for time-of-arrival-based source localization. *Neural Comput. Appl.*, 24, 109–116, 2014.
15. Patwari, N., Ash, J.N., Kyperountas, S., Hero, A.O., Moses, R.L., Correal, N.S. Locating the nodes: Cooperative localization in wireless sensor networks. *IEEE Signal Process. Mag.*, 22, 54–69, 2005.
16. Wang, J., Gao, Q.H., Yu, Y., Zhang, X., Feng, X.Y. Time and energy efficient TOF-based device-free wireless localization. *IEEE Trans. Ind. Inf.*, 12, 158–168, 2016.
17. Wang, J., Gao, Q.H., Pan, M., Zhang, X., Yu, Y., Wang, H.Y. Towards accurate device-free wireless localization with a saddle surface model. *IEEE Trans. Veh. Technol.*, 65, 6665–6677, 2016.
18. Wang, J., Gao, Q.H., Wang, H.Y., Cheng, P., Xin, K.F. Device-free localization with multi-dimensional wireless link information. *IEEE Trans. Veh. Technol.*, 64, 356–366, 2015.
19. Wang, J., Gao, Q.H., Yu, Y., Cheng, P., Wu, L.F., Wang, H.Y. Robust device-free wireless localization based on differential RSS measurements. *IEEE Trans. Ind. Electron.*, 60, 5943–5952, 2013.
20. Golestanian, M., Poellabauer, C. Localization in heterogeneous wireless sensor networks using elliptical range estimation. In *Proceedings of the International Conference on Computing, Networking and Communications*, Kauai, HI, 15–18 February 2016, pp. 1–7.
21. Zhang, P., Sun, Y. A new DV-Hop algorithm for wireless sensor networks. *Chin. J. Electron Dev.*, 33, 1–7, 2010.
22. Liu, P.X., Zhang, X.M., Tian, S., Zhao, Z.W., Sun, P. A novel virtual anchor node-based localization algorithm for wireless sensor networks. In *Proceedings of the Sixth International Conference on Networking*, Sainte-Luce, France, 22–28 April 2007, pp. 1–6.
23. Yi, T.T., Fang, Z.Y., Li, R.X. RMADV-Hop: An improved DV-Hop localization algorithm. In *Proceedings of the Seventh International Conference on Information Technology*, Las Vegas, NV, 12–14 April 2010, pp. 939–943.

24. Fang, H., Lei, J., Hu, K. An improved DV-Hop algorithm based on RSSI revising. *Commun. Technol.*, 45, 16–18, 2012.
25. Zhang, W., Yang, X.Y., Song, Q.X. DV-Hop localization algorithm based on RSSI correction. *J. Softw. Eng.*, 9, 188–194, 2015.
26. Xie, H., Li, W.S., Li, S.B., Xu, B.G. An improved DV-Hop localization algorithm based on RSSI auxiliary ranging. In *Proceedings of the Chinese Control Conference*, Chengdu, China, 27–29 July 2016, pp. 8319–8324.
27. Peyvandi, M., Pouyan, A.A. An improved DV-Hop localization algorithm in wireless sensor networks. In *Proceedings of the Signal Processing and Intelligent Systems Conference*, Tehran, Iran, 16–17 December 2015, pp. 153–158.
28. Shi, H.Y., Peng, L. An improved DV-Hop node localization algorithm combined with RSSI ranging technology. In *Proceedings of the 5th International Conference on Electrical Engineering and Automatic Control*, 2016, pp. 269–276.
29. Chen, H., Sezaki, K., Deng, P., So, H.C. An improved DV-Hop localization algorithm for wireless sensor networks. In *Proceedings of the 3rd IEEE Conference on Industrial Electronics and Applications*, Singapore, 3–5 June 2008, pp. 1557–1561.
30. Chuang, P.J., Jiang, Y.J. Effective neural network-based node localisation scheme for wireless sensor networks. *IET Wirel. Sens. Syst.*, 4, 97–103, 2014.
31. Borenovic, M.N., Neskovic, A.M. Comparative analysis of RSSI, SNR and noise level parameters applicability for WLAN positioning purposes. In *Proceedings of the IEEE EUROCON*, St. Petersburg, Russia, 18–23 May 2009, pp. 1895–1900.
32. Mahfouz, S., Mourad-Chehade, F., Honeine, P., Farah, J. Non-parametric and semi-parametric RSSI/distance modeling for target tracking in wireless sensor networks. *IEEE Sens. J.*, 16, 2115–2126, 2014.
33. Huang, G.B., Zhou, H.M., Ding, X.J., Zhang, R. Extreme learning machine for regression and multiclass classification. *IEEE Trans. Syst. Man Cybern. Part B Cybern.*, 42, 513–529, 2012.
34. Luo, X., Chang, X.H., Ban, X.J. Regression and classification using extreme learning machine based on L1-norm and L2-norm. *Neurocomputing*, 174, 179–186, 2016.
35. Luo, X., Chang, X.H., Liu, H. A Taylor based localization algorithm for wireless sensor network using extreme learning machine. *IEICE Trans. Inf. Syst.*, 97, 2652–2659, 2014.
36. Luo, X., Chang, X.H. A novel data fusion scheme using grey model and extreme learning machine in wireless sensor networks. *Int. J. Control Autom. Syst.*, 13, 539–546, 2015.
37. Chang, X.H., Luo, X. An improved self-localization algorithm for ad hoc network based on extreme learning machine. In *Proceeding of the 11th World Congress on Intelligent Control and Automation*, Shenyang, China, 29 June–4 July 2014, pp. 564–569.
38. Xing, H.J., Wang, X.M. Training extreme learning machine via regularized correntropy criterion. *Neural Comput. Appl.*, 23, 1977–1986, 2013.
39. Tomic, S., Beko, M., Dinis, R. Distributed RSS-based localization in wireless sensor networks based on second-order cone programming. *Sensors*, 14, 18410–18432, 2014.
40. Man, D.P., Qin, G.D., Yang, W., Xuan, S.C. Improved DV-Hop algorithm for enhancing localization accuracy in WSN. *Appl. Mech. Mater.*, 543–547, 3256–3259, 2014.

41. Tian, S., Zhang, X., Liu, P., Wang, X. A RSSI-based DV-hop algorithm for wireless sensor networks. In *Proceedings of the 3rd International Conference on Wireless Communications, Networking and Mobile Computing*, Shanghai, China, 21–25 September 2007, pp. 2555–2558.
42. Benkic, K., Malajner, M., Planinsic, P., Cucej, Z. Using RSSI value for distance estimation in wireless sensor networks based on ZigBee. In *Proceedings of the 15th International Conference on Systems, Signals and Image Processing*, Bratislava, Slovakia, 25–28 June 2008, pp. 303–306.
43. Santi, P. Topology control in wireless ad hoc and sensor networks. *ACM Comput. Surv.*, 37, 164–194, 2005.
44. Yang, X., Pan, W. DV-Hop localization algorithm for wireless sensor networks based on RSSI ratio improving. *Transducer Microsyst. Technol.*, 32, 126–128, 2012.
45. Huang, G.B.; Zhu, Q.Y.; Siew, C.K. Extreme learning machine: A new learning scheme of feedforward neural networks. In *Proceedings of the IEEE International Joint Conference on Neural Networks*, Budapest, Hungary, 25–29 July 2004, pp. 985–990.
46. Erdogmus, D., Principe, J.C. An error-entropy minimization algorithm for supervised training of nonlinear adaptive systems. *IEEE Trans. Signal Process.*, 50, 1780–1786, 2002.
47. Santamaria, I., Pokharel, P.P., Principe, J.C. Generalized correlation function: Definition, properties, and application to blind equalization. *IEEE Trans. Signal Process.*, 54, 2187–2197, 2006.
48. Liu, W.F., Pokharel, P.P., Principe, J.C. Correntropy: Properties and applications in non-Gaussian signal processing. *IEEE Trans. Signal Process.*, 55, 5286–5297, 2007.
49. Vapnik, V. *The Nature of Statistical Learning Theory*. Springer: New York, 1995.
50. Chen, B.D., Principe, J.C. Maximum correntropy estimation is a smoothed MAP estimation. *IEEE Signal Process. Lett.*, 19, 491–494, 2012.
51. He, R., Zheng, W.S., Hu, B.G. Maximum correntropy criterion for robust face recognition. *IEEE Trans. Pattern Anal. Mach. Intell.*, 33, 1561–1576, 2011.
52. Yuan, X., Hu, B.G. Robust feature extraction via information theoretic learning. In *Proceedings of the 26th International Conference on Machine Learning*, Montreal, Québec, Canada, 14–18 June 2009, pp. 1193–1200.
53. Rockfellar, R. *Convex Analysis*. Princeton University Press: Princeton, NJ, 1970.
54. Boyd, S., Vandenberghe, L. *Convex Optimization*. Cambridge University Press: Cambridge, MA, 2004.
55. Wei, Q.R., Liu, J., Han, J.Q. An improved DV-Hop node localization algorithm based on unbiased estimation for wireless sensor networks. *Journal of Xi'an Jiaotong University*, 48, 1–6, 2014.
56. Ren, H., Zhu, L., Yang, A. Localization algorithm for sensor node based on RSSI ranging and DV-Hop error correcting. *Comput. Meas. Control*, 20, 2863–2866, 2012.

Chapter 15

Intelligent Situation Assessment to Secure Smart Cities with Cryptography

Pushpinder Kaur Chouhan,
Jorge Martinez Carracedo,
Bryan Scotney, and Sally McClean

Contents

15.1 Introduction

Smart cities are rapidly moving from visions to reality with the Internet of Things and a host of new technologies to build powerful industrial and enterprise systems. Smart cities offer conveniences and efficiency to achieve better quality of life. However, challenges exist to fully enhance smart city facilities. A number of these challenges have been presented in [1]. Nevertheless, cyber security is now the top concern of smart city stakeholders.

Key services, such as energy, water, transportation, public health, and safety are managed by gathering timely logistic information so as to provide efficient and safe environments to smart city users. Various technologies are implemented to automize the data exchange, service deployment, and asset safety in the smart cities. As all these services become interconnected, cyber security appears as the topmost priority to protect data/information, and devices of smart cities.

Cyber security consists of technologies, processes and controls designed to protect internet-connected systems, including hardware, software and data, from cyber-attacks. However, cyber security definitions vary considerably in the level of detail to which they are considered:

- The devices to be protected
- The techniques used for protection
- The nature of the attack

Proper deployment of cyber security in smart cities is needed to provide the protection of data, devices, services and infrastructure. Cyber security in smart cities can be achieved via smart surveillance technologies, analytics, and deployment of effective response systems.

15.2 Smart Cities

The smart city is not only about implementing smart physical, technical and automation methodology to provide city-related services effectively and efficiently; in addition, it is a huge concept to support several services which facilitate the dynamic living of citizens. To achieve the objective of smart cities, several devices interact and communicate through networks. The smart city is about smartening the process of several computer-related sciences such as artificial intelligence, cloud computing, embedded computing, and biometrics in order to reduce resource consumption, wastage and overall living costs.

The smart city architecture can be understood through the five layers: sensor, communication, data, application and smart. The technology across these layers works in an integrated manner to deliver smart city services (Figure 15.1).

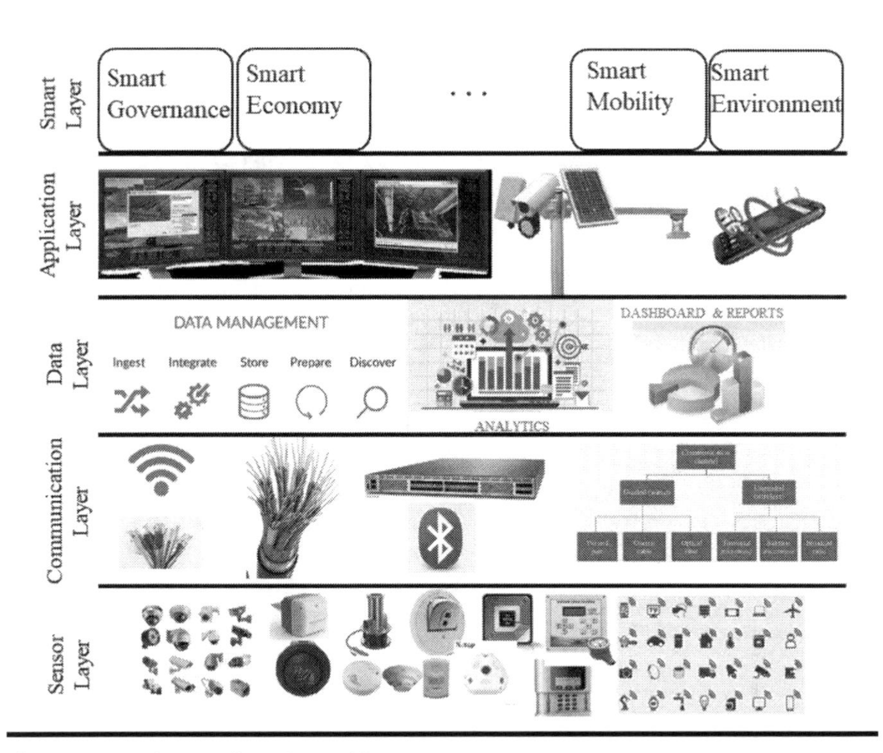

Figure 15.1 Smart city ICT architecture.

The smart layer represents the smart city services, the activities that use data, and applications derived by the exchange of information. Sectors of activity relevant in the context of a smart city are energy, infrastructure, safety and security. Broadly we can divide smart city services into four groups: smart governance (private, public, and civil organizations; infrastructure; government and utilities), smart economy (e-business, e-commerce, production), smart mobility (transport, logistic systems, traffic) and smart environment (energy, water and waste management, clean environment, controlled pollution). To protect and provide reliable services, this layer of security should focus on cyber-attacks because any attack at this layer will cause maximum loss both in terms of finance and time, along with the efforts of bottom layers.

The application layer represents technologies used to access, process and transfer information and data that will be used by the smart layer. The application layer consists of applications such as video management systems, integrated traffic management systems, waste management, water management, telemedicine, flood monitoring systems, parking management systems, and other enterprise applications/APIs.

The data layer represents the information or the data that is collected from the sensor layer and processed and transmitted to the application layer. Various types of information and data are pertinent in the context of smart cities. Data are gathered from many different types of devices, and data may be related to location, traffic, infrastructure usage, energy consumption, surveillance and monitoring, cyber security threats and incidents, etc.

The communication layer represents the transmission medium for data and information sharing from connected devices and APIs. Communication media can be either wired (e.g., twisted pair, optical fiber, coaxial cable) or wireless (e.g., radio, Bluetooth, ZigBee). Technologies such as 6LoWPAN, IEEE 802.15.4, and HC-06 Bluetooth are exclusively used for data exchange between devices and data centers. The communication layer is very relevant from a cyber security point of view.

The sensor layer consists of the physical devices that detect and measure a physical property to send for further analysis. Some examples of devices at the sensor layer are surveillance cameras, audio detection sensors, parking sensors, water level detectors, leakage detectors, smoke detectors, speed detection cameras, red-light violation detectors, smart meters, and traffic detection systems.

15.3 Security Challenges with Smart Cities

A fundamental feature of smart cities is optimizing the city in a dynamic way. This introduces a wide range of new security risks and challenges to smart cities, both at the implementation phase and the utilization phase. Security technologies will be required to protect smart cities from both information attacks and physical tampering. Smart city–specific threats are aggravated by a number of factors:

1. Numerous heterogeneous connected devices
2. Devices with little to no built-in security
3. No standard and formalized process to secure all devices
4. An increase in devices to access/provide personal information
5. Collected information passed as unencrypted data
6. No standard or formalized mechanism for secure data transfer

Each layer of the smart city architecture has different security risks and thus uses different technologies for security. However, all layers should adhere to any or all the five main security parameters: Integrity, Authenticity, Availability, Non-repudiation, and Confidentiality.

Integrity means assuring and guaranteeing the accuracy and completeness of information/data over its complete lifecycle. It signifies that data/information cannot be altered in an unauthorized manner. For data integrity, the data should be delivered intact and should not be modified. It is essential for protecting the data integrity at rest, in transit and in use. Only authorized devices, developers and applications/services should be communicating to access the data/information.

Authenticity focuses on associating a message, user, or device with a valid source. Human authentication can be achieved by a combination of the following characteristics:

- Knowledge—something you know (e.g., a password)
- Possession—something you have (e.g., a smart card)
- Inherence—something you are (e.g., a fingerprint)

Single-factor authentication uses a single characteristic to grant access. For example, any one of the entities such as password, biometric, PIN, or security token will be sufficient for the user to be granted access. Security can be further improved by deploying multi-factor authentication. For example, combine two or more entities such as a fingerprint along with a smart card or iris scan with password but never two entities of same characteristic. Methods to authenticate a device include use of device/user's digital certificates, digital signature, multiple users of a single device and use of two-factor authentication.

Availability is the state of being able to be used when needed. Systems (application, devices, technologies) should be available to serve its purpose. This means the systems used to store and process the information/data, the communication channels and the security controls are properly deployed and are functioning correctly. Ensuring availability prevents denial-of-service attacks of the target system and similar attacks.

Non-repudiation ensures that nobody can deny their actions. For example, a defender cannot deny that certain messages were sent, or specific services or data were modified by them. Thus, messages should be certified with a digital signature. In addition, a public-private key can be deployed to send and receive data/information, thus avoiding non-repudiation.

Confidentiality ensures that data/information is not read by any unauthorized individual. Thus, data/information need to be protected, in transit, at rest and in use, with both symmetric and asymmetric encryption. In smart cities, setup of standard encryption and protocols requires extensive efforts due to the wide range of devices and various services. In addition, all smart city encryption deployment should be assisted by equivalent full encryption key lifecycle management processes. Otherwise, overall security will be compromised due to poor key management.

These security parameters have threats associated with them in the form of various attacks and other malicious activities. Table 15.1 shows how these security parameters can affect different layers of smart city architecture layers. For example, denial of service is an availability threat and unauthorized access or manipulation/corruption

Table 15.1 The Security Parameters with Smart City Architecture Layers

Security Parameters	*Sensor Layer*	*Communication Layer*	*Data Layer*	*Application Layer*	*Smart Layer*
Availability	✓		✓	✓	✓
Integrity			✓	✓	✓
Authenticity	✓	✓	✓	✓	✓
Confidentiality		✓		✓	✓
Non-repudiation	✓	✓		✓	✓

of information/data are integrity threats. Authenticity is to be secured while sending, receiving and using different types of messages/information. Confidentiality threats include the unlawful collection of data through eavesdropping or the illegal analysis of the network traffic. Device denial or denial of sleep attacks that drain batteries can be caused by defective communication protocols.

These threats can broadly be divided into two parts: threats from intentional attacks (eavesdropping, wiretapping, unauthorized use, unauthorized access, tampering, alteration, theft, distributed denial of services, loss of reputation, denial of services) and threats by accident (hardware failure, hardware malfunction, operator error, user error, software error, electrical and frequency disturbance, interferences, end of support obsolescence, acts of nature, environmental incidents).

Overall smart city threats compromise capacity in various ways, ranging from disruption of some small function of a device to a security attack that could even halt the overall setup. Threats can bypass the privacy and security of data/information by gaining illegitimate access to individual devices or the system as a whole. Security measures can be categorized as passive or active actions. Passive action will prevent access through secure protocols. Active action will prevent access through refusals of service. Thus, it is beneficial to continuously monitor the status of devices and deployment software/systems to detect any changes that could be classified as malicious. Situation assessment is a methodology that could facilitate threat avoidance in smart cities.

15.4 Situation Assessment

Smart cities truly provide the opportunity to affect and transform businesses and lifestyles. However, this emerging evolution can lead to unforeseen security issues/outcomes. Therefore, it is important to carry out situation assessment to identify possible security risks and to develop a complete picture of secure smart city deployments. Situation awareness and assessment can be defined for both human and autonomous systems as *the perception of environmental elements and events with respect to time or space, the comprehension of their meaning, and the projection of their status after some variable has changed, such as time, or some other variable, such as a predetermined event* [2].

Nowadays, security is considered as the topmost priority by all smart city stakeholders. To facilitate smart city security, situation assessment should be considered prior to IoT deployment. Correct assessment of the situation will help with implementation of proper steps to provide full security to the IoT model development and deployment. The 2016 Mirai botnet attack [3], which was orchestrated as a DDoS attack through 300,000 vulnerable IoT devices such as webcams, routers, and video recorders, showed just how situation awareness and assessment could be useful.

Steps are being taken towards smart city security enhancement, as ENISA [4] has released two detailed guidelines for cyber security of smart cities: *architecture model for public transport* and *security and resilience for smart health service and infrastructure.* In addition, the EU has released the NIS directive [5], which mentions that member states for European cyber security should raise EU citizens' awareness of cyber security. The framework [6] seeks to ensure an EU-wide certification scheme consisting of comprehensive rules, technical requirements, standards, and procedures. The CRISALIS [7] program has been launched, aimed at providing means to secure critical infrastructure environments from attacks caused by malware and threat agents such as Stuxnet and Duqu.

Security comprises three aspects: *protect, detect,* and *respond. Detect* is the most relevant to situation assessment. In detection, situation assessment helps especially with security monitoring and assessment (for the purpose of responding). Situation assessment could play a vital role for a Security Operations Center (SOC) for monitoring not just the network but also smart cities end-to-end.

Situation awareness and assessment are fundamental for any system that aims to operate efficiently and proactively. This requires perception of the environment along with comprehension of the meaning and prediction of the future, particularly for dynamic systems operating in highly variable environments. Such state-of-the-art systems provide and integrate data from diverse sources, such as heterogeneous sensors and other devices as part of smart cities. Such data typically have large volume and are streamed, meaning that they provide a steady flow of updates containing new information with potentially new and better knowledge of developing situations. However, in order to provide informative and usable situation identification and assessment we must first resolve problems of noisy and heterogeneous sensor data subject to incompleteness, uncertainty, and imprecision. The data, context, domain knowledge, and spatial and temporal models must then be integrated and abstracted to inform high-level concepts. As such, a situation can be thought of as an abstraction of the events occurring in the real world derived from context and hypotheses.

All smart city architecture layers are important in understanding application and technology aspects, which in turn are essential for the detailed assessment of cyber security requirements to establish appropriate controls. For example, the status of sensors should be monitored continuously to assess the situation because if a sensor is being tampered with or starts malfunctioning, then analysis of all the top layers will result in faulty execution [8] presented a hierarchical network threat situation assessment method for DDoS based on Dempster–Shafer evidence theory.

Another aspect of security is *protect*, which can be addressed with cryptography. Cryptography is usually defined as the study, development and comprehension of techniques that provide secure communications when an adversary is present.

15.5 Smart City Security Enhancement Using Cryptography

Historically, the main goal of cryptography was to provide message confidentiality and in order to achieve that goal, new cyphers were designed. That is what is called classic cryptography.

One of the first examples of the use of classic cryptography is Caesar's Cypher, used in 53 BCE to protect military orders between armies. In Caesar's Cypher, every letter of the message is substituted for another letter defined by a fixed shift. By using this method, a confidential message could be sent between different battalions. However, if we study this method with our twenty-first century knowledge it turns out to be very easy to break.

The arrival of new technologies has increased security problems, both in number and type. The growth in our mathematical knowledge has made it possible to design new protocols that can tackle different types of security problems: confidentiality, integrity, non-repudiation, and authentication. These kinds of new techniques are known as modern cryptography.

Modern cryptographic algorithms are mostly designed considering computational assumptions that make them (in a practical way) impossible to break by any adversary. That means that an adversary cannot break the algorithm within a reasonable period of time.

However, the arrival of quantum computers will change this status-quo. Algorithms widely used such as RSA and elliptic curve algorithms will be easily broken under the attack of a quantum computer. New cryptographic schemes are being designed to tackle this issue, and this field is known as post-quantum cryptography.

Below we outline some common techniques in modern cryptography and provide an overview of post-quantum cryptography.

15.5.1 Asymmetric Cryptography

Public key schemes refer to any algorithm having two different keys. Those keys are usually known as public and private keys. The public key, as its name states, is known by everybody and anybody can use it to cypher a message. On the other hand, the private key is known by only one person and will be used to decipher the message.

Most public key algorithms are built around two mathematical problems: the factorization problem and the discrete logarithm problem. These two problems have an exponential computation time, which makes them hard to break by a computer within a reasonable period of time.

Public key algorithms are a basis of secure communications nowadays as they guarantee confidentiality, integrity, and non-repudiation. Some of these algorithms also provide digital signatures or key distributions.

The best-known public key algorithm is RSA. It was developed in 1978 [9] and constructed based on the practical computational hardness that the factorization of the product of two large primes has. RSA is a slow algorithm and is mostly used to share the keys of a symmetric algorithm.

Another common approach to public key cryptography is the elliptic curve, where the algebraic structure of elliptic curves over a finite field is a key point in the algorithm. The main advantage of these kinds of algorithms is that they guarantee a level of security similar to RSA, while ECC uses smaller keys.

As a third example, we cite the ELGAMAL algorithm [10]. This algorithm is defined over a cyclic group, and it is based on the computational difficulty of solving an equation involving powers in a group (the discrete logarithm problem). It is used in the free GnuPG software, amongst others.

- *Digital signatures*: Amongst the problems that public key algorithms have fixed are authenticity and non-repudiation. These problems are tackled by using public key digital signatures, which can be broadly defined as a mathematical algorithm to verify the authenticity of the digital data.

15.5.2 Symmetric Cryptography

Symmetric key algorithms use the same key (or a direct transformation of it) for encryption and decryption. The key is shared between the parties that undertake private communication. A major weakness compared with public key cryptography is that the key is known by every party. This type of algorithm is lighter than the public key algorithms, which makes them more suitable for use in constrained devices.

The main exponent of a symmetric cypher is AES [11]. It is a block cypher chosen in a contest in 1997 that was organized by the NIST (National Institute of Standards and Technology) and it is supposed to be efficient in both software and hardware.

It is important to note that the development of symmetric algorithms has been huge in the last decades. Algorithms such as PRESENT, Salsa20, and Chacha are good examples of this development. In recent years the search for algorithms suitable for highly constrained devices has become a hot topic in cryptography.

- *Hash functions*: In symmetric cryptography it is important to mention hash functions. A hash function can be defined as any mathematical function that maps data (of any size) into fixed-size data. For these functions to be useful in cryptography, they have to hold three mathematical properties: one-wayness, collision resistance and second preimage resistance. One function holding these three properties can guarantee the integrity of the message.
- *Message authentication codes* (*MACs*): MACs are the symmetric key tool used to provide authentication. On input, a secret key and a message, a MAC-tag, is produced, and the recipient can check if the tag matches the pair message-key.

15.5.3 Post-quantum Cryptography

It is well known (thanks to Shor's algorithm [12]) that the most used public key algorithms such as RSA, ECC, and ELGAMAL cannot resist an attack performed by a quantum computer. Post-quantum cryptography refers to algorithms (in general terms, public key algorithms) that are supposed to be secure against these kinds of attacks.

Different approaches have been considered in this field. In general terms, the mathematic approach to this kind of algorithm is always highly complicated. The use of complex mathematical structures and/or techniques is required to provide security against quantum computers. Two examples are shown here to illustrate the complexity:

- Multivariate cryptography, where multivariate polynomials over a finite field are used to build the algorithms
- Supersingular elliptic curves, where properties of those mathematical objects are used to define the algorithms

As shown in Table 15.1, availability is not listed because device availability cannot be tackled using cryptography. However, integrity, authenticity, confidentiality and non-repudiation can be addressed using cryptographic techniques.

Integrity can be guaranteed using either hash functions or MACs. Thanks to the collision resistance property, the hash value of a modified message will not match the hash value of the original one.

Authenticity can be addressed using both symmetric and asymmetric cryptography with the use of MACs and digital signatures, respectively. Only a person knowing the correct key will be able to compute the MAC or a valid signature for a particular message.

Using symmetric and asymmetric cyphers, confidentiality can be guaranteed. Knowing only the appropriate key, it is possible to recover the plaintext from the cyphered message.

Non-repudiation can be tackled only using digital signatures. Whereas MACs can be produced by both the sender and the recipient (since both know the common shared key), digital signatures can be produced only by the owner of the corresponding secret key. Therefore, the sender cannot deny having sent the signed message.

15.6 Discussion

Smart city architecture can be utilized to enhance environment security by providing monitoring, analysis and response systems. Various applications can be used to analyze and correlate feedback from the smart cities.

The application layer follows a secure software development lifecycle process for custom developed applications and provides privileged access to servers for authorized users only. To improve security, it is important to build authentication mechanisms for all applications and APIs, and create a role-based access control list derived from the principle of least privilege. Secure application communication should be provided through encrypted protocols such as HTTPS over TLS 1.2 and above. User-provided inputs should be validated at the server side, and error-handling mechanisms should be implemented on end-user inputs.

At the data layer user authentication is implemented to access databases and provide database access to authorized users only on a need-to-know basis. In addition, the database server is deployed into a segmented zone, separate from the app server and web server. Perform hardening for all database servers as per minimum security baseline guidelines. Channel encryption is performed to ensure security of data in transit. All sensitive data is encrypted and encryption keys stored in a trusted key store. Regular backups of the database should be made, and backup media encrypted.

The communication layer can be secured by segmenting the data center network into multiple zones such as demilitarized zone, trusted zone, management zone, production zone, and user zone, and then implementing policies, procedures and minimum baseline security guidelines accordingly. All edge devices, including Wi-Fi, sensors and IoT devices, are placed on a separate firewall-monitored network. All communications to and from edge devices are encrypted. To secure the data center network an external firewall, web application firewall, intrusion prevention and detection system and other security products are deployed. Inter-component communication is encrypted with secure protocols such as HTTPS over TLS 1.2, SSH, and SFTP. Encrypted channels are used, such as a virtual private network, while connecting remotely to the data center network. To prevent unauthorized access, it is beneficial to disable unused network or telecommunication access points. In addition, authentication and hardening are implemented for all the devices on the network.

At the sensor layer, the first thing is to change default passwords of all edge devices and then authenticate based on physical characteristics such as device ID and MAC ID. This will secure the access to the edge devices, even remotely. To prevent software modifications, physical interfaces in the edge devices are disabled. All edge devices should be hardened and configured to connect to authorized wireless networks only. Digital certificates can be securely loaded onto devices at the time of manufacture or could also be installed post-manufacture. These digital certificates can then be activated/enabled by third-party PKI software suites. Edge device firmware should be updated regularly to prevent known attacks. Encrypted channels are used to secure over-the-air updates to edge devices.

Authentication and privilege should be configured under the principle of least privilege. In addition, implement the software restriction policies to prevent access to critical resources so as to avoid any usage breach. For example, if all the vulnerability patching is agreed but the basic security strategy of authentication for privilege is not configured, a security breach will result.

15.7 Conclusion

Clearly, smart cities are interdependent and huge complex systems, and that will facilitate human living. However, smart cities will lead to several technical, economical, and social problems and challenges. The range of areas where cities can become smarter is extensive. Data and information generated should be secure throughout the lifecycle. We have concluded that information security and data privacy are critical, and cryptography can help to protect a smart city from harm. However, if that could not be prevented fully in time then situation assessment can detect, and appropriate action can be taken to improve the system state. Finally, all the devices, interfaces, and data need to be protected to provide confidentiality, integrity and authentication to smart cities.

By using different cryptographic techniques, it is possible to address four of the five main security issues in smart cities. Different techniques are designed to tackle each particular problem and it is important to keep in mind that no single technique can address all of them at the same time. On the other hand, the eventual arrival of quantum computers generates the need for research and development of new post-quantum algorithms able to resist attacks performed by such computers.

In addition, situation assessment is a continuous process of routine monitoring, fusing disparate and distributed knowledge and data, and evaluating the results to provide feedback and/or actions. Thus, cryptography can be used to secure the activities between the first step "detect" and the last step "response" based on the event detected.

References

1. T. Braun, B. C. M. Fung, F. Iqbal, B. Shah, Security and privacy challenges in smart cities. *Sustainable Cities and Society (SCS)*, 39, 499–507, 2018.
2. P. K. Chouhan, S. McClean and M. Shackleton, Situation assessment to secure IoT applications. *2018 Fifth International Conference on Internet of Things: Systems, Management and Security*, Valencia, pp. 70–77, 2018. IEEE.
3. Mirai (Malware), Wikipedia 7 June 2019. Available: https://en.wikipedia.org/wiki/Mirai_(malware).
4. European Union Agency for Network and Information Security (ENISA) Guidelines for Cyber Security of Smart Cities, (1) Cyber security and resilience of smart hospitals November 24, 2016 (2) Architecture model of the transport sector in smart cities January 12, 2016, ENISA. Available: https://www.enisa.europa.eu/topics/iot-and-smart-infrastructures/smart-infrastructure?tab=publications. Retrieved 7 June 2019.
5. European Union (EU) Network and Information Security (NIS) Directive for Sectoral Supervision, ENISA Available: https://www.enisa.europa.eu/topics/critical-information-infrastructures-and-services/cii/nis-directive. Retrieved 7 June 2019.
6. Certification Framework for Devices, European Commission. Available: https://ec.europa.eu/digital-single-market/en/eu-cybersecurity-certification-framework. Retrieved 7 June 2019.
7. Critical Infrastructure Security Analysis (CRISALIS) Programme. Available: https://www.chalmers.se/en/projects/Pages/CRitical-Infrastructure-Security-AnaLysIS-QCRISALISQ.aspx. Retrieved 7 June 2019.
8. L. Zihao, Z. Bin, Z. Ning and L. Lixun, Hierarchical network threat situation assessment method for DDoS based on D-S evidence theory. *2017 IEEE International Conference on Intelligence and Security Informatics (ISI)*, Beijing, pp. 49–53, 2017.
9. (a) R. Rivest, A. Shamir, L. Adleman, A method for obtaining digital signatures and public-key cryptosystems. *Communications of the ACM*, 21(2), 120–126, 1978. (b) P. L. Montgomery. Record number field sieve factorisations. http://krum.rz.uni-mannhein.de/cabench/sieve-record.html. Retrieved 7 June 2019.
10. T. ElGamal, A public key cryptosystem and a signature scheme based on discrete logarithms. *IEEE Transactions on Information Theory*, 31(4), 469–472, 1985.
11. J. Daemen, V. Rijmen, AES Proposal: Rijndael (PDF). National Institute of Standards and Technology. http://www.eng.tau.ac.il/~yash/crypto-netsec/Rijndael.pdf. Retrieved 7 June 2019.
12. P. W. Shor, Polynomial-time algorithms for prime factorization and discrete logarithms on a quantum computer. *SIAM Review*, 41(2), 303–332, 1999–2001.

Index

Note: Page numbers in italic and bold refer to figures and tables, respectively.

E

F

G